History of Leather-working Castes in India

Social Transformation and Challenges

History of Leather-working Castes in India

Social Transformation and Challenges

Edited by

Vikram Harijan & Thallapally Manohar

MEENA BOOK PUBLICATIONS

Delhi (India)

ISBN : 978-93-85957-25-3

First Published 2018

Meena Book Publications
Regd. Office:
H.N.140, Street No. 9C, Prem Nagar,
Karawal Nagar, Delhi - 110094 (India)
Mobile : +91-9868280998

Sales Office:
21/4648, Ansari Road,
Daryaganj, New Delhi - 110002 (India)
Tel. : 011-23277141, 9899953194
E-Mail: meenabookpublications@gmail.com

Printed in India

Dedicated to

Anjali Chaterjee

and

Smt. Sonmati Devi

Contents

Acknowledgement

In acknowledging the help, I have received from others in the work presented here. I must begin by recording that my greatest debt to Indian Council of Historical Research and Indian Council of Social Sciences Research, New Delhi, both played very significant contributions by sponsoring the Seminar. I special owe to Honorable Vice – Chancellor Prof. Ratan Lal Hangloo who was always ready to help and solve my problem. As mentor, he was always come forward to help me. He was very instrumental to shape ideas about the seminar. He is one who suggested me to call upon the Key Note speaker, Prof. Umesh Kadam of JNU who really very suit the theme of the seminar. I take this opportunity place on record my special indebtedness to him. The Dean, Prof. K.S. Misra has extended his hand whenever I needed his help. My Head of the Department of Medieval And Modern History, who encouraged me to undertake the seminar forward and was available any time when I required. He adviced me time to tome for success of the seminar. I must thanks to Director, Badri Narayan Tiwari of G.B.Pant social science institute for proving me help regarding accommodations and seminar, auditorium for conducting the seminar. I am very grateful to him.

I express my gratitude to Prof. Sashi kant Rai who readily agreed to become Organizing Secretary of the seminar. Without him, seminar was nearly impossible. In the capacity of Organizing Secretary, he helped me a lot which lack words. My Colleague, Dr. Alok Prasad was also Organizing Secretary who was also available to me when I needed him. I am also very thankful to Prof. Prakash Sinha of Ancient History who taught me how to organize a seminar. He was very specific to account. Within limited fund, he made me learn how to handle a seminar. The head of Ancient history, Prof. Puspa Tiwari who give me motherly affection and encouraged to conduct the seminar. My Deparmental Colleagues Prof. Lalit Joshi, Prof. P.L. Vishwakarma, Prof. Yogeshwar Tiwari, Prof. Vandita Verma, Dr. Sanjay Srivastva, Dr. P.H. Harish. I also got support from Sumit Saurabh Srivastva, Prof. Pankaj, Prof. Ashsih Saksena, Prof. Pardeep Sharma, Prof. Bhure Lal and so on.

I am very very thankful to My teacher and and Prof. Harbansh Mukhia who always encourage me and guide me. Sir always give to tips for success. He always wish for my success. I also indebted to my supervisor Prof. Yogesh Sharma who always encouraged to take me the research of The occupational Caste groups, Lower caste and so on.

I am very thankful to Prof. Vivek Kumar, Prof. JNU, New Delhi, played very significant in shaping the my life. There is no word to describe this. Regarding seminar, he gave ideas how to organize the seminar. I very thankful to him.

I am also beholden to the former finance officer , Sri Kanojia ji who was readily agreed to open joint account for this gesture, I am very thankful to him. The current F.O Sri Sanjay Uppadhya ji also helped me a lot .The University Registrar, Dr. Pradeep Sharma, secretary to Vice-Chancellor to whom I am very thankful to him. I am very thankful to Neerala Ji (P A to VC), Pandey ji (P A To V C). Prof. Harsh Kumar, PRO of the university,

Sri Amit ji, OSD to VC and all the office staff of Vice-Chancellor office.

My special Thanks to Prof. Chinna rao who not only gave me valuable advice for the work but also helped me how to organize the seminar. He also extended his warm love and affection and showered upon me enthusiasm and energy especially on problem solving occasions. I also extend my sincere thanks to my friends. B. Ram Chandra Reddy, Srinivas, T. Manohar, Mohan Rao garu, Jay Kumar Garu, Prashant kain, Devi Dayal Gautam, Swadesh, Prashant, zafar, Shant Sundaram, Vikas Rathi, and so on.

I also extend my sincere thanks to my Deparmental guest faculties and research Scholar such as Dr. Narender Singh, Dr. Bhavesh Dwedi, Dr. Anil Yadav, Dr. Refaq Ahmed, Dr. Vinita Misra. Among research Scholars, Ajay kumar Ahirwar, Ranjeet Kumar,Rakesh Singh, Kamlesh Singh, Anirudha kumar, Pankaj Kumar, C.B. Bharti, Nishant yadav and so on.

My undergraduate and post Graduate students such as Goind Misra, Saumya Singh, Pratima Patel, Amarjeet Chakravarthy, Tushar, Suyas Misra, Kum Kum Yogesh, Ajit Ranjan, Soni, Nidhi, Eklabhya (Delhi), Anrag (Delhi), Narender, T. kumari. Riya Kumari, Ranjeet and so on.

I am also very thankful to my office staff, Sri Misra Ji, Sri Bhanu Ji, Imam Ji, Razzak Ji and so on.

I express my heartfelt gratitude to my parents. Their unceasing support and prayers had been an incessant sources of strength and happiness for me, in spite of the hectic scheduled in the course of my research.I express my deep love to Aditya, Sabhya, Guddu, Jhinkanu,Riya, Pappu, Sangeeta, Gita, Nitesh, Prianka and Paramjeet.

My special thanks to my friend Suresh Chaudhuri who is one who cares me a lot in Allahabad. I also thankful to Surender Chaudhuri, my friend who also treat me as younger brother. Bhai Parusharam of Lucknow who is very instrumental in my life for doing very positive work. Friend like Dewa Ji cares a lot in Lucknow. Bhai Parusharam of Lucknow who is very instrumental in my life for doing very positive work. Friend like Dewa Ji cares a lot in Lucknow.

My Desiner friend Saurabha Chaudhuri who had taken a lot of pen for successful of the seminar. He was ill during the seminar. He, still, worked for me. His wife (bhabhi JI) also served coffee to me when we (me and Saurabha bhai) tried.

The book is being published by Meena Publications, Delhi. I am very thankful to Hardutta Sharma ji who has taken pain to publish this work within the short time, virtually no time.

Editors

Editorial Introduction[1]

The occupations of tanning and leather work was specialized and recognized as a significant crafts in early India. The earliest known literary work of India, the Rigveda, refers to various types of skin/ leather items. They include the skin to carry water, liquor, poison, honey and curds, the musical instrument skin bagpipe, garments made of the skins of cow and sheep, strong reins and straps made of cow leather. The Maruts was depicted as a god carrying antelope skins on his shoulders and Indra was praised as the one "giving the skin of the deer, well-pressed honey at the winning of prizes".[2] The skins of the deers were seems to have been used to sit on during penance. The first reference of a leather worker, more precisely tanner, also found mentioned in the Rigveda. The hymn runs as follows. "He (Kasu, the lord of the Cedi) who (previously) bestowed on me a king's ten (horses?) of golden appearance- beneath the feet of the lord of the Cedis are (all) the communities, the 'hide-tanning' men all around".[3]

W. Briggs states that the "tanners (*charmamna*) are mentioned in the Rig Veda, later Vedic literature and in the Brahmanas. Tanning, *mla, mna,* is also spoken of in the Rig Veda and certain details of stretching and wetting hides probably refer to the process of manufacture. Ox-hides were used in the pressing of the soma and ox-hides and antelope and tiger skins were used in sacramental and ceremonial rites. The use of skins for clothing is mentioned in the Satapatha Brahmana and in other early literature. The Maruts wore deer skins and the wild ascetics seem to have been clothed in skins".[4] Briggs also mentions that there are references to the thong, *yoktra*, used for yoking the chariot or cart, the bow-string, *jya*, made of ox-hide, reins of leather, leather bags, *driti* and *dhmata*, for holding liquids, leather bottles, *bhastra* and thongs used for couches, *vardhra* for door fastenings, *paricarmanya* and for bridles, *syuman*.[5] The Mahabharata referred to the use of leather variously as the hand guard for the bow, shields (ox-hide/ bear skin), cuirass and abreast-plates and the sword sheaths. It further attests that the war chariot was protected with shields of leather, the box of the chariot was fixed to the axle with thongs of leather, the horses were yoked to the pole of the chariot with leather straps and reins and the drums, especially the great kettle-drums, were fashioned with leather heads.[6]

Manusmriti curiously mentions that shoes were one of the items to be gifted to his teacher by a student after the completion of his studies.[7] In the event of damage done to leather or to the utensils of leather, a fine of five times to the value should be imposed.[8] For killing adulterous women of four castes, a person must give, in order to purify himself, respectively a leathern bag, a bow, a goat or a sheep.[9] Three days fasting was prescribed for stealing leather[10] and no punishment should be inflicted when the leather thongs, the rope around the neck or bridle were broken and when the driver (of a chariot) loudly called to make way.[11] However, Manu opines that Karavara, who works in leather, sprang up due to the union of a Nishada man and Vaideha woman.[12] The leather working communities were referred to with various *jati* names in different parts of India among whom there were hardly any marriage relations that presupposes that each one was a distinct community of its own. However, they were known in various names in india.They were called

Madigas of Andhra Pradesh, the Chakkiliyans and the Vettiyans of Tamil Nadu, the Madiga, Mochi and Samagara of Karnataka and the Tolkollans of Kerala, the Chamara ,Jaiswara of North India.Chakkiliyan were also known as Chukler. In many accounts they were as inferior to the Paraiyans.[13]

Various scholars, census enumerators, colonial administrators and others have composed rich reliable source materials on leather working castes in India. In Fact, W.G.Briggs[14], who probably first who has done pioneer work on leather Caste. He collected many local records, manuscripts, legends, copper plate inscriptions and so on. Another pioneer study done by Edgar Thurston and K.Rangachari[15] on South India which is very pioneering studies in terms of leather working caste. At the same time, H.A. Staurt[16], F.R. Hemingay[17], Colin Mackenzie, W.W. Hunter, Sir Herbert risley[18], Abbe Doubis[19], Record of fort St. Geroge[20]. Further, Syed Siraj ul Hassan[21] also contributed in terms of leather working caste in India.

Some secondary sources also need to be consulted like, Stephen Fuchs[22] who has given great description of leather Castes. Bernard Cohan[23] greatly focused on Chamar caste of Janupur of up. Thallapally Manohar[24] new book also important to know the Madigas Caste of Andhra region.

Context

Allahabad University has always occupied an esteemed place among the universities of India for over a century now. Established on 23rd September 1887, it is the fourth oldest university of India after Calcutta, Bombay and Madras University. The credit for conceiving a large Central College at Allahabad, eventually to develop into a University, is due to Sir William Muir, then Lt. Governor of United Provinces. As a result of his initiative the foundation stone of the Muir Central College (named after him) was laid on Dec. 9 1873 by His Excellency Lord Northbrook. Sir William Muir said on that occasion: "The establishment of a central college at Allahabad has been my earnest desire ever since I assumed my present office. Shortly after coming here I found that a strong wish prevailed among the chief people of the place for a better means of education at Allahabad; and being myself deeply impressed with the same conviction, I took occasion at the first Darbar which I held here to urge upon those present the necessity of showing that they were sincere and in earnest, by contributing to the work. The appeal was widely and liberally met, a considerable sum was subscribed and address was presented to me in 1869, praying for the establishment of the college here." On September 23, 1887 Act XVIII was passed which established the Allahabad University. Like the Universities of Calcutta, Bombay and Madras, the Allahabad University also started as a degree conferring institution. Its first entrance examination was held in March 1889. In 1904 the Indian Universities Act was passed which limited the territorial jurisdiction of Allahabad University to the United Provinces of Agra and Awadh, the Central Provinces including Berar, Ajmer, Mewar and most of the states of Rajputana and Central Indian Agencies. Between 1887 and 1927 at least thirty-eight different institutions and colleges of this area were affiliated to Allahabad University. With the promulgation of the Allahabad University Act in 1921, the Muir Central College lost its independent existence. Between 1922-27 the University had its internal and external wings which were subsequently separated from the University to give the latter a purely unitary and residential character. In fact the Allahabad University was started with a preliminary loan of Rs. 5240/- from the government to meet its expenses. The loans were repaid in two years. Henceforth, its main source of its income was from the examination fees and sale of Prospectus & Calendar. Being an examining body it met its incidental expenses easily.

The History department has given very renowned historians of the World. The department produced historians like R.P. Tripathi, Banarshi Das Saxena, Dr. Iswari Prasad, B.N.S. Yadav, Dr. Tarachand, Dr Sahafat Ahmed Khan and so on. Therefore it came to know the "School of Historiography". Continuing this tradition, the department of history has organized two day national seminar on the " the History of leather Working Caste in India: Social transformation and Challenges" which was held on 28th and 29th October, 2017. This seminar is funded by Indian Council of Historical Research, New Delhi, and Indian Council of Social Science Research, New Delhi. This is the proceeding of the seminar.

Endnotes

1 For editorial I have taken help of my friend Ram Chandra Reddy and Manohar sir.

2 *Rigveda*, 1, 85, 5; I, 191, 10; IV, 23, 8; , IV, 45, 1; V, 34, 7; VI, 49, 18; VIII, 5, 19; VIII, 48, 5; IX, 2, 7 and IX, 70, 7. Stephanie W. Jamison and Joel P. Brereton, Tr., *The Rigveda: The Earliest Religious Poetry of India*, Oxford University Press, New York, 2014, pp. 215; 398; 594; 629; 699; 841; 1036; 1129; 1236 and1303.

3 *Rigveda*,VIII, 6, 37, Stephanie W. Jamison and Joel P. Brereton, Tr., *op.cit.*, p.1037.

4 Geo w. Briggs, *The Religious Life of India: The Chamars*, Association Press, Calcutta and Humphrey Milford, Oxford University Press, London, 1920, pp. 11-12.

5 *Ibid.*, p. 12.

6 *Ibid.*, pp. 12-13.

7 G. Buhler, Tr., *Manusmriti: The Laws of Manu, Sacred Books of the East, Vol. 25*, Clarendon Press, Oxford, 1886, Chapter II, Verse No. 246. The other preferable items to be gifted were a field, gold, a cow, a horse, a parasol, a seat, grain and vegetables.

8 *Ibid.*, Chapter VIII, Verse No. 289.

9 *Ibid.*, Chapter XI, Verse No. 139.

10 *Ibid.*, Chapter XI, Verse No. 167.

11 *Ibid.*, Chapter VIII, Verse No. 292.

12 *Ibid.*, Chapter X, Verse No. 36.

13 Niels Brimnes, Constructing The Colonial Encounter, Right and Left Hand Castes In early Colonial South India, Curzonpress, Great Britain, 1999, p. 256.

14 W. Geo. Briggs, *The Religious Life of India: The Chamars*, Association Press, Calcutta and Humphrey Milford, Oxford University Press, London, 1920,

15 Edgar Thurston and K. Rangachari, *Castes and Tribes of Southern India*, Asian Educational Services, New Delhi and Madras, 2001 (originally published in 1909),

16 Manual of the North Arcot district which is written by H.A Stuart.

17 F.R. Hemingway, Godavari, District Gazetteer, in two volumes ,vol 1, Asian Educational Services, New Delhi, 2000

18 Sir, Herbert Risley, the people of India,London,1915.

19 A.J. Abbe Dubois, A description of the character , Manners and customs of the people of india and their institutions religious and civil, translated from the French Ms with notes, corrections and additions by Rev G.U. Pope, Third edition, Asian Educational Services, New Delhi, First published in 1879, reprinted in AES in 1992.

20 Reocrd consists several volumes like *Diary and Consultations, Monograph and so on.*

21 Syed Siraj ul Hassan, *The Castes and Tribes of H. E. H. the Nizam's Dominions*, Vol. I, Times Press, Bombay.

22 Stephen Fuchs, At the bottom of Indian Society, Munshiram manohar,1981, Delhi.

23 Bernard Cohan Omnibus with foreward by Dipesh Chakrabarthy, An anthropologist among the other historians and other essays, Oxford University Press, 2004.

24 Thallapally Manohar, Cultural history of Madigas: A brief Study,Pragma Publications, 2016.Hyderabad.

List of Contributors

1. **Akulapally Kumaraswamy,** Deapartment of History and Tourism Management, Kakatiya University, Warangal, Telangana.
2. **Amardeep,** Assistant Professor in History, Govt. College, Birohar, Jhajjar, Haryana. He obtained his Phd from JNU, New Delhi. His area of research is Dalit and History.
3. **Anjali Yadav,** Post Doctoral Fellow, Department of History, University of Allahabad.
4. **Dr. B. Rama Chandra Reddy,** Head and Associate Professor,Department of History, Bhrathidasan Government College for Women, Puducherry.
5. **Prof. G. Samba Siva Reddy,** Dept. of History & Archaeology, Yogi Vemana University KADAPA, Andhra Pradesh.
6. **Dr. Jayaram Gollapudi,** Post Doctoral Fellow, Assistant Professor (F&C), Tagore National Research Scholarship (2013-15) Scheme of Tagore National Research Fellowship award from Ministry of Culture, Government of India.
7. **Dr. Muneer Illath,** Assistant Professor, Department of Sociology, University of Allahabad, Allahabad.

8 **Prsahant Kain,** Assistant professor, English and Foreign languages University, Hyderabad.

9 **Paramjeet Kaur,** Doctoral Fellow, Jamia Millia Islamia, New Delhi.

10 **Refaq Ahmad,** Guest Faculty, Department of Medieval and Modern History, University of Allahabad.

11 **Ronki Ram,** Professor, Shaheed Bhagat Singh Professor of Political Science, Panjab University, Chandigarh.

13 **S.K. Chahal and Narender Singh,** Professor & Chairman, Department of History, Kurukshetra University, Kurukshetra.

14 **Sashi Kant Rai,** Associate professor, Department of Ancient History and Archaeology, University of Allahabad.

15 **Dr. S. Babu,** Head and Associate Professor, Department of History, Avvaiyar Government College for Women, Karaikal.

16 **Theegala Sreenivas and Prof. Thallapally Manohar,** Department of History and Tourism Management, Kakatiya University, Warangal, Telangana.

17 **S.Victor Babu,** Professor and Head, B.B. Ambedkar University Lucknow.

18 **Vivek Shukla,** Ph.D. Scholar in Department of Ancient History, Culture & Archaeology, University of Allahabad, Allahabad (U.P.)

19 **Dr. Vikram Harijan,** Assistant Professor, Department of Medieval and Modern History, University of Allahabad, U.P.

1

Leather Working Caste During Medieval Period

Dr. Anjali Yadav*

In India caste structure was based on the individual professions and this profession was being passed on from one generation to the other; soon the castes came to be known by this hereditary occupation. The occupational caste that came to be associated with the leather craft in Northern India was the Chamar.[1] There are thought to be some 3,000[2] castes in India in which some are derived from tribal or racial elements, some are occupational, being of the nature originally perhaps of guilds of artificers or craftsmen, some are territorial, some religious and so forth. The Leather working caste i.e. *Chamars* whose traditional occupation was related to working with hides and skins were responsible for removal of dead animals and female *Chamars* function as midwives.[3]

Charmakara, the Sanskrit word for which this caste draws its name mean a worker in Leather, denoting that the *Chamar* by name as well as by his hereditary occupation was the man who worked in Leather. Manu traces their origin to the mixed marriage between a Nisada male to a Vaidehi female. A Brahman parent on either side of his ancestry should have given the *Chamar* some respectability but this was far from reality because neither could this

* Post Doctorate Fellow, University of Allahabad, Allahabad.

help him in raising his social status nor remove the stigma attached to his work.

Chamars were the traditional workers in Leather but with the passage of time number of sub castes were also associated with this craft arising from the adoption of new occupations or of changes in the original occupations which could have given rise to subdivision of the caste ultimately developing into entirely distinct castes.[4] These distinct castes were engaged in Shoe making, sandal making or oil can making we can see that these traditional leather workers came to be organized into a hierarchy of sub castes, specializing in one or another aspect of leather industry. In this hierarchy playing job was highly degrading. The workers in this branch were regarded as the most inferior of all the leather workers due to their direct, association with flesh. The tanners came next, while the *mochis* or other workers who were engaged in manufacture of leather products enjoyed the highest status, within the community. Few other sub groups were also associated with this community and they were *Rangias* and the *Khalrangas* specialized in dyeing the leather, *Dhalgars* made shields, *Kuppesaz* restricted to making of *kuppis,* the containers for holding oil and ghee.[5] The elementary division among the leather workers was into two major classes the butchers and the leather workers. Both were equally important components of leather making. While the former ensured the availability of the raw material the latter worked on it to produce the final products.

As per W. Crooke survey which he mentioned in his book, "The tribes and castes of North western Provinces and Oudh", we find that the butchers were generally Muslims, the leather workers of whom *Chamars* were in majority with 99.77% were Hindus. Here the *Chamars* were the traditional workers in leather, while *Dabgar, Dhalgar* and *Mochis* were functional castes which were formed because of the specialization in their work.

Till early medieval time we can see that the *Chamar* castes showed peculiarity, marking it off from the untouchable classes. Kalhan[6] has narrated the tale of 'charmakrit', leather worker, and 'padukrit', shoemaker, who lived in the capital city of Kashmir in the reign of king Chandrapida (A.D. 682). We also find that by the time the Muslim conquest started, the stratification of the caste system had been completed. In the medieval period a new class of professionals, the butchers or *Qassabs* made an appearance, chiefly due to the dietary habits of the Mohammadans. Meat formed a very important part in the diet of the Muslims, especially in the mass feeding *Khanqahs* of the Sultanate on festive occasions and in the Kitchens of the aristocrats. In the Kitchen of Mohammad bin Tughluq alone 200 sheep and 2500 Oxen were consumed each day.[7] The appearance of this class of professionals had a direct impact on the leather craft both in terms of the quantity and quality of hides available to the leather workers who till this time had to depend on the hides of worn out fallen cattle, the quality of which invariably was deplorable.

The *Qassabs* were later divided into three important offshoots differentiated on the basis of the animal slaughtered, thus we had the *Chiks*, the *Khatiks* and the *Qassabs* all working as butchers. *Chiks* were Mohammedans, who worked on goat and sheep skins, [8] and they used these skins to make coloured leather.[9] *Khatik*, Sanskrit meaning butcher or a hunter, gave an indication of their profession. This was cultivating, Labouring and vegetable selling caste found all over the United Provinces. The *Khara* and the *Khalrangas* were exclusively engaged in dyeing leather. *Qassab's*, Arabic word meaning, 'to cut' and earlier used for the entire class of butchers was now one of the castes involved in this profession.

By the advent of Muslim rule in India, Muslim religion also entered in Indian society and this Muslim caste system is a result of Hindu influence; the Indian Muslims have acquired the system from the Hindus through content and continuous culture contact, the system of caste groupings itself resulted in the concept of social distance between the two communities the Hindus and the Muslims.[10] It is often assumed that there was no place for a concept related to caste in Islamic society, and hence any caste- like structures in Indian Muslim Society must be the result of accretions or borrowing From the ambient Hindu society or customs inherited from pre-Islamic times.

Since Muslim were in limited numbers so they tried to convert Hindu into Muslim community for this they take help of Sufis. The chief reason of Hindu conversion into Muslim religion is particularly the attractiveness of Islam, as an egalitarian faith, for the lower castes especially the untouchables. The cities and Qasba established by the new conquerors would have been spaces of liberty; Muslim community had permitted the most disfavored people to rise in the social hierarchy, by opening new economic outlets.

According to Arnold,[11] "A Hindu will naturally be attracted by a religion which receives everybody without discrimination; and : "It is the absence of class prejudice which constitutes the real force of Islam in India and which allows it to win so many converts from Hinduism". In the context of conversion to Islam in Bengal, Rice and W.W. Hunter wrote that the Islamic armies "were welcomed by the out- cast Chandals and Kaibarrta"[12]. As per Habibs quotes the medieval Muslim rule in India involved considerations of urban labour, and the preference of Indian workers for the new religious law:

> "Face to face with the social and economic provisions of the Shari'at and the Hindu Smritis as practical alternatives, the Indian city worker preferred the Shari'at. And the decision of the city worker was decisive."[13]

When we kept all factors in mind then we find that during The Ghurian Conquest of Northern India, there was division of the people into small water tight sub caste groups which results into the total annihilation of any sense of common citizenship or of loyalty to the country as a whole.[14]

With the establishment of Muslim rule in India, we find that Muslim community was also started getting divided into various castes which arises caste system in Muslims too, Dr. B.R. Ambedkar took cognizance of the existence of castes even in Muslim Bengal, Ambedkar noted:

> "The conventional division of the Mohammedans into four tribes- *Sheikh, Saiad, Moghul* and *Pathan* has very little application to this Province (Bengal) The Mohammedans themselves recognize two main social divisions, (1) Ashraf or Sharaf and (2) Ajlaf. Ashraf means 'noble' and includes all undoubted descendants of foreigners and converts from high caste Hindus. All other Mohammedans including the occupational groups and all converts of lower ranks, are known by the contemptuous terms, 'Ajlaf', 'wretches' or 'mean people': they are also called *Kamina* or *Itar*, 'base or *Rasil*, and corruption of Rizal, 'worthless'. In so me places a third class, called Arzal or 'lowest of all', is added. With them no other Mohammedan would associate, and they are forbidden to enter the mosque or to use the public burial ground".

Within these groups there are castes with social precedence of exactly the same nature as one finds among the Hindus.[15]

According to M.K.A. Siddiqui there are several caste groups among the Muslims in Calcutta, Siddiqui discusses several different ways in which inequality manifests itself- restrictions on commensality, hyper gamy, pollution by contact etc. He divides the castes into three categories. The castes in any one category can accept food from the others in the category, but not from castes in lower categories. It has been found that as Lower caste in Hindus were treated inferior in the society, in the same way the Lal Begis (who roughly correspond to the *Bhangi* caste in Hindu society) were also not given equal status in Muslim community as they are generally regarded as unclean on account of their humble occupation- "they often experience difficulty in getting their dead buried in the common Muslim burial ground". We can also see that Hypergamy is widely practiced in the highest category, meaning that women from lower castes can be married into the higher castes (Sayyad and sheikh), but not vice versa. The children of these mixed marriages are called "Sayyadzada" and Sheikhzada" respectively. They do not attain the full status of their fathers and are expected to make alliance with people of their status.

The Hindus who are converted into Muslim Community are generally characterized as New Muslims and they are looked down upon by the social groups which are known to be descendants of Foreign Sources or who have succeeded in eliminating the stigma of recent conversion. This gave rise to certain differentiations in the adjustment of the *Sheikh Siddiques* after their conversion to Islam in the different villages. In villages that were largely or predominantly Hindu, the sheikh *Siddiques* were excluded from the Framework of interaction with the Hindu castes but they continued to enjoy a somewhat superior status as a Muslim group. But in villages where there were numerous other Muslim groups of superior status, the *Sheikh Siddiques* were not merely excluded from the social hierarchy of Hindu castes, but were also relegated to a somewhat lower position even within the hierarchy of Muslim castes.

The continued prestige of the *Siddique Sheikhs* in their native villages even after conversion can probably be explained by the fact that they were already a community which enjoyed prestige among the Hindus. They were allowed to retain their prestigious occupation as land record keepers. Since they were not *Ashraf* so they did not get much prestige in Muslim dominated villages. This shows that Hindu converted into Muslims were not getting as much respect as they expected after conversion.

One more example of conversion of Hindu into Muslim was Hindu fishermen called *Mukkuvans* called *Pusalars*. Their conversion took place relatively late. Because of their low occupation of fishing they are alloted a low status in the Moplah society. The Pusalars are spread all along the coastline of Kerala and they still continue their traditional occupation of fishing.

As we see that if an Asiatic converts to Christianity, he does not obtain the rights of the European community but if any Persian, Indian, European or Asiatic converts into a Muslim religion then his sole fact of conversion, one immediately becomes equal of other Muslims in rights. We noticed that due to the conversion of Barber, weavers and tanners to the Islam, opened for them new economic outlets- and this is precisely the reason for their conversion; their conversion in no way improved their status.

Ansari says that social hierarchy had already become part of Islamic society by the time it entered India in the twelfth century and at last even untouchability entered Islamic society. The plight of Muslim untouchables is described by Ansari in moving detail:

> A Bhangi, either Muslim or non- Muslim, is not permitted to enter a mosque no matter how clean he may be at the time. Although in theory of a Muslim *Bhangi* or *Chamar* is allowed to offer his prayer(s) in a mosque, but in usual practice their entrance into such pious places as mosques and shrines of Muslims saints is socially disapproved and thus it is resisted. Even if they could get into a mosque or shrine, provided they have had a bath and are dressed in clean clothes, they do not usually proceed beyond the entrance steps. In contrast to the Hindu caste system, Muslim Bhangis

are allowed to learn Quran, but they are not expected to teach it.

While studying the 1921 census we find that in the caste wise break up of the Hindu, Muslim and Sikh communities in the Northwestern province of Punjab, the very lowest castes Chamars (Leather- workers) and Chuharas (Scavengers/ Sweepers) did not convert to Islam at all. This shows that it's not necessary that the lower castes Hindus were converted to Muslim in order to seek relief from oppression.

Till now we see that medieval historians do not focus on the problem of caste. The Poet Amir Khusrau confirm that the Hindu noblemen who rebelled against the King had *chandals* and meos among their retainers. Thus, to the extent that Amir Khusran's work can be regarded as historically sound, it actually supports the contention that the lowest castes were among those who opposed Muslim rule.

So we can say that the breakdown of caste notions in Muslim Communities is probably because of the small size of nuclear Muslim communities which had to abandon caste notions in order to survive.

References

1. Manab Chakaraborty, et.al "Leather workers", India's Artisans, A status Report (New Delhi, Shruti, 1995) p. 60
2. J.H. Hutton, Caste in India its nature, function and Origin, p.2.
3. Bernard. S. Cohn, India: the social anthropology of a Civilization (New Delhi, Oxford University Press, 2000)
4. Herbert, Risley, The People of India (2nd ed.), Delhi Oriental Books Reprint Corporation, 1969, p. 76
5. Manab Chakraborty, "Leather workers", India's Artisans A status Report, op. cit., p. 50
6. Rajtarangini, IV, pp. 58-76

7. H.K. Nazvi, agricultural, Industrial and dynamism Under the Sultans of Delhi (1206-1555), Munshiram Manoharlal Pub. p. 72
8. H.G. Walton, A Monograph on tanning and working in Leather in the United Provinces, p. 26
9. W. Crooke, The Tribes and castes of North Western Provinces and Oudh, vol. III, Op. cit., pp. 257-58.
10. Muslim caste in Uttar Pradesh (A study of culture contact) Ghaus Ansari, Lucknow, 1960, p. 66
11. The Preaching of Islam, pp. 188-119.
12. Dr. James wise, "The Muhammadans of Eastern Bengal", J.R.A.S.B, (Calcutta Asiatic society of Bengal, 1894) No.1, p. 32
13. Introduction to Elliott & Dowson's History of India, vol. II (reprinted with Introduction by Professor M. Habib & supplement by K.A. Nizami), cosmopolitan Publisher, Aligarh, 1952, p. 32
14. Politics and society during the Early Medieval Period: Collected works of Professor Mohammad Habib, Vol. 1, ed. K.A. Nizami, 1974, People's publishing House, p. 155
15. Pakistan or the Partition of India, B.R. Ambedkar, thacker & Co. Ltd., Bombay, pp. 218-219.
16. Tughluq Namah of Amir Khusrau, Majlis-i-Makhtutat-i-Farsi.

2

How to Uplift the Scavengers, Cobblers and Tanners: A Critical Study of the Gandhian Approach to the Dalit Problem

S.K. Chahal* & Narender Singh*

This paper seeks to critically examine the approach of Mohandas Karamchand Gandhi (1869-1948), popularly known as Mahatma Gandhi, vis-à-vis the Dalit problem, i.e., the problem of 'Untouchables' in India, with particular reference to the Cobblers, Tanners and Scavengers. In the first part of the paper, we have critically examined the ideological framework and of Gandhi with regard to the problem of Dalits who had been the victims of caste discrimination and untouchability in the country through the ages. In the second part, we have specifically discussed strategy and initiatives which Gandhi had come out with for upliftment most depressed sections of the Untouchables, i.e., Cobblers, Tanners and Scavengers. The paper suggests that the religious ideology of Gandhi largely affected his all movements including the movement for attaining *'Swaraj'* (self-rule) and the movement for the uplift of 'Harijans' (i.e., Dalits). His idea of 'Harijan uplift' was based on *Varnashrama Dharma*. He took the

* Department of History, Kurukshetra University, Kurukshetra.

problem only as a socio-religious problem of the Hindus. He wanted to reconstruct the Hindu society strictly on the basis of the institution of four *Varnas* and, therefore, wanted to eliminate the *Panchama Varna* or the fifth caste of the outcast Untouchables. It emphasized that only Hindus, particularly the caste Hindus, could work for the eradication of untouchability. The approach did not insist much on human rights of Dalits and only adhered on charity works on the part of the caste Hindus for the Untouchables. The above approach could be described as a 'paternalistic approach.' Having such an approach, Gandhi came out with his strategy and initiatives for the upliftment of Untouchables, particularly its most depressed sections like the Cobblers, Tanners and Scavengers.

Before we discuss the approach of Mahatma Gandhi to Dalits, it is necessary to us to know a little bit about his religious ideology which was actually the very basis of his ideas and strategy concerning Dalits. Gandhi hailed from an orthodox Hindu Bania family. He always called himself a '*Sanatanist* (orthodox) Hindu' belonging to the *Vaishnava* sect. He believed in "all that goes by the name of Hindus scriptures", e.g., scriptural purity, idol worship, doctrine of '*Karma*' (action), theory of rebirth, cow protection, '*Varnashrama Dharma*' (four fold order of society and life) and institution of caste.[1] But at the same time he 'disbelieved' in untouchability. He once argued that India was "indebted" to the Brahmins as they taught that even a Chandala (outcast) or a prostitute could attain *Moksha* (salvation), if he/she had purified his/her heart.[2] About *Manusmriti*, the Hindus' text of law which legalized caste as well as untouchability, Gandhi opined, "*Manusmrit* and the similar treatises put before us seem to be different today from what they were in their original form....What I said about untouchability is that there is no sanction in *Shastras* (scriptures)."[3]

This religious ideology of Gandhi largely affected his all movements including the movement for attaining '*Swaraj*' (self-rule) and the movement for the uplift of 'Harijans' (i.e., Dalits) Just as '*Ramraj*' (reign of Rama) inspired his idea of '*Swaraj*', his idea of 'Harijan uplift' was based on *Varnashrama Dharma*. He wanted to reconstruct the Hindu society strictly on the basis of the institution of four *Varnas,* (i.e., the Brahmin, the Kshatriya, the Vaishya and the Shudra) and, therefore, wanted to eliminate the *Panchama Varna* or the fifth caste of the outcast Untouchables.[4] The Mahatma suggested that the Untouchables and outcasts should be regarded as touchable and castemen of Shudra status. "A Panchama does the work of Shudra and he, therefore, is naturally classified as such when he ceases to be regarded as Panchama."[5]

When Gandhi returned to India from South Africa, he established Sabarmati *Ashram* in Ahmadabad in 1915 and admitted in it a poor sweeper family of Dudhabhai.[6] Discarding untouchability was one of the eleven vows which every inmate had to take before he was admitted to the *Ashram*.[7] Hence, Gandhi entered in the Indian National Congress with a *Sanatanist* ideology and a personal emotional touch with the 'Dheds', 'Bhangis' (sweepers), 'Chamars' (cobblers) etc. In short, the Gandhian approach to the Dalit problem had following features:

1. The Dalit problem is basically a 'religious' problem. It is not a political problem at all.
2. The problem is an internal matter of the Hindus and non-Hindus have nothing to do with it.
3. The problem could be solved only by the abolition of the notion of untouchability. There is no need of annihilation of *Varna* or caste for the removal of untouchability.
4. It is the caste Hindus who had to reform themselves by the way of 'change of their heart' for the Untouchables.

5. The activities of 'sanitation work' etc. among the Depressed Classes are also necessary for their 'moral upliftment.
6. God lives in the poor, they are *'Daridranaryana'*. So the caste Hindus should develop among themselves the feelings of 'pity', 'obligation' and 'fellow-feeling' for them.[8]

The above approach was in fact, based on a 'paternalistic approach.' Towards oppressed/lower sections of society including Dalits, *Adivasis*, women, workers and peasants. The paternalistic approach was a major component of Gandhism.[9] As regards Dalits, it did not recognize political and communitarian aspects of the Dalit problem. The approach took the problem only as a socio-religious problem of the Hindus.[10] It emphasized that only Hindus, particularly caste Hindus, could work for the eradication of untouchability.[11] Gandhi convinced the Indian National Congress to follow this paternalistic approach with regard to the problem of Dalits.

The Gandhian approach to the Dalit problem basically took its shape in 1920s. It was the time when Gandhi decided to launch a national Non-Cooperation Movement. He made his position clear on the issue in *Young India* dated 27 October 1920 saying, "Though the Panchama problem is as dear to me as life itself, I rest satisfied with the exclusive attention to national Non-Co-operation, feel sure that the greater includes the lesser."[12] The first resolution of the Congress on untouchability appeared in the last paragraph of its lengthy and historic resolution on Non-Co-operation adopted in the Nagpur annual session held in December 1920. It read:

> ...As the Movement of Non-Co-operation can only succeed by complete co-operation, the Hindu delegates of this Congress call upon the leading Hindus to settle all disputes between Brahmins and Non-Brahmins wherever they may be existing,

> and to make a special effort to rid Hinduism of the reproach of untouchability, and respectfully urge the religious heads to help the growing desire to reform Hinduism in matter of its treatment of the suppressed classes.[13]

Hence, the Dalit problem was now a 'reproach to Hinduism' rather than a 'hardship' to the Untouchables. During the Non-Cooperation Campaign Gandhi specially focused on the 'propaganda work' against untouchability which was an integral part in the Non-Cooperation programme. During the movement Gandhi put forth a programme of 'self purification' comprising of four items of which 'giving up the practice of untouchability' was second.[14] In his speeches he always mentioned the Dalit problem. He normally urged the people to treat the Untouchables as 'touchable Shudras' and often asked them a question, "...(Will you) treat the Antayajas in the same way as you treat the Shudras? Raise your hand in support...."[15]

Gandhi generally mentioned the subjection of the Hindus under the British rule and compared it to the subjection of Dalits by the caste Hindus. He argued that the *Swaraj* was impossible unless we would not liberate the 1/5 of our brothers and sisters from socio-religious bondage.[16] He compared the atrocities of the caste Hindus on Dalits with that of 'O. Dyerist' atrocities.[17] While declaring his promise of attaining '*Swaraj* within one year', he appealed the people that they would have to eradicate untouchability during this short period of one year and not after attaining *Swaraj*.[18] His speeches often included a warning to the caste Hindus. For instance, in his speech at Haryana Rural Conference held on 15 February 1921 at Bhiwani, which was presided over by Lala Lajpat Rai, he warned the people that as long as they would treat millions of their countrymen as Untouchables, they also would continue to be treated as 'Chamars' and 'Bhangis' by the British.[19] He called the British rule 'satanic'.

Similarly he also called the oppression of the Untouchables by the caste Hindus as 'satanic'.[20] He passionately warned the caste Hindus, 'The groans of innocent Untouchables are sufficient to keep the *Swaraj* away from us." [21] Speaking in a public meeting on 18 April 1925, he further said:

> I am only a Bhangi, a Chamar, a farmer and a servant.... Hinduism is not likely to perish even if *Khadi* and spinning wheal are wholly forgotten....But unless the practice of untouchability is rooted out, we shall perish, Hinduism will perish. How can you accept a person like me, a Bhangi, unless you have given up untouchability?[22]

When Mahatma Gandhi began his Civil Disobedience Movement in 1930, he again reminded the people 'basic conditions of *Swaraj*' including the 'untouchability work.' During this movement he propagated that the foundations of the *Swaraj* were being laid by those who regarded communal unity and removal of untouchability as articles of faith.[23] He hoped that under *Swaraj* public temples, public schools and public wells would be used "equally by Brahmins and Bhangis."[24] He asked the people to celebrate 'national weeks' for the purpose of 'self-purification' and appealed to the caste Hindus to do 'constructive work' especially 'untouchablity work' during such celebrations.[25]

By his arguments he continued to propagate that untouchability had no sanction in the Hindu scriptures and, therefore, the Untouchables should be treated as touchable caste men. He was of the view that untouchability was a system which was introduced as an *'Apad Dharma'* (urgent duty) during the days of social decay and the 'form' in which it was being practiced currently was to be condemned altogether.[26] He also argued, "*The Sanatana Dharma* will not be saved by defending every verse printed in the scriptures."[27] He pleaded that the *Bhagawad Gita* does not justify any difference between a Brahmin and a Chandal.[28] He further argued that untouchability was "not in keeping with the teachings of *Vedas*" and was "foreign to the principles of Hindus religion."[29] He, therefore, denounced "the sort of untouchability which is being practiced" in the name of *Shastras*, and described it as "sinful."[30] He observed, "Untouchability is a sin against God and humanity."[31]

Gandhi laid great stress in his propaganda that he took up it "purely out of the consideration of *Dharma*"[32] and also that he advocated abolition of untouchability for a "purely religious motive."[33] He pointed out that it was his 'conscience' which told him that "untouchability can never be a part of Hinduism."[34] He wrote in *Navjivan* dated 1 May 1921 :

> My prayer is this: The only thing dear to me is *Moksha* (salvation). My whole effort is to attain *Moksha* at the end of this very life. It is with this aim that I have taken up so seriously a movement of Non-Cooperation. However, if I do not have my aspiration fulfilled at the end of this life and if the sin of untouchability will not have disappeared by then, I would pray that I may have my next birth in an Antayaja family so that I could suffer all that they do rigorous *Tapashya* (asceticism) to mitigate their sufferings.[35]

Gandhi urged the people that we should have a "fellow feeling" for the "poor, down-trodden and depressed people" as it was the "essence of *Varnashrama Dharma*."[36] Sometimes, during his earlier days, this 'fellow feeling' of the Mahatma even took the shape of superiority complex. For instance, he wrote in *Navjivan* on 18 September 1921, "Yudhisthra refused to enter the gates of heaven without his dog. Do we hope to get into the temple of *Swaraj* ourselves leaving our Bhangi (and Chamar) brothers behind and running at top speed towards it?"[37] He repeated the same 'argument' even in 1927 in a public meeting at Mysore.[38] He uttered that Balmiki had written that Ramchandra provided justice even to a dog, and Tulsidas said that Rama made friendship with a Chandal.[39] He further argued that Rama ate berries already savored by Shabri (a low caste woman) and he hugged the king of Nishadas (Dalits).[40]

In addition to his efforts for convincing the caste Hindus against untouchability, Gandhi simultaneously appealed to Dalits that "they should never permit in their mind the thought that they are not Hindus...(as) a person does not leave his family because he is harassed by other members but tries rather to reform them."[41] While speaking at an Antayaja Conference at Sagitra on 16 January 1925, he appealed to Dalits:

> Why should you give up your religion? It is I who has to make atonement. Why should you give up chanting the name of Rama? It is the way of Rama to make his followers and servants suffer and it is thus he tests their devotion.[42]

As regards the inter-caste relations, Gandhi was totally against in earlier days. While giving an interview to a periodical on 23 September 1920, he opined on the issue:

> I am against both (i.e., inter caste dinning and inter-caste marriage) on hygienic and spiritual grounds. Eating is as dirty a business as evacuating, the only difference is evacuation is a matter of relief.... Suppose my son wants to marry my daughter, I will not stand in the way of marriage. But one thing I will do. I will not allow them room under my roof.[43]

He further clarified in *Young India* on 2 February 1922, "When I ask you to eradicate untouchability, I don't mean that you should eat and drink in the company of Antayajas or have marriage ties with them or drink water out of jug used by one of them. The Hindu religion does not compel anyone to use any article from which another has eaten."[44] Similarly, he was also against that "Bhagis,

Chamars etc. should give up their vocations."[45] He had, however, to change his views in the matter due to growing criticism by the progressive people as well Dalits. For instance, he was criticized on this issue by his friends like C.F. Andrews and Rabindranath Tagore. When the caste Hindu boycotted and attacked those Dalits in Gujarat who tried to send their children to schools and to give up their hereditary occupations, Gandhi called it a "*Swadeshi* Dyerism" and opined in *Navjivan* dated 14 December 1924:

"...Other castes have also given up these old occupations.... Today the Chamar's vocation has been taken up by others also. I see no impurity in carrying carcasses to where they belong. However, how could I force others to do that or any other work?"[46]

After some days, the Mahatma also spoke on inter-caste relations in a political conference at Bhawnagar in a changed tone, "I have personally no objection to sharing my meal with him (Untouchable)."[47] Though he also made it clear that, "I am not asking you to inter-dine or inter-marry with him."[48] He gave liberty to the people in this matter saying, "this is a matter of your own choice."[49] He would also not oppose the Chamars, Dheds etc. who had given up their caste occupations, he still ideally regarded the caste occupations as a 'healthy division of work based on birth.'[50]

After 1925 Gandhi included in his propaganda against untouchability the teachings of saints and poets. He stressed upon the element of compassion found in their teachings for the down-trodden. His first favorite saint poet was Akha, a Gujarati Dalit poet of 17th century who, according to Gandhi, described the idea of anyone being defiled by the touch of another human being as a "superfluous limb."[51] He mentioned another Gujarati poet Pritam in his speeches who sang "At sight of the purifying flame of the path of love, people run away in fear." Gandhi argued that the path of love required that "we should not mind touching the so-called Untouchables."[52] He further argued that Vallabhacharya and Chaitanya "lifted up thousands of people who were regarded as Untouchables."[53] But it was Narsinh Mehta, a famous Gujarati saint poet, whom Gandhi admired greatly. He usually sang his famous *Bhajan* (prayer) in between his speeches which means that 'he is a true Vaishnavte who understands the sufferings of others.'[54]

Though Gandhi quoted scriptures against untouchability, yet, when the orthodoxy refuted him by giving evidences of the existence of untouchability in the Hindu scriptures, he warned that the *Shastras* would become "death traps" if we were to regulate our conduct according to "every detail given in them or according to that of character therein described."[55] He quoted *Bhagwad Gita* at many a time in his anti-untouchability propaganda. To him, the banishment of untouchability meant translating into action the great message of *Bhagwad Gita* which read, "Treat the Bhangi and the Brahmin alike if you would but know God."[56] He further argued that how could any Hindu practice untouchability when he proclaimed faith in *Advaita* (the theory of non-duality)?[57]

During the course of time, the tone of Gandhi against untouchability became sharper. In 1930s, he fell heavily on the prejudicial attitude of the caste Hindus towards Dalits.[58] He went on to say that the sufferings of the Untouchables could not be compared with those of any other class in India or the world and "even the slavery of Negroes is better than this."[59] He treated all professions as equal and dignified. He spoke in his public meetings that a lawyer, a doctor or a collector did not serve the society "a whit more than a Bhangi or a Chamar"[60] indeed, the "Bhangi's services surely rank much higher than the services of these" because "if the former were to stop serving, what would be the plight of society?"[61] He warned the Hindus, "Assuming that the Bhangis on the bar sinister being not removed refuse to do our scavenging, we must be prepared to do it ourselves."[62] He declared, "It is by way of protest against this arrogation of superiority by one class over another that I delight in calling (myself) a Bhangi, that is sweeper, beyond which so far as I am aware inferiority does not travel."[63]

It is pointed out that in the public meetings the caste Hindus and the Untouchables used to sit separately during the earlier phase of Indian national movement. In order to get them mixed together, Gandhi used to ask them, "Do you want that this wall should disappear and that our Antayaja sisters and brothers should take their seats with us?" In response, many caste Hindus would raise their hands in support. Dalits then came and took seats with the rest.[64] This practice was fruitful. Gandhi also warned, "Let the Antayajas come in or permit me to go and sit in their midst. But remember that it is not proper for you to do anything out of the false regards for me and with the thought in your mind that you will take a bath after returning home."[65] In the public meetings Gandhi would also prefer to be welcomed by Dalit boys and girls. When he saw them being asked to sing from a distance, he uttered, "I can keep quite no longer....If the Antayaja girls are to sing from there, the presentation of the address on behalf of the Congress Committee would be a mere farce."[66] At such occasions he asked the caste Hindus that they were just "merely passing resolutions" and writing slogans on their welcome arches against untouchability which were only "for show."[67] There were occasions when people sitting in his meetings laughed over his touching references for the Untouchables. He would warn then people, "My friends, it is not a matter of laughter, but it is matter of shedding tears of blood."[68] He warned the caste Hindus to stop their atrocities against Dalits, otherwise their 'courage would ebb away."[69] He observed, "If Hinduism will bear untouchability, 22 crores of Hindus will perish which means India will perish."[70] He emphasized that the non-violence was "sole religion" and if the people believed in it as a "cardinal principle of their faith, they could not possibly face the world with the crime of untouchability on their head."[71]

In 1927 Gandhi witnessed untouchability in the Buddhist country Sri Lanka too. He spoke at Colombo on 25 November 1927, "I know that if India may take pride in having sent you Mahendra and the message of Buddha to this land, I had also to accept the humiliation of having sent you the curse of caste distinctions."[72] At Jaffna where Gandhi was welcomed by the Untouchables he said:

> I was delighted to receive two addresses from the Depressed Classes...living in a country over which the spirit of Buddha is brooding....Let us realize that it is a sin to consider a single human being as inferior to ourselves or Untouchable.[73]

Having such an ideological framework with regard to the problem of Dalits Gandhi came out with his specific initiative for the operation of his strategy of social amelioration of Dalits, particularly their most oppressed sections like Bhangis (scavengers), and Chamars (cobblers/tanners) which was also an important part of his 'Constructive Programme' vis-à-vis the problem of untouchability. His programme for social amelioration of the Untouchables included providing all necessary public and civil amenities, particularly water and education, to Dalits. Interestingly, the issue of temple entry was not included in this programme during the earlier period which, later on, became a prominent part of the 'Harijan work' of Gandhian Congress.

At Bardoli Taluka Conference held on 20 January 1922 Gandhi said :

> If there are separate schools for the Untouchables elsewhere, it may not matter, but here untouchability must positively be considered a sin. You cannot rest satisfied with having separate schools for Antayajas. It is your duty to persuade

> the Antyajas of those villages which have national schools to enroll their children in those schools and you should let them sit with your children.[74]

This speech was delivered in the historic Bardoli Conference. Here resolution on Civil Disobedience was passed which included 'Constructive Programme'.[75] Needless to say that it was Gandhi who made the Congress to take up the issue of social amelioration of the Depressed Classes. The party, however, did not contribute much to the cause except an expenditure of a sum of Rs. 43,381 out of Rs. 49.5 lakhs collected for the 'Telak *Swaraj* Fund' during 1921 to 1924.[76] In the Belgaum Session held in December 1924 under the chairmanship of Gandhi, the Congress adopted a resolution on the Dalit problem saying:

> The Congress notes with satisfaction the progress in Hindu opinion regarding the removal of untouchability but is of opinion that much yet remains to be done and, therefore, appeals the Hindu members of the Congress...to devote grater attention to the amelioration of the lot of Depressed Classes by ascertaining their wants.[77]

According to the Belgaum resolution, no school could be called 'national' where the Untouchables were refused admission. [78] But Gandhi soon adopted an 'impartial' approach and asked the Congressmen to "start a larger number of schools, especially for Antayaj children."[79] On 7 July 1927 he wrote in *Young India* that there were many schools for Dalit children being run in several provinces under the Congress and with Congress funds.[80] He further subscribed that those schools were also subsidized by the Government. The Congress also built 'Suppressed Class High Schools', particularly in Gujarat.[81]

It was further resolved by the Working Committee of the Congress on 24 March 1924 at Delhi to set up an 'Anti-Untouchability Committee' with M.M. Malviya, a prominent leader of Hindu Mahasabha, as President.[82]

He was to be assisted by Jamnalal Bajaj. Malviya appeared to have done very little work for the cause and, as such, Jamnalal Bajaj was left alone to do the work assigned to the Committee. The office of this Committee was opened at 395, Kalbadevi Road, Bombay.[83] The main objectives of this Committee were:

(i) to get public temples thrown open to the Antayaja;

(ii) to secure for the Antayajas the use of public wells;

(iii) to remove the restrictions which Antayaja children were facing in public schools;

(iv) to improve their conditions in respect of cleanliness; and

(v) to induce them to give up their habits of eating carrion and taking liquor.[84]

The Committee also expected from "every Hindu to help in educating public opinion for this work."[85] It is pointed out that Gandhi did not take up seriously the issues of wells and schools before 1932.[86] He, however, supported and admired the efforts of A.V. Thakkar who addressed an appeal to the public in March 1930 to donate to a Fund for digging wells for Dalits in Gujarat.[87] It was only after 1932 that Gandhi and party took seriously the issues of wells, schools and temples.[88] As of now, the Secretary of the Committee toured many parts of the country such as Madras, Central Provinces, Rajputana, Sind, Kashmir, Punjab and North West Frontier Province aiming at especially to convince the temple trustees in favour of 'temple reform.'[89] The Committee also organized three conferences in Bombay presidency in May and June 1929 at Bandra, Bombay and Poona.[90] Here workers took pledge to get at least one temple opened in near future by their 'humble efforts.'[91] But when these activities encouraged the Untouchables of Poona to launch a Temple Entry *Satyagraha* at Parvati temple, the Committee criticized their movement.[92]

It was after 1932 when Mahatma Gandhi did an intensive work for the cause of the Depressed Classes and, as such, made an operation of his approach to the problem on a wider scale. Actually, his clash with Dr. B.R. Ambedkar (1891-1956), the renowned Dalit leader, during 1930-32 over the issue of separate electorate of Dalits made him realize the seriousness of the problem.[93] He even undertook a fast-unto-death on 20 September 1932 against the grant of separate electorate to the Depressed Classes by the British Government.[94] By this act, he forced Dr. Ambedkar to agree to the joint electorate with reserved seats in the historic Poona Pact (24 September 1932)[95] It is, however, pertinent to note that during his fast Gandhi referred to the problem of untouchability and not the issue of separate electorate as a excuse of his fast which, for a short time, lit 'sacrificial fire' among the caste Hindus and made them realize about their 'sins' and prejudicial attitude towards Dalits.[96] It was the only positive outcome of his fast in the interest of the Depressed Classes as they were suddenly treated properly at places. Swaroop Rani Nehru, an orthodox Brahmin lady and mother of Jawaharlal Nehru, accepted from the hands of a sweeper.[97] In Shantiniketan Rabindranath Tagore began 'organized work' against untouchability.[98] Common caste Hindus at many places organized inter-caste dinners. Many temples were thrown open to Dalits at place like Bombay (Vithoba Rukmani temple), Poona (Parviti temple), Madras (Kanhaswani temple), Karachi (Jasraj temple), Nagpur, Gauhati etc.[99] After the conclusion of the Poona Pact some more temple were thrown open to Dalits, e.g., 100 year old Rama temple at Bombay, 80 year old Sindhi temple at Karachi and many other temples at Patna, Layallpur, Beawar, Rajwari, Calcutta, Baroda, Kashmir, Kolhapur etc.[100]

Gandhi who felt jubilant over such efforts, especially opening of temples, now decided to lead the Hindus to sustain their spirit of kindness for Dalits. Hence, the idea of 'Harijan Movement' took birth. During the Harijan

Movement, Gandhi operated his patronalistic approach to the Dalit problem on a massive scale. For operation of movement, a strategy was worked out wherein Gandhi retreated his stand on the issue.[101] He again declared the anti-untouchability work as an internal religious and social matter of the Hindus. He suggested that the caste Hindu 'reformers', whom he named 'Harijan *Sevaks*' (servants of Dalits), should take "this work as a purely religious work" and it must be "carried in a religious spirit."[102] He emphasized on a 'change of heart' among the caste Hindus towards Dalits by the peaceful means of 'reformers'. He made it clear, "Anti-untouchability movement is, as applied to the masses, for merely changing of heart and changing their (the caste Hindus') attitude towards Harijans, the vast majority of the caste Hindus do not need to interrupt their daily activity in order to serve the Harijans...."[103] He opined, "If reformers are truthful and humble, they can bring about a change of heart in the *Sanatanists*."[104] Gandhi still regarded *Varna* and caste as ideal social institutions.[105] Though he allowed the marriage of his adopted Dalit girl Laxmi with a Brahmin boy Maruti in August 1933, yet his opinion in the matter was that "I do not hold this marriage as an example for anybody to follow."[106] He only said that inter-caste dinning should be left entirely on "individual choice."[107] He promised Dalits that in free India's Constitution, the evil of untouchability would be abolished.[108] In short, Gandhi's position was still almost the same as was in 1920s.

Mahatma Gandhi tried his best to satisfy both Dalits as well as the caste Hindus during the Harijan Movement. He made clear his position on the question in very beautiful words:

> "I feel like the wife whom her many husbands profess to reject because the poor woman cannot give satisfaction to all her lords and masters... (though) the faithful wife (is) staunch in her loyalty."[109]

Gandhi said that he had undertaken the Dalit cause not in the 'spirit of patronage' but in the 'spirit of service.'[110] To this, however, Dalits would not agree. Their opinion was that the so-called 'spirit of service' itself indicated the spirit of patronage, as it reflected the feelings of pity, kindness etc. towards Dalits. Further, his 'spirit of service' had nothing to do with the capital issues concerning the problem, i.e., need of land reforms, political and economic empowerment of Dalits etc.[111]

In his statement to press after breaking his fast-unto-death on 25 September 1932, which reflected his future plans for the Depressed Classes, Gandhi said that he had decided to use the word 'Harijan' (people of God) for them saying he would like "henceforth to name them Harijans", and 'assured' his best to work for their cause.[112] After this he began his campaign against untouchability namely 'Harijan movement'. He also began to use the new name on a massive scale, despite the fact that it was disliked by both orthodox Hindus as well as Dalits. To proceed further, Gandhi decided to found an All India Anti-Untouchability League, a non-political organization of the caste Hindus, which was later on renamed as 'Servants of Untouchables Society', and finally 'Harijan Sevak Sangh.'[113] Gandhi started his Harijan movement with undertaking a 'penance fast' from 8th to 21th of May 1933[114] followed by the so-called 'Harijan tour', a most extensive journey in which Gandhi toured various parts of India continuously till nineteen months, i.e., from 7 November 1932 to 21 July 1934.[115] During this tour he made an extensive anti-untouchability propaganda and also collected a 'Harijan Purse Fund' worth Rs. 8 Lakhs which was contributed to the newly formed Harijan Sevak Sangh.[116]

In his fifth Statement on untouchability released on 14 November 1932, Mahatma Gandhi presented his guidelines for the Depressed Classes to the effect that "What Harijans could do in order to help the Movement."

He asked the 'Harijan Workers' to devote all their energies to:

(1) the promotion of cleanliness and hygiene among Harijans, and

(2) to improve the method of carrying on what are known as unclean occupations, such as, scavenging and tanning.

During the Harijan movement, Gandhi especially emphasized on 'Bhangi work' and asked the scavengers to become "ideal Bhangis."[117] He also suggested village tanners to use "modern scientific methods" for tanning work.[118]

The large part of the 'Harijan propaganda' regarding the Depressed Classes was often related to the 'Bhangi work' Even the Mahatma did not emphasize so strongly on cobbling or tanning word as he did in the matter of 'Bhangi work.' He was perhaps anxious about the problem of scavenging and sanitation in the caste Hindus' society, which could arise in the situation if the Dalit scavengers would deny to do their dirty work. This situation could cause a serious problem to the caste Hindus, as nobody would agree to work as their substitutes in any condition. That is why, the Mahatma always glorified the 'Bhangi work', and asked repeatedly scavengers to become 'Ideal Bhangis.'

But how was it possible for the scavenger to become an 'Ideal Bhangi', when he was branded by the Hindu Society as a "social pariah?" The Mahatma was equally worried about their conditions and that is why he repeatedly suggested the Municipalities to improve the working conditions of the scavengers. He pointed out that the municipal officials should help the scavengers by giving loans, constructing residential quarters, starting schools, arranging water facilities, and improving living conditions of the scavengers.[119] He also suggested the municipalities and local bodies to provide the sweepers "facilities for becoming clean" after doing their work.[120]

These "facilities" included, "bath and change of clothes", where were propagated by Heeralal Shah, a 'Harijan Sevak' and disciple of Mahatma Gandhi.[121] Mahatmaji also suggested the municipalities to purchase carts for the sweepers for scavenging the human excreta.[122] He also asked the sweepers to use "strong booklets in place of baskets for the disposal of night soil."[123]

Mahatma Gandhi simultaneously suggested the sweepers to do "proper disposal" and "wise use" of human excreta, as it could contribute "annual gain of 60 crores of rupees to the country."[124] He even supported the arguments of a medical men in favor of human excreta as "good food" for cows and cattle.[125]

So far as the cobblers and tanners were concerned, Mahatma Gandhi also tried his best to convince them to continue in their hereditary occupations. But he was anxious to the problem of eating carrion and beef by them, and wanted the Chamars to give up this practice at all. He was even ready to learn the craft of tanning so that he could help the Chamars to improve their conditions and also convince them to give up eating carrion: "I would have to learn how to skin the carcasses and tan the hides. This is necessary, if I am to deal with the habit of carrion eating..... This (habit) is a direct result of the criminal neglect of caste men and of compulsory segregation of the most useful members of our society...."[126]

In an article entitled, "Disposal of Carcasses" in *Harijan* dated 18 March 1933, Mahatma Gandhi expressed his views on this issue in these words:

> "There are several sections among Harijans, e.g. Chakkiliyans and Madigas in Southern India, and Chamars in Gujrat, who remove and dispose-off dead cattle, and eat their flesh.... We must show them the way out .... The removal (of carcasses) must be made condition as a promise, not to eat the carrion and no one shall be compelled to remove the dead cattle.... The carcasses should not

> be dragged as it presently (done) as it is damages the hide and decreases its value.... The way in which dead cattle are disposed... entails a loss of crores of rupees to the country.... They (bones) should be carefully collected and turned scientifically into manure.... The flesh...will be valuable for manufacturing grease for factories.... Municipalities and Local Bodies and State can immediately undertake the work of training volunteers in scientific skinning and hide carrying."[127]

Though, Mahatma Gandhi used the word "volunteers", it actually meant for the tanners.

When Prem Nath Bhargava, a 'Harijan Sevak', who was working in a tannery at Agra, asked him that would not the tanning of un-slaughtered cattle hides on a large scale by "modern scientific methods", helpful to "(a) economic upliftment of Harijan brethren and an immediate item of programme of work for the Servants of Untouchables Society, (b) improvement of living wealth of the country, (c) the creation of a new field of activity for the educated unemployed, and (d) protection of cows," Mahatmaji replied him that, "I have my doubts. Home or village tanning is necessary."[128]

In an important article entitled, "Village Tanning and its Possibilities", which appeared in *Harijan* dated 7 September 1934, Mahatma Gandhi said:

> "It is estimated that Rupees nine crores of raw hide is annually exported from India and that much of it is returned to her in shape of manufactured articles....

As a tanner, who is living at the Harijan Ashram, describing the scenes at his own now forsaken home, tells me, the whole family is drunk in joy at the sight of the dead animal.... Reformed tanning means the automatic disappearance of carrion-eating....

If the villagers and the public know the priceless and noble service the tanners render, they will provide easy and simple methods of carrying it so as not to injure the skin at all.... None, not even surgeons, do this work better or more expeditiously then the village tanner does with his village knife.... Doges however round the carcass, whiles it is flayed and take away some, if not all, of the bones.... There are several tanneries in India doing this work. The urbanization (however) do little good to the Harijans, much less to the villagers."[129]

In this way like scavenging, the tanning work was equally as important matter of the interest to Mahatma Gandhi. He would like the village tanners to do this work just like doing of scavenging work by the 'Bhangis.' But the cobblers and tanners were gradually developing a tendency of giving up their dirty and filthy occupations. In this regard, though Gandhi supported the right of Chamars to abandon or take up any work, he tried to convince them not to give up the profession of tanning because it would pay more to them than any other profession:

> "They have every right to abandon the work and take up anything else .... Often a carcass pays more..., for the dead flesh can be turned into fine manure. Bones need to be simply charred in order to be turned into rich manure, they are also used to make buttons, handles etc. Fat, which can be easily preserved, is precious for various purposes, the intestines are valuable for guts, for carding bows and musical instruments."[130]

When a Dalit asked him to make "some other arrangement for removal of the dead cattle, so that we may have no opportunity to remove or eat their flesh", Gandhi clarified:

> "The carcass of a dead cattle (firstly) belongs to him (the Chamar) ... Since he does not arrange

> for the proper disposal of the carcass, it means that he renounces his right over it. It, therefore, becomes the property of the State and the State should arrange for its disposal through Harijans by paying them suitably... He (the Chamar) may...hand over the hide to the State.... I have only suggested the easiest and simplest way which can be immediately adopted, of making the Chamars give up the practice of eating beef and carrion."[131]

The Mahatma further suggested to this effect that all dead cattle "should be declared state property and the cattle should be treated under the supervision of reliable officers and proper remuneration should be given to the Harijans, who may be willing to skill the carcasses...."[132]

It is pointed out that regarding tanning, Mahatmaji promptly suggested the state to take up the tanning work in situation of its giving up by Chamars. But as regards the 'Bhangi Work', he never suggested so and always propagated this work among the common Bhangis as a "sacred work." He also did not care much about other hereditary occupations of the Depressed Classes. It was perhaps so, that the as denouncing of all the occupations by Dalits other than scavenging, could not cause such a big trouble to the caste Hindus, as the denial of scavenging work could be. There was no possibility of adoption of scavenging work by the caste Hindus or even by non-Bhangi Dalits and this would cause a serious crisis to the Hindu society. That is why, Mahatma Gandhi put the idea of 'Bhangi Work', in the center stage of Harijan propaganda for the Depressed Classes. After his Harijan Movement, Mahatma limited his 'Harijan activates' only around the 'Bhangi Work.' He even began to live in a 'Bhangi colony' at New Delhi during his last days, uttering to them "I shall consider my faith among you amply sacred, if you give up all vices.... If you are keen that I should take food prepared by you, you can come here and cook food for me."[133]

During the Harijan movement Gandhi also guided K. Kelappan, a Congressman of Malabar, to launch a *Satyagraha* for securing entry of Dalits to the Krishna temple of Guruvayur in 1932-33.[134] Hence, the Guruvayur *Satyagraha* could not succeed and the temple remained closed to Dalits upto the independence of India.[135] Gandhi just presented a scheme of 'model temple' for "building new temples where necessary" for Dalits.[136]

After the elections of Provincial Assemblies in 1937, the Congress got majority in most of the provinces and formed Ministries.[137] The Congress Ministries made some legislations in the respective provinces for ensuring the access of Dalits to public places, particularly temples.[138] They gave financial aid to the branches of Harijan Sevak Sangh.[139] They also increased government funds for education of Dalits.[140] Especially in Bombay and Madras provinces, the Congress Ministries did a good work for the welfare of the Depressed Classes.

During this period, the most significant thing which appeared now in the approach of Gandhi was that his efforts and ideas - all witnessed a revolutionary change.[141] He attacked on the institution of untouchability in a very sharp language. His speeches were full of sincerity, passion and love for the drown-trodden. He now even made an attack on caste system and expressed his desire, like Dr. B.R. Ambedkar, to abolish it. He also reinterpreted *Varnashrama*. Said he:

> Today neither the *Varnas* nor the *Ashrams* (four stages of life) of my conception are in existence anywhere....The *Ashrams* have disappeared altogether and *Varnas* are found in the form of privileges. The claim of being a Brahmin, a Kshtriya, a Vaishya connotes pride. How can there be pride where there is religion? And the Shudras are not taken into consideration at all. Shudras are low and the Ati-Shudras (i.e., Dalits) are the

> lowest of the low. This is not religion, but negation of it.[142]

He further pointed out, "...If I had the power, I should declare that we are all Hindus, all of the same *Varna*....I do not know...when shall (we) be able to revive true *Varnashrama*."[143] He also openly advised inter-caste relations including inter-caste dinning and inter-caste-marriages: "So long as there are restrictions regarding inter-dinning and inter marriage, untouchability is bound to survive to some extent."[144] He advocated inter-caste marriage in most revolutionary manner:

> "If an educated Harijan girl marries a caste Hindu, the couple ought to devote themselves to the service of Harijans....It is certainly desirable that caste Hindu girls should select Harijan husbands....I would agree that at present the marriage of a caste Hindu girl to a Harijan is better than that of a Harijan girl to a caste Hindu."[145]

He also allowed Dalits to select the professions of their choice and not the hereditary ones. When he was asked by a Dalit, "We want the right of true citizenship, equal opportunity, I want my son to have equal liberty to be a *Vaqil* or Barrister or a Doctor according to his wish", the Mahatma replied, "There is no legal bar....Dr. Ambedkar is a barrister."[146]

Mahatma Gandhi asked repeatedly the 'Harijan *Sevaks*' and the *Savarnas* (caste Hindus) to work hard to remove all disabilities and difficulties of the Depressed Classes.[147] When the problem of finances confronted the Harijan Sevak Sangh after resignation of the Congress Ministries in 1939, Gandhi redoubled his efforts in collecting the donations for it from the people. He followed a practice of charging a price for his autographs for the cause of the down-trodden. He got few hundred of rupees every year by this practice.[148] When Gandhi began his Individual *Satyagraha* in 1940, he stated that only those Congressmen would be permitted to take part in the *Satyagraha* camps who worked against untouchability.[149] He waged a powerful struggle against the obnoxious custom.[150]

When the independence came nearer, Dalits began to ask him about their position in free India.[151] They were also worried about the special safeguards they got during the British period for their well being. A Dalit leader asked him pointedly:

Q. : What will be the position of the Harijans in future Constitution to be framed ?

Gandhi : In the Constitution I could influence...the so-called Untouchables would have seats reserved for them in all electoral bodies according to their population within the electoral areas concerned.[152]

And Gandhi agreed to give the Depressed Classes 15 percent reservation of seats in the Central and Provincial Legislature.[190] He came with the same generosity and kindness to Dalits when he, in a prayer meeting at New Delhi on 27 June 1947, declared his desire that he would like to see a Dalit to be the first President of the Indian Republic.[153] Actually, this idea came into his mind on the demise of Chakrayya, a Dalit disciple of Gandhi from Andhra Pradesh, in May 1947.[154] The Mahatma observed on his death, "He certainly did deserve to be the first President of the Indian Republic....If I had my way, I would put a suitable Harijan girl in the presidential chair. In free India. Knowledge of English would not be necessary for the President. She needs not to have knowledge of high politics.[155] All the learned statesmen of the country would help her to carry on the Government."[156] He again said in a prayer meeting at Delhi:

> Who will be the President of Indian Republic?... My answer is that ...(it) will be a chaste and brave Bhangi girl.... It is not necessary that President should be highly educated person knowing many

> languages....By electing a Harijan girl to that office we shall demonstrate our soul force....She should be chaste as Sita and her eyes should radiate light. Sita had such radiance that Ravana could not touch her. If I can find such a girl, she will be our first President. We shall all salute her and set a new example before the world....This is real moral power.[157]

Such a 'moral power' was, however, yet to develop among the Congressmen and the caste Hindus as nobody among them took the Mahatma's words seriously. Perhaps this old great man of modern India was, to them living in a world of dreams and old men's illusions (he was 78 then). But this was all said and done by Gandhi, the real Gandhi!

Endnotes

1 *The Collected Works of Mahatma Gandhi,* Navjivan Trust, Ahmadabad, d.d., Vol. XIV, pp. 73-74.

2 *Young India,* Ahmadabad, 4 April 1921.

3 *The Collected Works of Mahatma Gandhi,* Vol. XXIII, p. 292.

4 *Young India,* 23 April 1925.

5 *Ibid.*

6 Mukut Bihari Verma, *History of the Harijan Sevak Sangh (1932-1968),* Harijan Sevak Sangh Press, Delhi, 1971, p. 24.

7 *Ibid.,* p. 23.

8 S.K. Chahal, *Dalits Patronised: Indian Natural Congress and the Untouchables of India 1921-1947,* Shubhi Publications, New Delhi, 2002, p. 67.

9 *Ibid.,* pp. 67-68.

10 *Dr. Babasaheb Ambedkar: Writings and Speeches,* Education Department, Government of Maharastra, Mumbai, d.d., Vol. V, pp. 62-74.

11 *Young India,* 24 October 1920.

12 *The Collected Works of Mahatma Gandhi,* Vol. XVIII, p. 78.

13 Eleanor Zelliot, "Congress and Untouchables 1917-1950", in Richard Session & Stenly Wolpert, *Congress and Indian Nationalism: The Pre-Independence Phase,* Berkley, 1988, pp. 184-85.

14 *The Collected Works of Mahatma Gandhi,* Vol. XXI, p. 267.

15 *Ibid.*

16 *Sampurna Gandhi Vangmya* (Hindi), Navjivan Trust, Ahmedabad, d.d., Vol. IXXX, Document No. 17.

17 *Ibid.*

18 *Ibid.*

19 *Ibid.,* Document No. 177 and 267.

20 *Ibid.,* Document No. 267.

21 *The Collected Works of Mahatma Gandhi,* Vol. XX, p. 136.

22 *Ibid.,* Vol. XXVI, p. 524.

23 *Ibid.,* Vol. XLIII, pp. 264-68.

24 S.K. Chahal, *op. cit.,* p. 72.

25 *The Collected Works of Mahatma Gandhi,* Vol. XLIII, p. 340.

26 *Young India,* 8 December 1920.

27 *The Collected Works of Mahatma Gandhi,* Vol. XIV, pp. 73-74.

28 *Young India,* 11 May 1921.

29 *The Collected Works of Mahatma Gandhi,* Vol. XX, p. 510.

30 *Ibid.,* p. 510.

31 *Ibid.,* Vol. XXI, p. 132.

32 *Ibid.,* Vol. XV, p. 45.

33 *Ibid.* Vol. XXI, pp. 2-3.

34 *Ibid.,* Vol. XII, pp. 471-72.

35 *Ibid.,* Vol. XX, pp. 53-54.

36 *Ibid.,* pp. 335-36.

37 *Ibid.,* Vol. XXI, p. 143.

38 *Ibid.,* Vol. XXXIV, p. 212.

39 *Young India,* 26 February 1932.

40 *The Collected Works of Mahatma Gandhi,* Vol. XXVI, p. 4.

41 *Ibid.,* Vol. XVII, pp. 518-19.

42 *Ibid.,* Vol. XXVI, pp. 7-8.

43 *Ibid.,* Vol. XXI, pp. 185-88.

44 *Ibid.,* Vol. XXIII, p. 292.

45 *Ibid.,* Vol. XIV, p. 75.

46 *Ibid.,* Vol. XXXII, pp. 428-29.

47 *Young India,* 8 January 1921.

48 *Ibid.*

49 *The Collected Works of Mahatma Gandhi,* Vol. XXVI, pp. 130-32.
50 *Ibid.,* p. 539.
51 *Ibid.,* Vol. XXVI, p. 132.
52 *Ibid.,* Vol. XXII, p. 275.
53 *Ibid.*
54 S.K. Chahal, *op. cit.,* p. 76.
55 *The Collected Works of Mahatma Gandhi,* Vol. XXX, pp. 212-14.
56 *Ibid.,* Vol. XXXII, p. 513.
57 *Ibid.*
58 *Ibid.,* Vol. XVII, p. 471.
59 *Ibid.,* Vol. XIV, p. 73.
60 *Ibid.,* Vol. XX, p. 30.
61 *Ibid.*
62 *Ibid.,* pp. 262-63.
63 *Ibid.,* Vol. XXIII, p. 436.
64 *Ibid.,* Vol. XXVI, pp. 130-32.
65 *Ibid.,* Vol. XXVIII, p. 378.
66 *Ibid.,* Vol. XXVI, p. 477.
67 *Ibid.,* p. 478.
68 *Ibid.,* Vol. XXVI, p. 373.
69 *Ibid.,* p. 147.
70 *Ibid.,* p. 525.
71 *Ibid.,* Vol. XXIII, p. 525.
72 *Ibid.,* Vol. XXXV, p. 318.
73 *Ibid.,* p. 312.
74 *Ibid.,* Vol. XXVI, pp. 130-32.
75 B.R. Ambedkar, *op. cit.,* p. 21.
76 *Dr. Babasaheb Ambedkar : Writings and Speeches,* Vol. IX, pp. 35-36.
77 *The Indian Quarterly Register,* H.N. Mitra (ed.), Calcutta, 1924, Vol. II, p. 425.
78 *The Collected Works of Mahatma Gandhi,* Vol. XXVIII, p. 168.
79 *Ibid.,* p. 352.
80 *Ibid.,* Vol. XXXIV, p. 126.
81 *Ibid.,* Vol. XXXVI, p. 232.

82 *Ibid.*, Vol. XLI, p. 3.

83 *Ibid.*

84 *Ibid.*

85 *Eleanor Zelliot,* op. cit., p. 187.

86 S.K. Chahal, *op. cit.*, p. 87.

87 *The Collected Works of Mahatma Gandhi,* Vol. XLI, pp. 348-49.

88 *Ibid.*, Vol. XLIII, p. 191.

89 *The Indian Quarterly Register,* 1929, Vol. II, pp. 326-27.

90 *Ibid.*

91 *Ibid.*

92 Eleanor Zelliot, *op. cit.*, pp. 179-180.

93 B.R. Ambedkar, *op. cit.*, pp. 68-69.

94 *Ibid.*, p. 87.

95 *Ibid.*, pp. 88-89.

96 *The Collected Works of Mahatma Gandhi,* Vol. LI, pp. 117-18.

97 Mukut Bihari Verma, *op. cit.*, pp. 53-54.

98 *Ibid.*

99 Pyare Lal, *The Epic Fast,* Mohanlal Maghan Lal Bhatt, Ahmadabad 1932, pp. 142-45.

100 Mukut Bihari Verma, *op. cit.*, pp. 54-55.

101 Eleanor Zelliot, *op. cit.*, p. 191.

102 *The Collected Works of Mahatma Gandhi,* Vol. XLV, pp. 124-25.

103 *Ibid.*, Vol. LI, pp. 434-35.

104 S.K. Chahal, *op. cit.*, p. 163.

105 *The Collected Works of Mahatma Gandhi,* Vol. XLI, pp. 218-19.

106 *Ibid.*, Vol. LIV, p. 16.

107 *Ibid.*, Vol. LIII, p. 192.

108 *Ibid.*, pp. 362-63.

109 *Ibid.*, Vol. LII, p. 358.

110 *Ibid.*, pp. 157-58.

111 S.K. Chahal, *op. cit.*, p. 164.

112 *The Collected Works of Mahatma Gandhi,* Vol. LI, p. 145.

113 *Ibid.*, Vol. LIV, p. 18.

114 *Harijan: A Journal of Applied Gandhism,* Joan Bondurant (ed.), Garland Publishing Company, New York, 1973, Vol. I, 18 February 1933 and 16 September 1933.

115 Mukut Bihari Verma, *op. cit.,* pp. 85-86.

116 *Dr. Babasaheb Ambedkar: Writings and Speeches,* Vol. IX, p. 129.

117 *The Collected Works of Mahatma Gandhi,* Vol. LXII, p. 329.

118 *Harijan: A Journal of Applied Gandhism,* Vol. I, 18 March 1933.

119 *Ibid.,* Vol. XXXXI, p. 268.

120 *Ibid.,* Vol. LIII, p. 268.

121 *Ibid.,* Vol. LIV, pp. 109-110.

122 *Ibid.*

123 *Ibid.,* Vol. LV, p. 277.

124 *Ibid.,* Vol. LX, pp. 302-303.

125 *Harijan: A Journal of Applied Gandhism,* Vol. 3, 26 June, 1935.

126 *Ibid,* Vol. I, 8 April, 1935.

127 *Ibid.,* Vol. 1, 18 March, 1933.

128 *The Collected Works of Mahatma Gandhi,* Vol. LIII, p. 215.

129 *Harijan: A Journal of Applied Gandhism,* Vol. 2, 7 September, 1934.

130 *The Collected Works of Mahatma Gandhi,* Vol. LXIII, p. 43.

131 *Ibid,* Vol. LII, pp. 372-73.

132 *The Collected Works of Mahatma Gandhi,* Vol. LIV, p. 193.

133 *Ibid.,* Vol. LXXXIII, p. 360.

134 *Dr. Babasaheb Ambedkar: Writings and Speeches,* Vol. IX, p. 116.

135 *Ibid.,* p. 117.

136 *The Collected Works of Mahatma Gandhi,* Vol. LIV, pp. 335-37.

137 S.K. Chahal, *op. cit.,* pp. 200-01.

138 *Ibid.,* p. 205-10.

139 *Ibid.*

140 *Ibid.*

141 *Ibid.,* p. 210.

142 *The Collected Works of Mahatma Gandhi,* Vol. LXXX, p. 222.

143 *Ibid.,* Vol. LXII, p. 291.

144 *Ibid.,* Vol. LXV, pp. 182-83.

145 *Ibid.*, Vol. LXXXIV, pp. 388-89.

146 *Ibid.*, Vol. LXII, p. 292.

147 *The Collected Works of Mahatma Gandhi,* Vol. LXXI, p. 429.

148 *Harijan: A Journal of Applied Gandhism*, Vol. IX, 26 April 1942.

149 *Ibid.*, Vol. VIII, 25 May 1940.

150 *Ibid.*, Vol. X, 17 March 1946.

151 *Ibid.*, Vol. VII, 20 January 1940.

152 *Ibid.*, Vol. IX, 2 August 1942.

153 *The Collected Works of Mahatma Gandhi,* Vol. LXXXV, p. 102.

154 *Harijan: A Journal of Applied Gandhism,* Vol. XI, 15 June 1947.

155 *Ibid.*

156 *Ibid.*

157 *The Collected Works of Mahatma Gandhi,* Vol. LXXXVIII, pp. 224-25.

3

The Politics of Inclusion and Exclusion: The Case of Reconstruction of Jatav Identity

Dr. Amardeep*

"Hum koun the kya ho gaye,
ab to tumhe kuch dyan ho,
Bahu-kal bita gupt rahte
bhulo na Yadu santan ho."[1]

[Who were we, what have we become?\ Now you should pay some attention\ Long time has been spent living in hiding\ don't forget you are the sons of Yadu (dynasty)].[2]

These lines, inscribed on the cover, illustrate the essence of the book written by Pandit Sundarlal Sagar (1886-1952)[3], who acclaimed that the Jatavs [or Yadavs] are the successors of the Yadu dynasty to which the god, Krishna, belonged.[4] This ideology remained instrumental in the process of reconstruction of a new identity which would instill a sense of confidence and respect and further, remove the sense of inferiority. The idea of a new identity influenced the untouchables of the United Provinces (UP)

* Assistant Professor in History, Govt. College, Birohar, (Jhajjar), Haryana, E-mail: amardeepmuwal@gmail.com

in the early twentieth century. Two major untouchable groups evolved their ideology to achieve their aim. On the one hand, the Adi Hindu movement, launched by Swami Acchutanand in 1922, asserted that the untouchables were the original inhabitants of India. They were reduced to bottom of the Indian society by the Aryan Brahmans through malpractices and conspiracies. On the other hand, Pandit Sundarlal Sagar, a Jatav, was influenced by the Arya Samaj and accepted the Samaj's idea of Varna system, believed that the Jatavs were the Kshatriyas in the course of ancient Indian history. Now, they could reclaim their centuries' old status through the help of the Samaj. The present paper is an attempt to examine the work and efforts of the first Jatav leadership in social sphere to attain Kshatriya Varna status in the first half of twentieth century. The second part of the paper brings out the outline of their social and political movement where Jatavs were associating themselves with the scheduled castes and Dr. Ambedkar but not with Chamar. And finally they rejected the idea of Kshatrization and many of them embraced Buddhism.

I

The Jatavs were engaged in shoe and leather industries, which bloomed into a full-fledged industry in the 1920s. With leisure, independence, and security, the wealthier Jatavs had the scope to engage in intellectual activities. They aimed to live a privileged life through social mobility within the caste system. For them, a significant change came with the growth of mission schools and, more importantly, the growth of the Arya Samaj. The Arya Samaj became a reference group for *imitation,* since it was the Vedic practices of this group that the Jatavs tried to imitate their behaviour, rites, and beliefs. This meant that meat eating and scavenging were to be eschewed, and the practice of the Vedic *samskaras,* especially the sacred thread ceremony (*Janau*), was to be adopted. It is significant that the Arya Samaj taught not only the Vedic way of life but also that an individual's caste status was achieved not ascribed. This was translated by the Jatavs into group action for a change of status for the whole group. The notion of individual achievement and its legitimacy had been planted in the Jatav mind as an awareness of a potential alternative form of social mobility without questioning the caste order.[5]

The print media was utilized to achieve the task of reconstruction of a new identity. The first generation of the Jatav leaders published their books and started newspapers and journals to strengthen their claim. The process of Sanskritization[6] and Kshatriyaization[7] was adopted by Jatavs. Further, they spread the awareness and desire to accept a new mythological definition[8] of their caste rank and the means of legitimizing it. In this direction, a book *'Jatav Jivan'* (Jatav Life), written by Pandit Sundarlal Sagar, was used to justify the claim to *Kshatriya* status in 1924.[9] The writer made explicit the Jatav's denial of their untouchable status. He wrote,

"through this book we want to tell other castes that the Jatav race is
one of the sacred and highest races and is not untouchable.'
(Sundarlal Sagar, 1924)[10]

This book was written with an aim to reconstruct a glorious Jatav history. It categorically pronounced that the Jatavs were the Kshatriyas. It was further established by references by Swami Atma Ram, an Arya Samaj preacher, who wrote *'Gyan Samudra'* in 1888. The Jatavs, he said, were really the survivors of the ancient war between Parasurama[11] and the Kshatriyas. The occupations of shoemakers and contractors in building construction were adopted as a defense and a disguise to which Jatavs were reduced in order to escape the wrath of Parasurama.[12] "The main reason of the non-availability of our history is the jealousy of Parasurama and his disciples towards the Kshatriya [warriors] race."[13]

Pandit Sagar expressed his belief in the Vedas and the Varna system. As per Arya Samaj's ideology, he also had a notion that the Varna system is based on merits of the person concerned, and not on birth. It is interesting that he argued that the Varna system is prevailing in whole world. However, its nature, he continued, is different according to the social structures of different countries. Our Brahmin is called a professor in other countries. Our Kshatriyas, Vaishyas, and Shudras are called soldier, merchant, and coolie respectively in other countries. There is a difference in names only but not in principles.[14] It is worth mentioning that the author strongly opined that the Jatavs are not Hindus at all. Rather, they are the followers of the Vedic religion. He considered 'Hindu' as a *'kafir'*, one who believes in many gods.[15] However, the idea of rejection of Hinduism was established but acceptance of the Vedic religion was the result of influence of the Arya Samaj. They called themselves Aryans instead of Hindus.

Adopting a Brahmanical stance to legitimize their claim for Kshatriyahood, the author elucidated the word 'Jatav' as derived from 'Yadav'. He constructed a genealogy of their 'great ancestors' and *kula*. There were eighteen *kulas* (lineage) in the Yadu dynasty. These belonged to great kings like Sagar, Maurya, and great *rishis* (sage) like Shiva, Pipil, Harit, Kashyapa etc. In addition, to present the Jatavs as different from untouchables, he said Jatavs were not a *Jati* (caste) but were a lineage. He claimed that *Jati* came into existence with the immorality of a particular group. The *Jati* is the result of illegal relations between different Varnas. It is also called *'Varnashankar'* (mixed Varna origin). Significantly, the Jatav is not included in this version of *Jati* system. They allegedly belonged to the *'Jatav Vansh'* (lineage) and their origin was absolutely pious.[16]This was presented to show that the ancestors of the Jatav community were learned and powerful. They had never reportedly associated with any polluted or unclean work.[17] Even though they, like the upper castes, tried to separate themselves from the low castes, but Brahmans rejected the Jatav claim to Kshatriyahood.[18]

The Jatavs considered the *Manusmriti* and the *Gita* as their holy scripture. Manu, they claimed, wrote this *smriti* in the period of great king Yadu. The Yadu dynasty has produced many warriors like King Yadu, Krishna, Jatayu, Maya, Alha and Udal. But Parasurama's successors distorted their history to render them untouchables and compelled them to live a subjugated life. Sagar called to the Jatavs to come out from 'exile' and use their glorious Yadav title because now there was no fear of enemy Parasurama or his successors.[19]

The second part of this book was published in 1929 and both parts were put together in one book. Sagar entitled it ***'Yadav Jivan'*** because Jatavs belonged to the Yadav dynasty in their past. In the second part, the symbols and rituals from the birth to after-death have been discussed in detail to strengthen their claim for Kshatriya Varna. This book emphasises that a sense of superiority can be spread if a glorious history is produced.

The Jatav adopted Brahmanical approach to acquire their new social status within the caste system. They were facilitated by the Arya Samaj whose aim was to convert or to bring back the untouchables to the fold of Hinduism. This was initiated by the process of socialization that included an anticipated rise it status.[20] Their contempt towards the Chamar caste and their claim for Kshatriya status can be seen a major development of the Dalit literary discourse.

Pandit Sagar founded an organization, the *Shri Jatav Maha Sabha*, to commence the collective struggle against orthodox Hinduism and to legitimize their claim of Kshatriya Varna in Rajamandi in Agra in 1917. Pandit Lala Ram Nim, Pandit Chedilal Kadik, Pandit Prabhudayal Vyas and Dr. Jatavaveer Manikchand played important role in the foundation of *Shri Jatav Maha Sabha*. Baba Khemchand was elected its first president and Baba

Chokhelal was elected as a vice-president of the *Sabha*.[21] Under the banner of the *Shri Jatav Maha Sabha*, Pandit Sagar organized many big and small meetings and conferences to infuse new blood and feelings of living with dignity among his brethren. But it was only in Maharashtra, that he got the positive support of the Arya Samaj. Otherwise, in other places like Indore, Rohtak, Amritsar, Patna and various cities of the United Provinces, he received a negative response, even opposition, from the Arya Samajists. The Arya Samajists had thought that if these people became literate or civilized, then who would look after their menial and other degraded works.[22] In 1912, Swami Acchutanand, in an Arya Samajist school's inaugural function in Mainpuri, was shocked to see the untouchable students sitting on the ground while the upper caste students were sitting on a mat. He sought donations from people from all quarters for construction of this school under the aegis of the Arya Samaj. His wife, Durgabai donated her only golden ring. Nevertheless, he found that even the Arya Samaj was not free from caste discrimination. He then decided to part away with it.[23] It showed the double standards of the Arya Samajists because on the one hand they argued that the Arya Samaj had no belief in the caste system and untouchability and it considers all human being as of equal origin. On the other hand, despite the *Shuddhi* initiative, they remained untouchables and segregated from the mainstream life of the Arya Samaj.

Despite that Pandit Sagar also founded *'Jatav Pracharak Mahamandal'* on 1 January in 1924 in Agra to propagate the Jatav identity as a Kshatriya. Pandit Prabhudayal was elected as president and Babu Ram Prasad as a minister of this organization. In spite of limited education, Pandit Sagar acquired a very good knowledge of Sanskrit literature and of comparative religions by self-education. To spread his ideas, he edited a monthly magazine *'Jatav Granth Mala'* in 1920 and wrote *'Jatav Jivan'* in 1924. It provided ideological support to their claim that the Jatav belonged to Kshatriya Varna and they should struggle for their true identity. He also wrote other booklet "*Jatav Pratha Sangrah*" which was published by *Jatav Pracharak Mahamandal* from Agra but there is no information about its publication.[24] He personally felt that the Jatavs must get educated. Otherwise, their emancipation from orthodox Hinduism would be incomplete. Keeping these ideas in mind, he opened a *Jatav Pathsahla,* a primary school for the Jatav students in Agra.[25]

Another ideological strength was provided by Ramanarayana Yadavendu (1909-1951) who wrote *'Yadu Vansh Ka Itihaas'* which was published from the Navyug Sahitya Niketan, Agra in 1942. The author was also influenced by the Arya Samaj and adopted a Brahmanical approach to explain religion and history from an angle that is radically differed from the contemporary Adi Hindu movement. He described the Vedas as historical sources rather than as sacred literature. He considered the *Ramayana* as the oldest source of history. He lamented that the British government also played a crucial role in distorting the Aryan history. British writers presented a history of India in such a way that the Aryans did not feel proud of their ancestors.[26]

Despite the arguments of western scholars that the Aryans were aliens, the author believed that the Aryans were the original inhabitants of India. He argued that B.G. Tilak misunderstood hymns of Rig Veda which tells us regarding the six-month long day and night. Swami Dayananda believed that the Aryans belonged to Tibet. But the author pointed out the views of historian like A.C. Das and Pandit Chintamani Vinayak as they regarded the *Sapt-Sindhu* region as the home place of the Aryans. He maintained that Swami Dayananda's views were quite similar to those that referred to the *Sapt-Sindhu* region.[27] The author was trying to bring out the Brahmanical framework and to further strengthen the *Varnashrama* order based on Hindu caste hierarchy.

Like Sagar, he also claimed that Jatav were Kshatriya and belonged to the Yadu dynasty. But he did not consider Krishna as an incarnation of God Vishnu. He argued that the incarnation theory is against the Vedas and he maintained that God is immortal and He does need to take rebirth. Krishna was a great warrior and politician of the Yadav dynasty.[28]

In an interesting development, he refuted that Yadav warriors changed their name to Jatav due to wrath of Parasurama. He argued that Parasurama was contemporary of Rama and there was a big gap of thousand years between Rama and Krishna. During the time of Krishna, the Yadavs were powerful in the realm of politics and religion. He constructed a new narrative, derived from the Mahabharata: that after the war of Mahabharata, the Yadavs indulged in a civil war and Krishna and Balaram tried to prevent them. But they failed. Later, the Yadav empire was destroyed in Dvarika and, subsequently, the Yadav power became weak. Later on, they adopted various names such as Yadav, Jadav, Jadon or Jatav etc.[29] It has been seen that both Jatav intellectuals have evolved a different set of arguments in the process of construction of their new identity nevertheless their aim was profoundly one i.e. the claim for Kshatriya status.

The process of the Sanskritization was used to acquire the Kshatriya status. Therefore, the first generation of Jatav intellectuals gave ample importance to it. For instance, Ramanarayan Yadavendu always tried to root out bad habits of his community people like meat eating, drinking, child marriage and other evils. The bad habit of meat eating was enforced by caste Hindus upon the Jatav because caste Hindus had not left any other alternative for their livelihood and kept them in ignorance by depriving them of their right of education. He believed that until and unless the Jatav had not left the bad habits till then they could not raise awareness and consciousness among them and their struggle of emancipation from the clutches of orthodox Hinduism would be incomplete.[30]

II

The Jatav intellectuals were much influenced by the Arya Samaj. It seems that in their writings it was the ideology of the Arya Samaj that was reflecting rather than contemporary problems of the Jatavs. They were ideologically and culturally hegemonized by the Arya Samaj. Therefore, they demonstrated their contempt towards the untouchables and claimed that they have no relation with the Chamar caste. In the 1930s and the 1940s, some significant changes occurred in the Jatavs' movement. On the one hand, in politics, they expressed their inclination towards Dr. Ambedkar. And on the other hand, in social scenario, they still kept distance from Chamar caste; but to get various political and economic benefits, they sent resolutions to Govt. of India for their inclusion in the list of the scheduled castes as separate from Chamar caste. This type of strategy had a clear indication of their departure from the acquiring of the Kshatriya status. It seems that they have been clearly understood the futility of the Kshatriya status. The above mentioned negative approaches of the Arya Samaj towards Jatav's claim, as Sagar faced during his visits in various parts of India, also evolved some apprehensions in the mind of Jatavs. Even the orthodox Brahmans were not ready to accept Jatavs's Kshatriya claim in their routines life.

During the Round Table Conferences and the Poona Pact, a significant change came into their position when they associated with Ambedkar instead of Gandhi. The British government announced the Communal Award for the untouchables in 1932. According to it, the right of separate electorates was given to them. A separate electorate means an electorate composed exclusively of untouchable voters who were to elect an untouchable as their representative to the Legislature. Caste Hindus had agreed that a certain number of seats were to be reserved for untouchables to be filled only by untouchables. But they insisted that the untouchable who was to be the representative of the untouchables in the legislature should be elected by a mixed electorate consisting both of caste Hindus as well as of untouchables.[31] Gandhi responded to the Communal Award by announcing that he would "fast unto death".[32] Subsequently, a compromise, known as the Poona Pact, was signed. According to it the electorate was maintained as a joint one while the numbers of seats specifically reserved for untouchables was almost doubled.[33] It is noteworthy that after the Poona Pact, the Jatavs started to show their inclination towards the leaders of the Depressed Classes like Dr. Ambedkar. They were convinced that the Arya Samaj only provided them with a nominal respect but in reality, only their name was changed but they remained as subordinate as they were earlier.[34]

Ramnarayan Yadavendu laid down the foundation of *'Bhartiya Yadav Yuvak Parishad'* with the assistance of Ramswaroop Sagar, Ramdayal Sagar and Natthilal Yadav to undertake social reforms in their caste in 1930.[35] This society played a significant role to include the Jatav caste as a separate caste in the list of the Scheduled Castes. Soon, its branches were opened in Delhi, Punjab, Rajasthan and other places. On 5 January, 1931, they sent a memorandum to the Viceroy and to the Census Officer of the United Provinces to include the Jatav caste as a separate caste in their population enumeration of 1931. But their demand was not fulfilled. A circular was issued by the Education Department in the United Provinces that students from Jatav community can write their caste as Jatav/Chamar on January 11, 1938. It meant that the Jatav caste should be understood as a sub-division of the Chamar caste. In 1938, a session of *'Bhartiya Jatav Yuvak Prashad'* was convened under the presidentship of Ramnarayan Yadavendu. A resolution was passed to organize protest meetings and to resolve that they should send their memorandum to the Provincial Government against the circular. It was a result of 11 years long movement that on 9 December, 1941 the Jatav caste was included in the list of Scheduled Castes as a separate caste.[36]

In 1944-45, a branch of Ambedkar's All India Scheduled Castes Federation (AISCF) had been opened in Agra by the Jatavs. It was a major turning point in the Jatavs' definition of their social and political position. This is because earlier they had claimed their affiliation with the *Kshatriya varna* and denied their association with untouchable castes. Now, their reference group of identification became the Scheduled Castes (SC): the oppressed and deprived sections of the society. These characteristics of the SC became the basis of a new Jatav self–image which was a striking about turn from their march to Kshatriyahood. Ramnarayan Yadavendu, Dharam Prakash, Jatavaveer Manikchand and others played instrumental role in organizing a conference of the AISCF at Agra in the presence of Dr. Ambedkar, then Labour Member in the Viceroy's Executive Council in 1946.[37]

With the opening of branch of the AISCF in Agra, the Jatavs gave up the idea of Sanskritization. In the 1940s, however they still did not consider themselves as Chamars rather than they demanded a separate status from the Chamars in the list of the Scheduled Castes from the colonial government. Sanskritization as a process is not applicable to all movements for social mobility in post-independence India. When a caste, such as the Jatavs, rejects the Sanskritization and the caste system and opts for political participation and parliamentary democracy, the term does not apply.[38] Further, Lynch claims, in post-independence India the Jatavs rejected Hinduism and its core, the caste system, as well as the Congress party. Instead, many of them embraced Buddhism and joined Ambedkar's political party – the Republican Party of India – in 1957 for political liberation.

Conclusion

In Northern India, some protest movements were emerging against the hegemony and monopoly of caste Hindus, legitimized by Brahmanical religious texts in the early twentieth century. Swami Acchutanand initiated a movement for emancipation from the stigma of untouchability. He made a strong assertion for the Depressed Classes who had never raised their voice against their oppressions and oppressors. At the same time, the Jatavs of Agra tried to rise within the Varna system with the help of the Arya Samaj by claiming the Kshatriya status. They reconstructed a new Jatav history to remove the inferiority complex in brethren. They utilized the means of Kshatrization and Sanskritization to achieve their aim. It was a great legacy of their initiatives that a movement launched by them created an army of Jatavs who were equipped with 'the power of writing' and provided a new energy to the movement. It is striking that the means of social mobility for the Jatavs was based on an acceptance and not a rejection of the caste system. The Jatavs were not attempting to destroy the caste system, rather they were trying to rise within it. Their ideas were changed drastically during 1930s and 1940s. Now they opened two fronts to struggle for a respectful life: one is political and other social. After Poona Pact, they accepted Ambedkar's movement instead of Gandhi. They also opened branches of All India Scheduled Castes Federation in Agra. They believed that without political power, their social and economic conditions could not be improved. But at the same time, on societal perspective, they were still not associating themselves with the Chamar caste because of its untouchable and polluted status as told by orthodox Brahmans.

After independence, many Jatav intellectuals embraced Buddhism and rejected the idea of the Arya Samaj and Varna system. They declared futility of the process of Kshatrization. They paved the way for raising caste consciousness among Jatavs. At the same time, many Jatav intellectuals continuously struggled against Hinduism. They also joined the Republican Party of India in 1957. Until now, their movement is going on for the betterment of political, social and economic conditions of their fellow brethren. They are still continuing their struggle to establish a society based on the merits of human beings where they can live with self-respect and dignity.

Endnotes

1 From the cover page of Sundarlal Sagar; *Yadav Jivan (Part 1)*, Agra: Shri Jatav Maha Sabha, 1929

2 My translation from Hind

3 He was popularly known as a *Pandit* despite his non-Brahman background in his community. He didn't attain formal education, but he acquired knowledge and efficiency of Sanskrit and Hindi languages through self study.

4 Nesfield, J. C.; *Brief View of the Caste System of the North-Western Provinces and Oudh, Allahabad: North Western Provinces and Agra* Government Press, 1885, p. 22

5 Lynch, Owen M., "The Politics of Untouchability: A Case From Agra, India" in B.S. Cohn & Milton (ed.) *Structure and Change in Indian Society*, Chicago, 1968, pp. 212-217

6 'Sanskritization' is the process by which a 'low' Hindu caste, or tribe, change its customs, rituals, ideology, and way of life in the direction of high and frequently, 'twice-born' caste. (For more detail: M.N. Srinivas; Social Change in Modern India, Berkeley: University of California Press, 1966)

7 In this process, The Jatavs tried to acquire Kshatriya Varna status and denied their association with untouchable caste Chamar. They gave up the practices associated with untouchable status and followed the rituals like wear *Janau* (sacred thread) and acquire *Dhanush* and *Tir* (Bow and Arrows). (For more detail: Owen M. Lynch; The Politics of Untouchability: Social Change in a City of India, New York: Columbia University Press, 1969)

8 An Arya Samaj Brahman named Swami Atma Ram had written a book entitled '*Gyan Samudra*' (the Ocean of Knowledge) around 1888. In this book, the origin of Jatav

race has been traced from the *Gotra* of Lord Shiva and hence they considered to be as *Kshatriyas*.

9 Lynch, Owen M., *The Politics of Untouchability: Social Change in a City of India*, New York: Columbia University Press, 1969, p. 69

10 Ibid

11 Parasurama was a mythical Brahman and incarnation of God Vishnu who appeared in the Mahabharta and the Ramayana. His hostility to Kshatriyas was so great that he was alleged to have cleaned the earth of them twenty one times. (Dowson, 1961: 230-31)

12 Lynch, Owen M., *The Politics of Untouchability: Social Change in a City of India*, New York: Columbia University Press, 1969, p. 72

13 Sagar, Sundarlal, *Yadav Jivan (Part 1)*, Agra: Shri Jatav Maha Sabha, 1929, p. 30

14 Ibid, p. 45

15 Ibid, pp. 32-33

16 Ibid, pp. 46-52

17 Ibid, pp.25-27

18 Lynch, Owen M., "The Politics of Untouchability: A Case From Agra, India" in B.S. Cohn & Milton (ed.) *Structure and Change in Indian Society*, Chicago, 1968, p. 217

19 Sagar, Sundarlal, *Yadav Jivan (Part 1)*, Agra: Shri Jatav Maha Sabha, 1929, pp. 36-37

20 Lynch, Owen M., "The Politics of Untouchability: A Case From Agra, India" in B.S. Cohn & Milton (ed.) *Structure and Change in Indian Society*, Chicago, 1968, p. 216

21 Sagar, Sundarlal, *Yadav Jivan (Part 1)*, Agra: Shri Jatav Maha Sabha, 1929, p. 3

22 Personal interviews with Sudhir Sagar (age 56) and Sunil Kumar (age 52), Grandsons of Sundarlal Sagar, Agra on 26 February, 2008 at 6.15 pm

23 Personal interview with Guru Prasad Madan, (age 65), Dalit writer and publisher in Allahabad on February 21, 2007, 5p.m.

24 Sagar, Sundarlal, *Yadav Jivan (Part 1)*, Agra: Shri Jatav Maha Sabha, 1929, pp. 3-4

25 Yadavendu, Ramanarayana, *Yaduvansh Ka Itihaas*, Agra: Navyug Sahitya Niketan, 1942, p. 251

26 Ibid, pp. 1-9

27 Ibid; pp. 10-15

28 Ibid; pp. 38-39

29 Ibid; pp. 67-71.

30 Personal interview with Doli Devi, great granddaughter of Ramanarayan Yadavendu (age 28), Agra on 26 February, 2008 at 10.30 am.

31 Ambedkar, B.R., *Mr. Gandhi and the Emancipation of the Untouchables*, Jullundur: Bheem Patrika Publications, 1943, p. 25.

32 Hardiman, David, *Gandhi in His Time and Ours: the Global Legacy of His Ideas*, Delhi: Permanent Black, 2003, p. 131.

33 Dirks, Nicholas B., *Castes of Mind: Colonialism and the Making of Modern India*, Delhi: Permanent Black, 2002, pp. 268-69.

34 Personal interview with Daya Shankar (age 66), Buddhist writer, Agra, on April 26, 2008, at Vasntkunj, New Delhi at 10.30 am.

35 Yadavendu, Ramanarayana, *Yaduvansh Ka Itihaas*, Agra: Navyug Sahitya Niketan, 1942, p. 7.

36 Ibid; pp. 181-183.

37 Kshirsagar, R.K., *Dalit Movement in India and its Leaders 1857-1956*, New Delhi: M.D. Publishers, 1994, p. 231& Personal interview with Daya Shankar (age 66), Buddhist writer, Agra, on April 26, 2008, at Vasntkunj, New Delhi at 10.30 am.

38 Lynch, Owen M., "The Politics of Untouchability: A Case From Agra, India" in B.S. Cohn & Milton (ed.) *Structure and Change in Indian Society*, Chicago, 1968, p. 236.

4

Identity Changed but not Profession (?): The *Madigas* of the *Rayalaseema* Region of Andhra Pradesh

Prof. G. Samba Siva Reddy*

I

There are certain classes (sections of people), however, who, owing to the depth of degradation into they have fallen, are looked upon as almost another race of beings, altogether outside the pale of society, and they are perfectly ready to acknowledge their own comparative inferiority in the society.[1] Among so many such castes and sub-castes, the *Madigas* were, and still are, neglected in India. They were and are one of the leather working communities in India, from time immemorial. An attempt is made in this paper to unearth their hidden story in the Telugu speaking present Rayalaseema region or erstwhile Ceded Districts so as to give them their due identity and promote them to the realm of main stream castes and communities.

Leather and skins of all kinds, except those of the tiger and antelope, are considered particularly unclean. Caste Hindus must never touch with their hands the slippers or sandals that are worn on the feet. A person

* Dept. of History & Archaeology, Yogi Vemana University, KADAPA, Andhra Pradesh.

riding must always carefully cover with a cloth any part of the harness or saddlery that is made of leather. So it is that caste Hindus do not understand how any one can possibly wear anything made, as they say, of the remains of dead animals, such as boots, gloves, or leather breeches, without a feeling of horror and repugnance. A scrupulous Brahmin must look very carefully where he puts his feet when walking. He would be defiled and obliged to bathe if by accident his feet should touch a bone, a piece of broken glass or earthenware, a rag, a leaf from which any one had eaten, a bit of skin or leather, hair, or any other unclean thing.[2]

II

The *Madigas* are the prominent leatherworking caste or community of the Telugu country, and correspond to the Chakkiliyans of the Tamil area. At Hospet in the Bellary district, they were at once formed a strong opposition party and upset the British Raj. But they were so frightened by the British that they went in a body to live in the Muhammadan quarter of the town. At the Hospet weekly market a mendicant youth lying naked in a thorny bed of babul (Acacia arabicd] stems. A loathsome (hateful) spectacle was afforded by a shriveled old woman with mouth distended by a mass of mud the size of a cricket-ball, both eyes bunged up with mud, and beating her bare breasts with her hands. The market was infested by religious mendicants, some from Benares and Ramesvaram, and others from across the Hyderabad frontier, who cadged persistently for tobacco[3] leaves, an onion or brinjal (Solanum Melongend], a few chillies, a handful of grain, or a pinch of salt, and helped to deplete the slender stock of the marketsellers. A conspicuous feature of Hospet is the block-wheel carts with wooden wheels, solid or made of several pieces, with no spokes. Dragged by sturdy buffaloes, they are excellent for carrying timber or other loads on rough roads or hill-tracks, where ordinary carts cannot travel. During the breezy and showery season of the south-west monsoon, kite-flying is the joy of the Hospet youths, the kites being decorated with devices of scorpions and Hindu gods, among which a representation of Hanuman, one of the genii loci, soared highest every evening. It is fairly easy to distinguish a *Madiga* from a Bedar, but difficult to put the distinction in words. The *Madigas* have more prominent cheek-bones, a more vinous eye, and are more unkempt. The Brahman assistant, hunting in the *Madiga* quarters for subjects for measurement, unfortunately asked some Bedars if they were *Madigas*. To which, resenting the mistake, one of them replied "We call you the Madiga," and the Brahman stood crushed. The Hospet Madigas had their hair cropped short, moustache, and trimmed beard. They wore the customary threads or charm cylinders to ward off devils, and steel tweezers for removing the thorns of the babul, which is largely used as a fence for the fields of cholam and sugar. One man had suspended round his neck, as a hereditary talisman, a big silver Venkataramana bottu with the namam in the centre on an altar, and the chank and chakram stamped on it. As bearing on the social status of the Malas and Madigas, which is a subject of dispute between the two classes, it may be noted that all the billets in cotton factories which require any skill, such as engine-drivers, valve-men, moulders, turners, etc., are held by Malas.[4]

The Madigas are generally only three-anna wage men, and do such work as turning a winch, moving bales, and other trivial jobs. At a factory, at Adoni, there were three wells, viz. : for Malas, for Madigas, and for the rest of the workers, except Brahmans. And the well-water for the Malas was better than that for the Madigas. A Madiga chindu, or sword-dance, was prohibited in 1859 and 1874. But a petition, referring to its obscene nature, and its being the cause of frequent collision between the Malas and Madigoas, was submitted to the Collector of Kurnool in 1887, by a missionary. The dance was performed at festivals, held annually or triennially, in honour of the village goddess, and during the time of threshing corn, building a new house, or the opening of a newly-dug well.[5] The dance, accompanied by a song containing grossly indecent reflections against the Malas, was also performed, under the excitement of strong drinks, in the presence of the goddess, on the occasion of marriages. One verse ran as follows : "I shall cut with my saw the Malas of the four houses at Nandyal, and, having caused them to be cut up, shall remove their skins, and fix them to drums." "The right hand party," it is stated,[6] "resent the use by the left of palanquins at their marriages, and so the Malas are very jealous of the Chucklers (Madigas) carrying the bride and bridegroom through the streets, using tinkling ornaments, etc. Riots sometimes occur when a strong feeling of opposition is raised, to resent what they consider innovations." Narahari Gopalakrishnama Chetty writes, "that the Madigas belong to the left-hand caste, and often quarrel with the Malas, right-hand caste people. Their condition has slightly been improved with the arrival of the Christian Missionaries, who have established schools for their children and exercise a tacit influence in their favour. Many of these have become Christians, almost all the Protestant Christians are from these caste people. The favourite deity of the Madigas is Matanga, an ancient sage from whom their trace or claim their origin. In 1867 Madigas were converted en masse by the Baptist Missionaries in Markapur taluk of the erstwhile Kurnool district and the present Prakasam district. Immediately afterwards a malariour fever carried off many of them. They attributed the calamity to their change of faith and consequent displeasure of Matanga, and later many reverted to their former faith. They live by tanning leather and making shoes etc.[7]

In 1871 a Madiga, having contrived to obtain a red cloth as a reward from the Police Superintendent, wore it on his head, and went in procession on horseback by the main bazaar street. This resulted in a disturbance, in which a European Inspector was severely hurt by a Mala, who had mistaken him for the Superintendent. The two factions fixed, by mutual understanding, the streets by which each was to proceed, and no quarrels have since occurred."[8] During the celebration of village festivals, an unmarried Madiga woman, called for the occasion Matangi (a favourite deity), abuses and spits upon the people assembled, and they do not take this as an insult, because they think that her spittle removes the pollution. The woman is, indeed, regarded as the incarnation of the goddess herself. Similarly, the Malas use very obscene language, when the god is taken in procession to the streets of the caste people.[9] Concerning the Matangi, that she is an unmarried woman of the Madiga class, chosen after a most trying ordeal, unless she happens to be descended from a previous Matangi, to represent the goddess. She must vindicate her fitness by suitable prophetic utterances, and her nomination is not confirmed till she has obtained divine approval at the temple of a certain village near Kumbam in Kurnool. When she has been finally confirmed in her honours, she enjoys the privilege of adorning her face with profusion of turmeric and red powder, and of carrying margosa (Melia Azadirachta] leaves about her. She is unmarried, but without being bound by a vow of celibacy. Her business is to preside at the purificatory ceremonies that precede all festivities. When Malakshmi, or Poleramma, or Ankamma, or any other of the village deities is to have her festival, the nearest Matangi is applied to. Her necklace of cowry (Cyprcea monetd) shells is deposited in a well for three days, before she is allowed to put it on for the ceremony. She dons the necklace, and marches behind the master of the ceremonies, who carries a knife, wooden shoes and trident, which have been similarly placed for a time at the bottom of a well. The master of the ceremonies, his male and female relations, then stand in a line, and the Matangi runs round and round them, uttering what appear to be meaningless exclamations, spitting upon all of them, and touching them with her stick.[10] Her touch and saliva are believed to purge all uncleanliness of body and soul, and are invited by men who would ordinarily scorn to approach her, and it passes one's comprehension how she should be honoured with the task of purifying the soul and body of high class Reddis and purse-proud Komatis. It must be said that only very few Brahman families keep up this mysterious ceremony of homage to the Matangi. She is allowed to come into the house, that is to pass the outer gate. There she besmears a certain spot with cow-dung, and places upon it a basket.[11]

It is at once filled with cooked food. A layer of rice powder covers the surface of the food, and on it is placed a small lamp, which is lighted. She then holds out a little earthenware pot, and asks for toddy to fill it with. But the Brahman says that she must be content with water. With the pot in her hand, and wild exultant songs in her mouth, recounting her humiliation of Brahman and Kshatriya, of saint and sovereign, she moves quickly round the assembled men and women, scattering with a free hand upon them the water from the pot. The women doff their petticoats, and make a present of them to the Matangi, and the mistress of the house gives her the cloth she is wearing. The men, however, with strange inconsistency, doff their sacred threads, and replace them by new ones after a bath. The origin of the supremacy of the Matangi is obscure, and shrouded in legends. According to one of them, the head of Renuka, the wife of the sage Bhrigu, who was beheaded by her lord's orders, fell in a Madiga house, and grew into a Madiga woman. According to another legend, a certain king prayed to be blessed with a daughter, and in answer the gods sent him a golden parrot, which soon after perched on an anthill, and disappeared into it. The disappointed father got the ant-hill excavated, and was rewarded for his pains by finding his daughter rise, a maid of divine beauty, and she came to be worshipped as the Matangi.[12] It is interesting to note that Matangas were an ancient line of kings 'somewhere in the south,' and the Madigas call themselves Matangi Makkalu or children of Matangi or Durga, who is their goddess." The system of making Basavis (see Deva-dasi), which prevails among the Madigas of the Ceded Districts, is apparently not in vogue among those of the Telugu country, where, however, there are, in some places, a class of prostitutes called Matangi, Matamma, or Matha,who are held in much respect. In connection with the Basavi system, it is recorded, in the Madras Law Report, 1892, that "upon the whole, the evidence seems to be to establish that, among the Madigas, there is a widespread custom of performing in the temple at Uchangidurgam, a marriage ceremony, the result of which is that the girl is married without possibility of widowhood or divorce; that she is at liberty to have intercourse with men at pleasure; that her children are heirs to her father, and keep up his family ; and that Basavis' nieces, being made Basavis, become their heirs. The Basavis seem in some cases to become prostitutes, but the language used by the witnesses generally points only to free intercourse with men, and not necessarily to receipt of payment for use of their bodies. In fact, they acquire the right of intercourse with men, without more discredit than accrues to the men of their caste for intercourse with women who are not their wives."[13]

About ten miles to the south-west of Cumbum, in the then Kurnool district, and within a mile of the village of Tudimilla, there is a narrow pass between two hillocks known as Surabeswara Kona. Besides the more common presences, there were the following shrines :

(a) Sapthamathas (seven mothers).

(b) A curious temple, in which are found the idols of Jamadhagni Bagawan the father of Parasurama and the local rishi his wife Renuka Devi, and the Surabi.

(c) Opposite to this temple is the curious shrine, not very much bigger than a railway pointsman's box, dedicated to Mathangi. In this temple are found no less than five idols arranged in the following order :

(1) a three-headed snake

(2) another three-headed snake

(3) a female body, with the palms joined reverentially in the worshipping posture in front, with the lower half of the body snaky in form, and with a canopy of snaky hoods above

(4) Mathangi proper a female figure of about 15 inches in height, made of stone with a short skirt, below which the feet are visible, but no upper garment, and wearing a garland round the neck. The right hand holds a snake-headed stick, while the left has an adlika, a kind of sieve

(5) another similar figure, but without even the skirt.

"We shall now proceed to enquire who this Mathangi was, and how she came to be worshipped there. Jamadhagni Maharishi, known also as Bagawan on account of his godly power and virtues, married Renuka, the daughter of Renu, and had five sons by her, the youngest of whom was the famous Parasurama, an incarnation of Vishnu. 'Once upon a time,' says the Bhagavatapurana, ' Renuka having gone to the Ganga, saw the king of the Ghandarvas wearing garlands of lotus, to play with the Apsaras. Having gone to the river to fetch water, she, whose heart was some what attracted by Chitaratha (the king of the Gandharvas) who was playing, forgot the time of Yajna (sacrifice). Coming to feel the delay, and afraid of the curse of the Muni, she returned to the hermitage, and placed the pitcher before the Muni, and remained standing with folded palms. The Muni (Jamadhagni), coming to know of the unchasteness of his wife, got enraged, and said, O my sons ! kill this sinner.' Although thus directed, they did not do so. The said (Parasu) Rama, who was well aware of the power of the Muni in respect of meditations and asceticism, killed, being directed by his father, his mother along with his brothers. The son of Satyavati (Jamadhagni) was pleased, and requested Rama to pray for any favour. Rama desired the reanimation of those killed, and their forgetfulness of the fact of their having been killed. Immediately did they get up, as though after a deep sleep. Rama, who was conscious of the powers of his father in regard to asceticism, took the life of his dear ones.[14] "The version locally prevalent is somewhat different. Jamadhagni Bagawan's hermitage was near this Kona, and he was worshipping the god Surabeswara, and doing tapas (penance) there. One day, his wife Renuka Devi went, very early in the morning, to the river Gundlacama to bathe, and fetch water for her husband's sacrificial rites. She was accompanied, as was her wont on such occasions, by a female slave of the chuckler (leather-worker) caste, as a sort of bodyguard and attendant. While she was bathing, the great warrior Karthaviriyarjuna with a thousand arms happened to fly across the sky on some business of his own, and Renuka saw his form reflected in the water, and was pleased with it in her mind. It must be mentioned that she never used to take any vessel with her to fetch water, for her chastity was such that she had power to roll water into a pot-like shape, as if it were wax, and thus bring it home. On this day, however, she failed to effect this, try what she might, and she was obliged to return home empty-handed. In the meanwhile, the sage, her husband, finding that his wife did not return as usual, learnt through his 'wisdom sight' what had happened, and ordered his son Parasurama to slay his sinful mother. Parasurama went towards the river accordingly, and, seeing his mother returning, aimed an arrow at her, which severed her head from her body, and also similarly severed, with its unspent force, the head of the chuckler woman who was coming immediately behind his mother. Parasurama returned to his father without even noticing this accident, and when his father, pleased with his prompt obedience, offered him any boon, he prayed for the re-animation of his mother. Jamadhagni then gave him some holy water out of his vessel, and told him to put together the dismembered parts, and sprinkle some water over them. Parasurama went off in great delight and haste, and, as it was still dark and early in the morning, he wrongly put his mother's head on the chuckler woman's trunk, and sprinkled water on them.[15] Then, seeing another head and another body lying close by, he thought that they belonged to the female slave whom he had unwittingly killed, and he put them also together, and re-animated them. He was extremely vexed when he found out the mistakes he had committed, but, as there was no rectifying them without another double murder, he produced the two women before his father, and begged to be forgiven. The sage finally accepted the person with his late consort's head as his wife, and granted to the other woman the status of an inferior deity, in response to her prayers, and owing to her having his wife's body. This was the origin of Mathangi. "There are some permanent inam (rent-free) lands belonging to this shrine, and there is always a Madiga 'vestal virgin' known as Mathangi, who is the high priestess, or rather the embodied representative of the Brahman-chuckler goddess, and who enjoys the fruits of the inams. Mathangi is prohibited from marrying, and, when a Mathangi dies, her successor is chosen in the following manner. All the chuckler girls of the village, between the ages of eight and ten, who have not attained puberty, are assembled before the shrine, and the invoking hymns are chanted amid a flourish of trumpets, drums, and other accessories. The girl who becomes possessed on whom the goddess descends is the chosen vessel, and she is invested with the insignia of her office, a round sieve, a bunch of margosa (Melia Azadirachta] leaves, a snake-headed bamboo stick, a piece of cotton thread rope with some cowries (Cyprcea moneta shells) strung on it, and a small vessel of kunkuma (coloured aniline powder). A vow of lifelong celibacy is also administered to her. Curiously enough, this shrine is venerated by all castes, from the Brahman downwards.16 We were informed that, at the time of worship, the chuckler priestess dances about in wild frenzy, and she is given toddy to drink, which she not infrequently spits on her devotees, and even Brahmans regard this as auspicious, and not in the least polluting. We had the pleasure of witnessing a 'possessed dance' by the reigning Mathangi, with her drummer in attendance. She is a chuckler woman, about thirty years of age, and, but for the insignia of her office, not in any way differing from the rest of her class. Though unmarried she had several children, but this was apparently no disqualification. We were standing before the shrine of the seven mothers when the drummer invoked the goddess by chanting a Telugu hymn, keeping time on his drum. The meaning of the hymn was to this effect, as far as we could make out :

Sathya Surabesa Kona ! Gowthama's Kamadhenu !

the headless trunk in Sathya Surabesa Kona !

your father Giri Razu Kamadeva Jamadhagni Mamuni beheaded the trunk ; silently Jamadhagni cut off the arms ; did you, the headless trunk in Kamadhenuvanam, the headless trunk of Jamadhagni, your father's golden sword, did you ask to be born a virgin in the snake pit? "While chanting the above, the drummer was dancing round and round the woman, and beating wildly on his drum. The woman began to tremble all over, and soon it was visible that the goddess had descended on her. Then the drummer, wilder and more frantic than ever, began to praise the goddess in these words:

Are you wearing bells to your ankles, O mother ?

Are you wearing cowries, O mother ?

Dancing and singing, O mother !

We pray to thee, O mother !

Possessed and falling on the ground, I implore thee, O mother !

O mother, who went to Delhi and Oruganti with a sieve in the right-hand, with a wand in the left; with bells tinkling at her ankles, the mother went to Oruganti town, the mother went away.[17] "During this chant, the woman vies with the drummer, and dances fiercely round and round, always facing him. Then comes the appeasing chant, which the drummer drawls out in a quivering and solemn tone, and without dancing about:

By the feet of the thirty-three crores,

by the feet of the sixty crores,

by the feet of the Devas, peace !

"The woman then stands with closed eyes, panting for breath, and quite exhausted." On ordinary days, the Mathangi goes about the villages, collecting the offerings of her devotees, and, we take it, she is never in much want. There are also local Mathangis in other villages, but they are all said to be subordinate to the Tudimilla woman, who is the high Pontiff of the institution. We were informed that there was an old palmyra-leaf manuscript in existence, describing the institution and the ceremonies (mostly tantric and phallic) in detail." Among the Madigas of Tumkur in Mysore, the Matangis must apparently belong to one of two sects, Belliyoru or Malloru. The Madiga Asadis, who are males, have to go through an initiation ceremony very similar to that of the Matangi. But a necklet of pebbles is substituted for the bottu, and the Vakkaliga priest touches the novice's shoulders with flowers, turmeric powder, and kunkumam. The Asadis are musicians who sing songs and recite stories about Ellamma. They play on a musical instrument called chaudike, which is a combination of a drum and stringed instrument. The Matangis and Asadis, both being dedicated to Ellamma, are eminently qualified to remove pollution for many castes who are Ellamma Vokkalu or followers of Ellamma. A lotus device, or figures of Pothu Raja and Matangi, are drawn on the18 ground, after it has been cleansed with cow-dung. The Matangi, with her insignia, sits in the centre of the device, and the Asadis, sitting close by, sing the praises of Ellamma to the accompaniment of the chaudike. The Matangis and Asadi then drink toddy, and go about the house, wherein the former sprinkle toddy with the margosa twig. Sometimes they pour some of the toddy into their mouths, and spit it out all over the house. The pot, in which the toddy is placed, is, in some places, called pallakki (palanquin). The Asadis' version of the story of Ellamma is as follows. She is the goddess for all, and is present in the tongues of all except dumb people, because they have to pronounce the syllable elli (where) whenever they ask a question containing the word where. She is a mysterious being, who often exhibits herself in the form of light or flames. She is the cause of universe, and the one Sakthi in existence thereon. She is supposed to be the daughter of Giriraja Muni and Javanikadevi, and the wife of Jamadhagni Rishi. Her son is Parasurama, carrying a plough. The town where she lives has three names, Jambupuri, Isampuri, and Vijayanagara, has eighty-seven gates, and is fortified by seven walls. She is believed to have for her dress all kinds of snakes. Several groves of margosa trees are said to flourish in her vicinity. She is worshipped under many names, and has become Lakshmi, Gauramma, and Saraswati in Brahman houses, or Akkumari in Vakkaliga houses. To the Idigas she is Gatabaghya Lakshmi, to the Kurubas Ganga Mari, to the Oddes Peddamma and Chinnamma, and so on. She is said to have proceeded on a certain day to the town of Oragallu, accompanied by Jana Matangi. On the way thither, the soles of Matangi's feet blistered, and she sat down with Ellamma19 beneath a margosa tree. After resting a short time Matangi asked Ellamma's permission to go to a neighbouring Idiga (Telugu toddy-drawer), and get some toddy to drink. Ellamma objected, as the Idiga Gauda was a Lingayat, and Matangi would be compelled to wear the lingam. When Matangi persisted, Ellamma transformed herself into an ant-hill, and Matangi, in the guise of a young woman, went to the Idiga Gauda with her cane (Jogi kolu) and basket, and asked for toddy. The Gauda became angry, and, tying her to a date-palm (Pkcenix sylvestris], beat her, and gave her cane and basket to his groom. Matangi was further ill-treated by the Gauda and his wives, but escaped, and went to the Gauda's brother, who treated her kindly, and offered her toddy, of which he had sixty loads on bullocks. All this he poured into the shell of a margosa fruit which Matangi held in her hand, and yet it was not filled. Eventually the toddy extracted from a few palms was brought, and the shell became full. So pleased was Matangi with the Idiga's treatment of her, that she blessed him, and instructed him to leave three datepalms untapped as Basavi trees in every grove. She then returned to Ellamma, and it was resolved to afflict the Gauda who had treated her badly with all kinds of diseases. Still disguised as a young woman, she went to him with sweet-smelling powders, which he purchased for a large sum of money. But, when he used them, he became afflicted with manifold diseases, including small-pox, measles, cancer, asthma, gout, rheumatism, abscesses, and bed-sores. Matangi then appeared before him as an old fortune-teller woman, whom the Idiga consulted, and doing as he was told by her, was cured. Subsequently, learning that all his misfortunes were due to his want of respect to Matangi, he became one of Ellamma's Vokkalu.[20]

Mr. H. A. Stuart informs us, "The Madigas will not take food or water from Pariahs, nor the latter from the former, a prejudice which is taken advantage of in the

Kalahasti Raja's stables to prevent theft of gram by the Pariah horse-keepers, the raw gram being sprinkled with water by Madigas in the sight of the Pariahs."[21] There are Telugu proverbs to the effect that "under the magili system of cultivation, even a Madiga will grow good crops," and "not even a Madiga will sow before Malapunnama." Writing concerning the Madigas, the Rev. H. Huizinga states that "they live in hamlets at a respectable distance from the villages of the caste people, by whom they are greatly despised. Their habits are squalid in the extreme, and the odour of a Madiga hamlet is revolting. They perform all the lowest kinds of service for the caste people, especially bearing burdens and working in leather. They take charge of the ox or buffalo as soon as it dies. They remove the skin and tan it, and eat the loathsome carcase, which makes them specially despised, and renders their touch polluting. Some of the skins are used for covering the rude drums that are so largely used in Hindu festivals, and beaten in honour of the village deities. The caste men impress the Madigas into their service, not only to make the drums, but also to beat them at their feasts. It may be mentioned that nearly ten per cent, of the Madigas are nominal Christians, and, in some parts of the Nellore district, the Christians form over half of the Madiga population. This changes their habits of life and also their social position. Eating of carrion is now forbidden, as well as beating of drums at Hindu festivals, and their refusal in this particular often leads to bitter persecution at the hands of the caste people. The main duty of the Madigas is the curing and tanning of hides, and the manufacture of rude leather articles, especially sandals, trappings for bullocks, and large well-buckets used for irrigation. The process of tanning with lime and tangedu[22] (Cassia auriculatd] bark is rough and simple. As did their forefathers, so the Madigas do to-day. The quality of the skins they turn out is fair, and the state of the development of the native leather trade compares very favourably with that of other trades such as blacksmithy and carpentry. The Madiga's sandals are strong, comfortable, and sometimes highly ornamental. His manner of working, and his tools are as simple as his life. He often gets paid in kind, a little fodder for his buffalo, so many measures of some cheap grain, perhaps a few vegetables, etc. In the northern districts, the Madigas are attached to one or more families of ryots, and are entitled to the dead animals of their houses. Like the Vettiyan in the south, the Madiga is paid in kind, and he has to supply sandals for the ryots, belts for the bulls, and all the necessaries of agriculture ; and for these he has to find the requisite leather himself ; but for the larger articles, such as water-buckets, the master must find the leather. Of late years there is a tendency observable among Madigas to poach on each other's monopoly of certain houses, and among the ryots themselves to dispense with the services of family Madigas, and resort to the open market for their necessaries. In such cases, the ryots demand payment from the Madigas for the skins of their dead animals. The hides and skins, which remain after local demands have been satisfied, are sold to merchants from the Tamil districts, and there is generally a central agent, to whom the various subagents send their collections, and by him they are dried and salted and sent to Madras for tanning. In the Kistna district, children have little leather strings hanging from the left shoulder, like the sacred cord of the Brahman, from which is suspended a bag containing something put in it by a Madiga, to charm away all forms of disease from the infant wearer."[23]

In some places bones are collected by the Madigas for the Labbais (Muhammadans), by whom they are exported to Bombay. The god of the temple at Tirupati appears annually to four persons in different directions, east, west, north and south, and informs them that he requires a shoe from each of them. They whitewash their houses, worship the god, and spread rice-flour thickly on the floor of a room, which is locked for the night.

Next morning the mark of a huge foot is found on the floor, and for this a shoe has to be made to fit. When ready, it is taken in procession through the streets of the village, and conveyed to Tirupati, where it is presented at the temple. Though the makers of the shoes have worked in ignorance of each other's work, the shoes brought from the north and south, and those from the east and west, are believed to match, and make a pair. Though the worship of these shoes is chiefly meant for the Pariahs, who are prohibited from ascending the Tirupati hill, as a matter of fact all, without distinction of caste,[24] worship them. The shoes are placed in front of the image of the god near the foot of the hill, and are said to gradually wear out by the end of the year.

At a pseudo-hook-swinging ceremony in the Bellary district, as carried out at the present day, a Bedar is suspended by a cloth passed under his arms. The Madigas always swing him, and have to provide the hide ropes, which are used.25 In an exceedingly interesting account of the festival of the village goddess Uramma, at Kudligi in the Bellary district, Mr. F. Fawcett writes as follows. "The Madiga Basivis (dedicated prostitutes) are given alms, and join in the procession. A quantity of rice and ragi flour is poured into a basket, over which one of the village servants cuts the throat of a small black ram. The carcase is laid on the bloody flour, and the whole covered with old cloths, and placed on the head of a Madiga, who stands for some time in front of the goddess. The goddess is then carried a few yards, the Madiga walking in front, while a hole is dug close to her, and the basket of bloody flour and the ram's carcase are buried. After some dancing by the Madiga Basivis to the music of the tom-tom, the Madigas bring five new pots, and worship them. A buffalo, devoted to the goddess after the last festival, is then driven or dragged through the village with shouting and tomtoming, walked round the temple, and beheaded by the Madiga in front of the goddess.

The head is placed in front of her with the right foreleg in the mouth, and a lamp, lighted eight days previously, is placed on top. All then start in procession round the village, a Madiga, naked but for a few margosa (Melia Azadirachta) leaves, and held by two others, leading the way. Behind him are all the other Madigas, carrying six hundred seers of cholum (Sorghum : millet), which they scatter ; and, following them, all the other villagers. It is daybreak, and the Madiga who led the way, the pujari (priest), and the women who followed him, who have been fasting for more than twenty-four hours, now eat. The Madiga is fed. This Madiga is said to be in mortal terror while leading the procession, for the spirit or influence of the goddess comes over him. He swoons before the procession is completed. At noon the people collect again at Uramma's temple, where a purchased buffalo is sacrificed. The head is placed in front of the goddess as before, and removed at once for food. Then those of the lower Sudra castes, and Madigas who are under vows, come dressed in margosa leaves, with lamps on their heads, and sacrifice buffaloes, sheep and goats to the goddess."[26]

A further account of the festival of the village goddess Udisalamma, at Bandri in the Bellary district, is given by Mr. Fawcett writes, "A Madiga naked but for a few leaves round his waist, leads the procession, and, following him, are Madigas with baskets. Fear of the goddess comes on the Madiga. He swoons, and is carried to the temple, and flung on the ground in front of the goddess. After a while he is revived, bathed, and given new clothing. This man is one of a family, in which this curious office is hereditary. He must be the son of a married woman, not of a Basivi, and he must not be married. He fasts from the beginning of the festival till he has done what is required of him. A young ram the sacrifice sheep is taken up by one of the Poturazus, as if it were a child, its hind legs at either side of his waist and its forelegs over his shoulders, and he bites its throat open and shows his bloody mouth to the people. He throws it down, and the Madigas remove it."[27]

Some of their children are named after these deities, while others receive Muhammadan names in fulfilment of vows made to Masthan and other Pirs. When asked concerning their caste, the Madigas always reply "Memu pedda inti vallamu," i.e., we are of the big house. The following legend is current in the Cuddapah district concerning a pool in the Rayachoti taluk called Akkadevatalakolam, or the pool of the holy sisters. "A thousand years ago, there lived near the pool a king, who ruled over all this part of the country. The king had as his commanderin-chief a Madiga. This Madiga made himself powerful and independent, and built himself a residence on a hill still called Madiga Vanidoorgam. At last he revolted, and defeated the king. On entering the king's palace, he found seven beautiful virgins, the king's daughters, to all of whom he at once made overtures of marriage. They declined the honour, and, when the Madiga wished to use force, they all jumped into this pool, and delivered their lives to the universal lord."[28]

The following are some of the more important endogamous sub-divisions among the Madigas : Gampa dhompti, basket offering. Ginna or thel dhompti, tray or cup offering. Bhumi do. earth offering. Chatla do. winnowing basket offering. Sibbi do. brass vessel offering. Chadarapa do. square space on the ground offering. These sub-divisions are based on the way in which the members thereof offer food, etc., to their gods during[29] marriages, e.g., a Gampa dhompti places it in a basket, a Bhumi dhompti on the floor. Each sub-division possesses many exogamous septs, of which the following are examples : Belli-silver, Chinthala-tamarind, Chatlawinnowing basket, Darala-thread, Emme-buffalo, Gavala-cowry shells, Golkonda-a town, Jalamslowness, Kambha-post, Kappala-frog, Kalahasti- a town, Kaththi-knife, Kudumala-cake, Kuncham-tassel, Midathala-locust, Mallela or malli-jasmine, Nannuru-four hundred, Pothulabuffalo, Pasula-

cow, Ragi-Eleusine Coracana, Slkili- broom, Thela-scorpion, Kaththe-donkey.

There seems to be some connection between the *Madigas*, the *Mutrachas*, and *Gollas*. For, at times of marriage, the *Madiga* sets aside one thambulam (betel leaf and areca nut) for the *Mutracha*, and, in some places, extends the honour to the *Golla* also. At the marriage ceremonies of the *Puni Gollas*, an elaborate and costly form of Ganga worship is performed, in connection with which it is the *Madiga* musicians, called *Madiga Pambala vandlu*, who draw the designs in colour-powders on the floor.

The *Madigas* observe the *panchayat* or tribal council system for the adjustment of disputes, and settlement of various questions at issue among members of the community. The headman is called *Pedda* (big) *Madiga*, whose office is hereditary ; and he is assisted by two elected officers called *Dharmakartha* and *Kulambantrothu*.

Widow remarriage (udike) is freely permitted, and the woman and her children are received in *Madiga* society. But care is taken that no one but the contracting parties and widows shall witness the marriage ceremony, and no one but a widower is allowed to avail himself of the form. A man may get a divorce from his wife by payment to her of a few rupees. But no money is given to her, if she has been guilty of adultery. The bride's price varies in amount, being higher if she has to cross a river. The elaborate marriage ceremonial conforms to the Telugu type, but some of the details may be recorded. On the *muhurtham* (wedding) day, a ceremony called *pradhanam* (chief thing) is performed. A sheep is sacrificed to the marriage (araveni) pots. The sacrificer dips his hands in the blood of the animal, and impresses the blood on his palms on the wall near the door leading to the room in which the pots are kept. The bridegroom's party bring betel nuts, limes, a golden bead, a bonthu (unbleached cotton thread), rice, and turmeric paste. The maternal uncle of the bride gives five betel leaves and areca nuts to the *Pedda Madiga*, and, putting the bonthu round the bride's neck, ties the o-olden bead thereon. The ceremony concludes with the distribution of pan-supari in the following order : ancestors, *Mutrachas, Gollas, Madigas*, the *Pedda Madiga*, and the assembled guests. The *Pedda Madiga* has to lift, at one try, a tray containing cocoanuts and betel with his right hand. In his hand he holds a knife, of which the blade is passed over the forefinger, beneath the middle and fourth fingers, and over the little finger. This ceremony is called *thonuku thambulam,* or betel and nuts likely to be spilt on the floor. The bridegroom, after a bath, proceeds to the temple, where cloths, the *bashingam, bottu* (marriage badge), etc., are placed in front of the god, and then taken to a jammi tree (Prosopis spicigera}, which is worshipped. The bottu is usually a disc of gold, but, if the family is hard-up, or in cases of widow remarriage, a bit of turmeric or folded mango leaf serves as a substitute for it. On the third day, the wrist threads (kankanam) are removed, and dhomptis, or offerings of food to the gods, are made, with variations according to the dhompti to which the celebrants belong. An illustration may be taken from the Gampa dhompti. The contracting parties procure a quantity of rice, jaggery (crude sugar), and ghi (clarified butter), which are cooked, and moulded into an elongated mass, and placed in a new bamboo basket (gampa). In the middle of the mass, which is determined with a string, a twig, with a wick at one end, is set up, and two similar twigs are stuck into the ends of the mass. Puja (worship) is performed, and the mass is distributed among the daughters of the house and other near relations, but not among members of other dhomptis. The bride and bridegroom take a small portion from the mass, which is called dhonga muddha, or the mass that is stolen. The bottu is said to be "usually tied by the Madiga priest known as the Thavatiga, or drummer. This office is hereditary, but each successor to it has to be regularly ordained by a Kuruba guru at the local Madiga shrine, the chief item in the ceremony being tying round the neck of the candidate a thread bearing a representation of the goddess, and on either side of this five white beads. Henceforth the Thavatiga is on no account to engage in the caste profession of leather-work, but lives on fees collected at weddings, and by begging. He goes round to the houses of the caste with a little drum slung over his shoulder, and collects contributions."[30]

The Madiga marriages are said to be conducted with much brawling and noise, owing to the quantity of liquor consumed on such occasions. Among the Madigas, as among the Kammas, Gangimakkulu, and Malas, marriage is said not to be consummated until three months after its celebration. This is apparently because it is considered unlucky to have three heads of a household within a year of marriage. By the delay, the birth of the child should take place only in the second year, so that, during the first year, there will be only two heads, husband and wife. At the first menstrual period a girl is under pollution for ten days, when she bathes. Betel leaves and nuts, and a rupee are placed in front of the Pedda Madiga, who takes a portion thereof for himself, and distributes what remains among those who have assembled. Sometimes, just before the return of the girl to the house, a sheep is killed in front of the door, and a mark made on her face with the blood.[31]

The Madigas dispose of their dead both by burial and cremation. The body is said to be "buried naked, except for a few leaves. Children are interred face downwards. Pregnant women are burnt. The bier is usually made of the milk-hedge {Euphorbia Tirucalli) plant." The grave is dug by a Mala Vettivadu. The chinnadhinam ceremony is performed on the third day. On the grave a mass of mud is shaped into the form of an idol, to which are offered rice, cocoanuts, and jiggery (crude sugar) placed on leaves, one of which is set apart for the crows. Three stones are arranged in the form of a triangle, and on them is set a pot filled with water, which trickles out of holes made in the bottom of the pot. The peddadhinam is performed, from preference on a Wednesday or Sunday, towards the close of the third week after death. The son, or other celebrant of the rites, sets three stones on the grave, and offers food thereto. Food is also offered to the crows by the relations of the deceased, and thrown into a river or tank (pond), if the crows do not eat it. They all go to a tank, and make on the bank thereof an effigy, if the dead person was a female. To married women, winnows and glass bangles are offered. The bangles of a widow, and waist-thread of a widower, are removed within an enclosure on the bank. At night stories of Ankamma and Matangi are recited by Bainedus or Pambalas, and if a Matangi is available, homage is done to her.[32]

In some places, Madigas have their own washermen and barbers. But, in the northern districts, the caste washerman does their washing, the cloths being steeped in water, and left for the washerman to take. Francis writes, "The Madigas may not use the wells of the better classes, though, when water is scarce, they get over this last prohibition by employing some one in the higher ranks to draw water for them from such wells, and pour it into their chatties. In other districts they have to act as their own barbers and washermen, but in Anantapur this disability is somewhat relaxed, as the barbers make no objection to let them (and other low castes such as the Malas) use their razors for a consideration, and the dhobis will wash their clothes, as long as they themselves first unroll them, and dip them onto the water. This act is held to remove the pollution, which would otherwise attach to them."[33]

Another notable thing in the same district was the custom of dedicating Basavis of Boyas, Malas and Madigas to the temple. According to this practice, a girl who is dedicated at a temple as a Basavi does not marry but lives in her parents' house under the protection of some men of her own or an equal or higher caste who is expected to maintain and clothe her. Her children belong to her father's and not to her temporary husband's family and she herself is treated as, and inherits like, a son instead of a daughter.[34]

In the Kurnool district of the region, the Madigas (1,17,870) and the Malas (61, 286), who form the two principal sub-castes under the Harijans, are largely labourers, both agricultural and non-agricultural. Some of them also hold land as tenants. Tanning and shoemaking are also pursued by many of the Harijans. The Malas also take to weaving of coarse white cotton cloth. These classes also perform services pertaining to the public needs of the village as a whole.[35] The Madiga caste people used participate in the Chindu dance in the same district. But that activity led to clashes between the Malas and Balijas on the one side and the Madigas and Gollas on the other at Koilakuntla (Kovelakuntla) in A.D.1938.[36]

III

Even though some of the above mentioned stories of Madigas are mysterious and strange, but majority of these customs and their religious and cultural practices are in vogue in the present scenario of their day to day life. On the other hand there is a sea change in their contemporary socio-economic and cultural life style in the light of urbanization, their migration to foreign countries particularly to the countries of the Persian Gulf and metropolitan cities to earn their livelihood. But still it is a pity and unfortunate that their segregation from the upper strata of the society and main stream life is continuing. Atrocities against them and oppression and suppression of them are continued unabated in many rural areas of the region.

Notes and References

1 Abbe J.A. Dubois, *Hindu Manners, Customs & Ceremonies*, Delhi, 2008 (rpt.), (1st pbd. 2006), pp. 53-54.

2 Abbe J.A. Dubois, *Hindu Manners, Customs & Ceremonies*, pp.205-206.

3 Edgar Thurston & K.Rangachari, *Castes and Tribes of Southern India*, Madras, 1909, vol. IV, p. 292.

4 Edgar Thurston & K.Rangachari, *Castes and Tribes of Southern India*, vol.IV, p.294.

5 Edgar Thurston & K.Rangachari, *Castes and Tribes of Southern India*, vol.IV, p.295.

6 Edgar Thurston & K.Rangachari, *Castes and Tribes of Southern India*, vol.IV, p.295.

7 N.Gopalakrishnamah Chetty, *Manual of the Kurnool District*, Hyderabad, 1886, pp.141-142.

8 N.Gopalakrishnamah Chetty, *Manual of the Kurnool District*.

9 Edgar Thurston & K.Rangachari, *Castes and Tribes of Southern India*, p.296.

10 *Madras Mail*, 1902 (Tamilnadu Archives (TNA)).

11 Edgar Thurston & K.Rangachari,*Castes and Tribes of Southern India*, p.297.

12 Edgar Thurston & K.Rangachari, *Castes and Tribes of Southern India*, vol.IV, p.297.

13 Edgar Thurston & K.Rangachari, *Castes and Tribes of Southern India*, vol.IV, p.298.

14 Edgar Thurston & K.Rangachari, *Castes and Tribes of Southern India*, vol.IV, p.301.

15 Edgar Thurston & K.Rangachari, *Castes and Tribes of Southern India*, vol.IV, p.302.

16 Edgar Thurston & K.Rangachari, *Castes and Tribes of Southern India*, vol.IV, p.303.

17 Edgar Thurston & K.Rangachari, *Castes and Tribes of Southern India*, vol.IV, p.304.

18 Edgar Thurston & K.Rangachari, *Castes and Tribes of Southern India*, vol.IV, p.305.

19 Edgar Thurston & K.Rangachari, *Castes and Tribes of Southern India*, vol.IV, p.306.

20 Edgar Thurston & K.Rangachari, *Castes and Tribes of Southern India*, vol.IV, p.307.

21 Arthur F.Cox, *A Manual of the North Arcot District in the Presidency of Madras*, Madras, 1880.

22 Tangedu is said to be cut only by the Madigas, as other classes think it beneath their dignity to do it. For more details see Narahari Gopalakrishnamah Chetty, *A Manual of the Kurnool District in the Presidency of Madras,* Madras, 1886.

23 A.Chatterton, *Monograph of Tanning and Working in Leather,* Madras, 1904.

24 Edgar Thurston & K.Rangachari, *Castes and Tribes of Southern India,* vol.IV, p.310.

25 John Kelshall, *Manual of the Bellary District,* Madras, 1872.

26 John Kelshall, *Manual of the Bellary District,* Madras, 1872.

27 John Kelshall, *Manual of the Bellary District,* Madras, 1872.

28 J.D.B.Gribble, *A Manual of the Cuddapah District in the Presidency of Madras,* Hyderabad, 1992 (rpt.), (1st pbd:1875, pp.363-364)

29 Edgar Thurston & K.Rangachari, *Castes and Tribes of Southern India,* vol.IV, p.318.

30 John Kelshall, *Manual of the Bellary District,* Madras, 1872.

31 Edgar Thurston & K.Rangachari, *Castes and Tribes of Southern India,* vol.IV, p.322.

32 Edgar Thurston & K.Rangachari, *Castes and Tribes of Southern India,* vol.IV, p.322.

33 W.Francis, *Andhra Pradesh District Gazetteers, Anantapur District Gazetteer,* Hyderabad, 1993 (rpt.) (1st pbd:1905), pp.45-46.

34 W.Francis, *Andhra Pradesh District Gazetteers, Anantapur District Gazetteer,* p.47.

35 M.V. Rajagopal, *Andhra Pradesh District Gazetteers, Kurnool,* Hyderabad, 1974, p.61.

36 M.V. Rajagopal, *Andhra Pradesh District Gazetteers, Kurnool,* p. 164.

5

The Leather Communities and the English East India Company in South India During 17th to 19th Centuries

Dr. Vikram Harijan*

Historians like Sanjay Subrahmanyam, Kanakalatha Mukund, S. Arasaratnam, Burton Stein, Susan Baylay etc. have ignored the specific studies on the leather working communities. Leather working communities like the Madigas of Andhra Pradesh, the Chakkiliyans and the Vettiyans of Tamil Nadu, the Madiga, Mochi and Samagara of Karnataka and the Tolkollans of Kerala, the Chamara, Jaiswara of North India. However, these leather working communities played a very important role in the economy. For instance, under the English East India Company these groups become the cogs of wheel for the economy. They not only contributed the economy but also in the growth and development of the English establishment during 17th century in Madras. They also led several riots in Madras under the leadership of the merchants. They were the sources of tension for the English company. Various ethnographer and colonial social scientist have penned on the leather communities which are of course is not enough but historians have totally ignored the said issues. My paper will try to analyze objectively their role in the

* Assistant Professor, Department of Medieval and Modern History, University of Alahabad, Alahabad

English company, their participation in the development of the English company, their assertion, their women role, the impact of religion, conversion to the new religion and of course their empowerment . The present study is mainly based on the English sources particularly the Records of fort st. George, Travelers account and census report.

Introduction

The tanners of leather, the preparers of skins, the manufacturers of leather articles and the makers of shoes belonged to well defined class in the Indian social order. Most of these workers in upper India were included under the general term Chamar.The word leather (hide) *Charman, Charma* was known in both the older and the later portions of *the Rig veda*. In the *Athava veda*,in the books of the Yajur vedic schools, in the Brahmans and in the later literature. In these books we found references to the thong, yoktra, used for yoking the chariot or cart; the bow-string, jya made of ox-hide;reins of leather; leather bags, driti and dhmata for holding liquids; leather bottles, Bhastra and thongs used for couches vardhra for door fastenings, paricarmanya, and for bridles, syuman.From the Mahabharat we learnt that leather was used for the hand guard for the bow that the hands and fingers were procted with leather; that the soldier used a shield made of ox-hide or bear-skin: that he had a cuirass and a oreast – plate of leather ; and that his body-armour was made of iron and leather. We found also that sinews were used to bind the feathers upon the arrow, and that sword was sheathed in leather. The war chariot was procted with shield of leather. The box of the chariot was fixed to the axle with thongs of leather. The horses were yoked to the pole of the chariot with leather straps.The reins were of leather.Sometimes the horses were even covered with leather robes which served as armour. Drums, especially the great kettle-drums, were fashioned with leather heads.[1]

The old literature also knew the shoemaker, *carmakara, Charmakrit, Padukara, pudukrit*. Shoes made of skins and of leather were mentioned in the Brahmanas, in Manu and the older laws books, in the Mahabharat, in the ramayana and in the Vishnu Purana.Thus there were well known and fully developed in Ancient India, the occupations of tanner and leather worker. Probably from the early aryans times the village life in India was organised somewhat as it " is today, with its cultivators resident within the village, and the lower orders of labourers attached to its outskirts. To this latter class belonged the common labourers and those who, an account of the disgusting aspects of the work and life, were deemed to be unclean and untouchable.[2] However, they were known in various names in India. They were called Madigas of Andhra Pradesh, the Chakkiliyans and the Vettiyans of Tamil Nadu, the Madiga, Mochi and Samagara of Karnataka and the Tolkollans of Kerala, the Chamara, Jaiswara of North India. Chakkiliyan were also known as Chukler. In many accounts they were as inferior to the Paraiyans.[3]

Cobblers Caste

Abbe Dubois informed us about the cobblers castes. He says that the Chucklers, or cobblers, were also considered inferior to the Pariahs all over the Peninsula, and, as a matter of fact, they (cobblers) show that they were of a lower grade by their more debased ideas, their greater ignorance and brutality. They were also much more addicted to drinking and debauchery. Their orgies take place principally in the late evening, and their villages resound, far into the night, with the yells and quarrels which result from their state of intoxication. Nothing will persuade them to work as long as they have anything to drink; they only return to their labour when they have absolutely no further means of satisfying their ruling passion. Thus they spent their time in alternate bouts of work and drunkenness. The women of this wretched class did not allow their husbands to outshine them in any vice, and were quite as much addicted to drunkenness as the men. Their modesty and general behavior may, therefore, be easily imagined. The very Pariahs refuse to have anything to do with the Chucklers, and did not admit them to any of their easts.[4] Abbe Dubois informed us about the cobblers castes. He says that their manners were more gross, and they were more addicted to gluttony and intemperance.[5]He further pointed out that they got merry towards the evening and it was not long before the villages resounded with the cries and quarrels occasioned by their cups. They were all wretchedly poor. However, they were rarely enjoyed but wretched Chakili or cobblers existed in absolute indigence. They also could less complain, as their misery arose chiefly out of their ebriety. He further explained the nature of the this wretched people is that they will never work while they had any pre-plan to have drink, and they never returned to their work till their purse was exhausted. He further informed us about their women is that their equally involved in this kind of behavior. Lastly he has given a very painful or disturbing kind of sentence and I quote 'and nothing more need be said of their morals or behavior'[6] He also informed that they were also a very dreadful creatures. I quote "One would not easily guess the cause of this dreadful commotion. It arouse forsooth from a chakili, at a public festival, sticking red flowers in his turban, which the Pariahs insisted that none of his caste had a right to wear."[7]

The Moochis, or tanners, though better educated and more refined than any of the preceding classes, were the lowest in the social strata. The other Sudras never allow them (cobblers) to join in their feasts; indeed, they would hardly condescend to give them a drop of water to drink. This feeling of repulsion was caused by the defilement which ensues from their constantly handling the skins of dead animals and eating of careasses.

As a rule, the mechanical and the liberal arts, such as music, paintings, and sculpture, were placed on very much the same level, and those who followed these professions, which were left entirely to the lower castes of the Sudras, were looked down upon with equal dis favour[8]. As far as he knew, only the Moochis took up painting as a profession. Instrumental music, and particularly that of wind instruments, was left exclusively, as he have already mentioned, to the barbers and Pariahs[9]. He informed us their low and degraded position also that music was nearly confined to the Barber and pariahs .Mochi were not allowed to use the music.[10]K.K.Pillay also informs us as follows:TheChakkiliyar form one of the lower castes. There is no mention of them in early Tamil literature. They seem to have come from the Telugu and Kannada regions. Though they are now Tamil speaking people, their earlier mother tongue was Telugu or Kannada. Perhaps they came to Tamil nadu in the wake of the Vijayanagar invaders. They are workers on leather. It is their duty to remove the dead cattle from villages. In return the Chakkiliyar have to supply leather for agricultural purposes. In the Madurai District a distinguishing feature is that the men of the *"Chakkiliya"* caste belong to the right hand caste while their women belong to the left.[11]

F.R. Hemingway had given also information about the leather working communities regarding the Telgu area of Godavari. He pointed out that The *Madigas* were a numerous caste whose traditional occupations were tanning and shoemaking. Some of them informed that they were the descendants of a saint or demi-god called Jambha-muni and women called *Puramasi* who disturbed the saint in his contemplation and became his wife.[12]They were subdivided into the occupational classes ofnMadigaDasaris(priests), MadigaPayikis (sweepers),the Kommalas (who blow horns) and the ordinary Madigas who followed the traditional callings of tanning and shoe-making. These will not dine together or intermarry. The last of them was by far the most numerous. The Dasaris were considered socially the highest and the Payikis the lowest of the sub-divisions.[13]

W.G. Briggs introduced the caste by writing that and I quote "The tanners of leather, the preparers of skins, the manufacturers of leather articles, and the makers of shoes belong to a well-defined class in indian social order.Most of these workers,in upper india, are today included under the general term Chamar"[14] In south India at Tamil region, they were called Chakallyan.They were leather worker.[15]The great leather –working caste of the Telgu country was the madiga.[16]This occupational groups may be traced back to very early times.Tanners(*Charmamna*) were mentioned in *the Rig veda,* in the later vedic literature, and in *the Brahmans*.Tanning, mlamna was also spoken of in *the Rig Veda,* and certain details of stretching and wetting hides probably refered to the process of manufacture.Ox-hides were used in the pressing of the soma, and ox-hides and antelope and tiger skins were used in sacramental and ceremonial rites. The use of skins for clothing was mentioned in *the Satapatha Brahmana,*and in other early literature . The Maruts wore deer skins, and the wild ascetics seemed to have been clothed in skins. The use presupposes the preparation of skins.[17]

The word leather (hide) *Charman,Charma* was known in both the older and the later portions of *the Rig veda*.In the *Athava veda,*in thebooks of the Yajur vedic schools, in the Brahmans and in the later literature.In these books we found references to the thong,yoktra,used for yoking the chariot or cart;the bow-string, jya made of ox-hide;reins of leather; leather bags, driti and dhmata for holding liquids; leather bottles, Bhastra and thongs used for couches vardhra for door fastenings, paricarmanya, and for bridles, syuman. From the Mahabharat we learnt that leather was used for the hand guard for the bow that the hands and fingers were procted with leather;that the soldier used a shield made of ox-hide or bear-skin: that he had a cuirass and a oreast –plate of leather ;and that his body-armour was made of iron and leather .We found also that sinews were used to bind the feathers upon the arrow,and that sword was sheathed in leather .The war chariot was procted with shield of leather. The box of the chariot was fixed to the axle with thongs of leather. The horses were yoked to the pole of the chariot with leather straps.The reins were of leather.Sometimes the horses were even covered with leather robes which served as armour .Drums, especially the great kettle-drums, were fashioned with leather heads.[18]

The old literature also knew the shoemaker, *carmakara, Charmakrit, Padukara, pudukrit.* Shoes made of skins and of leather were mentioned in the Brahmanas, in Manu and the older laws books, in the Mahabharat, in the ramayana and in the Vishnu Purana.Thus there were well known and fully developed in Ancient India, the occupations of tanner and leather worker.Probably from the early aryans times the village life in India was organised somewhat as it " is today, with its cultivators resident within the village, and the lower orders of labourers attached to its outskirts. To this latter class belonged the common labourers and those who, an account of the disgusting aspects of the work and life, were deemed to be unclean and untouchable.[19]

Syed Siraj ul Hassan introduced Madiga caste with various connotations. He pointed out that Madiga, Madigowd, madigaru, Madru, Dher, Chandal, Antyaja, Ettiwandlu, Peddintiwandlu, Panchamollu, Matangi, Makallu, Gosangi, Kamathi, Bendar, Chambhar –a very numerous caste of leather-workers and rope-maker,many of whom were engaged as village watchmen and musicians.[20]

Francis Buchanan, fellow of the royal society and of the society of antiquaries of London, came India in early 19th century, has supplied some information pertains to the *Madiga*caste of the South India. He pointed out that the *Madigas,* or *Madigaru* were looked upon as a very low caste. They dress hide, made shoes and some of them cultivate the ground, acting as servants to the farmers. They were divided into small tribes of ten or twelve houses and intermarry with the daughters of these houses only, in order to be certain of the purity of their race; of which they seemed to be as fond, as those castes that were esteemed infinitely superior in rank. Some of the richer among them took two wives; but this was not common as a girl's father required from 30 t0 80 fanams. They never divorce their wives for any crime, except adultery. They ate carrion and all manners of animal food and avowedly drink spirituous liquors. Their religious worship seemed to be exactly the same with that of the *Coramaru*;but they had a priestly tribe.whoneverintermary with the laity, who lived entirely on their countributions, and were called *Jambu*. There was a *Matam*of Jambu at Cuddapa; and the office of high priest there was hereditary. This person took frequent rounds through the country, collecting money and admonishing his followers. He never seen any of the Jambu; and; if they had any learning among them, they kept it entirely to themselves, as none of the laity could either read or write.The Madigaru, who by the English of Madras were called Sirlars, had no hereditary chiefs; but, in case of any fault being committed by a person of the caste, the elders assembled and punished him according to custom.[21]

Edgar Thurston, who was super indent of Madras Government Museum, had written extensively on caste and Tribes of south India. He was assisted by K. Rangachariwho had influenced upon Edgar Thurston. While writing on leather community (Chakkiliyan) Edgar Thurston had taken a great part of the H.A Stuart[22], Abbe Dubois[23], Mr. A Chatterton[24] and so on. Edgar Thurston quotes Mr. H.A. Stuart "The Chakkiliyans are the leather –workers of the Tamil districts, corresponding to The Madigas of the Telugu country. The Chakkiliyans appear to be immigrants from the Telugu or Canarese districts, for no mentions are made of this caste either in the early

Tamil inscriptions, or in early Tamil literature."[25]Edgar Thurston quotes the Madura manual 1868 that Chakkiliyans were the dressers of leather and makers of slippers, harness and other leather articles.[26]

Left and Right Hand Caste and Power of the Leather Communities

Fort St. George recorded certain castes, which belonged to Right Hand castes and the Left Hand castes. Firstly, the right hand caste includes Chetti,[27] Pariyar,[28] oilmen,[29] and other castes while the left hand castes also includes Chettis,[30] bricklayers, carpenters, weavers,[31] boatmen, watermen, fishermen, barbers,[32] and other come to the left hand castes.[33] M. Srinivasa Aiyangar also classified the right-left hand divisions according to their occupation:[34]

Occupation	Right Hand	Left Hand
1. Traders	Balija	Beri Chetti
	Banajiga	Vaniyans
	Komati	(who yoke two bullocks)
	Vellan Chetti	
2. Weavers	Jandra	Devanga
	Saliyan	Kaikolan
	Seniyan	
3. Artisans	Nil	Kammalan
	Kamsali	
	Panchalas	
4. Leather workers	Maidga or	Ditto (males)
	chakkilyan (females)	
	Malaiman	Bedar
	Nattaman	
5. Field labourers	Palli (females)	Pallis (males)
and soldiers.	Vedan or Vettuvan	Pallan
	Paraiyan, Mala and Haleya	

H.D. Love quoted Captain Colin Makenzie, which according to him, there were 39 castes in 'Buljewar[35] caste (right hand caste). They were Komati, Moochi, Vullickar, Tellanwar, Paniayar, Vullawar, Gundapodikar and Shaunar castes while in the left hand castes (Naggaret)[36] he gave eleven castes. They were Chitti, Pully, Chakkilyan, Panchalas and Kaikolan.[37] None the less, his reporting also makes very great confusion. Makenzie excluded Chitti caste from the Right hand caste while Aiyangar included in both sides. Ayangar includes Chakkilyan females in Right hand and male in Left hand caste. Makenzie also quoted fewer number of left hand castes, while Aiyangar gave almost equal numbers.

Abbe Dubois informed us that whole South India was divided into Right and Left hand castes. Untouchable's castes were also divided into Right and Left hand castes. The Pariah caste was in the right hand caste while Chakilan caste was in Left hand caste.Abbe Dubois informed us that he was present at one dispute which was happened between right hand pariah caste and Left hand Cobblers or Chakili castes. Abbe Dubois informed us that it was most dreadful and dangerous. I quote, 'The dispute was between the castes of Right and Left hand castes. and the Cobblers or Chakili, where it happened, that many of the peaceable in habitants had begun to remove their effects and to leave their villages for a place of greater safety, with the same feelings as when the country sees an impending invasion of a Mahrata army, and with the same dread of savage treatment. Fortunately in this instance, matters did not come to an extremity, as the principal inhabitants of the district seasonably came forward to mediate between these vulgar castes, and were just in time, by good management to disband the armed ranks on both sides that only waited the signal of battle. One would not easily guess the causes of this dreadful commotion. It arose forsooth from a Chakili at a public festival, sticking red flowers in his turban, which the

Pariahs insisted that none of his caste had a right to wear.'[38]

Francis Buchanan, a traveller, who visited Madras, Mysore, Canara and Malabar, in the early 19th Century has also reported on the right-left hand divisions. He recognized nine castes in left hand side (Idangai).[39]

1. Panchalas: in Panchalas, there were five castes: i) Cubbinadava or blacksmiths; ii) Badiga (carpenters); iii) Cunsugaru (coppersmiths); iv) Culbadiga (Masons); v) Akala, (gold and silver smiths).
2. Beri Chette, a merchant who pretended to be of the Vaisya caste.
3. Devanga, a class of weavers.
4. Heganigaru, oilmakers, who used two oxen in their mills.
5. Gollur or Golawanlu, who transported money.
6. Paliwanlu and Palawanlu, the two tribes of cultivators.
7. Baydaru, a hunter.
8. Madiga, tanners or shoemakers.

Francis Buchanan also indicated nineteen right hand caste groups:

1. Banijiguru, who were traders and divided many religions. The two were most important as; i) Panchum Banijiguru, who were traders and weaned linga; ii) Taliga Banijiguru.
2. Wocligaru, cultivators of the Sudra caste.
3. Joti Phana, oilmakers, who used one bullock in the mill.
4. rungaru, Calico printer and tailors.
5. Ladaru, a kind of Muslim traders who were followed by all artificers of the same religion.
6. Gujarati, merchants of Gujarat.

7. Komati, persons who were really of Vaisya caste.
8. Jain, worshippers of Jain.
9. Curubaru, shepherds, blanket weavers and cultivators.
10. Cumbaru, potters.
11. Agasa, washermen.
12. Besta, palanquin bearers.
13. Padma Shalayvaru, a kind of weavers.
14. Naindaru, barbers.
15. Uparu, person who dug tanks and builds rough walls.
16. Chitragaru, painters.
17. Goallaru, keepers of cow and buffalos.
18. Whalliaru, the paraiyar caste who formed the active part of the right side.

Francis Buchanan's classifications of the dual division produce much confusion. Generally, washermen, barbers and painters caste belonged to the left hand caste while Buchanan included them in the Right hand castes. Even weavers and boat makers were in both sides. Buchanan accepted that the divisions was often controversial.Francis Buchanan pointed out in the context of Telgucounty that it was Madiga who was most violent caste. I quote ' *The madigaru, in all disputes, from the most active combatants; on which account, a their own name was reproachful, they are commonly called the Eddagai cast, as if they were the only persons belonging to it.'*[40].

F.J. Richards had also pointed out that it was the untouchable groups who started the riots first. I quote " TheParaiyans belong to the right hand and the Chucklers to the left, and it is between these that rows begin."[41] It had been noticed as a curious fact that in the Madura district, while the men belonged to the right hand factions, the women belonged toand were most energetic supporters of the left. It was even said that during the entire period of a faction riot, the Chakkiliyan women kept aloof from their husbands and denied them their marital rights.[42]Edgar Thurston quotes Mr. N.G. Chetty[43] that the Madigas belonged to the left hand castes and often quarreled with the Malas(Right hand caste). In 1871 a Madiga, having contrived to obtain a red cloth as reward from the policesuperintendent wore it on his head, and went in procession on horseback by the main bazar street. This resulted in a disturbance in which a European inspector was severely hurt by a Mala, who had mistaken him for the superintendent. The two factions fixed by mutual understanding, the streets by which each was to proceed, and no quarrels had since occurred.[44]In 1783, Tipu sultan intervented in a dispute between Paraiyans and Chakkiliyans in Sreingapatnam and personally sanctioned anumber of 'Customs', which were to be preserved.[45]

Causes for the Riots

Various records and writings on the subject agreed that pride, honours, symbols, physical and social space and status were the most important causes for the conflicts and disputes in Madras. However, the new urban economies, which provide new avenues for occupational[46] upward social mobility to the merchants were one of the main causes for the various disputes including the riots.[47] Numerically, the right hand caste merchants were more dominant than the left hand caste groups. However, because of their influential position and economic status the left hand caste groups started to claim an equitable status on par with the right hand caste. This had brought about constant conflicts between the two groups, which sometimes broke out into open riots. Apparently, the left and right hands were fighting for physical and social space. However, if one goes deeper, the booming economic conditions provided the base for the continuing conflicts between the two. The fact that Madras witnessed most frequently of those caste riots in comparison to the hinterland and other port towns suggest that the flourishing trades and the booming economy of Madras was the main cause of the conflicts.

Another chief cause was urbanization. Since the Chola period, urbanization started to gain importance as the state practised both domestic and foreign trades. Decidedly, it contributed to the weakening of the state and brought about dramatic social change. It especially became importance during the Vijayanagar period and later during the British time.[48] Most of the scholars who are working on the caste riots like Burton Stein, Arjun Appadurai and S. Arasaratnam etc. agreed that urbanisation was the principal factor for the riots. Arasaratnam says that urbanization factors brought many differences into caste, productions and performance of many caste related ceremonies, weddings and funerals.[49]

Migration also played a very significant role in the disputes because people from Telugu and Kannada region moved in madras and got new opportunities in the English company as Burton stein explained. Burton Stein explained that the forging of significant links among a variety of dependent peoples of diverse localities, which could transcend the boundaries of the nadus or basic territorial units, into which the Chola agrarian system was highly fragmented. As the Chola agrarian system spread to new territories, new social groups were assimilated into the existing dual social system, and particularly the Left side'.[50]

Stein argues that the earlier (Chola) period, there was only one recorded instance of major conflict, and frequent hostility was a feature of only the later (Vijayanagar) period. Extending his argument, Stein says that this hostility, in fact, became more pronounced with progressive urbanization in the late Chola and Vijayanagar periods, which essentially meant a realignment of the interests of the two – insofar as groups the occupational absorption/ engagement is concerned and changes in the power structure, since the 'mobile craftsmen and traders who were the core of idarigai groups' began to gain economic and social advantage vis-a-vis the land based valarigai groups and, finally,[51] Appadurai's analysis of the basis of the conflict is far more complex and provides a theoretical framework for its context. Outwardly, the disputes were about 'the respective monopolies of the two sides over certain practices, emblems and spaces', but the metaphor of a bifurcated social body itself is a 'root paradigm in South Indian history,' and 'the function of this particular metaphor is to give expression to a wide variety of empirical conflicts and antagonisms. Though the body is divided, he adds, 'the metaphor also simultaneously expresses the unity of the conflicting units'.[52]

I am very surprise that they were so violent and so dreadful then how come they were very low and their status is so degradeful? It a question mark .I also see the power of the caste. Power" is the main concept which is at the heart of social stratification. Max Weber has pointed out that power is the fundamental concept in stratification with which class, status and party were the serious concern in three separate dimensions. Classes were the outcome of the distribution of economic power. Status was a kind of normatively defined social power; and parties were groups active in the political spheres in pursuit of various goals. Power is, therefore, a social relationship. Power thus defined by Weber in general terms as the probability of persons or groups carrying out their will even when opposed by others.[53]

Weber made further observations concerning the nature of power in his political sociology. Few groups in society base their power purely on force or military might. Instead, ruling groups attempt to legitimate their power, and convert it into what he termed "domination". According to Weber there are three bases of domination: traditional, rational-legal, and charismatic.

Steven Lukes points out that power is an essentially contested concept.[54]

According to Weber status is related to the power. To me "caste' is statuses which confirm our place in the society. Caste is very much associated with power. Each caste carries power within the caste occupation. With this occupation Castes people were in bargaining position.To, me belongigng to the bottm line of the status and become so violent and become leaders of the caste that means you carray alots of meaning.it is the power of the who display lots of courge.

Social Status

Julia Maitland was born in London and got married James Thomas, attended Haileybury College, arrived madras in December 1836 who had witten several letters addressed to his family and relatives and friends which is really a valuable documents to understand the south indian Histories. She pointed out in her fifteenth letter and I quote "The Castes are not now so unmixed as when first invented. Indeed I believe that some of the original divisions no longer exist; but they make up for it by subdividing the Sudra or Merchant caste. Ayah continually tells me " that man of moochy (Carpenter) caste or bearer caste &c.The shoemakers, I believe are the lowest of any. The Pariahs are of no caste at all."[55]

F.R. Hemingway had given also information regarding the leather working communities regarding the Telgu area of Godavari. He also informs about the social positions of the Madiga communities in south india. He pointed out that Madigas were much despised by other castes because they were leather-workers and eat beef and even Carrion, and they took much the same low social position as the Malas. Their curious connections with the Komatis had been mentioned in the account of that caste above. Their marriage and other ceremonies were very similar to those of the Malas. Their special caste Goddess was

Matangi, who herself from him under the 'tanning-pot in a Madigas house. At Pongal they worship their tanning-pots, as representing the Goddess, with offerings of fowls and liquor.[56] It was also said that they used to give poison to the cattle because they were habitual to take the dead meat of the cattle for food. They used to hide the cattle for killing them.[57] Maridamma,(goddess) who in many respects corresponds to the Mariamma of the south, was purely malevolent in character and was not in the habit of conferring benefits. She brought disease upon the villages, but could be included by becoming worship to hold her hand. She was offered animal sacrifices whenever serious sickness visited a village. Sometimes a small car was made to which pigs and fowls were tied and which was then dragged through the village. Every household pours offerings of rice, etc., upon it and it was at last left outside the village limits to symbolize the departure of the goddess. The animals were taken away by the Malas and Madigas.[58]The good shoes were made by Madigas.[59]F .j Richardshas supplied some information pertains to the lower caste of South india. He categorized lower caste into *serf castes.* He wroteand I quote " The serf castes, including the pallars of the Tamil country and the outcastes, the paraiyans, panchamas or Adi-Dravidas of the tamil, the sakkiliyas (Chucklers) and Madigas and Malas of the Telugu country and the Holeyas of Kannada"[60]Edgar Thurston quotes Mr. H.A. Stuart that Chakkiliyans occupied the lowest rank,though there was much dispute on this point between them and the Paraiyans.[61]Edgar Thurston quotes Sonnerat[62] in eighteenth century that the Chakkiliyans were in more contempt than the Pariahs, because they used cow leather in making shoes.[63]Edgar Thurston quotes Mr. A. Chatterton who writes as follows "The position of the Chakkiliyansin the south differs greatly from that of the Madigas of the north, and many of his privileges are enjoyed by a s sub-sect of the Pariahs called Vettiayans.These people possess the right of removing dead cattle from villages and in return have to supply leather for agricultural purposes. The majority of Chakkiliyans are tanners, but leather workers and instead of getting the hides or skins direct from the vettiyans.

Syed Siraj ul Hassan had supplied some information pertaining to the social status of the Madiga.The social rank of the Madiga was the lowest in the Hindu social system. They used to eat the leavings of any cattle except the Erakalas, Domars, Pichakuntalas, Buruds;Jingars and Panchadayis, while ate food cooked by them. They lived on the outskirts of villages, in thatched one-storied houses, with only one entrance door. Their habits were very dirty, and their quarters extremelyfilthy. The village barber will not shave their heads nor will the village washermen wash their clothes and they had to employed barbers and washermen from among their own community.Their touch was regarded as unclean by all respectable classes,and a Brahman touched by a madiga was required to obtain purifications by bathing himself, washing his cloths and changing his sacred thread for a new one. The diet of a madiga was in keeping with his degraded positions and he used to eat beefs, houses, flesh, pork, fowls, mutton as a representative of their ancestor jambavant was held in special respect and noMadiga will injure or kill animal.[64]

They prefer to purchase them ready tanned from traders, who bring them from the large tanning centres. When the chuckler starts making shoes or sandals, he purchases the leather and skin which he requires in the bazar and taking it home, first proceeds with a preliminary currying operation. The leather is damped and well stretched and dyed with aniline, the usual colour being scarlet R.R. of the BadischeAnilin Soda Fabrik.

Madigas served as a menial and as a scavenger.Many madigas were pracrically serfs.Most of them were field labourers. They beat drums at festivels. In some part of the country they still had their perquisites (jajman), but those were diaapearing under the competitions .[65]

Funerals

F.R. Hemingway had given information about the funerals of the Mala and Madigas. It is also applicable to all castes in south India. The dead were usually brunt, but children were buried and some simple rite was performed, such as the pouring of milk, either alone or mixed with rice or oil and ghee,on the grave. The ceremonies at the funerals of adult were much the same in all non –Brahman castes. The body was bathed and was borne to the burning-ground on a bier. He mala and Madigas carried in it their arms in a sittings posture. The corpse was set down three times on the road while rice was placed the pyre, the son of the deceased walked thrice round it with a pot of water in which three holes had been made, and lights the pyre with face averted. The relatives then went home and worship a lamp. Further ceremonies were performed on the eleventh day afterwards and on some day between the second and fifth after it, which was called the small day. On the latter the bones and ashes are collected and were offered a ball of cooked rice. The party then returned home and feasts.[66]

Dependent Caste

F.R. Hemingway had given information of Dependent communities of Madiga. He pointed out that the begging castes specially attached to the Madigas were Dekkalas, Mastidis and Tappitas or Bagavatas. Of These the Dekkalas were musicians who sing the praises of their patron's ancestors. The Mastidis were gymnasts and the Tappitas were the same as the MadigaBogams and were the dancers and prostitutes of the caste.[67]

Dress

F.R.Hemingway had given description of Dress of Madiga caste. He penned that Mala and Madiga wore only languti.[68]

Food

Edgar Thurston quotes Mr. H.A. Stuart that they indulged very freely in intoxicating liquors, and will eat any flesh including beef, porketc. Hence they were called par excellence, the flesh-eater.[69] They were men of drunken and filthy habits.[70]They were described as coarse and filthy,as an eater of unclean food,and as a user of obscene language.[71]

Occupations and Mobility

A Catalogue of the different kinds of work which the Chamars performs, showed that he belonged to the great class of unskilled labour.They were grass-cutter, coolie, wood-cutter, budle-carrier, drudge, doer of odd jobs,maker and repairer of thatch and mud of walls,field labourer, groom crrier, house servant,peon,brick-maker,and even the village watchman. They were the common labourer along railways and in the great cities. They also did a good deal of weaveing.They repaired the underground rooms and made the bins where the grains was stored, and prepared the threshing-floors. Besides, they beat drums, ring bells, and blew trumpets at weddings or when cholera or other epidemics were being exorcised from the village. They used to make musical instruments. Some sub caste names were illustrations of occupational functions: for example, Mochi (shoe-maker), Chamkatiya (leather –cutter), Chamar (leather-maker), Chamar mamgta or mamgatiya (beggar), katua (leather-cutter), Tamtua (maker of leather thongs), Zingar (maker of saddles) and nalchhind (one who cuts the navel cord).[72] They made shoes according to the English model. [73] It was because the shoes were in great demand in the Englishcompany.

Syed Siraj ul Hassan who was compiled Castes and Tribes of The Nizam's Dominions, had pointed out the occupation of the leather community that is Madiga. He pointed out that their original occupation of the caste was believed to be the skinning of dead animals, leather dressing and the making of leather ropes, leather buckets for hauling water from wells and other leather articles used in husbandry. Like the Malas they were field servants and supply the farmers with the above articles, for which they got, as their perquisite, a fixed quantity of grain for each plough. They made shoes of various kinds,but especially chapals (sandals), of which they produced the best varieties. They were engaged as scavengers,village watchmen, guides, executioners and begaris, or forced coolies. They also served as musicians at the marriage and other ceremonies of high caste Hindus. Their rights to carcassed were often disputed by the Malas and tedious litigations result. At some places they hold inams lands, in lieu of services rendered by them to the village community as messengers and carriers. They also worked as village criers, announcing by beat of drum any public orders. Some of them got enrolled in the Indian army, where they passed under the name of Bedars or Gosangi Bantus. Many served as menials in the houses of Muhammadan Landlords. A few only had taken to agriculture.[74]

It showed that there was greater caste occupational mobility was there. I used caste occupational mobility not caste mobility. Because I believe there in no mobility in caste, the mobility possible in occupations only.

Leather Tanning Technique

F.R.Hemingway supplies some information that coarse leather for the manufacture of country shoes was made by the Madigas all over the low country. Their method of tanning that was very elementary. The hides and skins were soaked in a solution of chunam to remove the hair, then in clean water for a day, next for ten days in decoction of the bark of the babul tree, and finally they were stitched into bags, which were filled with babul bark and soaked for a week in water.

Francis Buchanan has given a detail account of leather manufacturer. He informs us that leather was tanned here (telugu country) by a class of people esteemed of very low caste and called *madigaru*caste.He tells about the technique that to dress the raw hides of sheep or goats, the Madigaru in the first place washed them and cleaned and then rub each with the fourth part of a kind of soft paste, made of 6 *Dudus* weight of the milky juice of the *yecada(Asclepiasgigantean)*, and about 6 *Ddudus*(2——426\1000 ounces) of salt (*mauriate* of Soda),and twelve *Dadus*weight of *ragy, sanguty,* or pudding of the Cynosuruscoracanus, with a sufficient quantity of water. This paste was rubbed on the hairy side, and the skins were then exposed for three days to the sun; after which they were washed with water,beating them well on a stone, as was usual in this country. This took off the hair. Then powder 2 Secrs(1 -213\1000) of *ArulayMyrobalans*and put them and one skin into a pot with 5 or 4 seers measure of hot water, where it was to remain for three days. The skin was then to be washed and dried.This tanned skin was dyed black as followed: took of old iron, and of the dross of iron forges, each a handful; of plantain and lime skins, each five or six; put them into a pot with some *ragy kanji* or decoction of ragy, and let them stand for eight days. Then rub the liquor on the skins, which immediately become black.[75]

These skins may be dyed red by the following process: took of ungrabled*Lac 2 Dudus*weight(about 13 drams) of *sujacara*or fine soda, 1 Dudu weight, and of Lodu bark 2 Dudus weight . Having taken the sticks from the lac, and powdered the soda and bark boil them all together in a seer of water (68 1\2cubical inches) for 1 1\2 hour. Rub the skin, after it had been freed from the hair as before mentioned,with the decoction;and then put it into the pot with the Myrobalans and water for three days. This is good cplour, and for many purposes the skins were well dressed.[76]

The hides of oxen and buffaloes were dressed as follows : For each skin took 2 *Sers (1-213\1000 lb) of* quick lime, and 5 or 6 *seers*measure for eight (about 1 1\2 ale gallon) of water; and in this mixture kept the skins for eight days,and rub off the hair.Then for each skin took ten seers, by weight, (about 6lb) of the unpeeled sticks of the *Tayngadu (cassia auriculata),* and 10 seers measure of water (about 2 1\2 ale gallons),and in this infusion kept the skins for four days. For an equal length of time, add the same quantity of *Tayngadu*and water. Then wash, and dry the skins in the sun, stretching them out with pegs. This leather was very bad.[77]

Leather Trades Institute and School for Lower Castes

Jullia maitland opened a school which was for all Castes. She obserbed and I quote "Our shool is now opened with about twenty-five boys, and more coming. All castes boys. A—thinks it better to teach them whenever one can, as it is far more difficult to get at them than at the Pariahs,and also the educations of the upper rank has much more influence than that of the pariah. We have a Bramin to teach Gentoo,and David Gonsalves, the half-caste, to teach English. I went to see them at the other morning. The Bramins and Merchant boys sat together;there was another row of the Moochy or workman caste; another of Mussulman boys"[78]

The leathers Trades institute was opened in 1915, and was run partly as a model tannery and school, and partly as a research institute. The course extended over three years. The number of students under instruction last year was thirty-four.[79]

Women of Leather Wworking Communities

Chakkiliyan Women

Edgar Thurston quotes Sonnerat that their women were held to be of the Padmani kind, i. e., of peculiar beauty of face and form, and were also said to be very virtuous. It was well known that Zamindars and other rich men were very fond of intriguing with them, particularly in the neighborhood of Paramagudi, where they lived in great numbers.[80]However, unlike the Madigas, they did not carry out the practice of making Basavis (dedicated prostitutes).[81]Chakkiliyans did not worship Matangi who was the special deity of the madigas. Their gods included Madurai Viran, Mariamma, Muneswara, Draupadi and Gangamma.[82]As a usual things their girls were not married before puberty. Widows were re-married. Divorce was common and easily secured.Their women were beautiful, and from amongst them was usually chosen the woman for the coarser form of sakti worship.[83]

Madiga Women

Madiga woman were having a very low position in the society and officially they were temple prostitute. Many ethnographers have written on the Madiga woman but Edgar Thurston had given details about the Madiga woman in the temple prostitutions. The system of making Basavis as well law was which was taking about the Madiga woman had right to have intercource with men at her plesure.While Syed Siraj ul Hassan had given different opinon that they were made temple prostitue on some conditions which I will discuss later on.

The English company also provided the laws for the Devdasi which are following which were argued in the Madras High Court;[84].

The accused, a Madiga of the Bellary district, dedicated his minor daughter as a Basavi by a form of marriage with an idol. It appeared that Basavi is incapable of contracting a lawful marriage, and ordinarily practices promiscuous intercourse with men, and that her sons succeed to her father's property. It was held that the accused had committed an offence under the Penal Code, why lays down that "whoever sells, let to hire, or otherwise disposed of any minor under the age of sixteen years, with intent that such minor shall be employed or used for the purpose of prostitution, or for any unlawful and immoral purpose, shall be punished, etc." The Sessions judge referred to evidence that it was not a matter of course for Basavis to prostitute themselves for money, and added: "The evidence is very clear that Basavis are made in accordance with a custom of the Madiga caste. It is also in evidence that one of the effects of making a girl Basavi is that her male issue becomes a son of her father, and perpetuates his family, whereas, if she were married, he would perpetuare her husband's family. In this particular case, the girl was made a Basavi that she might be heir to her aunt, who was Basavi, but childless. Siddalingana Gowd says that they and their issue inherit the parent's property. There is evidence that Basavis are made on a very large scale, and that they live in their parent's house. There is no evidence that they are regarded otherwise than as respectable members of the caste. It seems as if the Basavi is the Madiga and Bedar equivalent of the "appointed daughter" of Hindu law (Mitakshara, Chap. I, s. xi, 3). Upon the whole, the evidence seems to establish that, among the Madigas, there is a widespread custom of performing, in a temple at Uchangidurgam, a marriage ceremony, the result of which is that the girl is marred without possibility of widowhood or divorce; that she is at liberty to have intercourse with men at her pleasure; that her children are heir to her father, and keep up his family; and that Basavi's nieces, being made Basavis, become their heirs. The Basavis seem in some cases to become prostitutes, but the language used by the witnesses generally points only to free intercourse with men, and not necessarily to receipt of payment for use of their bodies. In fact, they seem to acquire the right of intercourse with men without more discredit than accrues to the men of their caste for intercourse with women who are not their wives.*

During the celebrations of the village festivals, an unmarried Madiga women, called for the occasion Matangi (a favorite deity), abused and spits upon the people assembled, and they did not take this as an insult, because they thought that her spite removes the pollution. The woman was indeed regarded as the incarnation of the goddess herself.[85]

Syed Siraj ul Hassan pointed out in the context of temple prostitute that Madiga women were dedicated to the temple on some conditions which is as follows; Girls for whom husbands could not procured or who were vowed by their parents to the service of temples were dedicated to their tutelary deities. Such girls were called Joginis or Basavis,and were sometimes married to an idol and sometimes to a dagger. The girl who was to undergo the ceremony was dressed in new clothes and taken to the temple. Her forehead was smeared with kum kum (red lead powder), a lighted lamp was waved round the idol or dagger, and the girl, bearing the lamp on her head, walked three times round the symbol of the deity. The joginis become prostitute, but their children were admitted to the full privileges enjoyed by the legitimate members of the caste. Unmarried girls, becoming pregnant were also devoted to the service of gods. A girl on attaining puberty was unclean for five days. On the 5th day she bathed, touched a green leaf and becomes ceremonially pure.[86]

During the celebrations of the villagefestivals, an unmarried Madiga women, called for the occasion Matangi (a favorite deity), abused and spits upon the people assembled, and they did not take this as an insult, because they thought that her spite removes the pollution. The woman was indeed regarded as the incarnation of the goddess herself.

Caste Violence and View of the English Company and Outlook Towards Leather Community

The English Company viewed the caste system was an exploitative structure. The caste system of south India was merely the expression of the law of endogamy. Many factors combined in India to give this law greater rigour than anywhere else in the world. First, pride of race, clannishness, the natural reluctance of a man to give his daughter in marriage to a stranger whose standard of living differs from his own, especially if that stranger was his social inferior. Secondly, there were strong economic reasons for keeping the clan group intact, the interest of real estate, it might be, or the trade-union instinct which holds together those who had common vocation and enables them to transmit their skills from generation to generations. Language and religion too come into play. A difference inlanguage almost always and a difference in religion not seldom were bars to intermarriage between communities otherwise closely alike. All these fluid human prejudices had in south India been crystallized by traditions and scripture and society was a mosaic of infusible tesserae.The four caste theory of Brahmanic writ did not fit the facts of Dravidian India. Kshattriyas of the classic Rajput type were missing. So also, but for the claims of Telugu Komatis were Vaisya. Claims to Kshattriyas or Vaisya rank were from time to time put forward, but such claimes were usually met by ridicule or violence. The general frameworks of the society in the Tamil, Telugu and Kanarese areas were much the same.[87]

The English company's opinion was very harsh a having very bad opinion. For the English authority such disputes was regarded as the "factious madness"[88] which needs to be taken seriously as they destabilized the smooth functioning of trade and commerce.Dubious, A.J. Abbe, has also informed us that the rights and privileges for which the Hindus were ready to fight such sanguinary battles appear highly ridiculous, especially in the sight of an European. Perhaps the sole cause of the contest was the right to wear slippers or to ride through the streets in a palanquin or on horseback during marriage festivals. Sometimes that was the privilege of being escorted on certain occasions by armed retainers, sometimes that of having a trumpet sounded in front of a procession, or of being accompanied by native musicians at public ceremonies. Perhaps it was simply the particular kind of musical instrument apt to such occasions as was in dispute; or, perhaps, it may be the right of carrying flags of certain colours or certain devices during these ceremonies. Such, at any rate, were a few of the privileges for which Hindus were ready to cut each other's throats.[89]

Proverb and Saying

There are so many proverbs which a kind of violence. These proverbs also find the kind of language that is used by the society. There are following proverbs;[90]

1. Beti chamar ki Naam rajrania.!(The daughter of chamar and their name is Rajrania!).The meaning of this proverb is that a girl belonging to the Dalit girl could not be named a good name like Raj Rani.
2. Bhukhe ke etewar, chude ke chamaiin!.(A person who is on the fast and will have a sex with woman of chamar caste !). The meaning of this proverb is when a upper caste person having a fast, Ideally he should not have sex with the chamr caste (dalit)woman.The hard truth is that a person belonging to the upper or OBCs or Hindu Hegemonies person can have sex any time or anywhere because their sexual organs are very cheap and very easily accessible. This is a idea behind this proberb.Therefore, we have numerous example of this kind where upper caste or OBCs people kept dalit women as concubine .Even they produce children .But when a dalit woman tried to marry to upper caste or OBCs they refuse, even they tried to excuse to give parental name.
3. Chaapal per chamaien chale,Sandel per Dhobiniya, Hai more Rama Badal gai Duniya.(The Chamar

caste woman walks by wearing chappal and the washers woman walks by wearing Sandel,Oh! My lord Rama, The world has been change). The meaning of this proverb is that now the low caste women like chamars and washers women started wearing chapel and Sandals, which should not be happen but now the world has been change, the low caste women started this which in not a good indications.

6. Chamaien aurato se pet nahai chupta hai.(The chamars women cannot hide their illegitimate pregnancy). The meaning of this proverb is that these women are know for their illicit relationship and after having sex it is made publicly that this particular woman is pregnant.
7. Chamaien aurato ko shamaan diya to aanag me chal aaiye.(If you give respect a low caste chamar womam,then she will trun to our courtyard).The message of the proverb that these low caste women are not worth giving respect. They deserve disrespect. But very surprisingly, during sex with low caste women they do not see any caste tabbo.This is caste system.
8. Chakkili girl and the ears of the millet are very beautiful when mature.[91]

Why are no Source and no Work on Leather Communities?

W.G. Briggs had penned details about the Chamar community of India in general and North India Particular who was of course a British official .But apart from that no ethnographer or any historians have done work on the leather communities. Kunal Chakraborty has pointed out that if leather communities' reference were mentioned in early text then why they have been ignored. It's a very serious question which we should address in near future.[92]Publisher's observation is also same. He pointed out that "The Chamars are a much neglected community, not only in Uttar Pradesh, Bihar and other states of mid-land, but also in some far flung areas. Their association with certain professions is so common that generally looked down upon and even now discriminated against in various ways."[93] Of course their unclean profession brought a bad name because of this reasons they were much neglected community. W.G.Briggs's chapter *'The outlook'* is very crucial for understanding the problems and solutions of the caste. He blames Indian social system. He pointed out that "In the real sense the Chamars are the product of the social and religious teachings of their own land. According to the doctrine of karma a man is what he is because of what has happened, and he finds himself just where, in the very nature of things, he belongs. Chamars, and their neighbors in the social scale, are foreordained to menial tasks with no outlook towards better things in this life.Ignorance,grinding poverty, servitude and degradation are lot."[94]

To me, it is caste based privileges, caste based discriminations, and pre-conceived notions of purity or non-purity and Caste based hegemony which forbids the, particularly historians who ignored the specific studies on the leather communities in India or south India in general.

Conclusion

The leather working communities during 17th to 19th acquired very low status in the society because of their unclean and leather professions. But at same time documents also mentioned that they were most violent castes and they were fist that started the caste disputes or riots. At one points we can say that they were the leaders of the caste. We need to discover the point further. At the questions of Basavi, we have to look the ideas of Edgar Thurston and Syed Siraj ul Hassan views because both views contradict. We have to look that why there are so less reference of the caste while their presence was from the earliest time I.

Endnotes

1 W.G. Briggs, the Chamars, p. 13.

2 W.G. Briggs, the Chamars, p. 13.

3 Niels Brimnes, Constructing The Colonial Encounter, Right and Left Hand Castes In early Colonial South India, Curzon press, Great Britain, 1999, p. 256.

4 Dubois, A.J. Abbe, Hindu Manners customs and ceremonies, translated from the author's later French Ms and edited with notes, corrections and biography by Henry K.Beauchamp, Low price publications, Delhi, First published in 1906, reprinted in LPP in 1999, p.61.

5 Dubois, A.J. Abbe, A description of the character, Manners and customs of the people of india and their institutions religious and civil, translated from the French Ms with notes, corrections and additions by Rev G.U. Pope, Third edition, Asian Educational Services, New Delhi, First published in 1879, reprinted in AES in 1992, p. 332.

6 Ibid, p. 333.

7 Ibid, p. 9.

8 Those who follow these liberal arts are treated with more respect in these days. At all events, they are not looked down upon with disfavour. There are now many Brahmins in Southern India who are professional musicians, though they play on certain instruments only.

9 Classes superior to the barbers and Pariahs also play wind instruments at the present time.

10 Dubois, A.J. Abbe, A description of the character, Manners and customs of the people of India and their institutions religious and civil, p,334.

11 K.K .Pillay, The caste system in Tamil Nadu, MJP Publishers, Chennai, first published in 1979, second reprint, 2007, p.61.

12 F.R. Hemingway, Godavari, District Gazetteer, in two volumes, vol 1, Asian Educational Services, New Delhi, 2000,p,60.

13 Ibid,p,60.

14 W.G.Briggs,The Chamars,Low Price Publications,Delhi,First published in 1920 and reprint several, last reprint,1995, Delhi,p,11.

15 W.G. Briggs, the Chamars,p,31.

16 W.G. Briggs, the Chamars,p,31.

17 W.G. Briggs, the Chamars,pp,11-12.

18 W.G. Briggs, the Chamars,p,13.

19 W.G. Briggs, the Chamars,p,13.

20 Syed Siraj ul Hassan, Castes and Tribes of the Nizam;s Dominions, in 2 volumes, first published in 1920, reprint in 1990, vintage Books, New Delhi, vol. 2, p. 409.

21 Francis Buchanan, a journey from Madras through the countries of Mysore, Canara and Malabar, in three volumes, Vol. 1, London, 1807, pp. 251-252.

22 Manual of the North Arcot district which is written by H.A Stuart.

23 Dubois, A.J. Abbe, A description of the character, Manners and customs of the people of india and their institutions religious and civil, translated from the French Ms with notes, corrections and additions by Rev G.U. Pope, Third edition, Asian Educational Services, New Delhi, First published in 1879, reprinted in AES in 1992

24 Monograph of tanning and working in Leather, 1904.

25 Edgar Thurston, vol, ii, p, 2.

26 Edgar Thurston, vol, ii, p, 3.

27 Diary and Consultations, 1708, p. 7.

28 Diary and Consultations, 1716, p.155.

29 Diary and Consultations, 1708, p.7.

30 Diary and Consultations, 1708, p.36.

31 Diary and Consultations, 1708, p.5.

32 Dispatches to England, 1707-8, p.76.

33 Fort St. George records did not mention clearly about Chettis in which group they belong.

34 Appadurai, "Right and Left Hand castes in South India", p.217.

35 Mackenzie write "Buljewar" for right hand caste and it is also in terms of Merchants. He says that these groups exported and imported commodities. Although, he included Pariyar caste who were not merchants.

36 Captain Colin Mackenzie uses term "Naggaret" from left hand caste. These castes were not a trading communities. The term is not connoting trading communities. The term Naggaret implied "living in a habitation".

37 Captain Makenzie as cited in H.D.Love, Vestiges of Old Madras, 1640-1800, AES, New Delhi, Madras, 1996, vol.I, p.124.

38 Dubois, A.J. Abbe, A description of the character, Manners and customs of the people of India and their institutions religious and civil, p,9.

39 Buchanan, Francis, A Journey from Madras through the countries of Mysore, Canara and Malabar, London, 1807, vol.I, pp.77-80

40 Francis Buchanan, a journey from Madras through the countries of Mysore, Canara and Malabar, in three volumes, vol 1, London, 1807, pp. 77-78.

41 Madras Handbook Mcmxxii,first published in 1921, The Madras Diocesan Press, 1921, Madras. P. 114. In that handbook the article of F .j Richards which is on a note on the anthropology of South India.

42 Edgar Thurston, vol, ii, p, 4.

43 Manual of the Kurnool district, 1886.

44 Edgar Thurston, Vol. iv, p. 295.

45 Niels Brimnes, Constructing The Colonial Encounter, Right and Left Hand Castes In early Colonial South India,Curzon press,Great Britain,1999,p,25.

46 'Occupation' is my word. I use the upward occupational mobility because mobility in caste was not possible.

47 Mukund, K., The Trading World of the Tamil Merchants, p.148.

48 Stein, Peasant State and Society, p.204.

49 Arasaratnam, Merchants, Companies and Commerce, p.256.

50 Burton Stein, Peasant, State and Society in Medieval South India, Delhi, 1980, pp. 173, 182.

51 Burton Stein, Peasant, State and Society in Medieval South India, Delhi, 1980, pp. 479-80.

52 Appadurai, 'Right and Left hand castes in south India', p. 221.

53 Marshall, Gordon, Dictionary of sociology, published by Oxford University press,1994(first edition), 1998, 2004, 2005, 2007, Delhi, p. 519.

54 Ibid, p. 520.

55 Jullia Maitland,letters from Madras during the years 1836 - 1839, with Introduction,notes and appendices by Alyson Price, Oxford University Press, New Delhi,2003,p,103.

56 F.R. Hemingway, Godavari, District Gazetteer, in two volumes, Vol. 1, Asian Educational Services, New Delhi, 2000, p. 60.

57 F.R. Hemingway, Godavari, District Gazetteer, in two volumes, vol 1, Asian Educational Services, New Delhi, 2000,p,15.

58 F.R. Hemingway, Godavari, District Gazetteer, in two volumes, vol 1, Asian Educational Services, New Delhi, 2000,p,48.

59 F.R. Hemingway, Godavari, District Gazetteer, in two volumes, vol 1, Asian Educational Services, New Delhi, 2000,p,248.

60 Madras Handbook Mcmxxii,first published in 1921, The Madras Diocesan Press, 1921, Madras. P.114.In that handbook the article of F.J. Richards which is on a note on the anthropology of South India.

61 Edgar Thurston, vol ii, p,2.

62 Voyage to the East Indies, 1774 and 1781.

63 Edgar Thurston, vol ii, p,2.

64 Syed Siraj ul Hassan, Castes and Tribes of the Nizam;s Dominions, vol,2, p,420.

65 W.G. Briggs, the Chamars,pp,31-32.

66 F.R. Hemingway, Godavari, District Gazetteer, in two volumes, vol 1, Asian Educational Services, New Delhi, 2000,p,50.

67 F.R. Hemingway, Godavari, District Gazetteer, in two volumes, vol 1, Asian Educational Services, New Delhi, 2000,p,60.

68 F.R. Hemingway, Godavari, District Gazetteer, in two volumes, vol 1, Asian Educational Services, New Delhi, 2000,p,44.

69 Edgar Thurston, vol ii,p,2.

70 Edgar Thurston, vol, ii, p, 3.

71 W.G. Briggs, the Chamars,p,31.

72 W.G. Briggs, the Chamars,p,56.

73 W.G. Briggs, the Chamars,p,57.

74 Syed Siraj ul Hassan, Castes and Tribes of the Nizam;s Dominions, in 2 volumes, first published in 1920, reprint in 1990, vintage Books, New Delhi, vol. 2, p,420.

75 Francis Buchanan, a journey from Madras through the countries of Mysore,Canara and Malabar, in three volumes, vol 1,London,1807,, pp,224-225.

76 Francis Buchanan, a journey from Madras through the countries of Mysore,Canara and Malabar, in three volumes, vol 1,London,1807,, pp,224-225.

77 Francis Buchanan, a journey from Madras through the countries of Mysore,Canara and Malabar, in three volumes, vol 1,London,1807,, pp,224-225.

78 Jullia Maitland,letters from Madras during the years 1836 - 1839,p,89.

79 Madras Handbook Mcmxxii,first published in 1921, The Madras Diocesan Press, 1921, Madras. P.64. In that handbook there was an article of H.H. Duncan who was principal of the presidency College, wrote ' General Education in Madras'.

80 Edgar Thurston, vol ii, p,3.

81 Edgar Thurston, vol ii, p,3.

82 Edgar Thurston, vol ii, pp,6-7.

83 W.G. Briggs, the Chamars,p,31.

84 Edgar Thurston, vol ii, p,145. See also,W.G. Briggs, the Chamars, p, 32. *Ibid., Vol XV, 1892.

85 Edgar Thurston, vol iv, p,295.

86 Syed Siraj ul Hassan, Castes and Tribes of the Nizam;s Dominions,vol 2, pp,414-415.

87 Madras Handbook Mcmxxii, pp, 110-111.

88 *English Factories in India*, 1651-54, p.155.

89 Dubois, p,26.

90 S.vikram (Vikram Harijan), edited, Dalit women:Safar Itihaas se Bartmaan Tak, Natraj Prakashan, 2010, pp, 307-311.

91 Edgat Thruston and K. Rangachari (edited), Castes and Tribes of Southern India,in 7 volumes, volii, C-to J, Cosmo publications, Delhi, 1975, p. 3.

92 Kunal Chakrabarthy is a professor of Ancient History in Jawhaharlal Nehru University, New Delhi. He is a currently also fellow at Indian Institue of Advanced Study, Simla, Himachal pradesh.

93 Publishers notes in W.G. Briggs, the Chamars, p. 7.

94 W.G. Briggs, the Chamars, p. 240.

Bibliography

Primary sources

1. Dubois, A.J. Abbe, Hindu Manners customs and ceremonies, translated from the author's later French Ms and edited with notes, corrections and biography by Henry K.Beauchamp, Low price publications, Delhi, First published in 1906, reprinted in LPP in 1999
2. F.R. Hemingway, Godavari, District Gazetteer, in two volumes, vol 1, Asian Educational Services, New Delhi, 2000,
3. W.G.Briggs,The Chamars,Low Price Publications,Delhi,First published in 1920 and reprint several, last reprint,1995, Delhi,
4. Syed Siraj ul Hassan, Castes and Tribes of the Nizam;s Dominions, in 2 volumes, first published in 1920, reprint in 1990, vintage Books, New Delhi.
5. Francis Buchanan, a journey from Madras through the countries of Mysore,Canara and Malabar, in three volumes, vol1,London,1807
6. Manual of the North Arcot district which is written by H.A Stuart
7. Madras Handbook Mcmxxii,first published in 1921, The Madras Diocesan Press, 1921, Madras
8. Jullia Maitland,letters from Madras during the years 1836 - 1839, with Introduction,notes and appendices by Alyson Price, Oxford University Press, New Delhi,2003
9. English Factories in India, 1651-54.

10. EdgatThruston and K. Rangachari (edited), Castes and Tribes of Southern India,in 7 volumes,volii,C-to J, Cosmo publications, Delhi, 1975.
11. Fort St. George Records, Madras Government Press, Madras, 1895, (Photocopy in DSA Library, JNU). Dispatches: from England: 1670-1677 to 17117-17(11 Vols.) and to England: 1701-01 to1710-1711 and 1722-1714 to 1727 (3 Vols). Diaries and Consultation Books: 1672-78 to 1720 (41 Vols.). Letters from Fort St. George: 1689-1711 (11 Vols). Letters to Fort St. George: 1681-82 to 1719 (14 Vols.). Census Report of the Town of Madras, 1871, St. Fort George Gazetteer Press, 1873.
12. Love, H.D., *Vestiges of Old Madras, 1640-1800* (3 Vols.), Asian Educational Service, Madras, New Delhi, 1996.

Secondary Sources

13. Mukund, Kanakalatha, *The Trading world of the Tamil Merchant, Evaluation of Merchant Capitalism in the Coromandel,* Orient Longman, Hyderabad, 1999
14. Stein, Burton, *Peasant State and Society in Medieval South India,* OUP, New Delhi, 1994
15. S.vikram (Vikram Harijan), edited, *Dalit women:Safar Itihaas se Bartmaan Tak,*Natraj Prakashan,2010,pp,307-311.
16. Arasaratnam, S., *Merchants, Companies and Commerce in the Coromandel Coast 1650- 1740,* Oxford University Press (OUP), New Delhi, 1986.
17. K.K .Pillay, The caste system in Tamil Nadu, MJP Publishers, Chennai, first published in 1979, second reprint, 2007, p.61.
18. Niels Brimnes, Constructing The Colonial Encounter, Right and Left Hand Castes In early Colonial South India, Curzon press, Great Britain, 1999.

Articles

1. Appadurai, Ajun "Right and Left Hand castes in South India," *Indian Economic and Social History Review (IESHR),* 14.1,1974, pp.217-259

6

Cultural Transformation of *Madigas* Under the Islam Guidence

Dr. Akulapally Kumaraswamy*

Introduction

In their *Varna* system, it can be inferred that the Aryans have termed the tanners as those born out of inter-racial mixture. They have classified those not in tunes with them as *Chandalas, Panchamas, Antyahas,* and untouchables, and in the same breath have called the *Madigas* as *Chandalas, Panchamas* or untouchables. The *Madigas* are the largest Telugu speaking community considered untouchables in South India. They lived on the outskirts of the village on the eastern side and close to the water bodies. They cleansed animal skins and then prepared gardening equipment with them. They ate the meat of the animals they skin as their primary food and led lives without any sense of cleanliness. Scarcely clothed, tall, dark, and well-built, they consumed the locally available liquor and smoked and led a carefree life. Besides pursuing their occupation of tanning the animal hide, they played drums (*Dappu*) during both auspicious and inauspicious occasions in the households of the village and were also engaged as bonded-labour and agricultural labour. *Madiga*

* Department of History & Tourism Management, Kakatiya University, Warangal, Telangana

has *Nulka Chandayya, Baindla, Chindu, Masti* and *Dakkalis* as dependent castes.

Madigas are classified to belong to a certain class based on their occupation. Those working as bonded labour are known as *Begaris* or forced workers, those working with animal hide or called chambers, which is corrupted from of the Sanskrit term *Charmakar*, those toiling as menials are termed *Kamatis*. Similarly the *Madigas* playing on drums are known as dappu *Madigas*, based on the reverence to the presiding deity of *Madigas Ellamma* or *Pedda Devara* (nude goddess) they are also known as *Peddintivaru* the descendent of progeny of *Mathangis* the incarnation of goddess *Ellamma* they are known as *Gosangis* besides because of their participation in battles they are also known as *Gosangi* solders. The *Vetti Madigas* of Telangana along with the other artisan castes and service castes had to random services freely throughout the year to the feudal lord, *Jagirdars, Doras*, government officials like Police *Patel, Malipatel, Patwari* and even other visiting officials like police *Amin* and *Girdavar*. The *Madiga* woman cleaned the cattle sheds of the Dora and made dung cakes apart from helping their men in agricultural occupational activates *Madiga* woman has equal liberty par with that of *Madiga* man like consuming beef smoking and alcoholic drinks.

Despite the normative ideal of social ostracism the *Madigas* had continues inter connections with cultural and religious movements of India tired to alleviate the ignominious social status of these leather workers in to its creed. Even some of the members of this community gave some gifts to the sacred institutions of Buddhism as attested by the inscriptions. Some of the leather workers were ardent *Vaishnavites*. Ramanuja the founder of *Sri Vaishnava* sect named the Dalit as Tirumaldar (of the family of god) and tied to secure them a degree of social status and allowed a restricted entry in to the temples. *Virasaivism* an egalitarian religious sect was started by Basava admitted these communities in to its rank and life. The *Virashaiva* hagiologies produced by Palkuriki Somanadha have numerous references of devoted Shaivite leather workers. The Initiation of unmarried *Madiga* girls as *Basavis* is a standing testimony for the affirmation of the leather workers to *Shaivism*. Veerabhrahmam 16th century social reformer of the Andhra region admitted the leather workers in to his creed. Kakkayya a *Madiga* was one of his important disciples. The ideology of human equality as a propagated by *Sree Veerabhrahamam* had a pre found influence on these ostracized communities.

As a sizable number of leather workers of the Telugu region followed his precepts. Emma Clough refers an esoteric sect based on ritual equality known as the Charmanista sect which was popular among the *Madigas*. The same author mentions another sect known as the Nasraiah sect who preached its followers not to steal not to worship ideals and to abstain from spirituals liquor and practice equality of human beings. Islam as a religion had also significant important on the leather working communities with its philosophy of human equality some members of the leather working community come in contact with the hide dealers belonging to Islam and were attracted towards it. Hence one can see that some of the members' leather workers are visiting the *Dargahas* and even name their children like *Yakub, Peeraiah, Sardar* etc.

Siraj-ul-Hassan in his book, *Castes and Tribes of HEH Nizam's Dominion* states that the term *Gosangi* gets its origin from *'Go Hamsaka'*, which means 'one who kills cows'.[1] Supporting this argument of Siraj-ul-Hassan, Nagendra K. R. Singh states that the *Gosangis* are cowherds and earned their livelihood by selling the meat of the animals they kill.[2] He adds further explanation stating that they are known as *Gosikas* and sold meat to the villagers, and the epithet *Gosika* over time got corrupted to *Gosangi*. Singh further states that the *Gosangis* are found in the Muslim community too. The *Gosangis* who have converted to Islam are known as Sheiks, Syeds and Pathans and are dependent on the *Madigas* seeking alms from them for subsistence.[3] On the basis of these opinions, it can be concluded that the *Madigas* were classified into sub-castes based on their occupations. These sub-castes, over time, split into dependent castes, sub-castes or castes of their own identity. The *Gosangis*, a part of the community, led the lives of cowherds and sustained through the sale of beef.

Madigas before the Islam Conversion

As the caste system gained strength, there started the *Kula Puranas* that depicted the origins of each caste. To demonstrate these *Kula Puranas* through dance or ballads umpteen number of sub-castes emerged. Yet, in the Andhra Pradesh and Telangana, the *Madiga* caste itself has so many castes that no other caste has. Of these, the *Madiga Jangam* (*Nulaka Chandayyas*), *Baindlas, Dakkalis, Madiga Mashthi, Chindu Madiga*, or *Bhogam Madigas*, and *Kommu Madigas* are prominent based on their occupations. Of these, the case of *Kommu Madigas* is a distinctive feature. Apart from being the dependent caste for the *Madigas*, the *Kommu Madigas* are equally dependent for the *Gollas* who belong to the *Sudra* class under the caste hierarchy. The important aspect of the dependant castes is that the people belonging to these castes are all, by profession, balladeers. The dependant castes seek patrons among the families and eke their livelihood by narrating the *Kula Purana*s in the form of narratives, stories, or using scrolls. Every *Kula Purana* stands testimony to the fact that their narration in itself is to boast that they are of a better social status. All the Castes that have been classified as *Sudra*s have only one objective – to project that these castes are socially not of inferior status, nor are their occupations disrespectful.[4] Their purpose is to propagate that their castes and the occupations are respectable, sacred, and honourable too. Not with standing their status as dependant castes, the narrators will have to be acknowledged as those who have been preserving the literature that reflects their culture for generations. They are literates and also skilled in arts, which they exhibit with great pride. The *Nulaka Chandayyas, Dakkalis, Kommus,* and the *Baindlas* know the script. While the *Nulaka Chandayyas* noted down *Jambapurana* on rolls of paper, the *Dakkalis, Kommus,* and *Baindlas* wrote down the *Jambapurana,* the ballads of Katamaraju, and stories of *Ellamma* respectively on palm leaves. What is ironic is that the patron caste *Madigas* have no knowledge of the script, but their dependant castes do.

The unwritten agreement between the patron and dependant castes is what is known as *Tyagam* (remuneration), translated literally, the term means 'sacrifice', but it is more of remuneration paid out of reverence. Every year, they approach their respective patrons, sing/narrate the mythologies and seek remuneration. This agreement between many artisan castes and their dependant castes are prevalent even to this day in the villages.

In every village the *Grama-Devata* is periodically worshipped and propitiated. The system, as it now exists, combines many different ideas and customs, and has probably resulted from the fusion of various forms of religion.[5] One of the most striking features of the worship of the village deities is the absence of anything like a sacerdotal caste in connection with it, but is presided over by one among the depressed classes, which affords a sense of self-respect and a sense of their own worth in the community.

The practice of worshipping guardian deities or village deities under the supervision of the priests belonging to dependant castes is known as *Kolupulu*. This has been an ancient practice, in which elaborate arrangements are made to offer the food and liquor they regularly consume to the deity. These festivities are organised when the crops they sow yield good harvests, when a family member has fallen ill, when a child is born in the family, or when they are faced with serious famines.[6] The *Madigas* believe that the deities are pleased when such festivities are organised and bless them with bliss, happiness, and prosperity. It is for this reason that festivities dedicated to *Matamma, Ellamma, Pochamma, Maisamma, Nannuramma* are organised.

Impact of Islam Religion

Elaborating further about the *Gosangis*, Siraj-ul-Hassan states that the *Madigas* working as soldiers in the armies of the rulers were known as *Gosangi* soldiers.[7] Reference to these *Gosangi* soldiers appears in the history of the Telugu Chodas of the Middle Age. After the entry Islam into India, who converted to Muslim religion they mingle with the *Shaiva* and *Vaishnavites*. Foreign tribes, who came in to India Afghans, Iranians, and Turkish are called their own race. Here there is a small difference between the Indian Muslims and Foreign Muslim tribes. Consequently Muslims are ruled almost seven centuries. They influenced to the *Madigas* by their customs and traditions especially south Indian untouchable. Obtain to breadth the Islam preachers or saint Peer Mahaveer Khurdhayat 1304 A.D. in Bijapur region nascent Islam preaching village by village roves.[8] The Muslim administrators constructed many masques commemoration of their progenitor names or saints and other beloved persons. An account of the chief saint of Muslims lived in Hyderabad. He did not visit to the villages. Because mullahs and fakirs are honored by preaching's of Islam.

Consequently 13th and 14th centutries of Muslim preaching's influenced in south India and significantly in Telangana region. Later Mughal rulers occupied of Hyderabad state is increased to expanse the Islam religion. In the same way, one of the Hyderabad *Nawab* Mir Mahaboob Ali Khan was identified as an ideal person of Hindus and Muslims. When he died in 1911 A.D., So many tombs built in different places of Telangana that tombs called as "*Mahaboob Bhasha Dargha*".[9] But also, the tradition started that flag was tied to peak of the tomb. End of the supremacy of the last Nizams, Urdu was continued as official language. It is influenced to both Telugu and an Urdu language speaks out the people by makes the matrimonial relationship. Until now in Telangana town's people were used Telugu and Urdu and followed the both traditions. Who changed into Islam was called *Dudekula* or *Noorbhasha*. Telangana people both of Hindus and Muslims are celebrate *Holi, Dussera, Diwali, Ranzan, Bhakrid,* and *Moharram* by all together. According to Vattikota Alwarswamy, the religions changes of untouchables are the main causes for the change of untouchables emancipate the *Vetti* and atrocities of forward classes through the ages they face the difficulties from them.[10] The Administrators of Islam rulers were superior to the Hindu forward classes. They hope that, if to take Islam religion better for revenge up on the Hindu forward classes.

To strengthen above the argument in Nalgonda district reports Bahaduryar Jung the leader of Muslim Itte-hadul-Muslimin perpetuated and established fifteen branches. He appointed permanent preachers to them. He expended in eleven months for 1129 people provoked to change into Islam religion. Apart from this in Warangal district 700 people, in Devaruppala 400 people, Kadavendi 300 people, Ramannagudem 100 people, Ramaram 400, Kodakandla 400, Narasimha puram 100, Edunuthala 200 and Mondrai 300 were changed in to Islam. All these villages belonged to Janagon *Taluk*.[11] In Hanamkonda Dalits were engrossed in to hands of Peesari Veeranna a Dalit Leader Worked at the favor of Muslim Missionaries and earned lot of money.[12] He fame as a Sardar Ali. In 1935 March 17th held a huge meeting. In this meet *Madigas* leader N. R. Babayya speaking the words "Not we change the religion for *Moksha*, we need socio economic changes in our lives we desire for to hinder the injustice for we are changing the religion".[13]

Main causes of Untouchables changed their religion, Islam and Christianity introduced by Europeans and also their primary food was beef. Due to this they converted in to Islam and Christianity but need not change their habitual food. Addition to Health and Education they got equality and honourable place at the house Hindus are discriminate the untouchables and they use them for economic profits.

The impact of Agricultural sector was industrialized, the leather tools are lost their significance and man power decreased too. So, Leather workers of *Madigas* were preferred to other occupations. According to K R Nagendra Singh, Islamic *Madigas* were slaughtering cows and sale the beef in some areas. It indicated that the *Madigas* changed their religion but they did not leave their occupational skills. Now a day, some of *Madigas* were collect the dry bones, leathers of animals to sell as Muslim traders that are called *Labbis* in various areas. Those who settled as *Labbis*, they continue their traditional leather skills. Some rich *Labbis* are established leather industries raw material supplied by another *Labbis*. In this way they collect bones and leather from various villages, consequently they bargain with *Madigas* and earn from their faith by telling of their oriented about their changing the religion. Subsequently they reached to near to the *Madigas* and collect from cow, ox, sheep and goats skins and bring out to leather industries of *Labbis*. The *Labbis* are collect unused bones of animals from the garbage or out skirts of the village to earn the income by selling them and become a rich. Although they changed religion, they continued their traditional occupation and the relationship with the mother caste of *Madigas*.

Besides they followed the customs and dressing seems to be a Muslim, who absorbed that they stay away from Hindu traditions. Although, they continued their caste occupations. The matrimonial relationship for them with religion changed families. They did not like to say as

Madigas. They admired as Muslims or *Labbis*. The Muslim rulers and rich Muslims were built the *Madarsas* commemoration of their elder or loving saints. The *Madarsas* are learnt the education to the poor children. The Muslim mullahs are sheltered the untouchables and learnt their education[14] Because of this, if untouchable *Madigas* change their religion in to Islam, Muslims consider as them equally. The capital city of Hyderabad concentrated *Islam* and Hindu culture similarly in Secunderabad concentrated Hindu and Christian culture.[15] Another Hindus of the society obedient to the Muslim rulers. The converted *Madigas* also honored as Muslims. The *Madigas* of transformed as Muslims and keep their names reflected Islam culture. Lastly Peraiah called as Peeraiah, Yakaiah called as Yakub, Durgaiah called as Dargaiah etc. The coverted *Madigas* ignore the previous customs and traditions of erlier religion and continued Islamic traditions. Thallapally Manohar in his book "Land Issues in Telangana a selected Village" explained the process of celebrating *Moharram* in villages, Muslims celebrate the *Moharram* festival with pay attention to the devotional in the form *peers* to the commemoration Martyred for god Hassan, Hussein.

These festivals celebrate all together Hindu and Muslims. At the time of rally Muslims and Hindus invite the *peers* in their homes. The incarnation of Hassan and Hussein *Peers* touched by them and revived their mistakes in the past life. Mattapally Saraiah, Uppalaiah and Rookala Narsaiah were belonged *Sudra* people with accompanied the *Madiga* devotee Immadi Gattellaiah invite the *peers* to his home and blessed by them at Waddepally village in Hanamkonda Mandal of Warangal district.[16] An account of this situation there is no untouchablity among the Muslim festivals and to all are equal in front of the God the concept is raised. In the same way so many *Madigas* without change the religion, they celebrate the Islam festival especially *Moharram, Ramzam, Bhakrid* and *Ursus* and also they participate the "*Kandurus*".

The impact of Islam religion *Madigas* have been changing their customs and traditions influenced by the Islam religion in location of dwellings merged with *Sudras* and other poor Muslims. They wear the Muslim traditional full cloths of body. They freely entered in to the masques they got offerings and subsidies from the rulers for the change of their religion. They emancipated form the *Vetti* and *Begari* system from the village society and free form the atrocities by land lords. They maintained matrimonial relations with converted Muslims those different from Hindu communities they continues superior relationship with *Madigas* they marry from *Madiga* girl they did not give their daughter to them. They enjoyed equal rights along with other Muslims in festivals like *Bakrid* and *Ramzon*. They worked leather industries of Muslim organised sectors.

Conclusion

The present work is an attempt to show what the *Madigas* are. Apart from depicting their worship of female deities, the work attempts to depict the *Madigas'* status in the *Saiva* and *Vaishnava* cults, besides their culture and traditions. Notwithstanding the influence of the cults, the *Madigas'* culture has experienced tremendous changes after the advent of Islam and Christianity in India. However *Madigas* has been uplifting by the Islam religion in food habits dressing social relationship and emancipating from menial works.

Endnotes

1. Siraj Ul Hasan, Syed: The Castes and Tribes of H.E.H Nizams Dominions, Volume-I, The Times Press, Bombay, 1920, p. 409.
2. Nagendra K R Singh (Ed)., Global Encyclopedia of the South Indian Dalit Ethnographies, Volume –I, Global Vision Publishing House, New Delhi, 2006, p. 219.

3. Nagendra, K. R. Singh & Abdul Mahabub Khan (Eds)., Global Encyclopedia of the world Muslims, Tribes, Castes and Communities, Volume – I, Global Vision Publishing House, New Delhi, 2001, p. 485.
4. Manohar Thallapally(Ed)., Cultural History of Madigas – A Brief Study, Pragma Publications, Hyderabad, 2016, p.57.
5. Kinsley David, Hindu Goddess, Vision of the divine feminine in the Hindu Religious Tradition, Mothilal Banarasidas, Delhi, 1998, p. 103.
6. Manohar Thallapally(Ed)., Cultural History of Madigas – A Brief Study, Op. Cit. p.57.
7. Siraj-ul-Hassan, Syed., Castes and Tribes of H.E.H Nizams Dominion, Op cit, p. 420.
8. Satyanarayana, Y.B., Nayana Balaiah, Hyderabad book trust, Hyderabad, 2015, p. 70.
9. Egorova Yulia, & Shahid Perwez., the Jews of Andhra Pradesh, Contesting Caste and Religion in south India, oxford University Press, 2013, p.39.
10. Thirumali, I., Against Dora and Nizam, The People Movement in Telangana, 1939-1948, Khanishka Publications, New Delhi., 2000, p. 59.
11. Ibid and Golconda Pathrika, 23 September, 1937, and (FN.3/ 47F.H.D.1347F, 1938).
12. Venkataswamy, P.R., Ma vimukti poratam, Ambedkar Publication Society, Hyderabad, 2003, p. 306.
13. Ibid, p. 115.
14. Satyanarayana, Y.B., Ma Nayana Balaiah, Op.cit, p. 31.
15. Ibid, p. 41.
16. Manohar Thallapally., Land Issues in Telangana, A Selected Village, Pragma Publications, Hyderabad, 2015, p.69.

7

Religious Rituals of *Madigas*: *Ellamma* Cult – A Study

Sreenivas Theegala* & Thallapally Manohar*

There are certain classes of population in India that sustain themselves on the traditional occupation of tanning. The *Chamars* of North India, the *Dher*s of Central India, *Chamagar*s of Karnataka, *Chakkiliyan*s of Tamil Nadu, the *Tolkollan*s of Kerala, and the *Madigas* of both the Telugu speaking states of Andhra Pradesh and Telangana eke out a living primarily working on animal hide (leather). The *Madigas* are the largest community considered untouchables in Telugu speaking region. They lived on the outskirts of the village on the eastern side and close to the water bodies. They cleansed animal skins and then prepared gardening equipment with them. They ate the meat of the animals they skin as their primary food and led lives without any sense of cleanliness. Scarcely clothed, tall, dark, and well-built, they consumed the locally available liquor and smoked and led a carefree life. Besides pursuing their occupation of tanning the animal hide, they played drums (*Dappu*) during both auspicious and inauspicious occasions in the households of the village and were also engaged as bonded-labour and agricultural labour.

* Department of History & Tourism Management, Kakatiya University, Warangal, Telangana

The *Madiga* community is the patron caste to a number of dependent castes with varied occupations, the number that no other caste across the country has. The dependent castes of *Madigas* that are *Nulkachandayya* or *Madiga Jangam, Baindla, Chindu Madiga* or *Bhogam Madiga, Dakkali, Masti, Kommu Madigas*. The *Nulaka Chandayyas* are the priests for the *Madigas* and narrate *Jamba Purana* which the mythology that depicts the origin of the *Madigas*. Apart from performing traditional rites during both auspicious and inauspicious events, the *Baindlavaru* perform the ritualistic *Poojas* called *'Koluvu'* to goddesses *Ellamma* and *Matamma*. The *Chindu Madigas* entertain the *Madigas* by melodiously reciting *Jamba Purana, Ramayana* and *Mahabharata* and are also known as *Bhogam Madiga*. *Dakkalis* narrate the *Jambapurana* with the help of artistically painted scrolls. The frescoes transferred onto textile depict wonderful lively images with folk-artistic gusto. The *Madiga Mashtis* perform adventurous juggleries and craft wooden articles. *Kommu Madigas* are uniquely the dependent caste of *Gollas*. These dependent castes perform the traditional rites and seek alms from the *Madigas*.

An observation of the history reveals that the primitive man across the world worshipped the five elements of nature – Earth, Air, Water, Ether, and Fire – in the manifestation of a goddess, which is an undeniable truth. The probable reason for this could be that the Earth is regarded as female and the presiding deities of agriculture are mainly goddesses, because the idea of fertility and reproduction is connected with women. Each village seems to have been under the protection of some super-natural and incorporeal being, who is its guardian deity, although it is difficult to ascertain as to the origins. The worship of the village gods is the most ancient form of Indian religion followed by the people of Indus civilisation. As part of the Aryan migration, the village deities of ancient India have been aryanised and have been transformed as the consorts of the Aryan male gods. Yet, the *Madigas* of Dravidian origin have been worshipping goddess

Ellamma (mother for all in Telugu parlance – *Ellaraku Amma*) in a wide mouthed trough (*Landatotte* – the trough in which animal hide is soaked for treatment). *Ellamma* is the representation of human reproductive organ and is worshipped as such in the incarnation of *Jogulamba* at Alampur or as *Renuka Ellamma* by the *Madigas*. She is considered to be born in the trough in a *Madiga* household. This *Kolupulu* (rituals) to appease her are performed by the *Baindla* along with the *Matangi* and the *Chindus* even to this day across Telangana.[1] The main aim of this paper is to describe the rituals performed by the *Baindla*s and the *Chindus*.

*Baindla*s

The *Baindlas*, also known as *Kolupulavaru*, are the devotees of Goddess *Shakti* performing the rituals of *Ellamma* and are one among the sub-castes of *Madigas*.[2] They officiate during marriages and other ceremonial rites performed by the *Madigas*.[3] They are the priests for the village deity *Ellamma*, draw *Rangoli* patterns in the shrines and narrate *Ellamma*s stories. Besides, there are instances of them acting as mystic healers in the village to put a break on the spread of contagious diseases like cholera, chicken-pox, measles, small-pox etc. by providing talismans, amulets or sheets of metal with inscriptions of mystic diagrams called *Yantra*s.[4]

An attempt to probe the origins of the name *Baindla*, and the reason for their occupation as singers reveals that the name originated from name of *Bhavani* or Goddess *Shakti*. Those worshipping the Goddess are known as *Bhavaneeyulu*, which over time got corrupted to the name *Baindla*. According to *Andhra Bhasha Nighantuvu* (Telugu Language Dictionary) the term *Bavaneedu* means *Kshudra Sangha Prasamsi* (those who live by praising people of lower castes). Even the pure Telugu glossary (*Atcha Tenugu Padakosam*) conveys the same sense – *Kshudra Sangha Prasamsi*. References to *Sabdaratnakaram* and *Sree Surya Narayana Andhra Bhasha Nighantuvu* reveal the meaning of the term *Bavini* as a type of dance performed by a community during fairs, and that of the term *Bavineedu* as a person who narrates stories during fairs.[5] One can find reference to the *Baindla*s even in *Kreedabhiramam*.[6] Based on this, it can be inferred that the *Bavanis* existed during the Kakatiya rule, and that they recited the stories of *Ekaveera Mahadevi* – another name of goddess *Ellamma*. Edgar Thurston opined that the *Baineendlus* draw *Muggulu* (patterns drawn on the floor) and narrate the stories of *Ankamma* while officiating the funeral rites of *Madigas*.[7] The origin of their name is not just owing to their occupation, but also because of the musical instrument they play. According to Syed Siraj-ul-Hassan the *Baindla*s practice occult arts too to ward off evil spirits and to control them.[8] According to K. S. Singh, the *Baindla*s, also known as *Kolupulavaru,* are the priests of village deities, officiate as the priests for the *Madigas,* and inhabit the states of Telangana and Andhra Pradesh, besides Karnataka and Maharashtra.[9] Emma Rauschenbusch-Clough describes them as *Bainurudus* who narrate the stories of *Ellamma* and act as spiritual gurus.[10] According to Nayani Krishna Kumari's *Telugu Janapada Geya Gathalu,* the *Beneendlu,* also known as *Baindla*s and *Bavanis,* are the people among the *Madigas* who worship female deities.[11] Biruduraju Ramaraju opines that besides being the officiating priests of female deities, they are the mystic healers in the village to put a break on the spread of contagious diseases like cholera, chicken-pox, measles, small-pox etc. by providing talismans, amulets or sheets of metal with inscriptions of mystic diagrams called *Yantra*s.[12] The primary music instrument that they use is known as *Jamidika*[13]. It is also known as *Jamuku* and *Bavanika*. Based on this, it can be said that those who use the *Bavanikas* while narrating stories are called *Bavanis*.[14]

The *Baindlas* declare themselves to be the descendants of *Parasurama*. Legend has it that when *Parasurama* intent upon killing *Renuka* chased her, she hid herself in a wide mouthed trough (*Landagolem* – the trough in which animal hide is soaked for treatment) lying in the house of *Madigas*. On reaching there *Parasurama* picked-up a thin layer of skin soaked in the trough and using the nerves of a cow from its leg sewed the skin into a *Jamidika* and started drumming it up while with a loud voice commanded her to emerge from her hiding place (*Ellamma*). Hearing the sounds emitted from the *Jamidika*, the frightened Renuka emerged. Thenceforth, the *Baindlas* say, the *Jamidika* became their principal instrument of music, using which they sang the ballads of *Ellamma* to earn livelihood. They declare that *Parasurama* – the pioneer in making and using the *Jamidika* to command *Ellamma* emerge out of her hiding – is their primogenitor and the *Baindlas* of the present day, call themselves his descendants.[15]

Rituals to Appease the Deity

The *Madigas* worship *Ellamma* as their guardian deity and perform rituals to appease her with great devotion. They perform these rituals either enmasse or individually at their respective homes. Once the deity is sanctified at home, the families perform the rituals annually, triennially or quinquennially without fail. These rituals are usually performed during the period between *Sankranti* and *Ugadi* (between January and March) only on a Monday and Tuesday.[16] The *Baindla*s, while worshipping the deity, do perform all the rituals on behalf of the *Madigas*. The rituals involve removal of impurities, collection of formicary, performing the marriage of *Ellamma*, drawing of *Chandra Patam*, sprinkling of sacrificial blood, offering of *Bonams* and *Saka*. To begin the rituals, an auspicious day is decided and the previous day the deity's idol is sanctified and a temporary shrine is built at a corner of the house, or abutting the well or agricultural field. If the entire community is involved in performing the ritual, the shrine is erected at the centre of the settlement. During the festivities of *Ellamma*, the community paints the shrine of *Ellamma* with limestone, and decorate it with turmeric and vermillion powders. The pandal in front of the shrine is decorated with festoons of mango leaves.[17]

Removal of Impurity Upon Death in the Family

The tradition of observing impurity upon the death of a family member for a year – a period of mourning – is prevalent across the southern states of India – Karnataka, Tamil Nadu, Andhra Pradesh and Telangana. The families do not perform any auspicious ceremonies during the first year. However, upon the completion of the first year, the ritual of removal impurity of the men in the *Madiga* families is performed by the *Matangi* and the *Baindlas* together. Of late due to the non-availability of the *Matangis* these days, the ritual is being mostly performed by the *Baindlas* themselves. The ritual is performed at night on a Sunday. The family seeking to perform this ritual spreads a new mat in front of the house. Paddy grains are heaped across the edges of the mat thus joining its four corners – this is called *Maila Polu* (resembling the impurity in the family). On the heaps of grain, small earthen pots called *Gurigis* are placed in all the four directions. These pots are then joined with a thread. In the middle of these *Gurigis* a *Banduva*[18] earthen pot decorated with vermillion is placed. After thus arranging the *Maila Polu*, the men of the family are made to sit around it. They cover only the lower parts of their bodies and hold twigs of neem (margosa). The *Baindla* prepare a concoction of arrack, palm wine, jaggery, water and buttermilk. He then holds branches of neem and a chick with his right hand and carries an earthen pot filled with *Saka*in the left hand. Moving around the men seated there, using the branches of neem, he sprinkles this concoction on them. He does this three times. Then he takes a little concoction into his mouth and spits on the men – repeated three times. He then squats on the backs of the other family members seated there, and performs three circumambulations around them. The people sitting there then take bath, signifying the completion of the ritual and also the removal of impurity.[19]

Collection of Formicary

The *Baindlas* officiate during the festivities of the deity without any reservations about caste of the organising community. They officiate during the festivities dedicated to deities like *Ellamma* and recite their stories. While the *Baindla* priest officiates, the community goes in a procession to the formicary on the outskirts of the village, as *Muttayiduvas*[20] lead the procession holding *Mangalaratis*, to the accompaniment of drum beats of *Madigas*, and the *Baindla* blowing the *Jamidika*. The people carry water in five broad mouthed earthen pots called *Kadavas*, a crowbar, spade, a new basket made of bamboo slats. The water in the earthen pots is sprinkled on the mound to flatten it; *Rangoli* design is drawn on it using five different coloured powders. Five eggs, dry coconut shells, betel leaves and nuts, bangles, cowry shells, turmeric tubers, dry dates are placed on five different position of the *Rangoli*. In the middle, an earthen oil lamp is lit and a new basket made of bamboo slats is placed upside down on the arrangement. A white cloth is spread over the basket to make it inconspicuous and over this neem branches are placed. They leave three of the men to guard the lamp. In the evening the return to the pit to the accompaniment of drum beats, and remove the basket to find a new pit coming up. This they consider as the deity's blessing, dig it up and collect it into the basket. It is believed that when *Parasurama* slew his mother *Renuka Ellamma*, her head fell in the mound. Hence the pit is considered sacred. They pay obeisance to the pit, collect the mud to erect the deity's throne with it in the shrine.[21]

Preparing the Sacrificial Animal (*Jaldikelluta)*

The act of preparing the sacrificial goats and herding them to a nearby water body is known as *Jaldikelluta*.[22] The goat is garlanded and its forehead is decorated with vermillion. It is then carried in a procession to the water source. On reaching the water body, the family head holds both the ears of the animal and stands on the animal. The women of the family fetch potsful of water and pour it on the man and the animal. The man then leaves hold of the ears; the animal trembles convulsively (called *Jadataivvadam*) indicating that the deity has accepted the animal for the sacrifice. If the goat does not tremble, the women continue to pour water until it does. Despite all their efforts, if the goat does not tremble, they consider it as the deity's rejection of the animal as sacrifice and it is let off.[23]

Performing the Symbolic Marriage of *Ellamma*

A new mat is spread in front of the deity's shrine and rice is heaped on the four corners. On these heaps for earthen goblets (*Gurigi*)[24] are placed; joining these *Gurigis* a thread is tied; this arrangement is known as *Laggampolu*. At the centre of this arrangement, the sacred *Banduva* and trident (representing *Ellamma* and *Jamadagni*) are placed. Five sets of betel leaves, coconut kernels, betel nuts, incense sticks, tubers of turmeric, and dates are prepared and each set is placed at the four corners and at the centre. These five locations are considered to be the representations of the five elements of nature. The *Baindla*s commence the programme by singing a lullaby to wake the goddess up, while at the same time dancing in tune with the lyrics. While escorting the deity to the *Laggampolu* or while performing the subsequent event – *Chandra Patam* - the *Baindla*s welcome her saying that the she is worshipped by kings. They then place the *Banduva* and the trident at the centre of the arrangement and perform the marriage ritual. Throughout the night, *Ellamma*'s narratives are sung in the form of ballads.[25]

Chandra Patam

After the narration, a *Chandra Patam* is drawn in front of the shrine. This is the primary event among the rituals for the deity and is usually performed during the early hours of Tuesday. Vermillion is then sprinkled on the ground under the pandal, over which an impression of a slab with five different colours is made.[26] On the four corners of the impression small earthen pots called *Gurigis* are placed. The sacred trident and *Banduva* decorated with vermillion are placed at the centre. Beside each *Gurigi* and at the centre, five a piece each of dry coconut cups (*Kudukalu*), tubers of turmeric (*Pasupu Kommulu*), betel leaves (*Tamalapakulu*), betel nuts (*Pokalu*), dry dates (*Kharjura Pandlu*), incense sticks, and bangles are placed. The number five – of each item and location – represent oblations to the five elements of nature (*Pancha Bhootalu*). The figure of a goat is drawn in front of the *Chandra Patam*, over which a lamb is laid. The goat is then covered with neem branches, and the branches are covered with a white cloth. Some men attired strangely circumambulate the shrine and say that they are holy men sent by Goddess *Ellamma*, who had advised them to consume the lamb since they had insufficient food, and demand the assembled people to offer them the lamb. They agree to offer the lamb to the holy men on the condition that they have to kill the lamb without using a knife but must kill it with their mouths. The holy men kill it as they are asked amid drum beats and sounds of *Jamidika*. This event is known as *Gavu Pattadam* (sacrificing an animal). Next is the activity of sprinkling the sacrificial blood. Another lamb is sacrificed near the *Chandra Patam*, the head is separated, one of the fore-legs is broken into half, which is then horizontally inserted into the mouth of the lamb and the head is placed in front of the deity. The mid-portion of the body is cut to extract the lungs, heart, and liver, upper part of the fore-leg and all these are place in front of the deity.[27]

Sprinkling of the Sacrificial Blood

In the villages, there is significance to the sprinkling of sacrificial blood. A heap of specially cooked rice (*Bonam*) is placed in front of the *Chandra Patam*. Over this heap boiled millets are placed. The blood oozing out of the sacrificed animal is then mixed with the millets and cooked rice, which is then collected into a new *Cheta* (winnowing basket). This mixed ball of boiled millets, rice and lamb's blood is called *Bali Padartham*. This *Bali Padartham* is then mixed with a part of the yet to be digested food in the lamb's stomach called *Kasaru*. To the accompaniment of sounds from the drums, and the *Jamidika*, the *Bali Padartham* mixed with *Kasaru* is then sprinkled around the shrine. Apart from the organisers of the festivity, none is allowed to be present in the surroundings, for the reason that if those others eat the mixture or if it accidentally falls on them, the outcome of the entire proceedings accrue only to such persons.[28]

Offering of *Bonam* to the Deity

Turmeric is mixed with the rice before cooking. The cooked rice is then offered along with the meat of the sacrificed goat. In the evening on Tuesday, the daughters of the families, accompanied by sounds of drums and *Jamidika*s, come to the shrine in a procession and offer cooked rice to the deity. After this event, the *Banduva* (representation of the deity) and the trident along with the other articles of worship are moved into the shrine.[29]

Offering of *Saka*

Offering of *Saka* is the last event in the ritual. The *Baindla* priests attire themselves as the deity herself – they wear a white saree and red blouse, apply turmeric powder all-over their body and apply vermillion on their forehead; they wear necklaces made of cowries. He then sits with both his palms held together to make a cup shape; the families then offer him *Saka* by pouring it into his cupped palms. The *Baindla* consumes the *Saka*, symbolically, signifying that the families have offered the drink to the deity herself.[30] This then is the procedure to perform ritualistic worship of *Ellamma*.

Chindus

Chinduvaru, Chindollu, Sindollu, or *Bhogam Madigas* are the other names of the Chindu *Madigas,* a dependent caste of the *Madigas*. The *Chindu Madigas* entertain the *Madigas* by melodiously reciting *Jamba Purana, Ramayana, Mahabharata,* the ballads of *Ellamma, Alli Rani, Rukmini Kalyanam, Sita Vanavasam, Bala Nagamma* etc. In remuneration for these, the *Chindu Madigas* collect grain, clothes, domestic animals, and cash.[31] They are nomadic and the entire family moves around villages in a bullock cart performing their art. They make or prepare on their own all the paraphernalia like costumes, ornaments, cosmetics, curtains, maces, bows and arrows, sabres that are required for the performances. People of other castes who come to watch their performances also help them out within their means.

The *Madiga* chief hands-over the grain and money according to the pre-agreed terms. The *Chindu Madigas* visit the villages under their *Mirasi* rights, perform their art and may hike or reduce the remuneration, also called *Tyagam,* depending on the affordability of the community. Once all the performances are completed in a village, the *Chindu Madigas* meet the community chief of the patrons, discuss and organise festivities for the guardian deity – *Ellamma*. Although all the performances are male oriented, the role of Goddess *Ellamma* is played by *Chindu* woman or a *Bhogam* woman of the village.

Rituals Officiated by *Chindus* During *Ellamma Kolupu*

Before the commencement of festivities of *Ellamma,* the chief members of the *Chindu* community meet the *Madiga* chief and discuss about the operational activities related to the festivities. While the *Bonam* is readied at the house of the *Madiga* chief, the Goud community chief offers the required palm wine for the goddess. The *Chindu* community chief dresses-up as *Betala* and a woman from the community dons the role of *Ellamma*.[32]

Donning the Attire of *Ellamma*

As per the traditions, the *Chindus* bathes early in the morning and start making themselves up as *Betala* and *Ellamma* in the community head's house. Simultaneously the *Bonam* is prepared at the chief's house, and even the millets and *Senagalu* (Bengal gram) are boiled. The woman making-up herself as *Ellamma* leaves her hair loose, wears a crown, and applies turmeric to her face and then a vermillion mark on the forehead. She wears straps of cowries to both her forearms and also above the elbows; she is dressed-up with a saree with cowries attached to it and holds a sabre with a lemon at its end in her right-hand. A bell and a pouch filled with *Vadvyalabiyyam* are tied around her waist. Once the costumes are worn and the *Chindu* woman is ready to appear as *Ellamma*, her entry is announced by beating the drums in the presence of the chief.

Fetching the *Ghatam* (pot)

They follow her holding turmeric, vermillion and a lighted oil lamp along with the person carrying the *Ghatam* and go to the Goud head's house, where he welcomes them by sprinkling water on the ground in front of their feet. Both the chiefs break a coconut each near the *Ghatam*, which is by now decorated as *Bonam*. The *Madiga* head and his wife then hand over the new pair of clothes to the Goud head and his wife. They then sit on the mat facing the Goud couple. Amid chanting of mantras by the *Chindu Madigas*, the couples exchange *Kankanams*.[33]

After tying the threads around the wrists, amid sounds of drum beats the Goud chief pays obeisance along with his wife and then lifts the *Ghatam* to his head. The elders of the community accompany him up to the threshold of the house where a *Madiga* man approaches, pays obeisance to the *Ghatam* and takes it over to his head. The Goud chief's wife fetches a potful of water and pours it on the feet of the *Madiga* chief as he crosses the threshold.

If anybody in the gathering is hypnotised because of the intense sounds of the drum beats, he or she is assumed to have been possessed by the deity, and the *Chindu Madiga* casts a spell (*Mantrinchuta*) on a bunch of neem leaves that are in his hands, and administers them into the mouth of the possessed. Yet the possessed continues to be in that state, he then casts spell on a lemon, cuts into two, puts a piece in the mouth of the possessed, and squeezes the second half on the spot he or she is standing. With this the person comes back to normalcy. The *Ghatam* procession that had started from the Goud's house is welcomed by people living on the way. They pour potsful of water (*Neellu Aarapoyuta*) as a sign of welcome. The *Madiga* chief breaks coconuts at the shrines of *Pochamma, Nagulamma,* and *Uppalamma* that lie on the way back to the *Madiga* ghetto.[34]Amid chanting of sacred hymns, the *Chindu Madiga* throws up the lemon in his hand. He draws a circle around the spot at which the lemon lands on the ground, and at the middle of the circle the *Ghatam* is placed. A *Madiga* man is left to guard it.

Escorting *Ellamma*

Amid drum beats the gathering, of *Chindu,* Goud, and *Madiga* communities, leaves for the chief's house to fetch the woman donning the role of *Ellamma*. She is ready by then and her appearance is as follows: with her hair let loose, a crown on her head, red dots of vermillion on the face, strips of cowry shells tied at the wrists and to the upper arms, a cloth with cowries attached is wound around her waist, holds with her right hand a curved knife pierced into a lemon, ties a bell around the waist and a cloth containing *Odi Biyyam* is also wound round her waist. The gathering offers new clothes to the deity, breaks a coconut at the threshold of the house, and the *Chindu Madiga* escorts her out of the house. Simultaneously, another *Chindu Madiga* and another *Madiga* elder lift the *Bonam* and place it on the head of a *Madiga* woman. Amid drum beats, the *Muttayiduvas* then escort

Ellamma and *Bonam* bearer to the spot where *Ghatam* is placed. The *Chindu Madiga* carries a *Cheta* filled with boiled millets. On reaching the spot, the *Bonam* is placed beside the *Ghatam*.[35]

Sacrificing a Sheep

Ellamma stands between these two pots – *Ghatam* and *Bonam*. The *Chindu Madiga* draws a *Muggu* with rice flour mixed with turmeric in front of her. The *Madiga* chief brings a young sheep to the *Muggu* and makes it drink the palm wine that was brought in the *Ghatam*. On sprinkling a little palm wine on the animal it shakes its ears. Immediately *Ellamma* chops the animal's head with the curved knife in her hand. The *Chindu Madiga* inserts his hand through the animal's genitals into the belly and pulls out its heart and intestines. He cleans the intestines, knots one end, through the other end blows air into it, makes a garland and then wears it around his neck. He holds the animal's lungs with his teeth, applies the blood oozing out of the severed neck to his head, and mixes the rest with the boiled millets. He then applies *Bottu* to the foreheads of the *Madiga* chief and others with the blood of the animal. The head of the sacrificed animal is then separated from the body, the right fore-leg is severed and placed horizontally into the mouth, and the head is then placed on the *Muggu*.[36]

Sprinkling of the Sacrificial Blood

The drum beats start again; with the *Madiga* youth rushing ahead the *Chindu Madiga* lets loose his hair, applies three parallel lines across his forehead with the slain sheep's blood, a new *Cheta* containing boiled millets mixed with the slain animal's blood is held at his waist with left hand, and with the right hand he picks up fistfuls of the mixture and scatters it on all the houses in the ghetto.

Touching the Containers Filled with Harvest

On his return, the palm wine in the *Ghatam* is poured on the *Muggu* (*Naksha Poyuta*). *Ellamma* then consumes the wine from the *Ghatam* and starts from there to visit each house in the ghetto. She first visits the *Madiga* chief's house, where she is given the traditional welcome by pouring water across her feet. After entering the house, she touches the cutlery, and the containers to store the harvest. The household drops coins worth sixteen rupees into pot from which they drink water – *Kalikunda*. They also place a new sari over the pot. *Ellamma* breaks a coconut in front of the pot, picks up the sari and also the coins, and leaves the house. This ritual is repeated in all the households, though not all leave a new sari, but will invariably leave the coins in their *Kalikunda*s. Finally, she reaches the house of the community elder, who offers her a potful of palm wine and welcomes her into his house. She proceeds to the *Ellamma Muntalu* (small earthen pots dedicated to the deity), breaks coconut, lights incense sticks and fumigates the house with frankincense (*Guggilam*) and then changes her costumes. The community elder honours her with palm wine.[37]

Distribution of the Offering

While the elders of *Chindu* and *Madiga* communities follow *Ellamma* to each household, the skin of the slain animal is removed; the meat is chopped into small pieces. The *Bonam* rice cooked by the *Madiga* chief's wife is made into small balls. The rice balls and chopped pieces of meat are then distributed to each household. The piece of meat is mixed in the curries the household had cooked on the day, and the ball of rice is mixed with the cooked rice. It is considered that they are consuming the food that the deity has herself served them. It is thus the *Chindus* perform the rituals to appease the goddess *Ellamma*.

Conclusion

The human civilisation, since its beginning, has been worshipping the five elements as various manifestations of female deities. As part of this worship, a variety of female deities are revered as manifestations of Earth because the idea of fertility and reproduction is connected with women. In India, the melting pot of multiple religious faiths and traditions, the practice of worshipping the village deity or guardian deity, especially the female deities, is prevalent since ages. Each community within the society worshipped a variety of female goddesses as their guardian deities and performed rituals in a variety of ways. The *Madigas* worship the goddess *Ellamma* either as a community as a whole or individually. The *Kolupulu* (rituals) to appease her are performed by the *Baindla* along with the Matangi and the *Chindus*. Such ritualistic performances can be considered as recognising the matriarchy too.

Endnotes

1 Goddess Ellamma, also known as Renuka Ellamma is the guardian deity of the Madigas. The Madiga maiden so dedicated is considered to be the living representation of the deity. The practice of dedicating is called Jannekiduchuta in Telangana parlance. The Baindlas are the priests of the deity. The Madiga maids are initiated into the practice of Matangi in the temple complex dedicated to Jamadagni and Renuka Ellamma (popularly known as the hermitage of Sage Jamadagni) at Surabheswara Kona on the banks of the rivulet Gundlakamma near Cumbhum in Prakasam district. Also see: Thurston, Edgar & K. Rangachari: Castes and Tribes Of Southern India, Volume IV, Government Press, Madras, 1909, p. 304; Saskia C. Kersenboom: Nityasumangali – A Devadasi Tradition in South India, Motilal Banarsidass Publishers Pvt. Ltd, Delhi, 1998, p. 56; Clough, Emma Rauschenbusch: While Sewing Sandals: Tales of Telugu Pariah Tribe, New York, 1899, pp. 31-33.

2 Henry White Hood: Dakshina Bharatha Desamlo Gramadevathalu, Vishalandhra Publishing House,

Hyderabad, 2013, p. 39, and LalithaVakulabharanam: Jogini Vyavastha, Janachaithanya Vedika Andhra Pradesh Committee, Hyderabad, 2007, pp.32-33.

3 Naga Bhushanacharyulu, Chirravoori: Sanchara Jathulu (Nomadic Tribes), Deenathi Deenula Parisodhana Kendram, Narasaravupeta, 1977, p. 35.

4 Siraj Ul Hasan, Syed: The Castes and Tribes of H.E.H Nizams Dominions, Volume-I, The Times Press, Bombay, 1920, p. 412 & Rama Raju, B (Nayani Krishna Kumari – Tr): Andhra Pradesh Janapada Sahityam, Sanskruti, National Book Trust of India, New Delhi, 2001, p. 153.

5 Yadaiah, Chinthala: Janapada Vignanamlo Bavaneelu, Drushti Prachuranalu, Hyderabad, 1990, p. 14., and Sree Suryarayandhra Nighantuvu, Volume-5, Telugu Viswa Vidayalayam, Hyderabad, 1983, p.74.

6 Radha Krishna Murthi, Mikkilineni: Teluguvari Janapada Kalaroopalu, Telugu Viswavidyalayam, Hyderabad, 1992, 43, 422, 593 & Ramaraju. B: Telugu Janapada Geya Sahityam, Andhra Rachayithala Sangham, Hyderabad, 1958, p. 767.

7 Thurston, Edgar & K. Rangachari: Castes and Tribes of Southern India, Volume IV, Op Cit. p. 130.

8 Siraj-Ul-Hassan, Syed., The Castes and Tribes of H.E.H Nizams Dominions, Op Cit. 412.

9 Singh, Kumar Suresh: People of India - Communities, Volume-I, 1995, p. 496.

10 Clough, Rauschenbusch: *While Sewing Sandals:* Tales of Telugu Pariah Tribe, Op Cit. pp. 31-33.

11 Krishna Kumari, Nayani: Telugu Janapada Geya Gathalu, Hyderabad, Krishna Kumari, 1977.

12 Rama Raju, B (Nayani Krishna Kumari – Tr): Andhra Pradesh Janapada Sahityam, Sanskruti, National Book Trust of India, New Delhi, 2001, p. 153.

13 A kind of music instrument made of a layer of animal hide sewn to a wooden ring with the animal's nerve drawn from the legs.

14 Radha Krishna Moorthi, Mikkilineni: Teluguvari Janapada Kalaroopalu, Op Cit. p. 594.

15 Interview with Veeraiah Vallamdasu, Baindla, Mandalapuram Village, Nakrekal Mandal, Nalgonda District.

16 Oral interview with Ramesh Vallamdasu. Baindla, Mandalapuram Village, Nakrekal Mandal, Nalgonda District.

17 Oral interview with Saidulu Deshapaka. Baindla, Nakrekal Village and Mandal, Nalgonda District.

18 The pot, which is worshipped as symbol of Goddess Elamma. It is made by Potter (Kummari). On this snake symbols painted.

19 Oral interview with Ramaswamy Imadapaka., Baindla, Chandupatla Village, Nakrekal Mandal, Nalgonda District.

20 Sumangalis.

21 Oral interview with Buchaiah Kandukuri., Baindla, Ogodu Village, Nakrekal Mandal, Nalgonda District.

22 The water Compart area like well,tank,stream in the village.

23 Oral interview with Guruvaiah Puli., Baindla, Thatikal Village, Nakrekal Mandal, Nalgonda District.

24 small clay vessels Or pots.

25 Theegala Sreenivas., Nallgonda Jilla Nakrekal Mandalam Baindlavari Jeevana Vidhanam Oka Parisheelana, Unpublished M.Phil, Dissertation, History, Culture and Archaeology, Potti Sreemulu Telugu University, Srisailam Campus, 2010, p. 52-53.

26 Turmeric, Kunkuma, white floor or rice floor, green floor or floor of senna auriculeta leaf's, chandanam.

27 Oral interview with Buchaiah Kandukuri., Baindla, Ogodu Village, Nakrekal Mandal, Nalgonda District.

28 Oral interview with Ramaswamy Imadapaka., Baindla, Chandupatla Village, Nakrekal Mandal, Nalgonda District.

29 Theegala Sreenivas., Nallgonda Jilla Nakrekal Mandalam Baindlavari Jeevana Vidhanam Oka Parisheelana, Op Cit. p.56.

30 Oral interview with Anjaiah Kandukuri., Baindla, Machanapalli Village, Thipparthy Mandal, Nalgonda District.

31 Edgar Thurston & K. Rangachari., Castes and Tribes Of Southern India, Volume I, Government Press, Madras, 1909, p. 315.

32 Oral interview with Gajavelli Bhujangam., Chindu, Paanthani Village, Wardhannapet Mandal, Warangal District.

33 Oral interview with Bhaskula Babu., Madiga, Lyabarthy Village, Wardhannapet Mandal, Warangal District.

34 Oral interview with Madada Buchaiah Goud., Gouda, Lyabarthy Village, Wardhannapet Mandal, Warangal District.

35 Oral interview with Akulapelly Venkataiah., Madiga, Lyabarthy Village, Wardhannapet Mandal, Warangal District.

36 Oral interview with Gajavelli Vedantham., Chindu, Paanthani Village, Wardhannapet Mandal, Warangal District.

37 Oral interview with Gajavelli Ellamma., Chindu, Paanthani Village, Wardhannapet Mandal, Warangal District.

8

Tanneries and *Tijarat*: Social and Economic Vulnerabilities of Muslim Leather Workers in India[1]

Dr. Muneer Illath*

1. Introduction

The paper attempts to briefly address some of the pressing socio-economic issues faced by leather workers among Muslims in contemporary India. It is argued that when looked through the prism of historical sociology of the formation and growth of 'Muslim' in India, both caste and community invariably surface as powerful axioms and intersect each other in the case of Dalit Muslims. While gathering the sources of constituting a category called Muslims in India, it is felt that caste as an encompassing feature, if not central, of Indian Muslims too, seems to hold true.

1 The draft paper to be presented at the National Seminar on History of Leather Working Castes in India: Social Transformation and Challenges organised by the Department of History University of Allahabad, Allahabad. Please do not cite or distribute the paper without permission of the author.

* Assistant Professor, Department of Sociology, University of Allahabad, Allahabad, E-mail: muneerillath@gmail.com

A significant number of Muslim workforce in India is engaged in informal economy and involved in unorganised sector, making their lives more precarious and vulnerable. Many of them are historically involved in cattle trade and run abattoirs to process and sell meat in the local market. Leather workers in India are largely involved in processing, production and supply of hides, leather, garments and other leather products in India. As Muslims constitute a major chunk of this workforce along with Dalits, their weak socioeconomic position leads to multiple hardships in their day-today life. A Recent study (2017) reveals that apart from the social discrimination that they experience in the workplaces and elsewhere in society they are also faced with casualisation of labour force and poor organisation of trade union, making their position more risky, both economically and socially.

Caught between the identities and interventions of community, state and market, this paper makes an attempt to trace the sources of vulnerabilities of the present-day leather working communities among Muslims in India. The paper suggests that labour conditions of Muslim leather workers in India are a result of the deep rooted social and economic inequalities that the community is entangled in by virtue being a minority community with multiple discriminations based on historical location as well as poor access to resources for social development. Exploring these structural conditions becomes imperative in understanding the sources of backwardness among the present-day leather workers among Muslims in India.

This paper is divided into five major section which will separately explain the ways in which leather workers among Muslims in India experience different forms of discrimination and exclusion for being 'Muslim', 'lower caste' and economically vulnerable 'class'. The first part of the paper deals with the debate of 'community' and 'caste' among Indian Muslims by tracing the origin and trajectories of making a 'Muslim' in India. The second part attempts to explain how caste discrimination and oppressions were historically associated with Dalits in India and the extent to which economic empowerment of Dalits were seriously dealt at the corridors of political power. The third part of the paper touches up on the sources of economic vulnerabilities among informal labourers in India with a special focus on leather workers. The fourth section attempts to see the challenges ahead in a situation in which social and political location of some sections, especially Muslims and Dalits, of the population invariably impinge on their economic visibility and performance. The last part of this essay provides a brief summary of the debates and offers some concluding remarks.

Literature research focusing on the origin and growth of socio-economic inequalities among Muslims in India, especially the lowest strata among, constitute the thrust area of this study. This study specifically addresses the structural contingencies that feed into making India's leather workers more vulnerable with a special focus on Dalit Muslims and argue that the social location of being Muslim and dalit at a time amount to multiple susceptibilities and exclusion among Muslims in India. While looking through the prism of economic sociology, thus, one can argue that norms, values and institutions that are lying outside the conventional purview of economics and manifested through institutions like caste and ethnicity are strongly 'embedded' and thus deeply affect economy.

2. Debate on 'Community' and 'Caste' among Muslims in India

Dalit Muslims carry a double burden of exclusion from their fellow Muslim brethren as well as the society at large. However, much of the debates and discussions that emerged in the circles of Muslims in India are accused of its conspicuous focus on politics of identity and other pressing issues that might invoke a false consciousness of a homogenous community. Dalit Muslims invariably argue that selective invoking of the 'community' as the quintessential and primordial identity not only prevent internal democracy but also ignore the mechanisms and agencies that create and perpetuate inequality within the 'community'. For them, it is only an elite minority of Muslims who have benefitted from such a consciousness of collectivity which inherently disregard internal diversities within.

Offering a powerful critique to homogenising and primordialising identities, scholars have argued fluidity of identities and how they are being constructed both politically and socially (Brass 1991; Kurien 2002). For instance, Kurien observes that although religion may be a defining attribute, a religious community is always a multidimensional entity consisting of social, cultural, political and economic structures. For her, all these structures, together with its position in, and relationship to, the larger society shapes its central defining features (2002: 29). Thus, going beyond building an analytical contour on 'community', which otherwise had been the dominant scholastic position on Muslims in India, caste and other defining factors need to be recognised and empirically analysed further. As far as leather workers in India are concerned, by virtue of being considered as an impuring and polluting profession among Hindus and thereby Dalits and Muslims making up the majority of the workforce, both community and caste invariably surface and fuse together in the case of India's leather workers.

Development deficits of India's Muslims is said to have been a puzzling omission in academia as well as in the political discourse of the country. Historical deprivation and selective discrimination of the 'community' has been highlighted in some of the recent scholarly and administrative documents on the community's socio-economic profile (Khalidi 2004, Sachar Committee Report 2005, Basant & Shariff 2010). These developmental discrepancies have been largely attributed to some of their most pressing issues related to *identity, security* and *equity* visa-vis other socio-religious communities in the country. While Khalidi (2004) cites number of examples of informal discrimination against Muslims even in the formal sector, a recent work brought by Basant and Shariff clearly demonstrates discrimination in terms of access to basic facilities (2010).

It is observed that the issue of caste and community seems to intersect and feed into each other in the case of Muslims as a 'community' and Dalit Muslims as a caste. One of the pressing examples is India's meat industry where Muslims have historically dominated the slaughtering and sale of meat while Dalits and Dalit Muslims have predominantly engaged in processing of hides in tanneries. As the production and sale of meat has been banned in parts of the country and thousands of abattoirs were closed down in accordance with the increasing demand for the protection of cattle, tanneries and other leather related production units have faced huge financial setback. Obviously, the biggest casualty of these legal initiatives and the emergence of a new political atmosphere have been Muslims and Dalits as their economic fortunes in the tanneries and households leather works, where they have been predominantly engaged in, have directly come under serious threat.

Economic prospects of Muslims in India has been punctuated by sporadic incidents of communal violence that erupted in India's Muslim neighbourhoods devastating their material properties and causing much hardships to the long-cherished interethnic relations (Engineer 1984; Harris 2005; Khalidi 2006). While at one level Muslims in India have been accused as a threat to national integration, they are also depicted as incompetent and underperformed because of their own action. Sometimes they are also deems, like Sachar Committee Reports suggests, as "carrying a double burden of being labeled as "anti-national" and as being "appeased" at the same time" (2006: 11). Yet, concerns over the security of their lives and wealth have been haunting the community for long (Engineer 1984; Sachar Committee Report 2006).

Notwithstanding the concerns of security and identity that Muslims at large face on everyday basis, community as the most legitimised analytical axiom of Muslims in India seems to sidestep internal diversities among Muslims where caste, especially among leather workers, plays a significant role.

3. Dalits and Economic Discriminations: Exploring Sources of Exclusions

Apart from persistent economic distress, caste has been one of most encompassing axioms on which Dalits in India have been oppressed and discriminated against. Harris (2014) observes two kinds of oppression and discrimination -namely British and Brahmanical, against Dalits that had heavily influenced their lives and life chances in colonial and post-colonial India. It is pertinent to observe that modernisation and its political institutions like democracy had paved some paths of political empowerment for Dalits such institutional mechanisms hardly offered them any form economic power. It is believed that effective control of state power by the upper castes continue to offer fewer avenues for Dalits to effectively participate in political and economic spheres.

The institutions like caste and ethnicity, traditionally embedded in the economic institutions, have created an aura of hierarchy of occupations where Dalits continuously engage in activities associated with agricultural labour, sanitary work, skinning of animals and other forms of myriad jobs which society treats and menial and impure. Despite the tall promises of the advocates of modernity of being an active agent in destabilizing archaic forms of economic exchange where a particular section of the society has always been at the receiving end, the reality was that those sources economic emancipation had remained unreachable to, and, thus, 'non-starter' for Dalits in India.

Although many hereditary occupations have been historically disassociated from their corresponding castes leather work has been a profession which was historically looked through the prism of ostracism and thereby de-facto assigned to Dalits and Muslims. Hindus traditionally consider working with hides and skins as something which is polluting and impure and therefore allocate these assignments to Dalits and Muslims. While Muslims have been working in leather industry as a formidable workforce and traders, it is largely the Dalits and Other Backward Classes among Muslims who are largely involved in tanning, leather production and making shoes.

Among many axioms on which Muslims in India are internally differentiated, caste assumes greater significance. Although there are some cursory annotations on the anthropological presence of caste among Muslims it was the series of writing by Imtiaz Ahmed during 1970s and 80s that brought the Muslims lives in India to the centre of sociological debate. It was argued that notwithstanding a complete rejection of the practice of caste system in the great tradition of Islam, Ahmed (1972) observes some elements of caste system among Muslims as well. He claims that similarities can be seen the pattern of endogamy, a keen sense of pride in birth and descent and a notion of hierarchy.

In a relatively recent study Khanam observes that "social distance among different Muslim caste is not ideologically or structurally sanctioned but they observe social distance of superiority based on deference, privileges and descent". Thus, recruitment to the broader faith called Islam among the vast majority of what we label as 'Indian Muslims' has been partial and does not involve a complete denial or disengagement with the rituals and cultural attributes of their earlier faiths and castes. Vast majority of Muslims in India have embraced Islam from the intermediary and lower rungs of Hindu society where status was rigidly defined in terms of birth and maintained by strong social sanctions (2013: 116).

Among many features of caste system which had influenced the social location of varied population in India, hierarchical pattern of social grouping, endogamy and hereditary occupations are still present among Muslims in India (Ahmed 1973; Sachar Report 2006; Khanam 2013). The leather workers among Muslims in India are largely the converts from the erstwhile untouchable castes, i.e. Chamar, who are placed at the bottom of social hierarchy among Muslims. By virtue of their profession that is socially demeaning, like preparing row hides for tanning to producing leather goods, their social economic position has remained far below their Muslim brethren as well as the general population at large.

Meat and leather industries are mutually supportive and provide jobs for thousands of Muslims who are either involved in trading and butchering of the animals for consumption and export and sell the hides for producing leather. The recent statistics (June 2017) reveals that India's export of leather shoes has experienced a dramatic decline of 13 % much to the favour of secure supply for China and Pakistan in this area. This is in tune with the findings of Sachar Coommittee Report that "Displacement from traditional occupations has contributed to Muslims being deprived of their means of livelihood and has led to economic backwardness" (2006: 21). The report further highlights that some of the traditional industries where Muslims are predominantly engaged in, like "silk and sericulture, hand and power looms, the leather industry, automobile repairing, garment making, have borne the brunt of liberalization. Although the ban on cattle has been revoked the cow-vigilants in the recent past have been given free hand to attack the cattle traders. These trends reveal that the new political atmosphere that cause new hardships to the economic fortunes of Dalits and Muslims, who are predominantly involved in this industry, would make India's position in the global economy more vulnerable and self-defeating. Recent studies and reports also reveal that people who are traditionally involved in meat and leather industries continue to feel unsafe to trade buffalo, buy cow leather or engage in the profession dealing with hides due to adverse political atmosphere that looms large.

4. Informal Economy and New Vulnerabilities: The Case of Muslim Workforce

Many studies and report in the recent past conform to the fact that vast majority of the workforce in India is informal and unorganised in nature. It is to be noted that most of the labour acts and welfare measures predominantly cater to the needs and demands of workers in the organised sector who constitute just less than one-tenth of the total workforce in the country. In other words, unorganised workforce like leather workers lies largely outside the ambit of economic security and provisions for social welfare ensured by the labour laws and are constantly exploited in the hands of their employers and other corporate companies.

Informal economy outside the organised labour market is the resort that India's vast majority of Muslims are engaged in, either by their choice or by force. Poor participation of different social groups in the regular employment is greatly determined by their relative advantage in terms of 'attributes', like educational attainments and 'access' to basic facilities through network and influence (Basant & Shariff 2010). Their study finds that India's deprived social groups, especially Dalits and Muslims, are lagging behind other socio-religious groups in terms of their poor attributes, but lesser attention has been paid to reverse the attribute deficits, but rather focused on access (p 12).

Sachar Committee Report (2006) reveals that Muslims and Dalits have higher presence than the general population in the occupational categories related to tannery, shoe making and other leatherwork related professions. For instance, shoe makers & leather goods makers account about 0.6 % of the total urban workforce in India whereas this number is 0.8 % for Muslims and 1.8 % for Scheduled Castes. As casualization of labour has been widely present among this informal and unorganised sector, they face uncertainty in terms of job security and are denied welfare measures during their tenure as well as in case of casualties. They are devoid of minimum statutory and social security benefits which any formal workforce is entitled to get. The casualisation of labour force among dalits and Muslim leather workers, this study would argue, both shapes and are shaped by their social location as untouchables and minorities.

5. Towards Conclusions

Notwithstanding attempts and articulations to paint Muslims in India as a homogenising category or 'community', both in practice and experience they are heterogenous and strongly rooted in the local cultures and traditions. Caste has been one of the prominent, if not central, and much debated axioms on which Muslims in India are divided, economically, socially and politically. As far as Muslims in India are concerned, their access to resources, economic and social organisations and exchanges are drawn predominantly on their community and caste identities. The protracted discrimination that Muslims in India are subjected to is firmly rooted in their social position as Muslims and Dalits. Both these categories intersect in the compound manifestation of marginalisation and discrimination against Dalit Muslims. Intersections of these categories as well as measures to redress their grievances, though appears glaring, had been hardly addressed within the 'community' or by the state or civil society.

The paper suggests that any attempt to study the sources of vulnerabilities of leather workers among Muslims and offer any insights to ameliorate their conditions will have to see multiple roots and causalities in which this social category is embedded and organised. The intersectionality of 'caste' and 'community' in the case of Dalit Muslims and Muslim leather workers calls for a fresh academic engagement especially in the context of new political atmosphere at national level and globalisation of labour and market in the transnational front.

References

Ahmed, Imtiaz. 1973. *Caste and Social Stratification among Muslims in India* New Delhi: Manohar Publications

Ambedkar B.R. 2014. *Annihilation of Caste.* New Delhi: Navayana

Basant, Rakesh& Abusaleh Shariff eds. 2010. *Handbook of Muslims in India*. New Delhi: Oxford University Press.

Brass, Paul. 1991. *Ethnicity and Nationalism: Theory and Comparison*. New Delhi: Sage Publications

Breman, Jan. 2010. *Outcast Labour in Asia* New Delhi: Oxford University Press

Damodaran, Harish. 2008. *India's New Capitalists* New Delhi: Permanent Black

Engineer, Asghar Ali ed. 1984. *Communal Riots in Post-Independence India*. Hyderabad: Orient Longman

Government of India. 2009. Report on Leather Industry Including Footwear and Other Art Workers in India. Ministry of Labour and Employment

Harris-White, Barbara. 2005. *India's Market Society* New Delhi: Three Essays Collective

————2014. *Dalits and Adivasis in India's Business Economy* New Delhi: Three Essays Collective.

Hoefe, Rosanne. 2017. "Do leather workers matter? Violating labour rights and environmental norms in India's Leather Production" *India Committee of the Netherlands* (March)

Illath, Muneer. 2015. Muslim Entrepreneurship and Socio-political Shifts: Impact of Gulf

Migration in Kerala. Unpublished PhD Thesis, Department of Sociology, University of Hyderabad. Hyderabad.

Khalidi, Omar. 2006. *Muslims in Indian Economy*. New Delhi: Three Essays Collective.

Khanam, Azra. 2013. *Muslim Backward Classes: A Sociological Perspective*. New Delhi: Sage Publications

Kurien, Prema 2002. *Kaleidoscopic Ethnicity*. New Delhi: Oxford University Press

Lakra, Christopher. 2010. *Dalit Muslims* New Delhi: Indian Social Institute

Saberwal, Satish 2010. 'On the Making of Muslim in India Historically' in Shariff, Abusaleh & Rakesh Basant eds. *Handbook of Muslims in India* New Delhi: Oxford University Press

Sachar, Rajinder. 2006. 'Social, Economic and Educational Status of the Muslim

Community in India' *Sachar Committee Report*, Prime Ministers' High Level Committee. New Delhi: Government of India.

9

Ravidas as Intellectual Leather Worker in Medieval India

Parmjeet Kaur*

ABSTRACT

Various schools of historians have not evaluated Ravi Das's contribution to the society. As a leather worker, he did not hide his profession, rather he declared himself Moochi. He also did not hide his caste "Chamar" which was a bold step. Why historians did not pay attention towards his bold step, is a question mark on the tools of historians. Secondly, Ravidas was limited into the Hindi discipline which shows the narrowness of the Historians. My paper tries to this aspect. I will throw some of the important example so that we could reach where Ravidas wanted to go.

Introduction

Let me first give the definition of an intellectual which is very much required. There are several definition of the intellectual. According to oxford Dictionary that a person is and well educated and enjoying activities in which he and she has to think seriously about things or the ability to think in a logical way and understand things, especially at an advanced level.[1] In another word,an intellectual is a person who engages in critical thinking,

* Post Doctoral fellow, Jamia Millia Islamia, New Delhi.

research, and reflection about society and proposes solutions for its normative problems. Some gain authority as public intellectuals. Coming from the world of culture, either as a creator or as a mediator, the intellectual participates in politics either to defend a concrete proposition or to denounce an injustice, usually by rejecting, producing or extending an ideology, and by defending a system of values.[2] Dr . Ambedkar also says in this regard that " in every country the intellectual class is the most influential class, if not the governing class. The intellectual class is the class which cans foresee, it is the class which can advice and give lead. In no country does the mass of the live the life of intelligent thought and action. It is largely imitative and follows the intellectual class. There is no exaggeration in saying that the entire destiny of a country depends upon its intellectual class. If the intellectual class is honest , independent and disinterested it can be trusted to take the initiative and give proper lead when a crisis arises . It is true that the intellect by itself is no virtue .It is only a means and the use of means depends upon the ends, which an intellectual person pursues. An intellectual man can be good man but he can easily be a rogue. Similarly an intellectual class may be a band of high souled persons, ready to help, ready to emancipate erring humanity or it may easily be a gang of crooks or a body of advocates of a narrow clique from which it draws its support. You may think it a pity that the intellectual class in India is simply another name of the Brahmin caste."[3]

Tohi, mohi, mohi tohi, antar kaisa:
kanak katik jal tarang jaisa.

(There is no difference between you (God) and me as there is no difference between the gold and its ornaments, between water and its waves.)

- Guru Ravidas

In this regard, Ravidas was a great intellectual. He was not a rogue, rather, he was problem solver and pathfinder. I will, try to see the many verses which solve the problem of the society. H e also states the reality of the society. First of all, a brief introduction of Ravidas.Ravidas was a North Indian mystic poet-sant of the bhakti movement during the 15th to 16th century CE.[4] Venerated as a Guru (teacher) in the region of Punjab, Uttar Pradesh, Rajasthan and Maharashtra, the devotional songs of Ravidas made a lasting impact upon the bhakti movement. He was a poet-saint, social reformer and a spiritual figure. He is considered as the founder of 21st-century Ravidassia religion, by a group who previously were associated with Sikhism.[5] The life details of Ravidas are uncertain and contested. Most scholars believe he was born about 1450 A.D in a family that worked with dead animals and their skin to produce leather products, making them an untouchable Chamar caste. Tradition and medieval era texts state Ravidas was one of the disciples of the Brahmin bhakti sant-poet Ramananda.[6]

Concept of Caste and Solution

He was agreed that Caste was the curse of the society and so he tried to destroy the caste .He stated many a time that caste is very dangerous to society. He see caste solution in bhakti. However, he also saw that people are very shy about their caste and tried to hide the caste. So, he clearly declared his caste which a revolutionary stand. Even today people hide their caste identity and use caste name of Upper caste and so on. But he did not hide this. Today, it may be a very simple things but during the Mughal times it was great and very bold step to describe the the stand. For instance, Abul fazal informed that during the Medieval times means the time of Ravidas, the Caste situation was very dangerous. He says that the Hindus were considered there were certain caste like –A sweeper, a washer man, A fisherman, a sprit-seller, a tanner, a dyer, and oil men. They were unlearns things.[7]

This becomes the case of generalization. This has been similar to the Dog, as ass and so on. There were other things which were unclean such as woman In her courses, and one newly delivered during the period, a dog, (tame) swine, the dust that rises from off an ass, goat, sheep or broom, and the mud shaken out of a garment, a sinner guilty of the five great sins, or whoever touches such, a crow, a (tame domestic) cock, a mouse, a eunuch, the smoke from a burnt corpse and so on.[8] He further state that For the Chandal caste (Pariah), A pathway or water that had been polluted by the shadow of a Chandal (pariah) was again purified by sunlight, moonlight, and air.[9] Milk cannot be purified except only when the shadow of a Chandal may have fallen upon it. in which case it become pure by boiling.[10] Wooden vessels if defiled by the touch of Chandal cannot be made pure, but if touched by a Sudra or any unclean thing, may be purified by scraping.[11] If he touches a washer man, or a dyer, or a currier, or an executioner, or a hunter or a fisherman, or an oilman, or tame swine, he is purified by water only. But if he (ouch a woman in her courses or a lying in woman, or a sweeper, or a great sinner, or a corpse, or a dog, or an ass, cat, crow, domestic cock, mouse or a eunuch, or the smoke of a burning corpse, or the dust from an ass, dog, goat or sheep reach him. he must enter the water.[12]

Not only this Manucci says that "to give some conception of the infamy attached by The hindus to these blacks, I will say that there are no words to express the vileness of the esteem in which they are held"[13] Other travelers account the mention the same . Thevnote, Carre, Fryer and so on. During the rein of Jahangir, the outcaste was seeing a very disguise manner. Take an example. "On the same day Kalyan, son of Raja Bikramajit, came form Gujarat. Certain extraordinary proceedings on the part of this rebellious rascal had been reported to me. Amongst these was this. He had kept a Musulman luli woman in his house, and for fear this affair should become known had killed her father and mother and buried them in his house. I ordered that he should be imprisoned until I could enquire into his proceedings, and after ascertaining the truth I ordered first that they should cut out his tongue and place him in perpetual confinement, and that he should eat his foot with dot-keepers and outcasts."[14]

However, in such a situation Ravidas says followings

Ravidas himself stated that he belonged to Chamar Category. He state in flowing lines;[15]

1. "Kah Raidas Khalas Chamara.

   Jo ham-sahri so mit Hamara."

   (Ravidas says that he is from Chamar Community, who understand me, he is my friend).

2. "Jat bhi Ochhi, Karam bhi ochha, Ochha kasab hamara,

   Neech se prabhu Unch kiye hai , kah , raidass Chamara"[16]

   (my caste is mean, my ,my so far work is mean and my profession is mean. My God took me high from mean, this what Ravidas says)

3. "Aisi meri jati vikhyat Chamar,

   Hirdya ram Govind Gunsaar"[17]

   (my caste, Chamra, is so famous that in my heart The God resides)

4. "Ham Apradhi neech Ghar janame,[1818] Ibid, p, 30.

   Kutumb Log kare hashi,

   Jaha Jaoo, taha dukha ki rashi,

   Jo na Patiyae Sadhu hai Sakhi"

   (I am criminal because I born in a low Caste, , people laugh upon me or my caste, wherever, I go, I receive sorrow, those who do not believe in the caste system, he is a good human being)

5. "Darider Dekha sab koi hase, aisi dasa hamari,[19]
   Astadas siddhi kar, sab kirpa tumhari"
   (people laugh by seeing my poverty. But I could successed for Astadas Siddhi, because of the grace of Almighty God.)

The above doha says that Ravi Das was born in low caste but his profession was making shoes and he was a cobbler. But during that days being a saint he acquired a great place during the medieval time. When he was alive he got enormous respect and dignity. Certainly his profession was not high level but his status was very high.

Concept of State

What kind of state we need is a very contested terrain. Ancient India followed monarchy. It was followed by Medieval India state. Even Modern world also followed Monarchies in many countries. The state produced Ruler like Ashoka and Akbar to whom Amartya Sen considered best ruler of the world while in the same time The sates also produced ruler like Hitler and Mussolini and so on. So, therefore, it is contested question. Ram Punyani describe the role of state as well social scientist role .Ram Puniyani has written path provoking book on the biases on the history .He writers "Today, the social atmosphere has been vitiated due to the prevalence of biases against the minorities. These biases have been spread through a partial recount of the events of the past and a lopsided projection of the phenomenon of the present. This has led to the generation of strong communal venom. —This communal venom derives its sustenance from the mythical projection of history. Today, one witnesses the gross abuse of history in order to spread communal hatred towards the 'other' community. As a matter of fact, it is the favorite weapon in the hands of those who base their politics on religion. The Muslim and Hindu communal interpretation of history. 'Our past it seems has never been as crucial for our present and future as it appears now. History –

the image of the past – is being conveniently and indiscriminately used for political myth making. They have comparisons between the "good" British rule and "bad" Muslim rule'. It is another matter that the Muslim ruling clans were socially mixed up with the local elite and a synthetic culture evolved in contrast to the British who remained aloof from the natives at the social level. Nor did the Muslim rulers take away the wealth of the country like the British rulers. —Since the two contesting communal streams were Hindu and Muslim, the major period of history that has been subjected to such gross abuse is the medieval period when the Mughal emperors ruled a major part of the country. The same period of history is interpreted in two contrasting ways. While Muslims communal historians (MCH) glorify it, the Hindu communal historians (HCH) and the imperial historians project it as a period when the Muslims tyrannised the Hindus. While the MCH project Aurangzeb as the greatest Muslim ruler upholding the values of Islam, the HCH see him as the most bigoted and cruel king in India's history. Chausalkar has an important observation to make: 'The communalists used the history as the opium of the people. They build up illusions of a great past'. Similarly. Prof. Arjun Dev writes. 'The two antagonistic communal trends complemented each other each finding in Aurangzeb justification of his variety of communalism, the Hindu communalists by believing that Aurangzeb's fanaticism was the final proof of irreconcilability of Hindus and Muslims. The Muslim communalists found him to be the pious Muslim who in a way laid the foundation of Pakistan.—A correct and holistic understanding of history in general and some of the misrepresented events of the past can go a long way in promoting inter-community bonds to improve the status of human rights of the weaker sections of society. The argument that certain events, that took place in the past need to be avenged today is based on a fallacious understanding of society. The politics of the past has to be kept confined to the past, irrespective of its interpretation. The present can in no way redress the mistakes of the past. The communal political forces reawaken past antagonism to consolidate their social base. This is done by spreading myths about Muslim rulers destroying Hindu temples or disseminating the canard that the Taj Mahal was originally a Temple or God Shiva that was usurped by the Muslim Emperor Shahjahan and converted into a tomb for his beloved queen. Vainglorious tales about how Rana Pratap and Shivaji took on the might of the Muslim rulers are used to work the masses into a belligerent mood. The very root of this historiography is based on the mistaken assumption that Indian society comprises a number of religious communities that are hostile to one another. It also assumes that there is uniformity in the interests of a religious community. Through this opaque prism, politics is seen as nothing but an interaction of different religious communities. ———The communal view of history has serious flaws as it takes the religion of the ruler as the sole determining point of the politics of the time. It also takes a static view of religion, believing that it remains impervious to change despite interaction with the people. It also sees a religious community as a homogenous group ignoring the serious differences in the socio-economic status of its constituents. Actually, what we should study in history is 'the stage of development of society from one point to another, the change in the society's system of production and the resultant social organization, etc'."[20]

Ravidas want different type of state. He says that he need place or country which should be "Be-gham-pura" (The city without Sorrow, the city without segeration, where people were free to go wherever they wanted;[21]

> Where there is no affliction or suffering
> Neither anxiety nor fear, taxes nor capital
> No menace, no terror, no humiliation—
> Says Raidas the emancipated Chamar;
> One who shares with me that city is my friend.

Conclusion

Ravidas was an great intellectual who played a very important which was left out by the historians because of Caste. The above mentioned ideas of Ravidas had a great importance. It has great relevance even today.

Endnotes

1 A S hornby, oxford Advanced Learner's Dictionary of Current English,Oxford university Press, London,2010,p,809.

2 Pascal Ory and Jean-François Sirinelli, *Les Intellectuels en France. De l'affaire Dreyfus à nos jours* (*The Intellectuals in France: From the Dreyfus Affair to Our Days*), Paris: Armand Colin, 2002, p. 10.

3 Dr Baba Saheb Ambedkar writings and speeches, Education department of Maharastra, 1982, Vol, 1, p. 71.

4 james Lochtefeld The Illustrated Encyclopedia of Hinduism: N-Z, Rosen Publishing, 2002, page 569

6 David Lorenzen Praises to a Formless God: Nirguni Texts from North India, State University of New York Press, 1996, page 268

7 Abul Fazal, vol iii, p,319.

8 Abul Fazal, vol iii, p,319.

9 Abul Fazal, vol iii, p,320.

10 Abul Fazal, vol iii, p,321.

11 Abul Fazal, vol iii, p,321.

12 Abul Fazal, vol iii, p,322.

13 Niccolao Manucci, Storia do mogor, 4 vols.

14 The Tuzuk-i-Jahangiri or memoirs of Jahangiri,translated by Alexander Rogers and edited by Henery Beveridge, published by low price publication,bound in 2 vol,first published 1909-1914,reprinted in LPP, 1989, 1999, 2006, Vol. 1, p. 104.

15 Kanwal Bharti, Saint raidass : Ek Vishleshan,Bodhiswa Prakashan, 1985, p. 29.

16 Ibid, p. 29.

17 Ibid, p. 30.

18 Ibid, p. 30.

19 Ibid, p. 30.

20 Ram Puniyani, Communal Politics facts versus myths,Sage publications, New Delhi, first print, 2003 and fifth print, 2008, pp. 43-45.

21 Arundhati Roy, An introduction of Annihilation of Caste of Dr. B.R. Ambedkar, Navayana, 2014, p. 48.

10

Caste, Labour and History: The Leather Workers of Agra During the Colonial Period

Prashant Kumar Kain*

ABSTRACT

There is a consensus among the historians and specially the labour historians about the negative impact of colonial rule on India. The colonial rule has been blamed for ruining the traditional village crafts, indigenous works, industries and destroying the village based self sufficient economy. It is often argued that India was a very rich country before the colonial authorities plundered this country to satisfy their greed. These narratives define the colonial authorities as being the exploiter and villain and India as being victim and oppressed. These opinions, views and worldviews more or less are largely shared by nationalists, Marxists and ultra nationalists. There is a consensus on the bad effect of colonial rule on India but most of the thinkers and articulators are hesitant to talk about the situation before. Whether India was really a prosperous, equal, egalitarian and just society before the colonial rule?. Was colonial rule equally bad for all the people and section?. The discourse has been formed in such a way that we are not allowed to ask these questions or we do not come to these questions readily (or at all). Discussion on these questions will lead us into the more brutal, cruel and problematic area in history. This poses another question who is afraid of this and why they are afraid? This is where one senses the ideological and political factors playing a major role in determining the very nature, forms of knowledge generation processes. The nature of colonial rule was exploitative beyond doubt but they were not solely responsible for all the ills of the society as projected by many.

Introduction

The colonial rule was a major event into the history of India. It brought sudden, deep and dramatic changes in the Indian society. It fundamentally shook the foundations of the Indian society to the deep core. The dominants groups that have been feeding, flourishing and living on the labour of the downtrodden got firm treatment by the colonial authorities. Many of the rights and privileges which were restricted to particular groups and sections in the society became accessible to others for the first time in history. It was the British who brought modern and English education in India and also made it available to everyone (at least theoretically). They banned certain inhuman and cruel practices like Sati, allowed widow remarriage, banned slavery and slave trade, raised the age of marriage, introduced railways, opened ports, built roads, brought new opportunities in various industries and sector like coal, mineral extraction, jute, opened educational and health institutions, promoted trade and commerce, unified country (at least partly), introduced judiciary and uniform penal code and many other things. It was probably the first time in history that such vast development happened in such a short period of time. These developments were phenomenal and milestone in the history and these shook the very foundations of society and led to a new wave of economic and social transformation and social awareness in the society.

The Dalits as they are known today have been the victim of Brahmanical orthodoxy for centuries. They have suffered hereditary and inter-generational violence and subjugation throughout history. The kind of violence they have suffered can be imagined from the facts that even their shadow and sight was considered to be impure and defiling. This is exceptional and has no match in other societies of the world. The basic human requirements like the water, shelter, cloths and food was not available and accessible to them unlike others. This treatment of human by other human is exceptional in world history. They have lived a life worst than an animal and have been sold and bought like commodities in history before and during colonial period until it was banned by the British through an act. The colonial rule brought significant changes in the economy and society that affected different sections differently. It was during the colonial period that the education became accessible to the dalits due to the intervention of the colonial rule and also the activities of the missionaries. This was the beginning of the social and cultural awakening for the dalits in India.

The experiences from the society are negative and humiliating therefore they do not have a romantic, nostalgic and glorious account both of the history and society. The question of caste, critique of Brahmanism, the rejection of Veda and idea of the divine origin of the universe is central to the Dalit critique, narratives and worldview. The Dalit critique does not present a positive picture of the society it rather exploitation, discrimination and violence is central to their critique of the society. It is due to this reason the Dalit critique goes well beyond of the positivist tendencies of different school of thoughts. It therefore directly confront the nationalist, Marxist and ultra-nationalist version and imagination of the society and history. The worldview of untouchables is not fixed, static and submissive. It is rather critical, reflexive, open and emancipatory as it firms takes a stand against dehumanization. It is neither guided by narrow methods nor by narrow imagination of history and society. This worldview is very broad, pervasive and emancipator as it covers and confronts religion, culture, polity, economy, history in itself. It does not content itself by mere description of the social reality but also engage at various levels to transform it. This paper keeping this in mind the diversity and pervasiveness of the experiences of Dalits across time and space takes a critical approach towards history and society. It takes a broad and holistic approach while understanding their perspective and experiences both in the history and also empirically. This paper tries to go beyond the given narratives and explores the role caste played in the history and shaped up the experiences of diverse groups particularly the Dalits in India.

Caste, Ideology and Identity in India

In Hindu cosmology and worldview, 'People are divided into different Varnas on the basis of their Gunas. These three Gunas (qualities or nature) are Satva (goodness), Rajas (activity) and Tamas (darkness). When one of these three qualities predominates, the body becomes distinguished by that quality (Ketkar, 1909: 114). In this classical division certain human beings (as Varna) represent Satva, some Rajas and some Tamas. The Satva is a quality of supreme Varna, Rajas is the quality of higher yet lower Varna while the Tamas is the quality of inferior Varna. These qualities are intrinsic and permanent to the nature of human beings therefore are universal and non-contestable. These are ontological in nature therefore cannot be transferred, altered and changed by human consciousness and acts.

According to classical texts, the lord Brahma created this order in which 'The Brahmins were product of his brain; the Kshatriyas or Rajashs issues from his shoulders; the Vaisyas from his belly; and the Sudras from his feet' (Jodhka, 2015: 59). This division into high and low are the essential design of the Varna. Therefore graded privileged and duties are assigned on the basis of their place in the Varna order and also the order of their creation. The upper three Varna are called Dwija or twice born. They have to compulsorily undergo purification ceremony after their birth to attain higher ritual status.

The fourth Varna is called Shudra the lowest and at the bottom of this graded division and it was not prescribed for them.

The Shudra was considered to be of inferior origin and conduct. He is labeled meanest of the above three Varna. 'In the institutes of Manu, they (Shudras) are contrasted with the Brahmans, as being the opposite pole of the social order. The Sudra is declared to be unable to commit an offenses involving loss of caste (they are so low to lose their castes), to be unworthy, to receive a sacrament, and unqualified to hear, learn, recite, or teach the Vedas. The only occupation open to him is that of humble service to the three higher castes' (Woodburne, 1922: 529). The Shudra were further categorized into high and low on the basis of their purity. 'Sudras were of two kinds, "pure" or "not excluded" (Aniravasita) and "excluded" (Niravasita). The latter were quite outside the pale of Hindu society, and were virtually indistinguishable from the great body of people later known as untouchables (Basham, 2004: 144).

The scared religious texts also mention a category of people usually called avarnas (without varna) as contrasted with savarna (with varna). 'The avarnas were not part of Varna system they are called with different names like chandals, pischaha, acchut, panchama. They are often called the "untouchable" in contemporary world identified as dalits or SCs in government records and documents (Wagmore, 2007: 9, Thapar, 2002: 63). According to Deliege, 'Untouchables were known as *chandala, nishad*, a term that designates those who were not allowed to dwell in a town or a village but had to live in special quarters outside the village or town limits, in theory, their main task was the carrying and cremation of corpses...the law books stipulate that chandalas must eat their food from broken vessels and avoid any contact with higher castes, high castes individuals could be reduced to the stats of chandalas by merely touching the latter (Deliege, 2001: 11).

The Brahmins are located at the top of this social pyramid. They stand apart from, and above, the others in the social hierarchy for four principle reasons according to the Brahmin authors of Vedic texts: (1) they were created prior to others therefore take precedence; (2) they are the most complete and perfect instance of the human being; (3) they are learned in the Veda; and (4) they had a monopoly on the priesthood and control of the powerful sacrifice' (Smith, 1994: 32). This hierarchal and differentiated power arrangement was based on the basis of origin, order of origin and the Gunas (nature) they possess. Therefore, the studies of Vedas, austerity, and knowledge, and purity, etc. are of the quality of goodness. Delighting in adventure, want of firmness, indulgence in sexual pleasure are marks of the quality of activity. Cruelty, covetousness, evil life, etc. are marks of dark qualities'. (Ketkar, 1909: 114). Hence, According to Manu the scared law giver, Different categories of people have different kinds of role, duties, and function in this world. Therefore, Brahman has the exclusive right to 'knowledge' (Vedas). The Kshtriyas, as the warriors, have to rule the world as per the *dharmashastra*, he has to preserve the (given) order, the *vaishyas* to do the business and trade, and the fourth one the *shudra* to serve the above three categories (Thorat & Despande, 2001:71).

Farquhar argues, 'The whole system rests on the belief that mankind of not a unity but consists of a large number of species each of distinct origin, and that each man is born into that species or sub-species for which his karma fits him. If he is a very far advanced, in virtue and spirituality, he is born a Brahman; if less advanced, he is born a kshatriya; and so on' (Farquhar, 1919: 164). According to Leach, 'caste ideology presupposes that the separation between different castes is absolute and intrinsic. People of different caste are, as it were, of different species-as cat and dog. There can therefore be no possibility that they should compete for merit of same sort' (Leach, 1969:7). The caste as ideology denies equality and freedom to people by making their status fixed in the society. It forces caste (graded division) on the people as it has religious sanctions therefore it is spiritual, moral and legal according to *shastras*. There is no sphere of life which is not regulated by this principle of graded inequality (Moon, 1987: 107).

Caste: Pervasiveness, Rigidity and Consequences

One of the most severe implications of caste and Varna based division led to huge disparities between different groups. The Varna ideology categorized the roles, duties, functions, assets of different groups according to their place in the Varna. This resulted in clustering and concentration of resources in few hands. The Varna based division brought the Dharma, ritual purity, reincarnation and transmigration of the soul in the central stage. People gave more importance to devotion, worship, maintaining ritual purity, *bhakti, paap, punya, daan-dakshina, pooja-path, havan, karma-kanda, moh-maya, jap- tap, mokshya, samskara* etc. to achieve or raise their position in the next birth. The accumulation and acquisition of *Punya*, austerity, departure from the present became more important in achieving the higher position and mobility in the next birth. One has to continue the dharma prescribed duties, roles and functions in order to fix/reserve or achieve a higher position in the next birth.

The kings acquired the status of god or the incarnation of the god. 'Monarch was considered either the representative of god or next to god. Before the emergence of god as an entity the monarchs considered themselves to be living gods on earth...In course of time the monarch wanted to perpetuate this by justifying the ways of god to men through the institution of religion by constructing temples and maintaining them by grants. Temple became a major institution, hence required a high income. Temples seem to have been well placed because of the grants made by the kings, royal family members, chieftains, officials, corporate bodies such as *sabha, ur, nagaram* and rich and poor individuals...The Pallavas, the Pandyas and the Chola kings were great patrons of temples. The king used to make grants on the day of his birth day, coronation, at the time of leading expeditions, on the occasion of victory in a battle, on the birth of a son, for the prosperity of his son, at the time of renovating, or setting up of divinities, at the time of visiting the temple, while he was camping, for long life, health and victory, while performing *hemagarbha* and *tulabhara* and at the request of others' (Geetha, 2008: 1-18)[1].

The growing importance of the temple and dharma in the public life brought good fortunes to the Brahmins. The grants and gifts received by the temples became their monopoly and rights. The Brahmins had an absolute control over the land especially in some villages which were exclusively reserved for them. 'Apart from land monopoly, the incidence of landownership by Brahmins has traditionally been high in Thanjavur. In 1807, the Tanjore committee in its report recorded that "there is hardly a family of this colony which does not hold land on ordinary *Mirasi* tenure in Tanjore". To substantiate this statement, they quoted the fact that the Brahmins constituted over 27 percent of the total number of *Mirsadars* (62,048). An 1876-77 *Jamabandi* is even more revealing. Out of 136,532 *Pattas* the Brahmins held 37,736, although the entire Brahmin population formed only 6.42 percent of the district's total population' (Menon, 1979: 58).

The superiority of the Brahmins and kshtriyas virtually established all the other human beings inferior. Both of these castes were assigned the role of maintaining the order in the society though the powers vested in them by the sacred scriptures. The Brahmins and the kshtriyas exploited the people in every way possible. While the Brahmins exploited the masses in the name of religion the kshtriyas enjoyed lavish life on the hard work of the masses. They imposed various kinds of taxes on the people. On the other hand laymen professions were taxed and taxes were of primitive in character. *Enikkanam,*

Thalakkanam, Menipponnu, Polipponnu, Mulaivila, Thalaivila, Mulayattikkaram, etc were the taxes that levied from the occupational Jatis during the pre-colonial period. The above first two taxes were collected from toddy [intoxicating drink produced from coconut and palm tree] tappers and the subsequent one, *Menipponnu*, was a tax paid by the subaltern women for wearing gold ornaments Polipponnu was tax levied for marriages, Mulaivila, was a tax paid by workingwomen and Mulayattikkaram from beautiful subaltern [keezhala jatis] women. *Thalaivila*, was the tax collected from every individuals of the subaltern jatis. In addition to it all phases of economic activities were taxed and the Brahmins/Nambootiris and Nairs were exempted from all sorts of taxes' (Philip, 2005: 77-8). These taxes have been collected from the masses only to be donated to the temple and maintenance of the priestly castes' privileges.

The idea of god, divinity, sacredity and infallibility of the Veda and the fixed idea of the world, sacred origin of the castes etc. brought superstition, blindness and irrationality in their lives and customs. While exploring the social and economic life of the people in India, Briggs found certain beliefs and customs like 'New cloths must not be put on a Wednesday, to lend, or to borrow, on Saturday, Sunday or Tuesday is unlucky; and it is not wise to return from a journey on these days. Horses or cattle, or anything pertaining to them, such as leather, *Ghi* or cow-dung, should not be bought, or sold on Saturday or Sunday; and if cattle should die on one of these days, they should be buried. The year's plowing should not be begun on a Tuesday, a Wednesday, a Thursday or a Friday, or on the first or eleventh of the month, and reaping should be begun on a Thursday and finished on a Wednesday...the south is unlucky and the cooking-floor should not face that way, neither should a person lie with his feet to the south...when one is starting on a journey, it is inauspicious to see a jackal cross the road from the right, a crow on a dead tree, or a dog shake his head so as to flap his ears. Under such circumstances a man should return home at once...to see a cat or a crow throwing water on itself is a good omen' (Briggs, 1920: 158-60)[2].

The Brahmanical belief system and orthodoxy made people superstitious, irrational and dependent. This dependence was exploited by the priestly castes to extract as much from the masses. 'Natural calamities were interpreted as a divine wrath, and the people did not raise any doubt about absurd explanations for such calamities, Captain MacMurdo, a political Agent in Kutch, had given, a graphic description o f the attitude of the people of Kutch. When a severe earthquake in June 1839, took a heavy toll of property and people particularly in Kutch, and made people panicky. Belief of the people in divine wrath was exploited by the greedy Brahmins, who declared that those who did not offer feasts and alms to them would be punished, Even the publicity of a letter supposed to be written by a person from *Kashi* was enough to convince the people that after the year 1819, *Satya Yug* would dawn on the earth, only pious people, would be spared and sinners would meet their fate. In fact, people prepared themselves mentally to die on 24th September, 1839, the fateful day, The frightened Muslims declared that a letter from Mecca also indicated the imminent doomsday. The Hindus attributed the cause for this earthquake to a war between gods and demons. Thus, this earthquake gave an opportunity to many charlatans to exploit the superstitious beliefs of the people' (Raval, 1983: 9).

Caste created division led to the development of highly inhuman and cruel customs and practices. While writing about the religious life in India, Debois writes, 'In some districts there are castes which are not to be met with elsewhere, and which may be distinguished by peculiarities of their own. I am not aware, for example, that the very remarkable case of *Nairs*, whose women enjoy the privilege of possessing of several husbands, is to be found anywhere but in Travancore. Among these same people, again, is another distinct caste called *nambudiri,* which observes one abominable and revolting custom. The girls of this caste are usually married before the age of puberty; but if a girl who has arrived at an age when the signs of puberty are apparent happens to die before having had intercourse with a man, caste custom rigorously demands that the inanimate corpse of the deceased shall be subjected to a monstrous connexion. For this purpose the girl's parents are obliged to procure by a present of money some wretched fellow willing to consummate such a disgusting form of marriage: for were the marriage not consummated the family would consider itself dishonored' (Dubois, 1906: 16).

Food and water were one of the most important areas where caste rules were strictly applied. The magnitude and degree of fear of loosing one's caste was so strong among hindus was such that people often preferred to suffer/die rather than accept food and water from caste they assumed to be lower than their's, 'If a Brahman feel thirsty and has no other water but such as is brought by a Sudra near him, he cannot drink it; for caste forbids it at the pain of excommunication" during the times of famines, when there was shortage of food, they abide by their caste rules, they refused food offered to them by Europeans (Murdoch, 1896: 26). It was not only the lower or impure castes who became the victim of brahmanical belief system. But the most powerful authority of the time the empirical British officers too became its victim. In Maratha country, it is only the touch of the lower castes which polluted food. But soldiers from many northern castes are known to throw away their food simply because the shadow of an English officer falls on it. The pretensions of madras Brahmins go farther than that: their food is polluted if a man of low caste looks at it (Ketkar, 1909: 25). People preferred extreme sufferings and pain rather than defy their caste defined rules. Bose writes, 'should a Hindoo of inferior caste happen to touch one of the superior caste, while the latter is cooking or eating, he throws always everything as defiled: even in cases of extreme sickness, the one will seldom condescend to drink water out of the hands of the other (Bose, 1881: 170).

The prejudices against each other were at his height, the same Varna and caste people were not able to accept or tolerate each other. 'One subdivision of a caste feels strong repulsion to another subdivision, because among the latter the use of tobacco is customary; two sections of one caste do not intermarry and feel strong repulsion for each other because they use different kinds of shoes' (Ketkar, 1909: 28). The prejudices and repulsion to each other was so deep and strong that 'the five tribe of Brahmans in the north, known as Gour, would be excommunicated if they partook of a meal sitting together on the same carpet, sir W.W. Hunter says: "in 1864, I saw a Brahman felon try to starve himself to death, and submit to a flogging rather than eat food on account of scruples as to whether the birthplace of north-western Brahman, who had cooked it, was equal in sanctity to his own native district...Mr. Sherringt says: - "the curse of brahmanism has fallen on all native society and blighted it. Each caste, down to the lowest, is eaten up with self-satisfaction and self-admiration. Indeed, it is a notorious fact that the most debased castes yield to none in the punctilious strictness with which they observe caste prejudices and carry out caste regulations". (Murdoch, 1896: 20).

The women lost their as human beings and they became a commodity into the hands of Brahmins. The Brahmins used to keep numerous wives it was socially allowed to them through customs; the same right was not available to the Brahmins women. 'Ishwarchand Vidyasagar collected 133 *Kulin* Brahmin data on this practice in Hooghly district, Bengal. He was horrified to find the magnitude of the problem. One fifty year old man had married 107 times, Bholanath Bandopadhyaya,(age fifty-five) had 80 wives, Bhagaban Chattopadhyaya (age sixty four) had 72 two wives and so the documentation continued' (Forbes, 2004: 22). This data only revealed the situation of Hooghly district only. The situation must be horrible and equally pathetic in other parts of India where Brahmanism was strong. The upper caste women were definitely the victim of brahmanical orthodoxy but they were also the beneficiary of the exclusive upper caste privileges like their men. But the condition of the lower caste women was beyond imagination. The lower caste women were not allowed to wear cloths as mark of respect to the upper caste men and women. 'As an instance a women by name Yesudial of Vilavancode Taluk went to the market at Kaliyakkavilai for purchasing household goods with the upper part of the body covered with cloth. On seeing this, Palamadan Chetty, Pandaram Andipillay and Mallenpillay belonging to the upper class (caste) got angry and she was beaten by them and forced to rid off her upper cloth... even upper class women also did not like the low class (caste) women to cover the upper part of their body in front of them. They even behaved worst than men in performing this injustice. For instance, when the Attingal Rani went to attend a temple festival, a woman of a lower caste appeared in front of her with her body covered with cloth. On seeing her, the Rani got infuriated and ordered to cut off her breast' (Mila, 2009: 92-3). The lower caste had to fight a fierce struggle to cover their body by cloths. Government acts were passed in phases and parts to give them this right.

Besides of the concerns of defilement of one's caste by touch, they also had strong views about the acceptable and unacceptable food, 'when, about a century since, a body of sepoys were being brought from madras to Calcutta, the provisions ran short, till at last the only food consisted of slated beef and pork. Though a few submitted to the necessity of circumstances and defiled themselves, many preferred a languishing death by famine to a life polluted by tasting forbidden food. The *mussulman* governors often took advantage of this prejudice, when their exchequers were empty the *hindoo* would submit to the most excruciating tortures rather than disclose his hoard, but the moment his religious purity was threatened, he complied with any demand, if the sum asked for was within his means; if not, the man being linked to his caste fellows, the latter raised the required sum by subscription' (Bose, 1881: 169-170).

Caste created such fixation to the place of birth that it became a sin to go beyond certain limited both physically and ritually as it resulted in loss of caste. The crossing of the "black ocean" was forbidden for the caste hindus, those who did, were severely penalized and prescribed atonement. 'During in 1824 when the 47 regiment at barrackpur was ordered to go to burma. To the religious hindu, crossing the sea meant loss of caste. The Sepoys, therefore refused to comply. The regiment was disbanded and those who led to opposition were hanged'...in the same ways, Sitaram who had gone to Afghanistan found himself an outcaste not only in his village, but even in his own barracks. The prestige of being in the pay of the company was not enough to hold his position in the society; religion and caste proved to be more powerful (Chandra, 1989: 34).

The most educated and enlightened persons of their time like Ram Mohan Ray went to England, he sought to preserve his caste by taking a Brahman cook with him (Farquhar, 1915: 420). Crossing the boundaries of one's native place was so strong that, Mohandas karamchand. Gandhi was outcasted from his community, *modh bania* in 1888, when the community came to know about his proposed trip to London for study; they never rescinded the proscription (Zelliot. 1998: 71). Hindus did not have much problem to working under authority, but came to revolt when their religious feeling were hurt, the 1857 revolt started just for that. Sepoys proclaimed, 'it is all well known that in these days all the English have entertained these evil designs- first, to destroy the religion of the whole 'Hindustani' army, and then to make the people by compulsion Christians. Therefore we, Sepoys on account of our religion, have combined with the people, and have not spared alive one 'infidel' (Chandra, 1989: 33).

The caste ideology devalued labour and physical work. Dr. K. M Banerjea says, "in civilized countries, every encouragement is held out to the cultivators of the arts, specialty the fine arts. Their professions are esteemed honorable-their labours are simply rewarded by men of taste and refinement...the pernicious system of caste taught a different lesson to the Hindus. The civil architect is branded as a bastard. The carpenter and the goldsmith are accursed, because the Brahmans chose to take umbrage at them. How could the arts flourish in such a society? How could a person of sensibility aspire to distinction in the cultivation of arts which are considered so low?" (Murdoch, 1896: 23). Col. Munro the British Diwan in the Travancore state says, "The most important cause against the growth and progress of India as nation was its casteism (Philip, 2005: 7).

The pervasive and disastrous impact of caste was felt in every sphere of life. Pandit Shiva Nath Shastri while talking about the ill effects of caste on Indian society says, (1) 'it has produced disunion and discord, (2) it has made honest manual labour contemptible in this country (3) it has checked internal and external commerce, (4) it has brought on physical degeneracy by confining marriage within narrow circles, (5) it has been source of conservatism in everything, (6) it has suppressed the development of individuality and independence of character, (7) it has helped in developing other injurious customs, such as early marriage, the charging of heavy matrimonial fees, & c, (8) it has successfully restrained the growth and development of national worth; while allowing opportunity of mental and spiritual culture only to a limited number of privileged people, it has denied these opportunities to the majority of the lower classes, consequently it has made the country negatively a lower, (9) it has made the country fit for foreign slavery by previously enslaving the people by the most abject spiritual tyranny' (Murdoch 1896: 35-6).

The Condition of Untouchables

The caste ideology virtually reduced them to the status below even to animals. They were treated as an object with no subjectivity, feelings and emotions. The caste degraded and pushed them at the bottom in every spheres of life which brought only sufferings, pain and destitution. The basic requirements and natural resources like water, food, cloths, shelter were barely available to them although many animals like rats, snakes, peacock, cow had access to them as they were considered to be sacred. They were treated worst than animals. They face the various disabilities and sanctions in different parts of the country. They could not choose place of their living and were pushed to the most undesirable and non-habitable places. 'the *candala* (Chandala) was not allowed to live in an Aryan town or village, but had to dwell in special quarters outside the boundaries...according to law books the Candala should be dressed in the garments of the corpses he cremated, should eat his food from broken vessels, and should wear only iron ornaments...by Gupta times Candalas had become so strictly untouchable that, like "Lepers" in medieval Europe, they were forced to strike a wooden clapper on entering a town, to warn the Aryans of their polluting approach ((Basham, 2004: 146).

They lost their value as human beings and became a commodity which could be sold or mortgaged as per the will of their masters. Alexander walker drew upon his year of experience in Malabar to make the following observations: 'the *chermas* are absolute property; they are part of the livestock on an estate. In selling and buying land it is not necessary that they should follow the soil; both kinds that of property are equally disposable and may fall into different hands. The Chermas may be sold, leased, mortgaged, like the land itself or like any cattle or thing' (Menon, 2002: 1665). This clearly reveals that the dalits were treated like animals and they were sold without their consent like animals. 'In 1801 Buchanan remarked that in south Malabar, ...by far the greater part of the labour in the field is performed by slaves, or *churmar*[3]. These are the absolute property of their *devarus* or lords and may be employed in any work that their master please. They are not attached to the soil but may be sold or transferred in any manner that the master thinks fit. Only husband and wife can be sold but children may be separated from their parents and brothers from their sisters...Buchanan mentions three modes of transferring slaves here: i) *Janmun*, or sale, where the full value of the slave was given and the property entirely handed over; ii) *Kanam* or mortgage, where the proprietor got a loan and the quantity of rice, to show that his property in the slave was not extinguished, but could be resumed once the loan was repaid; iii) *Pattam* or rent, where the slave was hired out for an annual sum, the hirer paying the cost of maintenance' (kumar, 1962: 343).

There were various kinds of customs to control their access and mobility of the untouchable castes. There were time restrictions on their mobility and they could not spit on the road it their spit could pollute the land 'The untouchable jati Mahar were not allowed to enter the gates of towns after three O'clock in the afternoon and before nine O'clock in the morning because the shadows are at their longest at this time and there was the fear of the higher jatis being defiled of it. In Maharashtra the Mahar jati could spit only in small containers tied around their necks because of the fear that their sputum upon the road might defile some superior Hindus by touching feet. Often if some Brahmin passed their way the Mahars had to destroy the imprints of their feet with brambles and lie down at a distance in order to protect the Brahmin from their shadow' (Philip, 2005: 9). Not only touch, their shadow was impure, people take special care not to get their shadow on them. Consequently they were not allowed near upper caste hearths or wells and they were prohibited from entering the village temple.

The caste Hindu adopted some highly violent and inhuman markers, symbols and practices which separate them from untouchables. During the regime of *peshwa,'* if a caste Hindu walked on the road, the untouchable was not allowed to tread, lest his shadow should defile the high caste Hindus. The untouchable had to tie a black thread on his wrist or nest as a mark, lest the Hindus touch him by mistake. In Puna, the capital of the *peshwas,* the untouchables were decreed to move about with a broom tied by their waist; and, while walking, they were required to sweep off their foot marks with that broom, lest a hindu be defiled by stepping on those foot marks. In Puna, an untouchable had to tie a clay pot by his neck when he walked so that he would spit in that pot, for if he spat on the ground and a hindu stepped on it, the later would be defiled' (Pujari, 2011: 60). 'In south India they were forbidden to enter the streets in which houses of the upper caste were situated' (Velassery, 2005: 8).

Majority of the untouchable caste were landless, they were attached to the land as labourers. Due to the marginal status in land holding and other assets, they were largely dependent on manual work in agriculture. Bayly, writes, 'the lands of a typical Anvail desai would be tilled by household farm-servants whose displays of deference confirmed the status of their patron-propretor. Most of these receivers of the big man's largesse were known by the jati title *Dubla,* and also as *Halis,* a term implying service and maintenance ties which were perpetuated through the institution of hereditary debt-bondage or *halipratha'* (Bayly, 1999: 198). All the agricultural works were not available to them. There was a distinction, they were not allowed to enter in certain processes. Pandya, says, 'no caste restrictions exists in the field of agricultural labour where all sub-caste are found to be working together. Ploughing, sowing and winnowing operations are, however, prohibited to all scheduled caste persons in some parts of Ahmadabad district' (Pandya, 1959: 1).

Kathleen Gough, observes, before 1843 *pallans* (untouchables) were agricultural serfs of landlords of the dominant castes, and today are landless laborers. The *paraiyans,* who were also agricultural serfs in addition beat tom-toms for non-brahman funerals, guard cremation ground and remove dead cattle from the streets of landlords (Gough, 1969: 17). 'Untouchablity was acknowledged in every part of India but adherence to unapproachablity was a special privilege of the caste Hindus of Kerala. Untouchability and unapproachability and fear of pollution disabled the lower castes. The untouchables were not supposed to dress neatly, nor walk on the public roads where even animals like cattle and dogs free to stray wherever they pleased. Thus condition of slaves in Kerala was indeed very dreadful' (Philip, 2005: 50).

Colonial Intervention, Industralisation and Structural Changes

The colonial period was one of the most important phases in the Indian history. They seriously challenged the traditional authority and monopoly of the dominant caste groups. They forcefully or though coercion made the princely class accept their dominance in various spheres. It is especially after the 1857 revolt that they took some serious changes in their policies to govern the country. Kathreen Gough says, 'After the mutiny (1857), British rule and military preparedness became stronger than ever and the rural upper classes of landlord and prices were either crushed totally or co-opted by the British through concessions'(Gough, 1974: 1392). Numerous Indian rulers were deposed and puppets installed in their place, with each of the latter paying "compensation" to the British. The British demanded such wealth which they claimed they would have otherwise had from the plunder of each particular territory. Many of India's rulers preserved their people and territories from British rule by agreeing to pay this tribute. Others, yet to be disposed, were made to pay for the British armed forces used to keep them in bondage. When they had impoverished themselves due to these extractions, the rulers were loaned money by the British officials and others, with interest of around 50 percent per annum. Such payments forced the rulers to raise tax rates or to surrender portions of their land to the lenders' (Shastri, 2014: 4).

They introduced various system of revenue collection on the type, nature, productivity of the land. These systems are called *Mahalwari, Ryotwari and Zamindari*. 'The British gradually transformed land ownership into private property and established the legal basis for capitalist production relations among landlords, tenants, village servants, and agricultural labourers. After various experiments, the government made household of the managerial castes separately responsible for specific amounts of revenue in 1822-23. In 1865, it issue individual tile deeds to share of varying sizes in the village lands, although actual field were not permanently parceled out until 1891-92' (Gough, 1978: 29). British actions led to the commoditization and commercialization of the land and the crops.

On religion and culture, they studied the people, their customs, manners and attitudes, their social relationships, beliefs and practices, rituals and village structure. Before the British there was no attempt to study India it its fragmented diversity human population, animal livestock and natural resources. They introduced various social legislations to ban certain practices which they considered to be inhuman. Under the Diwanship of Col. Munroe the slavery was abolished in Travancore in 1812, By the royal decree, It became illegal to sell or buy the lower caste slaves in the territory of the state (Jebakany, 2011 :144). A similar measure had been undertaken by the rulers of the State of Cochin under the leadership of its able Diwan Nanjappa in the year 1821 of CE (Philip, 2005: 36-7). Later in 1843 the viceroy and his council decided to enact an act for the emancipation of slaves throughout India in 1843. (Beena, 2011: 188). In 1829 Widow burning was prohibited, in 1856 government passed an act legalizing the marriage of Hindu widows, in 1891 age of consent act was passed raising the age of marriage from ten to twelve. Under the pressure from the Christian missionaries and the British authority, the king of Travancore issued a Proclamation in 1863 that the women of Ezhavas and all other caste had the right to cover the upper part of their body (Mila, 2009: 113).

The British rule brought some fundamental changes in the country in different spheres and areas. It shattered the foundation of the Indian society to the deep. "England" Marx wrote in 1853, "has broken down the entire framework of Indian society without any symptoms of reconstitution yet appearing" it has, however, "a double mission to fulfill...one destructive and, and the other regenerative- the annihilation of old Asiatic society [or despotism]- and the laying of the material foundation of western society in Asia." . it has begun the latter by imposing political unity, now [1853] to be strengthened and perpetuated by the electric telegraph; by introducing the first free press in Asia, a " a new and powerful agent of reconstruction" by creating private property in land; by educating Indians and thereby producing " a fresh class...endowed with the requirements for government and imbued with European science"; by connecting India through steam navigation with itself and the world, thereby breaking the isolation " which was the prime law of its stagnation"; and by gifting India "with the means of irrigation and of internal communication [railroad] which will, when completed, liberate her productive powers by revitalizing agriculture and enabling her to exchange what she produces" (Rudolph, 1965: 976-7).

The introduction of railways brought both opportunities and mobility for those who were traditionally controlled by traditions within the village economy. 'Now they could move freely in search for new opportunities. 'the movement was something like an exodus: ' in some part of the country as many as 25 percent of the (the rural male Chamar) are away from home half the year', they were not all working in the tanneries, though tanning remained the occupation where they were most naturally acceptable. The western indian Mahars moved to 'the cotton mills, gin factories, and railways'. The Malas and Madigas of southern Andhra went to the gins and presses. Chattisgarh Chamars were found in the Assam tea gardens, in the railway workshops of kharagpur and chakradharpur, as porters in the railways stations all over the east, and of course, as labourers in Calcutta. Chamars and *moshis* formed the largest relatively homogenous component of labour in the mines and factories in Bengal (Roy, 1999: 170-1). Due to railways, the Dalits could travel to great distance which was not possible earlier.

The successive British policies commercialized and commoditized the land and crops. There occurred significant changes in the land relations both the land owners and the British authority and the labourers who worked on those land. The land became a transferable commodity subject to the payment of the revenue. Many were displaced due to non payment of the revenue or through coercive measures like succession. This also changed the relationship of people with the land. The jajmani system started collapsing which were the backbone of the traditional village economy and also the source of sufferings for the poor masses. The old system were collapsing, there were significant changes in the villages as there were now more means to seek employment in different areas which arose due to industrialization, emergence of railways, opportunities in public works and increase in the trade and commerce.

The labour acquired a new meaning and value during the rule of British; it became a scarce resource and a commodity. Those groups who were traditionally slave and attached to land though Jajmani system benefitted as new opportunities arose outside the village. Roy says 'Large streams of migration began from the mid-nineteenth century, aided by the railways and the telegraphy after 1850, to facilitate this huge reallocation of labour. Men increasingly had to leave home for careers elsewhere. And as competition for land intensified, those with inferior rights to land had to do so more often than before (Roy, 2005: 9). The labour which was till now controlled and regulated by the traditions and customs got freed from the village based traditional economy. The migration was not merely caused to get better livelihood but also caused by the famines, failure of crops, shrinking of agriculture activities, caste oppression in the villages etc.

Famines were the result of the British land and economic policies. The frequency, intensity, degrees of famines increased during British rule. The notorious Bengal famine of 1770 caused the death of 1/3 of the population of Bengal. The worst famines occurred between 1865 and 1899, and the most severe of all in 1896-97, when 97 million were seriously affected at least 4.5 million died. Another 650,000 died in 1898. And further 3.25 million in 1899. In 1860s the principle victims were landless labourers and unemployed weavers...there were 20,687,000 famine deaths in India between 1866 and 1943 (Gough, 1974: 1393). In Bihar and Uttar Pradesh which were traditionally agricultural areas, Samita Sen says, 'in Saran, Chamars, Nonias, Jolahs, Dusads, Binds and Ahars (Ahirs) were the one who applied for relief due to famines. In Patna, 75 percent of relief workers were landless, and in Bhagalpur, too landless laborer predominated. Except in the case of about 10 percent of the workers, most were accustomed to earthwork (Sen, 1999:65-6). One of the major reasons for the migration was the failure of the patrons towards their client. There was no responsibility of the patrons towards their clients. Whenever there was drought and famines, they simply pulled their hand off to take the moral responsibility to support the poor artisans and workers families. Therefore marginal groups tried to find alternative arrangement for their survival.

The frequent famines during British rule were also responsible for the large chunk of migration. Washbrook writes, 'the climate was highly unstable; markets were extremely imperfect; and the fortunes of war blew hot and cold. In the event of famine a continuous threat-notionally large wages and crop-shares might turn out to be worth nothing. Labourers must needs then turn to their patrons for protection and to see them through their difficulties. However, by the number of starving itinerants and vagrants who flooded into the fort and temple towns begging food and charity whenever crops failed, the generosity of regular patrons and employers was not particularly extensive and its quality suffered very little straining. Causalities during famines tended to be heavy, and composed, principally, of the 'labouring' and pariah classes' (Washbrook, 1993: 68).

Another cause of morality of the working groups was the frequent outbreak of epidemics like the plague, cholera and influenza. Twenty three million people died of the disease (cholera alone) in British India between 1865 and 1947. It is estimated that 10 to 15 million deaths occurred during the previous fifty years. Moreau calculated that cholera struck one tenth of the population of the British India and killed one-sixteenth. For the period 1817-31 he postulated an average annual mortality of one and a quarter million, amounting to eighteen million deaths in all. The other commentators elaborated on Moreauy's figures, suggesting that the whole of Indian the number of cholera deaths might have been as high as forty million in only fourteen years (Arnold, 1986: 120-1). The "Guntur famine" in the madras presidency in 1833, cholera killed over two million.

The introduction of railways brought both opportunities and mobility for those who were traditionally controlled by traditions within the village economy. 'Now they could move freely in search for new opportunities. 'the movement was something like an exodus: ' in some part of the country as many as 25 percent of the (the rural male Chamar) are away from home half the year', they were not all working in the tanneries, though tanning remained the occupation where they were most naturally acceptable. The western indian Mahars moved to 'the cotton mills, gin factories, and railways'. The Malas and Madigas of southern Andhra went to the gins and presses. Chattisgarh Chamars were found in the Assam tea gardens, in the railway workshops of kharagpur and chakradharpur, as porters in the railways stations all over the east, and of course, as labourers in Calcutta. Chamars and moshis formed the largest relatively homogenous component of labour in the mines and factories in Bengal (Roy, 1999: 170-1). Due to railways, the dalits could travel to great distance which was not possible earlier.

They migrated in groups, often related with each others on the basis of caste, village and kingship. Chandavarkar says, 'the dominant image of Indian workers has been cast in terms of their peasant character. Migration occurred within the framework of caste, kinship and village connections. Migrants to the city lived with their co-villagers, caste fellows and relatives and sought work with their assistance. In times of distress, it was within these social connections that they found relief. Caste and kinship appeared to form indivisible social units in the city's working class neighborhoods (Chandavarkar, 2002: 10). Caste, kinship and villages association provided that security in distress but it also worked in as divisionary ways when it separated people from each others on the basis of same. Those who migrated had their own social and occupational identity and history which determined their preferences in finding employment which suited their social status and identity.

Even while people were migrating in search of employment and opportunities, they did not loose their traditional identities. Some groups were more inclined towards certain kinds of work. They picked certain works which correspond to their traditional identity and status. People could not cut off their ties with their traditional occupation. When they moved to new working sites they carried their traditions and customs with them. The nature of work was changing; the sites of work were changing but not the notions about work and identities. The old association and identities were reproducing itself in new working sites in the matters of work and occupational preferences. In the early decades of the twentieth century, workers from artisanal castes were predominant among factory workers in kanpur. In 1906, koris constituted 21 percent and Muslims 33 percent of the total workforce in two textile mills. Koris were traditional weavers, and about a third of the total number of Muslims in the mills were julahas or handloom weavers (Joshi, 2003: 78-9).

In Gujarat, 'There was significant presence of 'scheduled caste' who found jobs though jobbers or village fellow men in the emerging textile industry of Ahmedabad... Dalits constituted 35 percent of the survey population...Most of them were vankars and chamars, two castes which were previously known in the Gujarati rural economy as weavers and leather workers respectively. Some processes like spinning, which was known traditionally as an unclean activity, was almost exclusively the domain of the Dalit castes as were many of the tasks that preceded it (working the frame and throstle, reeling). In the same way, a number of steps had to be taken before the actual weaving started (winding, warping, sizing and drawing-in). The specialists in these tasks were largely baxi panch and Muslims (Breman, 2005: 183-9).

Caste maintained its rigidity, and got produced in different work spheres. In most of the unorganized industries the employers get significant advantage of the situation. Structural factors like class, caste and gender have a decisive role in determining one's position in the employment hierarchy. Uma Ramaswami observes, 'mill workers come from wide variety of castes. Perhaps, the only notable aspect of the caste composition of the workforce is that there is very few Brahmins. The villages in the vicinity of the mills once had a large Brahmin population. But Brahmins accorded a poor rating to mill jobs. Most of them acquired education and moved out to the big cities' (Ramaswamy, 1979: 368).

Even when the Brahmins had a clear avoidance to the manual work in the mills and factories but they had a preference towards sitting jobs which did not require much manual labour. For instance, in the study of South Indian factory workers in Bangalore, Holmstrom that, high-caste Hindus (mainly Brahmans) are more represented in managerial and skilled occupations especially in one factory, and middle-caste Hindus are distributed in most jobs except cleaning while Harijans are mostly engaged in technically unskilled and menial jobs like cleaning and in the posts of watch man (Thresia, 2000: 37). There was a clearly production of Varna based caste hierarchy in the occupations and administrative jobs. Those Brahmins who were ready to do the technical, skilled and managerial works 'tend to be the sons of clerks, lower government officials, small businessmen or village landlords (Holmstrom, 1976: 34).

Besides this traditional association with certain work, the traditional villages hierarchies were also produced across different segments and work processes. Morris says 'there are some suggestions that in the spinning department of the Bombay mills, although untouchable groups are a significant proportion of the labour force, there they tend to be restricted to the least skilled classification of those departments' (Morris, 1960: 131).

Kelman writes, 'In many mills in Bombay no untouchable are allowed to work, but in other mills they are employed in the same department as caste Hindus and Muslims. There are curious distinctions, however. A group of Mahar working on front rows by themselves on the coloured side in a winding department "would not be tolerated" among the grey winders in the same room (Kelman, 1923: 86-7).

In Mumbai, 'The caste distribution within the workplace was related both to managerial preferences and to workers practices. The dominance of particular caste in certain departments, koris and julahas in weaving for instance, represented an effort by weaving castes to preserve their space within higher paid category' (Joshi, 2006: 83). In Bombay, Mahars made up slightly under 10 percent of this workforce, maintain from the districts of Satara, Tatnagiri and Ahmednagar. They were concentrated in the spinning depart and menial forms of work, since the more highly paid weaving department barred them from entry due to pollution prejudices (the practice of holding a broken thread in the mouth while repairing it) that in the end were broken by automation rather than any struggle (Omvedt, 2010: 141). Clearly caste has affected not only the composition of the workforce, but also its distribution across various processes within different industrial sites. These different processes were ranked high and low with differential economic gains. Those processes which were the elementary, unskilled, dirtiest, labour consuming and lowly paid were left out for the Dalits. The traditional caste structure was produced in a more secular ways within factories and industrial sites.

The Impact of British on Leather Work and Workers

The colonial rule was the most important phase in the development and expansion of economic activities in India. Leather work emerged as one of the most important and essential industries during British rule in Agra. Hence the impact of colonial rule was positive on leather industry unlike textile and handloom. The demand and supply of leather products during colonial increased phenomenally. Roy says 'Leather probably the most important quasi-services that commercialized during the colonial time' (Roy, 1999: 156). The reasons are many like steady demand for leather goods, investment in industry in the form of capital, technology and expertise, emphasis on quality, introduction of railways for transportation, opening of ports for exports, development and access to markets and emergence of leather trade etc. The work which was considered to be dirty acquired great economic value and dignity.

India was a resource rich country in terms of natural resources which were not tapped and utilized properly. British realized the huge resource base of India which was scattered, underutilized and untapped. They saw great potential and opportunities in animal live stock in India and its scope and potential for economic returns. To exploit the natural resources they brought whole of Indian under their direct jurisdiction and control. They systematically collected data on the animal livestock in India to know the exact numbers, types, and its abundance in different parts so that these resources are used to the optimum. British were the first one to systematically collect animal census in India. According to Royal Society for the Encouragement of Arts, Manufactures And Commerce (RSEAM&C) there were 180 million cattle and 87 millions sheep and goats in India in 1913. According to cattle census of 1924-25 the number of cattle is taken to be 183 million and 87 million sheep and goat (Tiwari, 1938: 1).

The inter-region trade prior to British was minimal due to frequent conflicts, tensions and disturbances between various kingdoms and lack of transportation. British opened various ports, built road network on the commercially important sites. Intelligence, army and police personnel were deployed for the safeguard of trade and controlling crimes. They encouraged trade of leather goods both within the region, outside region and also promoted exports to other countries. The hide and skin trade emerged one of the prominent goods exported from India. Sir Henry Ledgard showed that the total value of India's whole export was 162 million pound of which six commodities accounted for 140 million pound sterling, hides and skin being fifth in the list (RSEAM&C, 1919: 646). It is further mentioned that in 1846-47 the total value of hides was rupees 22,423 which increased to rupees 13,450,913 in 1912-13. The industry was changing so rapidly and showing phenomenal growth under British influence and patronage.

British played an important role in developing the trade related infrastructure for the transportation of the goods. The hide and skin trade emerged one of the prominent goods exported from India. 'The export of Indian hides are mainly to great Britain. But in the case of skins Indian occupies a superior position in the world market, as she produces about 1/3 of the world's exportable surplus of goat skins. No doubt goat skins are also exported by south Africa, china, brazil, Argentina, Mexico, Russia, morocco and turkey, but the position of India is strongest of all' (Tiwari, 1938: 2). There was phenomenal rise in the exports, employment and diversified products under British patronage, and influence.

The colonial authority maintained huge police personnel, military, intelligence and bureaucracy. They needed regular supply leather goods to meet their requirements. Moreover, the British were engaged on many fronts. They were fighting constant wars both within and outside India besides various regional uprisings. The uprising of 1857 and the growing demand for military and civil administrators necessitated the establishment of government harness and saddlery factory at Kanpur in 1867 to undertake tanning of leather to make harness and saddlery for the British army in India. They had to maintain an interrupted supply of leather goods. The few Englishmen that they brought with them were unable to handle the demand. Therefore they employed the low caste workers who were trained to manufacture British style shoes and other goods.

The trade in the hides and skin was increasing due to its steady demand abroad. Leather work as a result was commercialized during this period due to high demand of hides and skins. British moved to manufacture leather products for their military requirements locally. The establishment of factories in different parts led to migration from rural areas to cities where tanneries, abattoirs were established and traditional caste and communities benefited from the increased employment. When the British opened slaughter houses and tanning units it led to a significant change. The economy which was so far controlled and regulated due to religious and culture belief systems started witnessing changes. The animals did not remain mere animals including cows it became a commodity which had a commercial value. It drastically changed the commercial landscape of the cities. According to an estimate about one-quarter of the total 20 millions hides produced annually in the early 1920s came from the slaughter houses (Roy, 1999: 167). The rural leather workers who were earlier dependent on natural death of the animals now started getting more and more employment in the cities in these modern establishments.

Hindus never realized the potential of their own resources as they were governed by their traditional beliefs. They controlled huge livestock without being aware of its hidden value. They let the animals suffer and die natural death rather than put to some productive use. In India most of the animals die due to starvation, diseases and old age causing much suffering to the animals. Whatever leather was available and produced came from naturally dead animals. Roy says, 'The raw hide came exclusively from the 'fallen' animals, that is, naturally dead cattle, or *murdari* as opposed to *halali* in north Indian trade parlance (Roy, 1999: 158). Therefore the animal skin which was acquired from naturally dead animals was not sturdy and firm. It was not suitable for making goods which required toughness and could tolerate pressures. The British required standard quality of leather which they required for their army and civilian purposes. The requirement for leather goods was increasing due to constant engagement of British troops both within and outside in battle and wars.

British were very strict administrators and firm rulers. They had both authority and power to reinforce their will. They opened slaughter houses in various cities undermining and ignoring the religious beliefs of Hindus. Initially slaughter houses were opened in various cities like kanpur, Agra, Calcutta, Bombay which were major center of British activities. Given the associated values against slaughter it was the Muslims and untouchable castes who were employed in these units. The traditional leather workers benefited from it as it provided them not only employment in these factories but also help them establish links with the British directly. Besides working for them as collies, porters, and workers, some of them became contractors and agents who supplied labour of their own caste men to these factories and units (Lynch, 1974: 33). they opened leather tanning units and established factories to manufacture various items like boots, harness and saddlery, leather belts, revolver covers, straps etc which were to be used for police and also for military which was fighting continuous wars across different regions within India and also outside. As the demand of leather goods increased, the few English shoe makers who accompanied the English troops were unable to handle the work and they appear to have employed low caste artisans. According to oral history after some time, these artisans acquired the additional skills that enabled them to work independently (Knorringa, 1999:305).

Muslims and dalits have traditionally been eating meat. They do not have the same religious taboos either eating meat or handing dead animals. Therefore they have been related to meat and leather work traditionally. 'Though Muslims were associated with leather, they were only butchers and not makers of leather articles. Muslim merchant activity spread to leather, which generally considered as socially polluting job by non Muslims (Nihila, 1999: 80). Atul Chandra Chatterjee, observes in 1908 that 'after sugar and cotton, leather is the most important industry in the united province (Oudh). The report noted that there were 341,796 workers both full times and also those involved partially with the work (Chatterjee, 2013: 98). 'The traditional Muslims butchers had a relationship with chamars and acted as middlemen and collected skinned hides from them. With tremendous increase in foreign demand for raw hides and skins, Muslims merchants (leather traders) anmassed much wealth in a short time. The Muslims concentration here as a natural cause and consequence of caste hindu vegetarianism and abhorrence of cow slaughter' (Nihila, 1999: 80).

The first factory was established in Agra in 1892 by two Kashmiri Pandit brothers, Mr. Mohan Krishna Dar and Pyare Krishna Dar under the name of "the Stuart boot & equipment factory limited" in Tajganj on the banks of river Yamuna (Sharma, 1958: 3). Mr. Stuart was a british general who then stationed at Agra helped in obtaining order from military and hence the factory was named after him. This factory was under military patronage and was supervised by the British. After about six years the company failed because of the absence of patronage because of retirement of Mr. Stewart and other reason was tough competition from Kanpur. This factory was, later over taken by the 'Dayalbagh Satsang Sabha', a closed mercantile sect which promote the values of its 'gurus' and renamed it "Dayalbagh Taj Tannery".

The venture of Dar brothers gave a lead to some of the residents of Agra. The Muslim shoe makers and Jatavs established factories on piece work system. It led to huge migration from rural areas to urban and from one region to another. Thousands of Muslims and untouchable castes particularly chamars came and settled in Agra to avail opportunities. Most of the owners of the factories and shoe dealers were Muslims from Punjab and Delhi province. The change of shoe manufacturing from *Desi* shoes to the English shoes attracted many outsiders. Among the persons who came, the late Haji Sayed Munsi Raja Sahib with a humble and moderate background was one of the foremost famous local manufacturers (ibid: 4). Agra also emerged as one of the most important centre for leather tanning, collection and supply of hides and skins. The hides of Agra were superior in quality and were known by the same name because it came from government regulated slaughter houses therefore good in quality. 'In hide and skins trade the commissariat hides are the best possible hides in their class and are confined mainly to Agra and were so named because of the best hides come from commissariat slaughter houses (Tiwari, 1938: 9).

When the demand for leather products increased and large scale manufacturing units came into being during British rule. It was the Muslims and lower castes groups which came to pick up this occupations The British employed Muslims and lower castes in the large factories as they were readily available for this work. 'The colonizers recruited Muslims, who did not have the same notions of purity and impurity and as the Hindus, to manage the units and procurement of hides. But leather was handled strictly by certain lower castes...the Muslims then gradually gained a foothold in this sector. Some of them had been trained in management by the Europeans. Others started to create their own units. Along with the development of tanneries, they took over control of the networks within the British Empire. By the mid-nineteenth century, Muslims had the monopoly of both tanning and manufacturing, which then slowly mechanized (Lalgee, 2009: 37).

The standard requirement for military and civil purposes required standardization in the quality. Therefore they encouraged and promoted research and development in leather. One of the major achievements of transforming the leather industry in the 19th century goes to Charles de Susa, a French Eurasian of Pondicherry. He introduced improvements in the native methods of preparing skins which he had learned Mauritius. He started a tannery in Madras in which the French processes were introduced. He was able to check the tendency of coloration found in the Indian tanned hides on exposure to air. Encouraged by these results, a number of people took up tanning on a large scale. The first modern tanning unit was established in madras in 1845 in madras. This laid the foundation of the tanning industry in Madras but did not extend beyond this presidency. Until the end of the 19th century it enjoyed the monopoly of this segment, of the 48 tanneries in India were located in Madras, while 11 were in Sind, 3 in Calcutta and 2 each in Kanpur and Bangalore. (Sharma, 2003: 15). Besides this, British also introduced scientific method of cutting animal skin so that there are maximum extractions and utilization of skin and less wastage. They introduced new designs and patterns in shoes and other leather goods. The old tool like *raphi* was inadequate to do all the processing of leather work like flaying skin, cutting leather pieces, making shoes and other goods by a single tool. Therefore they devised new tools and machines which were necessary for standard military quality and requirements. These processes prevented large scale wastage of animal skin which incurred due to traditional techniques. They introduced new designs, patterns and shoe making techniques.

One of the important developments which affected the leather industry was the introduction of railways. The animal's hides start rotting if they are not treated soon. The undressed hides started moving from these regions to cities like Bombay, Calcutta and kanpur, Agra. The impact of railways was stronger in leather compare to textile in India. (Roy, 1999: 166). Now due to railways not only the collection of hides improved but these were reaching the tanning cities more quickly. It changed the industrial dynamics in many ways; it promoted inter-region trade which was limited earlier. The traditional centre of hides like Punjab, united province, central province, and western Bihar were connected which were traditionally agricultural regions with abundance of animal livestock benefited from railways immensely.

The World War I proved to be a boom for this industry. The production grew rapidly due to increase demand. The import was stopped due to political disturbances and now there was pressure to fulfill needs from the internal sources. In 1917 Dayalbagh footwear factory limited was established which was the biggest manufacturing factory that time. The increased demand for more shoes lead to more production thus the competition from kanpur and imported goods from Japan and Germany was over. The Cooper Allen Company of Kanpur, a major competitor had to divert its attention to the military requirements. Many new factories were established and leather trade grew significantly. Besides military requirements, these factories also started manufacturing many other goods. As soon as the war stopped the industry started seeing stagnation. The import of shoes from Japan and Germany resumed and factories started finding difficult to sustain. The industry also suffered from the world wide depression of 1930s.

In spite of the difficulties, the industry continued to grow, in 1914 it was 4 while it increased to 20 in 1929 during this period the small karkhanas also increased so was the home based business of Jatav tradesmen. The fortune of the industry changed further with the start of world war II. Military requirements increased. The military demands were fulfilled by big factories like Bata and Flex and hence the civilian demand was left for Agra shoe industry. The demand increased to such an extent that factories started functioning during day and night shifts and the number of workers increased further significantly. It is estimated that production of shoes in the year 1945 increased to 50,000 pairs per day (Sharma, 1958: 5). In the year 1939 the number of workers in the Agra leather industry was 37,000 which grew to 50,000 during 1943-44 (Sisodia, 1960: 6-7).

The untouchable and the Muslims acquired huge money due to the surge in demand of leather goods. Some chamars took to the profitable trade of shoe making and saddler, trading in raw hides and skins as legitimate entrepreneurs. They also found new outlets in large tanneries, especially around Kanpur and Aligarh, with relatively higher wages. In Agra, some families of the chamar caste came to be accepted as credit worthy merchants (Gupta, 2010: 313). It started transforming a traditional caste which was earlier dependent on fallen animals for their livelihood to a caste which now working as a partner in leather trade. The disadvantage of low caste was transforming into an advantage and privilege as they did not have competition from other castes.

The surge in demand of the leather products also resulted in the increasing value of the leather work and the value of workers. 'The price of leather has been increasing due to the leather being procured for the organized tanneries through agents. In the united province region of Oudh particularly in Kanpur the prices of hides and skin have risen 125 percent during the last few years' (Latifi, 1911: 102). The commercialization meant significant increase in opportunities both in terms of employment, profits and trade for those workers who were involved at different levels of work. Many of the low untouchable caste people became wealthy merchants due to their engagement with the hides and skin trade and emergence of factory work. these people were known as *seths* in their influential areas. two of the reputed merchants in the leather industry of Agra were Sita Ram and Man Singh. They acquired enough wealth that they opened many cotton mills before their death in 1890s (Lynch, 1974: 33).

The colonial engagement with the leather work changed the conditions of the leather workers. Besides economic upliftment it also brought social, cultural and political change. The emergence of entrepreneurs among the untouchable castes during the colonial rule also brought huge internal reforms in their own society. They became politically aware and sensitive of their conditions and aims. These rich people also worked for the promotion of education, employment and brought reforms. Their initiatives were carried out by their future generations which later on became more assertive. The new economic confidence also brought new thinking and political assertion. There were many societies, sabhas, associations, federations etc. were formed to further the community interests and goals. These initiatives show the emergence of assertion and political consciousness among the untouchables of Agra.

The untouchable of Agra particularly the Jatavs of Agra found a hero in Ambedkar. They Shared Ambedkar views and followed Ambedkar path which changed their relationship with their old relation and status. A major event in Agra when Ambedkar visited this city some 3000 people converted to Buddhism in 18-19 march 1956 much before the popular Nagpur conversion event. It is significant due to the fact that Jatavs were not from Ambedkar's caste but they shared the vision and goal of Ambedkar. Caste did not come in their way when they followed Ambedkar. There is substantial support for the BSP in Agra due to this historical legacy. The leather workers particularly the Jatavs are the most politically aware and sensitive caste which are the backbone of the BSP.

Conclusion

Most of the dominant approaches to knowledge like the positivist, Marxian and constructionist have blamed colonial period to be disastrous for the masses. It is interesting to see how the different school of thoughts blamed colonial authorities for the plunder of the resources and exploitation of the masses. Most of the dominant approaches to knowledge do not go beyond colonial period while writing the experiences of dalits. There is scant literature on the role of caste during the Muslim rule in the country. It is during the colonial period that rich literature on the Indian society was produced. The missionaries, officials and the colonial authority took serious initiatives to explore the life, habits, customs and the practices of Indian people. The reduction of the Indian history only to certain time frame especially to the colonial period is biased. It does not present and project a holistic and comprehensive picture of the reality in India. It does not take into considerations of the Dalits and their experiences which go well beyond the colonial rule.

The impact of colonial rule on the leather work and workers was positive. The colonial engagement, support and promotion created huge employment opportunities in the leather work. It made the untouchable independent, politically sensitive and provided them stability and boost up their confidence. The colonial rule was exploitative for the India but not everyone suffered equally. The historically marginalized caste groups for the first time witnessed changes which favored them. Their leather craft was acknowledged valuable and they were accorded respect, value and dignity unlike before. This is one of the reasons that colonial period is not seen by them as bad. They achieved considerable employment, success and opportunities due to the promotion of trade and commerce. In their narratives there is critique against the caste rather than the colonial rule. They lived a dehumanized life before the emergence of colonial rule and colonial authority and through missionary activities they managed to get education, dignity and opportunities.

References

Arnold, D. (1986). Cholera and colonialism in British India. *Past & present*, no. 113 (nov.), pp. 118-151.

Basham, A.L. (2004). *The Wonder That Was India: A Survey Of The History And Culture Of The Indian Subcontinent Before The Coming Of Muslims*. London: Picador.

Bayly, S. (1999). *Caste, Society And Politics In India From The Eighteenth Century To The Modern Age*. Cambridge, Uk: Cambridge University Press.

Bose, S.C. (1881). *The Hindoos As They Are: A Description Of The Manners, Customs, And Inner Life Of Hindoo Society In Bengal*, Calcutta: W. Newman & Co.

Breman, J. (2005). The expulsion of labour from the formal sector of the economy. In Bhattacharya, S., & Lucassen, J. (Eds.), *Workers in the Informal Sector: Studies in Labour Labour History 1800-2000* (pp. 177-210). New Delhi: Macmillan India Ltd.

Briggs, G.W. (1920). *The Chamars*. Calcutta: Association Press.

Chandavarkar, R. (2002). *The Origins Of Industrial Capitalism In India*. Uk: The Press Syndicate Of The University Of Cambridge.

Chandra, B., Mukherjee, M., Mukherjee,A., Panikkar, K.N., Mahajan, S. (1989). *India's Struggle For Independence*, New Delhi: Penguin.

Deliege, Robert. (2001). *The Untouchables Of India*. Uk: Berg.

Dubois, A.J.A. (1906). Hindu manners, customs and ceremonies. Oxford: the clarendon press.

Farquhar, J.N. (1919). *The Crown Of Hinduism*. London: Oxford University Press.

Forbes, Geraldine. (2008). *Women In Modern India*. New York: Cambridge University Press.

Geetha, V. (2008). *Land Grants To Temples In Tamilnadu, 550-1200 A.D.* (Unpublished Ph.D thesis). School Of Historical Studies, Madurai Kamaraj Uiversity, Madurai , Tamilnadu, (India).

Gough, E.K. (1969). Caste In A Tanjore Village, In Leach, E.R. (Ed.) *Aspects Of Caste In South India, Ceylon And North-West Pakistan*, Uk: Cambridge University Press.

Gough, K. (1978). Agrarian relations in southeast India, 1750-1976. Review (fernand braudel center), vol. 2, no. 1 (summer), pp. 25-53.

Gupta, Charu. (2010). Feminine, Criminal Or Manly?: Imaging Dalit Masculinities In Colonial North India. *Indian Economic Social History Review*, Vol. 47, No. 3, Pp. 309-42.

Holmstrom, Mark. (1976). *South Indian Factory Workers: Their Life And Their World*. London: Cambridge University Press.

Jebakany, C. J. (2011). *Socio-Religious Movements In South Travancore (1806-1956)*. (Unpublished Ph.D thesis). Department Of History & Research Centre, Nesamony Memorial Christian College, Marthandam, Manonmaniam Sundaranar University, Tirunelveli, (India)

Jodhka, S.S. (2015). Cast(e) On The Hill: ''Divine' Power, Social Cohesion And Hierarchy In Humachal Pradesh, *Economic And Political Weekly*, Vol. L, No. 21, Pp. 59-69.

Joshi, Chitra. (2006). *Lost Worlds: Indian Labour And Its Forgotten Histories*. New Delhi: Permanent Black.

Kain, P.K. (2006). *Barriers To Social Mobility And Its Implications For Well Being In The Footwear Industry: A Case Study Of Jatavs Of Agra*. (Unpublished M.Phil Thesis). Centre Of Social Medicine And Community Health, School Of Social Sciences, Jawaharlal Nehru University, New Delhi, (India).

Kelman, J.H. (1923). *Labour In India: A Study Of The Conditions Of Indian Women In Modern Industry*. London: George Allen & Unwin Ltd.

Ketkar, S. V. (1909). *The History Of Caste In India*, Ithaca, N.Y: Mkssrs. Taylor & Carpenter.

Knorringa. P. (1999). Artisan Labour In The Agra Footwear Industry: Continued Informality And Changing Threats. *Contributions To Indian Sociology*, Nos. 1 & 2, 33:303-328.

Kumar, D. (1962). Caste and landless in south India. *Comparative studies in society and history*, vol. 4, no. 3 (April), pp. 337-363.

Leach, E.R. (1969). Aspects Of Caste In South India, Ceylon And North-West Pakistan. Cambridge, Cambridge University Press.

Lynch, O. (1974), *The Politics Of Untouchability: Social Change In A City Of India*. New York And London: Columbia University Press. [Republished Indian Edition, New Delhi: National Publishing House (1974)].

Menon, D. M. (2002). Religion and colonial modernity: rethinking belief and identity. Economic and political weekly, vol. 37, no. 17 (apr. 27-may 3), pp. 1662-1667.

Menon, S. (1979). Response to class and caste oppression in Thanjavur District, 1940-1952: part two. *Social scientist*, vol. 7, no. 7 (Feb.), pp. 57-68.

Mila, D.R. (2009). *Social Upheaval In South Travancore*. (Unpublished Ph.D Thesis). Department Of History, S.T. Hindu College, Nagercoil, manonmaniam Sundaranar University, Tirunelveli, (India).

Morris, Morris David. (1960). 'Caste And The Evolution Of Industrial Workforce In India', *Proceedings Of The American Philosophical Society*, Vol. 104, No. 2, Pp. 124-133.

Murdoch, J. (1896). Caste: Its Supposed Origin, Its History: Its Effects: The Duty Of Government, Hindus, And Christians With Respect To It: And Its Prospects. London And Madras: The Christian Literature Society For India.

Omvedt, g. (2010). Dalits and the democratic revolution. New Delhi: sage publication

Pandya, B.V. (1959). *Striving For Economic Equality*. Bombay: Popular Book Depot.

Philip, G. (2005). *A Historical Anatomy of The Evolution Of Social Revolution In Travancore*. (unpublished Ph.D. thesis). School Of Gandhian Thought And Development Studies, Mahatma Gandhi University, Kottayam, Kerala, (India).

Pujari, V.K. (2011). *Dr. Ambedkar: Life Of Struggle*, New Delhi: Samyak Prakashan.

Ramaswamy, U. (1979). Tradition And Change Among Industrial Workers, *Economic And Political Weekly*, Vol. 14, No. 7/8, Pp. 367-376.

Raval, R.L. (1983). *Socio-religious reform movement in Gujarat*. (Unpublished Ph.D thesis). Department of history, Gujarat University, Gujarat, (india).

Roy, T. (1999). *Traditional Industry In The Economy Of Colonial India*. Uk: Cambridge University Press.

Roy, T. (2005). *Rethinking Economic Change In India*. London: Routledge

RSEAM&C (1919). Indian industries. Journal of the royal society of arts, vol. 67, no. 3484 (aug. 29), pp. 646-651.

Rudolph, L.I. (1965). The modernity of tradition: the democratic incarnation of caste in India. *The American political science review*, vol. 59, no. 4, pp. 975-989.

Sharma K.B. (1958). *Marketing Of Leather Goods At Agra*. (Unpublished Master's Thesis). Department Of Commerce, Raja Balwant Singh College, Agra (India).

Sharma, M. (2003). *Workers And Leather Industry In Kanpur From 1861 To1947: Transition From Craft To Factory Production*. (Unpublished M.Phil Dissertation). Centre for Historical Studies, Jawaharlal Nehru University, New Delhi, (India).

Shastri, N. (2014). *Economic Transition In The United Provinces Of Agra And Oudh Between 1828-1888*. (Unpublished Ph.D Thesis). Department Of Medieval & Modern History, University Of Lucknow, Uttar Pradesh, (India)

Sisodia, R.J. (1960). *Cottage Shoe Workers In Agra*. (Unpublished Masters Thesis). Department Of Commerce, Raja Balwant Singh College, Agra, (India).

Smith, Brian K. (1994). *Classifying The Universe: The Ancient Indian Varna System And The Origins Of Caste*. New York: Oxford University Press.

Thapar, R. (2002). The Penguin History Of Early India From The Origins To Ad 1300, New Delhi: Penguin Books.

Thorat & Despande, (2001). Caste System And Economic Inequality: Economic Theory And Evidence. In G. Shah (Eds), *Dalit Identity And Politics*. New Delhi: Sage Publications.

Thresia, C.U. (2000). *Work, Gender Relations And Health Of Women Workers In Cashew Processing Industry Of Kerala*. (Unpublished Ph.D thesis). Centre Of Social Medicine And Community Health, School Of Social Sciences, Jawaharlal Nehru University, New Delhi, (India).

Tiwari, R.D. (1938). Leather Industry: Its Transport Problem. *The Journal Of The University Of Bombay*, Vol. VI, Part IV.

Velassery, S. (2005). Casteism and human rights: towards an ontology of the social order. New delhi: Overseas press india pvt. Ltd.

Wagmore, S. (2007). Exploring The Unexplored: Dalit Worldview In Development Discourse. *The Indian Journal Of Social Work*, Vol. 68, Issue 1: Pp. 7-23.

Washbrook, D. (1993). Land and labour in late eighteenth-century south India: the golden age of the pariah?. In Robb, p. (ed.), *Dalit movements and the meaning of labour in India* (pp. 68-85). Delhi: oxford university press.

Woodburne, A.S. (1922). Can India's caste system survive in modern life?. *The journal of religion*, vol. 2, no. 5 (sept.), pp. 525-537.

Zelliot, E. (1998). Gandhi And Ambedkar- A Study In Leadership. In Mahar, J.M. (Ed.), *Untouchables In Contemporary India* (pp. 69-96). New Delhi: Rawat Publications.

Endnotes

1 For more details on this, read Geetha, V. (2008). Land Grants To Temples In Tamilnadu, 550-1200 A.D. (Unpublished Ph.D thesis). School Of Historical Studies, Madurai Kamaraj University, Madurai, Tamilnadu, (India).

2 For more details see chapter VII 'the mysterious' in the religious life of India by Briggs, G.W. pp. 158-197.

3 Buchanan's term churmar, or more properly cheruman, is the name of the caste that formed the bulk of the agricultural labourers in malabar.

11

The Saint Raidas so Called Ravidas, From Leather Worker Turn to Poet-Saint, Social and Religious Reformer of Medieval India: A Review

Dr. Refaq Ahmad*

It is a very glorious day when I am writing this article for National seminar (Edited book) on 'History of leather working castes in India : Social transformation and challenges'. My paper (chapter) is 'The Saint Raidas so called Ravidas, from leather worker turn to social and religious reformer of medieval India : A Review'. I have tried to know about leather worker Raidas in this article. How does Raidas change from leather worker to social and religious reformer. It is very important and attractive historical fact. Besides, I have seen many different issues about the Saint Raidas which provide us knowledge about leather worker Raidas in medieval India.

The age of Raidas was also the age of Bhakti movement in medieval India which was started from south India by great saint Shankaracharya.[1] Which had been moved further by Ramanujacharya, Nimbarkyacharya, Madhvacharya etc.[2] The most prominent saint Ramanand of Bhakti movement had made very popular of this, in

* Department of Medieval and Modern History, University of Allahabad, Allahabad

northern India which was the bridge between the Bhakti movement of the south and the north.[3]

Ramanands was born at Prayag(Allahabad) in a Kanyakubja Brahmin family. He was educated partly at Prayag and partly at Benares. His first teacher was a Vedantist of the monist school, but he became later the disciple of Raghavananda who belonged to Ramanuja's Sri sect. He had an independent mind, he travelled about the country broadening his outlook, and, according to Macauliffe, " It is certain that Ramananda came in contact at Benares with learned Mussalmans."[4]

The result of his experience and discussions was that he made a bold departure from the doctrines of the school to which he belonged. In theological belief he substituted the worship of Rama for that of Visnu and his consort, and he taught the doctrine of Bhakti to all the four castes without prejudice. He rejected the regulations of Ramanuja with regard to the preparation and partaking of meals, and admitted to his new sect disciples from all castes, from both sexes and even from among the Musalmans. The names of his twelve disciples who became famous were Anantananda, Kabir, Pipa, Bhavananda, Sukha, Sursur, Padmavati, Narhari, Raidasa, Dhana, Saina and the wife of Sursura.[5]

The main contribution of Ramananda was to preach the bhakti doctrine of love in the language of the people, bringing Hindu lower castes in contact with direct religious experience as distinct from religious ritual. Most of the eclectic Bhakti poets rose from lower castes.[6] Raidas, one of the disciples of Ramananda, a chamar (shoemaker) of the lowest Hindu caste, wrote verses condemning Brahmanical ritual and caste inequality[7], and used some pseudo-Persian vocabulary. The followers of the Bhakti movement gave themselves the name avadhutas (the emancipated ones) as they had freed themselves from the fetters of caste.[8]

The details of Ravidas' life are not well known. Most scholars said that he was born about 1450, and died about 1520.[9] Ravidas was born in the village of Seer Goverdhanpur, near Varanasi in Uttar Pradesh, India. His birthplace is now known as Shri Guru Ravidas Janam Asthan. His father was Raghram, and his mother was Mata Ghurbinia.[10] His parents belonged to leather working Chamar community, whose profession involved processing dead animals and their skins, which made them untouchable.[11]

While his original occupation was leather work, but he was not interested in this occupation because his nature was like saints and devotees from his childhood he was influenced from Bakhti movement which was tried to end of many evils of society, which was spread in society of that time. Besides, he was interested in the service of sadhus and saints and needy person of society. So, he spent his money on them.[12] He began to spend most of his time in spiritual pursuits as a Vaishnava Hindu in the Ramananda tradition.[13] Thereafter he spent most of his life in the company of Hindu saints, sadhus and ascetics.[14]

The text Anantadas Parcai, one of the earliest surviving biographies of various Bhakti movement poets, introduces the birth of Ravidas as follows.[15]

In Banaras, that best of cities, no evil ever visits men. No one who dies ever goes to hell, Shankar himself comes with the name of Ram. Where Sruti and Smriti have authority, there Raidas was reborn, in the home of a low-caste Shakta, his father and mother were both Chamars.

In his previous birth he was a Brahmin, he listened all the time to religious recitation, but did not give up meat. For this sin, he was born into a low-caste family. but he remembered his previous birth.

Medieval era texts, such as the Bhaktamal suggest that Ravidas was one of the disciples of the Brahmin bhakti sant- poet Ramananda.[16] He is traditionally considered as Kabir's younger contemporary.[17] His ideas fame grew over his lifetime, and texts suggest Brahmins (members of priestly upper caste) used to bow before him.[18] He travelled extensively, visiting Hindu pilgrimage sites in Andhra Pradesh, Maharastra, Gujrat, Rajasthan and those in the Himalayas. He abandoned saguna with attributes, image forms of supreme beings, and focused on the nirguna form of supreme beings.[19] As his poetic hymns in regional language inspired others, people from various background sought his teachings and guidance.[20]

There is no any evidential fact related to the early life of saint Ravidas. As the tradition was in medieval society, that people generally opt heredity profession to spend their life. Saint Ravidas also opted his heredity profession of leather working.[21] There is indication of leather working of Ravidas in his own lines.[22]

Kah Raidas khalas Chamara,

Aisi meri jaati vikhyat chamar.

It is said that earlier the father had involved him in his profession but later on his father separated him because he was not taking interest in his work and spending more money and time in service of saints. Then he started to live in slum behind his home. Now the Raidas was more free and remained pegged in the hymns of God.[23] It is also said that Ravidas never make shoes by killing animals instead he purchased the leather of dead animal to make shoes. It is also famous that he put on shoes to saints without taking its cost.[24]

People were attracted to him by his life of simplicity and contentment, and it is said that a Rajput queen accepted him as her Guru. His hymns breathe a sprit of humility and self-surrender. He did not indulge in high philosophic speculation about the nature and essence of God and his relation with the world and man. His cardinal doctrine are not different from those of Kabir, and like him he uses Rekhta, even the Persian language, and Sufi terms to show the identity of Hinduism and Islam, He believed in a God who was the Absolute Lord of all. [25]

"Govind is immovable, fromless, unborn, unique, of fearless gait, unlimited, beyond sight and reason, indivisible, unqualified, extreme joy."[26]

"Hari is in all and all is in Hari."[27]

And identical with self.

"Thou art I, and the difference between me and thee is like water in a vessel of gold and in the wave."[28]

Thus although he is one he is yet many,

"One is many and many is one Hari, how am I to say that there is a second," and

"He is one, and only two by illusion."[29]

But God is not identical with any of the incarnation,

"The Rama in whom the people recognize Him, they are in error about it, O brother."[30]

Raidas looks upon the world as the play of God, and is inclined to the view that it is illusory or at any rate not worth paying attention to,

"He arranges it like a player (Bazigar),
no one knows the secret of his play.
The play is false, only the player is true,
by knowing this the mind is satisfied."[31]

Again,

"The body is empty, the maya (nature) is empty,
emptily hast thou wasted life without Hari.
The temple and luxurious living are empty,
empty is the dependence on other gods."[32]

Raidas has complete faith in his grace:

"For did he not come to the help of Ajamila,

the elephant, the prostitute,

and if he broke their chains,

undoubtedly he will do the same for him."

Yet there is a pleasing conceit in his attitude:

"Thou hast bound me by chains of illusion (moh),

I have bound Thee with the ropes of love.

I am making an effort to emancipate myself,

but when I attain freedom then who will adore Thee?"[33]

The other attitude, of complete surrender and humility, is him.

"O Rama, Thou alone art wise, thou art eternity without guise,

Thou art King (sultan) of kings. I am thy ignorant broken (shikasta) servant (banda).

I have no manners, no fortune. I am senseless, foolish and given to evil.

I am a sinner, an alien (gharib), heedless, cowardly and black-hearted.

Thou art powerful (Qadir) and capable of taking me across the ocean.

I am greedy and cunning.

This body of mine is shattered and broken, and my mind is full of many apprehensions.

Raidas the slave begs his lord (Sahib) vouchsafe to me a sight (didar) of Thee,"[34]

And therefore he calls upon him out of the depth of his heart.

"Save me, save me, O holy Lord of three worlds."[35]

It is necessary then to give up all external rites, the pilgrimages, fasts, shaving of head, singing and dancing in temples, offering of leaves to idols, and to betake to the devotion of One only, by losing the self on him, as the river loses itself in the sea.

Although,

"My caste is low, my action are low, and even my profession is low,

Says Raidas, yet the Lord has raised me high."[36]

Most scholars believe that Ravidas met Guru Nanak Dev ji, the founder of Sikhism.[37] He is revered in the Sikh scripture, and 41 of Ravidas' poems are included in the Adi Granth. These poems are one of the oldest attested source of his ideas and literary works.[38] Another substantial source of legends and stories about the life of Ravidas is the hagiography in the Sikh tradition, named Premambodha.[39] This text, composed over 150 years after Ravidas' death in 1693, includes him as one of the seventeen saints of Indian religious tradition.[40]

The 17th century Nabhadas's Bhaktamal, and the Parcais of Anantadas, both contain chapters on Ravidas.[41]Other than these, the scriptures and text of Sikh tradition and the Hindu Dadupanthi tradition, most other written sources about the life of Ravidas, including by the Ravidasi (followers of Ravidas), were composed in the early 20th century, or about 400 years after his death.[42]

Anantadas, a writer who belonged to the bhakti poet-saint Ramananda group, wrote a biography of major bhakti poet-saints about 1600 C.E.[43] This text, called the Parcais or Parchais, included Ravidas among the saintwhose biography and poems were included. Over time newmanuscripts of Parcais of Anantadas were reproduced, some in different local languages of India.[44] Winnand Callewaert notes that some 30 manuscripts of Anantadas's hagiograohy on Ravidas have been found in different parts of India.[45]

Of these four manuscripts are complete, collated and have been dated to 1662, 1665, 1676 and 1687. The first three are close with some morphological variants without affecting the meaning, but the 1687 version systematically inserts verses into the text, at various location, with caste-related statements, new claims of Brahmins persecuting Ravidas, notes on the untouchability of Ravidas, claims of kabir giving Ravidas ideas, ridicules of nirguni and saguni ideas, and such text corruption.[46]

Examples of inserted verses in the 1687 version of Anantadas's hagiography on Ravidas, that are not found in the older versions of Ravidas' biography:

Then the king called Raidas , who went to see him along with his companions,

The king said : Listen Raidas; the Brahmins are disturbed and make a lot of noise. (inserted before Chapter 5, verse 1)

We organize donations and worship, but Raidas replied: Listen to me Brahmins,

You deceive the king and the people, you leave the right path and take them on the wrong path. (inserted into Chapter 5, verse 6)

In a low caste you were born, you have no right to perform rituals. (inserted into Chapter 5, verse 12)

Since the earliest times Brahmins have been respected, and even more so in this Kaliyug, Nobody will touch an untouchable, how can he become like a Dahma Brahmin. (inserted into Chapter 5, verse 15)

This nirgun devotion concentrating only one the Name, could not at all appeal to the queen. (inserted into Chapter6, verse 12)

——Winnand Callewaert, The Hagiographies of Anantadas: The Bhakti Poets of North India[47]

Winnand Callewaert considers the 1676 version as the standard version, his critical edition of Ravidas's hagiography excludes all these insertions, and he remarks that the cleaner critical version of Anantadas's parcais suggests that there is more in common in the ideas of bhakti movement's Ravidas, Kabir and Sen than previously thought.[48]

Ravindra S Khare similarly has questioned the textual sources on Ravidas, and mentions there are few "readily available and reliable textual sources on the Hindu and Untouchable treatment of Ravidas."[49]

The Adi Granth of Sikhs, and Panchvani of the Hindu warrior-ascetic group Dadupanthis are the two oldest attested sources of the literary works of Ravindas.[50] In the Adi Granth, forty of Ravidas's poems are included, and he is one of thirty six contributors to this foremost canonical scripture of Sikhism.[51] This compilation of poetry in Adi Granth responds to, among other things, issues of dealing with conflict and tyranny, war and resolution, and willingness to dedicate one's life to the right cause.[52] Ravidas's poetry covers topic such as the definition of a just state where there are no second or third class unequal citizens, the need for dispassion, and who is real Yogi.[53]

Jeffery Ebbesen notes that, just like other bhakti sant-poets of India and some cases of Western literature authorship, many poems composed by later era Indian poets have been attributed to Ravidas, as an act of reverence, even though Ravidas has had nothing to do with these poems or ideas expressed therein.[54]

Peter Friedlander says that Ravidas' hagiographies, though authored long after he died depict a struggle within the Indian society, where Ravidas' life gives a means to express a variety of social and spiritual themes.[55] At one level, it depicts a struggle between the then prevalent heterodox communities and the orthodox Brahminical tradition. At another level, the legends are an inter-communal, inter-religious struggle with an underlying search and desire for social unity. At yet another level, Peter Friedlander says, the stories describe the spiritual struggle of an individual unto self.[56]

There is no historical evidence to verify the historicity in these hagiographies, which range from Ravidas's struggle with Hindu Brahmins,[57] to his struggle with Muslim Sultan Sikander Lodi.[58] Peter Friedlander says that the dtories reflect the social dynamics that influenced the composers of the hagiographies during the 17th to 20th century. These are legends where Ravidas is victorious because God intervened with miracles such as making a stone float in water or making river Ganges to reverse course and flow upstream.[59]

David Lorenzen similarly says that poetry attributed to Ravidas, and championed by Ravidasi (his followers) from the 17th through the 20th century, have a strong anti-communal theme.[60] The legends, suggests Lorenzen, cannot be separated from the power and political situation of this era, and they reflect a strong element of social and religious dissent by groups marginalized during a period when Indian society was under the Islamic rule and later the colonial rule.[61]

The songs of Raidas discuss Nirguna-Saguna themes, as well as ideas that are at the foundation of Nath Yoga philosophy of Hinduism.[62] David Lorenzen says Ravidas's poetry is imbued with themes of boundless loving devotion to God, wherein this divine is envisioned as Nirguna.[63] In the sikh tradition, the theme of Nanak's poetry are very broadly similar to the Nirgun bhakti ideas of Ravidas and other leading north Indian sant-poets.[64] Most postmodern scholars (Karen Pechilis) consider Ravidas's ideas to belong to the Nirguna philosophy within the bakhti movement.[65]

Ravindra khare says that there are two divergent versions that emerge from the study of texts relating to Ravidas's philosophy.[66] The 17th century Bhaktamal text by Nabhadas provides one version, while the 20th century texts by Dalits[67] provide another.[68]

According to Bhaktamal text, Raidas was to pure speech, capable of resolving spiritual doubts of those who held discussions with him, was unafraid to state his humble origins and real caste.[69] Further, the Bhaktamal text states that Ravidas's teachings agreed with Vedic and ancient scripture, he subscribed to nondualism, discussed spiritual ideas and philosophy with everyone including Brahmins without gender or caste discrimination, and his abilities reflected an individual who had reached the inner content state of the highest ascetic.[70]

The 20th century version, prevalent in the texts of Dalit community, concurs with the parts about pure speech and resolving spiritual doubts.[71] However, they differ in the rest. The texts and the prevalent beliefs of the Dalit community hold that Ravidas rejected the Hindu Vedas, he was opposed by the Brahmins and resisted by the caste Hindu as well as Hindu ascetics throughout his life, and that some members of the Dalit community have believed Ravidas was an idol worshipper (saguni bhakti saint) while other 20th century texts assert that Ravidas rejected idolatry.[72]

In fact, there is always protest against excess of ritual and external pomp. Mahatma Buddha had also protested it strictly. It is also said in Upnishad that there is no salvation on the basis of it. This ritual will drown the people in the way without salvation.[73] Saint Raidas also protested traditional Idol worship. His statement was,

"Jo Avinasi sabka karta, Wyapi reh, yo sab thaur re.
Panch tat jin kiya psara, so yo hi kidhu aur re.
Tu tau kehat hau yo hi karta, yanku manic krai re.
Tarni Tarni shakti je yamai, to Aapn kyun na tirai re.
Aamhi bhrose sab jag budha, suni pandit ki baat re.
...Ya ki sev sool bhajai katai na sanshy fans re."

It's means: The God, who is the master of whole world and omnipresent, and is completely present in five element of world ever, His represented could not be this stone idol. On thinking all these he left idol worship.[74] In another place he described,

"Pati tore puji rachavai, taran tran kahai re.

Murti mahi basai parmesur, to paani mahi Tirai re."

It's mean : The test of the power of the Idol saying that If God dwells in Idol, he could be swim in water at least but it drowned itself.[75]

In fact, Ravidas has protested rituals, idol worship and blind faith which were in trend at that time; but it is necessary to clear here that Raidas has protested only the external form of it. While, he forced it's fundamental from, internal worship and life of purity.[76] Raidas said that when there is God's meditation instead of external display in the heart of a person then that person is not harassed by lust and anger and that devotee become got form of God himself. According to him, people should recognize the real and actual form of religion in place of religious rituals and external pomp.[77]

According to saint Ravidas, If any person do all the religious ritual and he have lack of humanity then his all these religious ritual are in vain. Raidas is completely the founder of devotional religious practice also in the field of religious practice. His statement is that the religious seeker should remember God day and night giving up religious dispute.[78]

The fundamental concept of religious practice of Raidas was social reform and public welfare. He consider saint only those people whose works is only public welfare.[79] Kabir also spread his voice for social welfare. While Raidas realized the pain of the society as that time and he solved it by spreading his voice. In the period of Raidas the traditionalism was controlled the society strongly.[80]

Although, the saint and social reformer of earlier period had also raised their voice to get it's solution but complex form of traditionalism was continue as earlier. Raidas, himself had faced this problem in various place of their life in extreme and he protested it at place to place.[81] Raidas was that first saint who presented the thought of this new era in acceptance form. Raidas also started his work of social welfare on religious basis, because in medieval period the social fram was based on religion.[82]

Raidas had given the view of social equality against social injustice at that time. He said about the equal right of every people in the field of religion and devotion. In this way, he declared the great need of new era. Raidas did not consider Hindu-Muslim culture as good. So, he had given the message of fundamental equality and mutual Harmony between these two. In fact, this was a great message of unity in that age of social stress.[83]

At last, Raidas was a North Indian mystic poet-saint of the bhakti movement during the 15th to 16th century.[84] Venerated as a Guru in the region of Punjab, Uttar Pradesh, Rajasthan and Maharashtra, the devotional songs of Ravidas made a lasting impact upon the bhakti movement. He was a poet-saint, social reformer and a spiritual figure. He is considered as the founder of 21st century Ravidassia religion by a group who previously were associated with Sikhism.[85]His family that worked with dead animals and their skin to produce leather products, making them an untouchable Chamar (leather) caste.[86] His name often include the honorific Bhagat, sometimes spelled as Ravidas, Raidas , Rohidas and Ruhidas.[87]

The people were inspired by his simple life and satisfaction.[88] He had protested the external form of religion spread in that society but supported the internal and basic form and emphasized on the devotion on God.[89] Raidas realized the condition of society of that time and had given a pratical solution through religion.[90] Raidas taught removal of social divisions of caste and gender, and promoted unity in the pursuit of personal spiritual freedoms.[91]

In this way Raidas, the symbol of simplicity and brotherhood, started his life from a leather worker and ended it as a famous poet, religious and social reformer. Who is very useful and relevant lesson for present India society.

References

1. Tara Chand, *The influence of Islam on Indian Culture,* Allahabad, 2012, 96.
2. Ibid, 84.
3. Ibid, 143.
4. Ibid, 144.
5. Ibid, 144-145.
6. Yusuf Husain, *Medieval Indian Culture,* London, 15.
7. Ahmed Shah, *Hindu Religious poetry,* Cawnpore, 1925, 40-42.
8. I. E. Carpenter, *Theism in Medieval India,* London, 1919, 428.
9. Arvind Sharma, *The study of Hinduism,* the university of South Carolina press, 2003, 220.
10. Yogender Singh, *The Saint Raidas,* Delhi, 1972, 23-24.
11. James Lochtefeld, *The illustrated encyclopedia of Hinduism* , Rosen publishing, 2002, 569.
12. Yogender Singh, *The Saint Raidas,* Delhi, 1972, 24-26.
13. Hardev Bahri, Harbans Singh, *Ravidas, encyclopaedia of Sikhism,* Patiala, Retrieved, 2017, 40.
14. Ibid, 45.
15. Winnand Callewaert, *The hagiographies of Anantadas : The Bhakti poets of North India,* Routledge, 2000, 307.
16. Rekha Pande, *Divine sounds from the heart-singing unfettered in their own voices,* Cambridge, 2014, 76-77.
17. James Lochtefeld, *The illustrated encyclopedia of Hinduism* , Rosen publishing, 2002, 570.
18. Yogender Singh, *The Saint Raidas,* Delhi, 1972, 19-20.
19. Hardev Bahri, Harbans Singh, *Ravidas, encyclopaedia of Sikhism,* Patiala, Retrieved, 2017, 50.
20. Ibid, 60.
21. Yogender Singh, *The Saint Raidas,* Delhi, 1972, 25.
22. Ramchandra Shukla, *Hindi Sahitya ka itihas,* Vani Prakashan, 2015, 74-75.
23. Yogender Singh, *The Saint Raidas,* Delhi, 1972, 25-26.

24. Ibid, 26.
25. Tara Chand, *The influence of Islam on Indian Culture,* Allahabad, 2012, 179.
26. *Raidas ki Bani,* 25; Tara Chand, *The influence of Islam on Indian Culture,* Allahabad, 2012, 179.
27. Ibid, 7; Ibid, 179.
28. Ibid, 15; Ibid, 180.
29. Ibid, 26; Ibid, 180.
30. Ibid, 6; Ibid, 180.
31. Ibid, 7; Ibid.180.
32. Ibid, 26; Ibid,180.
33. Ibid, 22; Ibid 181.
34. Ibid, 16; Ibid, 181.
35. Ibid, 39; Ibid. 181.
36. Ibid, 20; Ibid, 181.
37. James Lochtefeld, *The illustrated encyclopedia of Hinduism,* Rosen publishing, 2002, 567.
38. Ibid, 568.
39. Peter Friedlander, *Myth and Mythmaking : continuous evolution in Indian Tradition,* Routledge, 1996, 106.
40. Ibid, 107.
41. Winnand Callewaert, *The hagiographies of Anantadas : The Bhakti poets of North India,* Routledge, 2000, 308.
42. Peter Friedlander, *Myth and Mythmaking : continuous evolution in Indian Tradition,* Routledge, 1996, 107.
43. Winand Callewaert, *Pilgrims, Patrons, and place : Localizing sanctity in Asian* Religions, Columbia, 2003, 203.
44. Ibid, 203-223.
45. Winnand Callewaert, *The hagiographies of Anantadas : The Bhakti poets of North India,* Routledge, 2000, 303-307.
46. Ibid, 316-334.
47. Ibid, 315-316.
48. Ibid, 303-307.
49. Ravindra S. Khare, *The Untouchable as Himself,* Cambridge, 1985, 41-47.

50. James Lochtefeld, *The illustrated encyclopedia of Hinduism* , Rosen publishing, 2002, 570.

51. G. S. Chauhan , *Bani of Bhagats,* Hemkunt, 2009, 41-55.

52. Pashaura Singh, *Fighting Words: Religion, Violence, and the Interpretation of sacred texts,* California, 2012, 202-207.

53. J. Kaur, *The concept of peace and the Guru Granth Sahib,* The Indian Journal of political science, Vol. 66, N0.3, 649-660.

54. Jeffrey Ebbesen, *Literary India : comparative studies in Aesthetics, colonialism, and culture,* New York, 1995, 53-55.

55. Peter Friedlander, *Myth and Mythmaking : continuous evolution in Indian Tradition,* Routledge, 1996, 106-108.

56. Ibid, 109.

57. Ibid, 109-110.

58. Ibid, 108.

59. Ibid, 110-112.

60. David Lorenzen, *Bhakti religion in North India: community Identity and political action,* New York, 1995, 105-116.

61. Ibid, 292-303.

62. Peter Heehs, *Indian religion: A Historical Reader of spiritual expression and experience,* New York, 2002, 368-370.

63. David Lorenzen, *Bhakti religion in North India: community Identity and political action,* New York, 1995, 107.

64. Neeti M. Sadarangani, *Bhakti poetry in medieval Indian: Its Inception, cultural encounter and impact,* Swarup and Sons, 2004, 115.

65. Karen Pechilis Prentiss, *The embodiment of Bhakti,* Oxford, 2014, 21.

66. Ravindra S. Khare, *The Untouchable as Himself,* Cambridge, 1985, 41.

67. Ibid, 42.

68. Ibid, 43.

69. Ibid, 44.

70. Ibid, 45.

71. Ibid, 46.

72. Ibid, 163-164.

73. Yogender Singh, *The Saint Raidas,* Delhi, 1972, 72.
74. Ibid, 72.
75. Ibid, 72.
76. Ibid, 73.
77. Ibid, 73-74.
78. Ibid, 74.
79. Ibid, 117.
80. Ibid, 118.
81. Ibid, 118-119.
82. Ibid, 119.
83. Ibid, 119-120.
84. James Lochtefeld, *The illustrated encyclopedia of Hinduism* , Rosen publishing, 2002, 569.
85. J. Kaur, *The concept of peace and the Guru Granth Sahib,* The Indian Journal of political science, Vol. 66, N0.3, 649-650.
86. James Lochtefeld, *The illustrated encyclopedia of Hinduism* , Rosen publishing, 2002, 570.
87. Peter Friedlander, *Myth and Mythmaking : continuous evolution in Indian Tradition,* Routledge, 1996, 106-107.
88. Tara Chand, *The influence of Islam on Indian Culture,* Allahabad, 2012, 179.
89. Yogender Singh, *The Saint Raidas,* Delhi, 1972, 73.
90. Ibid, 120.
91. Ibid, 118-120.

12

Traditional Economy of Leather Working Madigas

Dr. B. Rama Chandra Reddy*

The occupations of tanning and leather work were specialized and recognized as a significant crafts in early India. The earliest known literary work of India, the Rigveda, refers to various types of skin/ leather items. They include the skin to carry water, liquor, poison, honey and curds, the musical instrument skin bagpipe, garments made of the skins of cow and sheep, strong reins and straps made of cow leather. The Maruts was depicted as a god carrying antelope skins on his shoulders and Indra was praised as the one "giving the skin of the deer, well-pressed honey at the winning of prizes".[1] The skins of the deers were seems to have been used to sit on during penance. The first reference of a leather worker, more precisely tanner, also found mentioned in the Rigveda. The hymn runs as follows. "He (Kasu, the lord of the Cedi) who (previously) bestowed on me a king's ten (horses?) of golden appearance- beneath the feet of the lord of the Cedis are (all) the communities, the 'hide-tanning' men all around".[2]

W. Briggs states that the "tanners (*charmamna*) are mentioned in the Rig Veda, later Vedic literature and in

* Head and Associate Professor, Department of History, Bhrathidasan Government College for Women, Puducherry.

the Brahmanas. Tanning, *mla, mna,* is also spoken of in the Rig Veda and certain details of stretching and wetting hides probably refer to the process of manufacture. Ox-hides were used in the pressing of the soma and ox-hides and antelope and tiger skins were used in sacramental and ceremonial rites. The use of skins for clothing is mentioned in the Satapatha Brahmana and in other early literature. The Maruts wore deer skins and the wild ascetics seem to have been clothed in skins".[3] Briggs also mentions that there are references to the thong, *yoktra,* used for yoking the chariot or cart, the bow-string, *jya,* made of ox-hide, reins of leather, leather bags, *driti* and *dhmata,* for holding liquids, leather bottles, *bhastra* and thongs used for couches, *vardhra* for door fastenings, *paricarmanya* and for bridles, *syuman*.[4] The Mahabharata referred to the use of leather variously as the hand guard for the bow, shields (ox-hide/ bear skin), cuirass and abreast-plates and the sword sheaths. It further attests that the war chariot was protected with shields of leather, the box of the chariot was fixed to the axle with thongs of leather, the horses were yoked to the pole of the chariot with leather straps and reins and the drums, especially the great kettle-drums, were fashioned with leather heads.[5]

Manusmriti curiously mentions that shoes were one of the items to be gifted to his teacher by a student after the completion of his studies.[6] In the event of damage done to leather or to the utensils of leather, a fine of five times to the value should be imposed.[7] For killing adulterous women of four castes, a person must give, in order to purify himself, respectively a leathern bag, a bow, a goat or a sheep.[8] Three days fasting was prescribed for stealing leather[9] and no punishment should be inflicted when the leather thongs, the rope around the neck or bridle were broken and when the driver (of a chariot) loudly called to make way.[10] However, Manu opines that Karavara, who works in leather, sprang up due to the union of a Nishada man and Vaideha woman.[11] The leather working communities were referred to with various *jati* names in different parts of India among whom there were hardly any marriage relations that presupposes that each one was a distinct community of its own.

The Madigas

Edgar Thurston and Rangachari state that "the Madigas are the great leatherworking caste of the Telugu country". [12] The first reference of leather working community of the Telugu region appeared from one of the Prakrit inscription of the Amaravathi *stupa* belonging to the early centuries before the birth of Christ. It refers to the gift of a slab with an overflowing vase (*punaghatakapato*) by the Carmakara (leather worker) Vidhika, the son of the teacher Naga.[13] It seems that the leather workers of the Telugu region were called as Carmakaras. As and when the caste name was changed to Madigas is not clearly known. However, from the available literary and epigraphical sources, they were known as Madigas from the medieval period. The etymology of the name 'Madiga' is uncertain. Different versions are forthcoming as to how they got the name of their caste. As per the manuscript of the Adi Jambava Maha Puranam, the caste history of the Madigas found with their teachers (*gurus*) known as Nulaka Chandayyas of Kolanupaka, when the Kamadhenuvu (the mythical cow) died in the rugged hills and none was able to remove the carcass, as per the divine direction one Mala Chennayya went to Sudimanu hills, where Adi Jambava, the ancestor of the Madigas, was undergoing penance and loudly called him "Maha Digi Ra" (O great, come down). He came down and while on his way to complete the assigned duty, the *prana linga* (the sacred phallus) tied to his neck dropped down when he decided to remove the carcass. He was cursed to be called henceforth as 'Madiga'. Hence 'Maha Digi Ra' was transformed into Madiga.[14] However, Gustav Oppert opines that the words Mang and Madiga are corruptions of the name Matanga, an outcaste sage and father of Arundhati.[15]

The Madigas were considered to be at the bottom of the Hindu social hierarchical ladder and were treated as untouchables. They were denigrated for removal of carcasses, peeling off skin of the carcass and eating of tabooed food including the carrion.[16] They were subjected to a variety of disabilities. They were denied to enter into the sacred spaces and dwelling places of elite classes, restricted entry into the village, denial of access to fetch water from public sources, denied the services of servicing communities etc. They were forced to dwell in separated hamlets outside the village known as *Madigapalli/ Madigawada* (Madiga hamlet) whereas it was referred to as *Velipalem/ Velivada* (outcaste hamlet) in the medieval Telugu literary texts.

The leather working Madigas are to be seen in Karnataka and Tamilnadu states also. Nanjundayya and Ananthakrishna Iyer inform that there were two main divisions of Madigas in the Mysore country based on the language they speak, the Kannada and Telugu Madigas, who do not inter-marry.[17] Likewise, the Telugu speaking leather workers, though mentioned as Chukkiliyans in tune with their Tamil counterparts, were found associated with the Telugu cultivating communities of the Tamil region. Hemingway explicitly describes the relations between leather workers and Reddi cultivators of Trichinopoly district[18] and Francis says that the leather workers of South Arcot district were Telugu speakers.[19] It seems that the Madigas migrated to the Kannada and Tamil linguistic regions during the medieval period due to political turmoil along with their patronizing cultivating communities as they strongly tied to them in the traditional patron- client relationship. Another wave of Madiga migration to the Southern linguistic regions took place during the colonial rule to settle in the cantonment areas for manufacturing and supplying the leather goods for military needs like saddles, reins, shoes, tents etc.

The Telugu literary works and the foreign travelogues occasionally made some references to the leather workers and goods. Though, Telugu was regarded as one of the oldest languages of India and some words of the language appeared in the inscriptions and literature before the Christian era, the first complete Telugu inscription appeared only in 575 AD at Kalamalla in Cuddapah district that was issued by the Renati Chola rulers.[20] But, the first Telugu literary work appeared five hundred years later in the eleventh century and Nannaya happened to be the first Telugu poet by translating portions of Mahabharatha into Telugu.[21] Perhaps, the first references pertaining to leather workers and goods appeared in Basavapurana and Panditaradhya Charitra written by Palkuriki Somanatha belonging to the twelfth and thirteenth centuries.[22] Both the works contain some stories of prominent Virasaivite devotees belonging to the leather working communities like the tanners and cobblers. They were emphatically called as *Pedda Bhaktulu* (great devotees). On occasions Somanatha used synonymous names of leather working community as pseudonyms for some characters and in this regard Svapachayya[23] (from Sanskrit *Svapach* for outcaste), Godagara[24] (same as Madiga), Madara[25] Dohara[26] (Tanner), Antyaja (base born) and Madiga[27] could be cited as examples. In the same texts some leather goods were mentioned. In the story of Surasani of Panditardhya Charitra of Palkuriki Somanatha, Lord Siva came to Porandla village in the guise of a Virasaivite Madiga devotee carrying a bundle of hides (*attala mopu*), leather strips (*varenalu*) and thick leather ropes (*mrokulu*) for sale along with his conspicuous implements i.e. a hand knife (*chetikatti*) and an awl (*ari*).[28] Stationed at Masulipatam on the Andhra coast in the early decades of the seventeenth century, Methold wrote that the 'Piriawes' (Madigas so mentioned by him) flayed all the dead cattle for skins and fed upon the flesh. They dressed the skins to make sandals to the Telugu people and shoes to the Muslims and use the remaining skins to 'embale merchandise to defend it against wet'.[29]

Some stray references to a variety of leather articles for various uses are forthcoming from the medieval and early modern literary sources and travelogues from South India, which will be mentioned at appropriate places. But none of them refers to the technology behind the manufacturing of the leather goods. The statement of Abbe Dubois on Hindu attitude towards leather is worth noting in this context. "Leather and every kind of skin, except those of the tiger and the antelope, are held to be very impure. They must never touch with their hands the pantoufles and sandals which they wear on their feet. A person who rides on horseback must have some stuff to cover the saddle, the bridle and stirrup leathers, to avoid all contact with skin. The most disagreeable of all European fashions in their eyes is that of boots and gloves and they hold a man to be extremely unrefined who does not shrink to touch the slough of a carcase. — In speaking or saluting a superior, he must cast off his slippers. He must do it also when he goes into his house. One is not permitted to enter into a cow-shed even, with leather shoes on his feet. Wherever he has occasion to go, he must invariably leave hiss slippers at the door. If he were to pass the threshold of his own house, or of any other, with any integument of leather, it would be considered on all hands as an enormous impropriety." [30] Perhaps, the same despise towards leather, leather goods and leather workers might have prevented the authors of literary texts of medieval period to record their technology. However, the technology of the leather working Madigas was intact till the modern period as it was orally transmitted from generations among the members of the community. Hence, Kancha Ilaiah says that "the Madiga life still remains in oratures, but not in literatures."[31] However, during the colonial rule their technology was registered in ethnographical and scientific reports which may be useful to reconstruct their traditional methods, though not completely.

Leather Tanning

Unlike other leather working castes elsewhere in India, the Madigas flay the skin of dead animals, tanners of hides and manufacturers of leather goods. Hence they are mentioned as 'the first major productive people of India'[32] and 'ancient scientists'.[33] From time immemorial, the Madigas removed the dead domesticated animals, may it be the goat, sheep, buffalo or ox. After carefully removing the skins of the dead animals without any damage, they eat the meat of the carcasses. In the process they share and distribute the meat among their brethren. The remaining flesh, if any, will be salted and dried for future consumption. The removing of the carcass and the eating of the carrion became central to their untouchability as the Hindus regard the dead animal as untouchable.

Then they start the process of tanning the hides, to make them usable leather. They developed the expertise in the art, perhaps, by trial and error method over a period of several centuries. Benjamin Heyne, a Danish surgeon, naturalist and botanist in the service of East India Company, scientifically explored most of the Telugu region at the orders of his superiors in the first decade of nineteenth century. He studied the tanning process in Andhra and says "tanning of leather is the particular province of shoemaker's women, as that of manufacturing it for the market belongs to their husbands".[34] Generally the skins of sheep and goat are used for manufacturing of straps of the chappals and the sole was made with the hides of buffaloes and bullocks. Heyne meticulously explained the tanning process, perhaps, which he witnessed as follows. The fleshy side of the goat skins was applied with quick lime and was soaked in a pot, locally known as *landa totte,* containing two gallons (around ten liters) of water for a day. Though not stated by Heyne, our enquiries revealed that the Madigas add common salt along with the lime while soaking in water. The skins were taken out on the next day and the hair was scrapped off by means of a broken pot or tile. Then two *seers* (about two pounds or a kilogram) of coarsely powdered bark of *Tangedu* (*Cassia Auriculata*) were put into a pot along with the hides and about a gallon (around five liters) water was poured upon them. The hides were allowed to soak for two days. They were then washed and again soaked for a day in similar quantity of bark and water. The process repeated in water containing two *vis* (about six pounds or three kilograms) of Myrobalan (*Terminalia Chebula* or *Karakai*) nuts broken into pieces without the kernels and *Tangedu* bark for a day. The skins were then washed and soaked in water containing one *seer* (half a kilogram) of *Tangedu* bark. After washing and drying, the leather was ready for use to manufacture footwear. The same process was followed in tanning the hides of buffaloes and bullocks, which was used for sole leather. The only difference in the process was the sole leather was soaked longer in the infusion of *Tangedu* bark.[35] Heyne commented that "at Ellore and some other inland places, they use the bark of *Cassia Fistula* (*Raela*) and *Mimosa Arabica* (*Nallatumma*) instead of *Cassia Auriculata* (*Thangedu*)"[36]

Another account of traditional leather tanning process of the Madigas of Bangalore is forthcoming from the account of Francis Buchanan, who journeyed the region around 1800 AD. Firstly the raw hides of sheep or goats washed and cleaned. Then the hairy portion of the skins were rubbed with a paste prepared with equal quantity each of milky juice of the *Yecada* (*Jilledu* or *Asclepias Gigantean*) and salt (*Muriate* of *Soda*) adding an equal quantity of pudding of *Ragi* (*Cynosurus Coracanus*).[37] The skins should be soaked in sufficient water and then the skins were exposed for three days to the Sun. After that the skins were washed and beaten on a stone to take off the hair. The skins were to be soaked again in three to four *seers* (about three to four liters) of hot water mixed with two *seers* (1 213/1000 lb or about 570 grams) of

Terminalia Chebula (*Arulay Myrabolans* or *Karakai*) for three days. Afterwards the skins were to be washed and dried.[38] The tanning of oxen or buffaloes slightly differs from that of sheep and goat. Each skin was soaked in five or six *seers* (1 1/3 ale gallons or around 6 liters) of water mixed with two *seers* (1 213/1000 lb or about 570 grams) of quick lime for eight days. The hair was rubbed off. Again the skin was to be soaked in the infusion prepared by adding ten *seers* (about 6 lb or around 2700 grams) of unpeeled *Tangedu* (*Cassia Auriculata*) wood with ten *seers* (about 2½ ale gallons around 11 liters) of water for four days. Again for equal length of time the skin was soaked in the infusion of water and *Tangedu*. Then the hides were washed and dried in the Sun.[39]

Nanjundayya and Ananthakrishna Iyer also referred to the process of 'primitive way' of leather tanning of the Karnataka region, though briefly, as follows. The Madigas first apply *chunnam* (quick lime) to the hides of cows and buffaloes and keep them for some days. Then in a pit known as *galle,* a lotion of the bark of the *Averlake* (*Cassia Auriculata* or *Tangedu*) plant is made and the skins were soaked in it. They then beat the skins with wooden mallets and stretch them in the sun to dry.[40]

It is clear from the above descriptions that lime, *Karakkai* and the barks of *Tangedu* and Nallatumma were prominently used in the native methods of tanning. Benjamin Heyne and Alfred Chatterton provided a list of natural leather tanning material available in South India. They were *Acacia Arabica* or *Mimosa Arabica* (*Nallatumma*), *Acacia Catechu (Nalla Sandra), Cassia Auriculata (Tangedu), Cassia Fistula (Reala), Mimosa Leucophloea (Tellatumma), Casuarina Equisetifolia (Saruguda), Melia Azedarach (Turakavepa), Mimosa Odorata (Chinduga), Rhizophora Mucronata (Uppuponna), Terminalia Belerica (Tandra), Terminalia Chambula (Karakai)* and *Terminalia Tamentosa* (*Nallamaddi*).[41]

Dyeing of Leather

The tanned leather was dyed in a traditional fashion by using natural products as mentioned by Buchanan. The leather was soaked in a pot for eight days in a decoction prepared by adding a handful each of old iron and the dross or rust of iron forges; five or six skins each of banana and lemon to the gruel of *Cynosurus Coracanus* (*Ragy kanji*). If liquor was rubbed to the skin, it would immediately become black.[42] Buchanan also explained the process of dying red to the skins. Two *Dudus* (about 13 drams or about 23 grams) ungarbled Lac, one *Dudu* (about 11.5 grams) of *Suja cara* or fine soda and Two *Dudus* (about 23 grams) of *Lodu* (*Caesalpinia Sappan?*) bark were powdered and boiled in a *seer* (68 5/8 cubical inches or about a liter) of water for 1½ hour. The decoction was to be rubbed to the leather and was to be put into a pot with Myrobalans (*Terminalia Chebula* or *Karakai*) and water for three days. Then the leather obtains the red colour.[43] Thus the tanned and dyed leather was ready for manufacturing of footwear.

However, the household tanning and dyeing disappeared with the establishment of tanning industries in South India especially in Madras, Ambur, Ranipet, Vaniyambadi, Tiruchurapalli etc. The traditional tanners became the major work force of these industries to eke their livelihood as they were unable to compete with mechanized process.

Manufacturing of Footwear

The references to footwear, though used by humans from time immemorial, are forthcoming from Telugu literary sources and travelogues from twelfth century onwards. In one story of Basavapurana, Svapachayya, a leather worker, covered his meat cooking pot with a sandal (*cheppu*) from the sight of a Brahmin, which would pollute the dish as per his belief.[44] Kridabhiramam, a Telugu text belonging to fifteenth century mentioned leather chappals that makes music at each step (*kirru cheppulu*) normally worn by people of high status.[45] Amuktamalyada, a Telugu work written by Emperor Sri Krishnadevaraya of Vijayanagara in the early part of sixteenth century, in an episode mentioned that a Brahmin went to the outcaste hamlet and purchased a pair of new leather footwear (*malaka*) and applied oil and tied *Tangedu* leaves to it.[46] Perhaps, Amuktamalyada is the earliest, if not the only Telugu literary source, to mention the importance of *Tangedu* in leather work. Some more varieties of leather footwear were forthcoming from medieval Telugu literary sources. *Metlu* (stepped) seems to be a kind of chappals whose heel was made with two or more layers of leather sheets and *godugupavulu* (umbrella chappal), perhaps, protect the feet from sun. The *orrachulu* (country footwear) and *ekavaru cheppulu* (single sheeted footwear) were preferred by the thieves as both of them did not make any sound while moving.[47] Hamsavimsathi, a Telugu work written by Ayyalaraju Narayanamatya, refers to leather footwear worn by a shepherd.[48] The Italian merchant who visited South India in the early part of fifteenth century mentioned that the people wore sandals with purple and golden ties and women had shoes made of thin leather, ornamented with gold and silk.[49] Domingo Paes, a Portuguese traveler, who visited the Vijayanagara kingdom in 1520 AD, mentioned different shoes with pointed ends and those that have nothing but soles, but on top were some straps which help to keep them on the feet.[50] With the arrival of Muslims into South India, shoes seem to have been used occasionally with a pointed raise ends. Invariably many more verities of footwear might have been manufactured by the South Indian leather workers in the past.

The implements of Madagas in the Mysore region as mentioned by Nanjundayya and Ananthakrishna Iyer were *rampi* (small saw), *ari* (awl), *goota* (peg or a hand hammer), *uli* (chisel), *adikallu* (stone to keep the leather while cutting), *kodali* (iron mallet) and *churi* (knife).[51] Kancha Ilaiah mentions that the *aare, rampe, gutam, teedgal, sandan* and *martole* are the key instruments of work of the Madigas.[52] However, our enquiry in the Telugu region revealed that different names of implements, though, used for the same purposes. They are *panrayi* (stone to keep the leather while cutting and smoothing), *ari* (owl), *gootam* (peg or a hand hammer), *kodavali* (sickle) and two to three verities of *kattulu* (knives) and *migkommu* (buffalo horn to keep a mixture of animal fat and ash to apply the awl while stitching).

The process of manufacturing chappal starts with measuring or taking the impression of the foot of the user. The bullock or buffalo leather was cut with sickle and knife into *achu / atta* or sole leather as per the size of the measured foot. The leather of sheep or goat was used to make the appropriate size of *ungutam* or toe loop and *guda* or foot fastener strap. A leather strip known as *mukvaru* was cut to joint *ungutam* and *guda*. Small strips known as *addavarus* were cut to decorate the sandal. By using his traditional instruments, holes were made to fix the strap and strips to the sole. Two or three small cut leather pieces were joined together known as *metlu*, if heel was needed to the chappal. The stitching process was completed by passing the leather thread through the holes made in the sole by an awl.

Silk, velvet, bronze and even gold was used to decorate the footwear. The esteemed of all the chappals of the Telugu region was *kirru cheppulu* also known as *kirrumetllu* normally worn by the people with power, wealth and high social status. They were a kind of chappals which make a creaking sound while walking.[53] The squeaky sound was produced by placing small crisped leather made by using coconut and lemon or by the seeds of *Ummetta* (*Datura Metel*) between the layers of leather.[54] Probably they were used to frighten snakes and scorpions while walking in the rural areas during the nights. The colonial paintings from Madras, Trichinopalli and Tanjore from 1800 onwards clearly reveal that the native cobblers were expertise to manufacture shoes worn by the Europeans. Huizinga, a Christian missionary from Ongole, says "the Madiga's sandals are strong, comfortable, and sometimes highly ornamental. His manner of working and his tools are as simple as his life".[55]

However, one can hardly see a Madiga involving in tanning the leather and making chappals in the rural areas now. The industrialization and corporatization of tanning and shoe making industries took away their livelihood. Many of them joined as industrial labourers and some more opened their own small manufacturing units. Most of them left the profession and a few are languishing in footwear repairing and polishing work mostly in urban areas.

Leather Dress

References to leather dress used by the common people were available during the medieval period, perhaps, manufactured by the Madigas. Amuktamalyada, while describing a Mala Dasari, an untouchable Vaishnava devotee, stated that he was wearing a leather shirt (*tolkubusambu*).[56] Hamsavimsathi, a Telugu work written by Ayyalaraju Narayanamatya, referred to leather shirt (*tolukullayi*) worn by a shepherd.[57] Domingo Paes also mentioned the tunics made of layers of very strong raw leather worn by horsemen.[58] But they seemed to have extinct and very costly leather jackets are manufactured by corporate companies are only available in the market, which are beyond the reach of a common man.

Leather Bottles, Bags and Pots

We came across leather bottles to carry water during the travel and leather bags to hold liquids during the medieval and early modern periods. Amuktamalyada mentioned the squeezing leather cases (*nannirutitti*) to sprinkle rose water.[59] The same work mentioned a Mala Dasari, was carrying leather water bottle (*doltitti*) over his shoulder.[60] Navarrete, a Spanish Dominican missionary, visited Masulipatam and Golconda in the last decades of seventeenth century informed that he purchased a leather bottle at Golconda to carry water during his travel. He stated that it was immensely useful in hot regions as the water poured into it would become very cool in a couple of hours. He praised that the leather water bottle was well worth for his money.[61] Fernao Nuniz, a Portuguese traveler who visited South India in 1535 AD, mentioned that while the Vijayanagara troops were moving, ten to twelve thousand men were supplying water with skin bags.[62] In the later part of seventeenth century Abbe Carre and Tavernier witnessed the transportation of toddy to Golconda in leather bags and bottles on horses and bullocks.[63] In ancient days, the leather bag was the only source of storage for oil, ghee etc. Leather bags were the best refrigerators with regard to liquids. Whatever was stored in leather bags survived for a longer period of time, while retaining quality.[64] In 1904 AD Chatterton stated that "the number of (leather) oil and ghee pots in use in the country (Madras Presidency) is very large, but owing to the nature of their contents their life is a long one. The pots are generally approximately spherical in shape and closed by a wooden bung which fits into a short neck. The use of leather vessels for this purpose is however on the decline as it is found much cheaper and more convenient to store oil in the ubiquitous kerosene oil tin and it is not improbable that eventually the industry will die out as it has done in other countries".[65] As predicted, these leather bottles, bags and pots went out of use in due course of time and they were replaced by tins, rubbers and plastics.

Basket Boats

Domingo Paes, who visited India during the early part of sixteenth century, mentioned the usage of the 'basket boat' to cross Tungabhadra river. He informed that it was made of cane and outside was covered with leather which was able to carry fifteen to twenty persons and even horses and oxen, if necessary.[66] While travelling to Golconda, Tavernier crossed a river in such boats. He described that the boats employed to cross the river were "like large baskets covered outside with ox hides, at the bottom of which some fagots are placed, upon which carpets are spread to support the baggage and goods, lest they should get wet. As for the coaches and carts, they are tied by the pole and wheels between two of these baskets. — There are four men to each basket, one at each corner, who stand and row with paddles. Should one of them fail to keep equal stroke with the others, or if all do not keep time, the basket turns three or four times round, and, the current carrying it down, it descends much lower than the spot where it was intended to land."[67] James Welsh also states that he crossed the Bhawani river near Erode in a 'wicker basket' or coracles covered with hides of considerable dimensions and informs that "in the absence of regular ferries, and having no pontoons with the force, a number of basket boats were made and covered with raw hides on which we contrived to cross all the rivers."[68] These basket boats or coracles are still used at Srisailam in Andhra Pradesh, Hogenakal in Tamilnadu and Hampi in Karnataka, perhaps for tourist attraction, but they are no longer covered with animal hide. Now, they make use of plastic sacking covered with tar as mean of waterproof.

Madigas and Agrarian Economy

The Madiga was invariably a member of the twelve *ayagars* of a village, despite of the variations in different available lists, as leather worker (*Madiga/charmakara*) as per the tradition.[69] As an *ayagar,* he was entitled to receive a piece of cultivable land free of tax. The Madigas were attached to one or more families of agriculturists of a village and were entitled to receive the carcasses of the dead animals of his master's houses.[70] The Madiga had to supply the chappals and the other leather goods needed like the leather bucket for *kabila* or *yatam*, leather straps used to keep the yoke and the plough together (*varena*), thick ropes (*moku*), collar belts (*patteda*), whip thongs (*chernakola*) etc.

Water was lifted from wells and other sources for irrigation in upland areas mainly by two methods namely *Kapile* and *Yatam* for which the services of the leather workers were indispensible. Both of the water lifts need leather buckets designed by the Madigas by stitching leather into a round shape. They were to manufacture and attend the periodical repairs of the buckets. The *kapile* or *kabalai* (Self-emptying *mohte* or bucket) was an ordinary South Indian bullock-lift. It was a big bucket of leather somewhat less than two feet in diameter, continued below a leather tube about four or five inches in diameter between two and three feet long. The oxen work on an inclined plane which slopes downwards from the edge of the well. Descending the slope they drag up the *kapile*, then they are made to back up the slope, and the *kapile* is lowered to the water level. When the *kapile* is being raised from the water, the top of the bucket and the end of the leather tube were level, each being attached to its own rope and the two ropes being dragged simultaneously by the oxen. But the rope attached to the bucket passes over a pulley about four feet above the ground level that attached to the tube, over a roller at the ground level. When the oxen were near the end of their run the open end of the tube was pulled over the roller and as the bucket was raised still higher towards the pulley, the whole of the water in the *kapile* was poured out.[71] The *Yatam* or picottah works on a balance mechanism. A lever or balance attached with a bamboo tied with a leather bucket that could hold nearly 40 liters of water was rested on a fulcrum. The far end of the lever would be loaded with mud or stones of requisite weight. One or two persons would be on the balance. The machine was wrought by man who walks along the balance; coming before the fulcrum, when he wants to sink the bucket and going back again when he wants to bring up the water. Another man attends to empty the bucket. On occasions, one man attending at the mouth of the well performs the whole labour.[72] A Madiga presence was indispensible for both types of lifting methods mainly to fix the leather buckets and to attend the periodical repairs of the leather buckets. Another variety of water lift from nearby ponds was known as *gooda,* a triangular or round shaped basket, which was covered with leather sheet for a possible leakage of water. It was fixed with two leather straps to be operated by two people to fill and drain water.[73]

Further, Athavanavyavaharatantram mentions that the Madigas supply leather ropes, buckets, sandals etc. to the cultivators who pay in return *kolva ginjalu* (grain for supplying ropes for cultivation), *hurihallu* (a tax on cultivators who pay in kind in lieu of straw) and *morabatta* (established fees of village servants). It was said that the Madiga income was substantial that included *morabatta, nijayam* (nearly 20 kg each as customary fees either on plough or field depending on the area), *kolata migulu* (left over grain after distribution between the government and ryot) and *mota cooli* (wages for carrying luggage)[74] Nanjundayya and Anantakrishna Iyer say that a village Madiga had to supply each person who contributes his yearly allowance of grain with a pair of chappals and some leather ropes. He had to supply leather buckets for lifting water with the hides provided by the peasant and attend their repairs. He was required to help at the harvest. For his services, the Madiga gets the bodies of dead cattle, one bundle of unthreshed crop and a winnow full of grain, the leftover grain after the measurement apart from food on important festive occasions.[75] Nanjundayya and Anantakrishna Iyer reported in1931 that "this qualified kind of serfdom has, however, all but died out, except in rural parts".[76] With the modernization and mechanization of agriculture oxen were substituted by tractors and oil and electrical pump sets replaced the traditional water lifting methods. Practically, the Madiga services are no more required to the cultivator and hence most of the Madigas of rural areas took up other occupations for their livelihood.

Madiga's Services to the Village

The Madiga performed many duties as servant of a village. With a beat of *Tappeta* also known as *Dappu*, his traditional musical instrument, a Madiga proclaim the important information or event of the village to the public (*chatimpu*).[77] In certain villages, the Madigas were employed as village watchmen known as *Talaris*, for which service they were entitled to *inam* (rent free) lands. In such cases, they bound to perform free services like carrying loads and acting as guides.[78] The presence of Madiga was mandatory in the festivals observed in honour of the village deities. They had to inform the villagers by their drum beat about the commencement of the festival and they beat tom-toms near the image of the goddess. As per the tradition a Madiga Chindu or sword dance in a rhythmic manner accompanied by the drum beat should be performed during one of the days of the festival. Due to the resistance of the Mala community and the riots associated during such events, the British prohibited the sword dance of the Madigas in 1859 and 1874 AD.[79] The festival of the village deities was always associated with the sacrifice of goats and buffaloes. A Madiga nearly always kills the buffalo with the sacrificial chopper in front of the goddess on the last day of the festival.[80] Then, a Madiga, generally the community head, takes the head of the buffalo with its foreleg in the mouth besmearing the forehead and nostrils with fat and placing a earthen lighted lamp on the buffalo head. The rice soaked with the blood of the animal was put in a basket and a Madiga carries it round the village followed by the males of the village with cries of *'poli, poli'* (food, food) sprinkling it on the ground as he goes.[81] The Madiga would get the sacrificial animal as his share which he partake with the people of his community. However, the festivals of village deities are rarely taking place in many of the towns and villages in recent days. Due to the government restrictions on the sacrifice of buffaloes to the deities and the ban of sword dance, the importance of Madigas in such occasions was lessened.

Madigas Contribution to Industry and Other Servicing Castes

The leather tanned by the Madigas was used in the native traditional iron smelting industry in the Telugu region, a part of which was exported to Persia for the manufacturing of swords. Fortunately, the traditional iron smelting methods of early nineteenth century South India survived in the accounts of Buchanan for Ramagiri region,[82] Heyne for Ramanakapetta,[83] where he saw nearly forty smelting furnaces and Voysey for Kona Samundram.[84] As per Buchanan, the furnace was fixed with two bellows, 'each consists of a whole buffalo's hide, removed without it lengthwise. Where it has been cut at the neck, it is sown up, so as to leave a small opening for a wooden muzzle'.[85] Heyne said that two pairs of bellows were applied to the aperture of funnel. Each pair of bellows was worked by one man. [86] However, Voysey reported that the fire was kept up in the furnace by a blast from four bullock skins, placed at right angles to each other: the muzzles resting on the upper edge of the furnace, so as to force the blast downwards.[87] Kancha Illaiah stated that the leather blowpipe "involved an essential principle of physics that empty space sucks in air. The blowpipe sucks in air from the atmosphere and pushes it in a controlled manner into the hearth. - - The Madiga scientists discovered such an air pumping mechanism several millennia back. And they applied that method to blowpipe in order to advance the production process and to develop an advanced technology of production".[88] The colonization of India and importing of iron and steel from England gave a death blow to the native iron smelting industry and the demand for bellows decreased considerably.

The productive and service castes used certain leather articles carefully manufactured by the Madigas for them. They supply leather for the bellows of the blacksmith (*kolimititti*) to pump air to his fire pit while manufacturing or sharpening of iron implements. Leather sheaths were supplied to carpenters, stone cutters and sculptors to protect their hands (*todugu*) from possible injuries and a leather bag (*titti*) to carry their instruments. The Madigas provided the barbers their leather cases or bags (*kalapapetti*) to carry implements and leather strips to sharpen their razors. The toddy tappers use leather waist belts (*mustyadu* or *patti*), leather covering to their ropes (*moku*) to support them while climbing the trees and *bandam* or *guji* worn around the ankles for safety from slipping which were supplied to them by the Madigas. They also supply the shepherds their waist belts (*nadumpatti*), small bags to keep flints (*chekumuki sanchi*) and leather water bottles (*tolutitti*). Finally, the weaver's looms and the spools were interconnected by leather cords.[89] Many of these items are substituted by rubber and plastic items and the above said communities are hardly depending on the Madigas now.

Madiga Contribution to Musical Instruments

The Madiga services were needed to manufacture many percussion musical instruments those have leather heads. *Tappeta* or *Dappu* was a characteristic musical instrument of the caste. It contains a round wooden ring which was covered on one side by a highly processed piece of leather preferably that of a sheep or goat, which produces a loud sound at the slightest touch. The *Tappeta* is generally slung over the shoulder with a leather strap. With a stick (*Sirre* or *chirra*) in the right hand and a very thin stick (*chitikanapulla*) in the left, the Madiga produces varying types of sounds.[90] It was with the instrument they proclaim any important public announcements (*chatimpu* or *dandora*) and events of the villages. The beating of *Tappeta* was a must for any festival associated with the little tradition.[91] Nanjundayya and Anantakrishna Iyer inform that the Madigas also use a musical instrument known as *Ramdholu*, the big drum for their proclamations in the village.[92] Mysore Archaeological Report informs that a drum by name *Dummana* was also known as *Ramdolu*.[93] It consisted of a bronze cylindrical shell with leather heads on both sides and the braces were thick cotton threads. The instrument was played with either hands or sticks. The drums were also used during the performance of *Oggukatha*.[94] Another typical Madiga musical instrument of the Andhra region was the *Titti*, a bagpipe-like instrument made from an entire goatskin, used while narrating the ballad of Katamaraju by Kommulavaru, a sub sect of the Madigas.[95] The instrument is described as a goatskin with a double-reed inserted into one leg, and a bamboo blowpipe into the other. Air was blown into the bag until it bloated and then released slowly by pressing the bag. The double reed attached to it would vibrate, producing the drone. Lalitha and Nandini inform that the *Titti* was once used in the festivals of Brihadeswara Temple at Tanjore.[96] Another musical instrument used by the Kommulavaru was *Kommu*, a hollow horn, which produces a thunderous noise while blowing. Nagabhushana Sarma opines that it was originally the horn of a bull or a ram polished and covered at both ends with brass.[97] Now the horn is completely made of brass or iron albeit retaining its original name *Kommu*. The *Jamidika* or *Javanika* was a musical instrument mostly played by Bavanidu or Baindla, a sub-sect of the Madigas. It was a barrel shaped drum with one end closed and covered with a thin skin of a sheep or goat. A string was tied at the center of the thin skin, which goes through the inside of the instrument fixed to a stick at the other end. *Jamidika* was used as an accompaniment while singing ballads. Kridabhiramamu, a fifteenth century Telugu work, praises the instrument as 'source of surpassing sound' (*vikaswaraswaravilasa srnivasambu*) and the performer Bavanidu as the 'virtuoso emperor' (*charutarakirthi bavanilachakravarthi*). [98]

The *Mridangam* is a classical drum which is an indispensable accompaniment to both vocal and instrumental music in South India. Its body is bored out of single block of wood. While describing a *Mridangam* of the Government Mueseum of Madras (Chennai), Sambamoorthy says that the right-head of it consists of three concentric layers of skin, the innermost being concealed. Calf skin is used for the outer ring and sheep skin for the inner ring. The left-head consists of two rings, the outer is of buffalo skin and the inner is of sheep skin. The skins fastened to leather hoops and tightened by leather braces are stretched over the two heads. Small cylindrical pieces of wood placed between the shell and the braces help in adjusting the pitch of the instrument.[99] The *Dolu* or *Tavil* is used along with *Nadaswaram* or *Sannai* on important occasions like marriage, temple festivals etc. It consists of a cylindrical shell hollowed out of a solid block of wood. The skins of the two sides are stretched over hempen hoops fastened to the shell and strained by means of leather thongs interlaced. A band of leather passing round the shell along the middle over the braces serves to tighten the instrument up to the desired pitch. The right head is played by the right hand, wrist and fingers and the left head is struck with a stick held in the left hand.[100] The *Tabla* and *Baya* are used in theatrical music and in the Hindustani music parties of North and South India. The shell of these one faced drums is either of wood or metal. The heads of these drums are covered with goat skin and a second skin is attached to the edges of basic skins. The heads are fastened by leather straps at the sides for adjusting the pitch. The *Dolak* is a simpler drum found all over India. The shell is hollowed out of a solid block of wood. The two heads are made of plain leather. The braces are of twine or of thick cotton thread which pass through circular rings of metal near the middle of the shell for tuning. The instrument is played with the hand and sticks.[101]

The *Nagara* is the large hemispherical kettle-drum covered with hide and is used in temples. The shell is of copper or brass riveted together. The skin is strained upon hoops of metal and stretched by leather thongs passing round the underside of the shell. It is beaten with two curved sticks. Bigger varieties of this instrument, known as *Bheri* and *Dundubhi* were used in battles. The Indian epics make mention of these martial drums. The battle drums were regarded with great veneration and capture of these drums by the enemy meant the defeat of the army.[102] The *Damaru,* attributed to Lord Siva, is made of wood or metal with leather drum heads at both ends. The strikers are beads fastened to the ends of leather cords or a leather knot at the end of a string wound round the middle. As the player waves the drum using a twisting wrist motion, the knot strikes the two faces at the centre alternately. The *Damarum* is the pair of conical drums placed on a bullock and seen preceding every temple procession. The shell is of wood and the braces are of leather. It is played with two sticks, one curved and the other straight. *Pambai* or *Pambajodu* is a pair of cylindrical drums made of metal and covered with skins. It is played with two sticks. The twine braces pass through metal rings which help in tuning. Leather is also used in the manufacturing of other percussion instruments like *Udukkai, Davandai*. *Suryamandalam* and *Chandramandalam* used in the temple of Sri Kalahasti, *Timila, Idakka* etc.[103] Invariably, the leather workers might have supplied the leather used in the making of all these instruments. Many of these instruments are used even now in the temples, rituals and festivals. It is a million dollars question as to why leather and its manufacturer became unclean and untouchable in Hindu tradition despite of using leather musical instrument even in the inside of the temples. Perhaps, leather is sanctified whereas its manufacturer remained untouchable.

Leather Puppets

In Andhra Pradesh the coloured shadow leather puppetry, *Tholu Bommalata* literally means "the dance of leather puppets", was a primitive dramatic art in the rural areas which popularized Hindu epics and local folk tales among the people. It was one of the most popular forms of entertainment in the Telugu region atleat from the medieval period. The skins of deer and goat were used in the manufacturing of leather puppets. Deer skins were used for auspicious characters like gods and epic heroes and all other puppets were made from goat skin. However, due to scarcity of deer skins, those of goats were substituted in due course of time. No process of tanning was involved while preparing the skin in the preparation of leather puppets. The wet skin of goat or deer was dipped in warm water and the hair was completely removed by means of a sharp knife. The properly cleaned skin was allowed to dry and the entire process will take nearly two weeks. The dried skin looks very clear, white, translucent, thin and of about 1/32 inches in thickness. The skin should be devoid of any smell or odour.[104] The skin was ready for being cut into the shape of the required figure. Generally three dried skins are required to complete a figure with the moving parts namely the head, trunk and the limbs .Nagabhushana Sarma informs that a total of ten pieces were required for a large puppet. [105] The puppeteer with his skilled artistic capacity draws the outline of the figure on the dried skin from which he has to produce a figure by stitching. Then they were painted with different natural colours, but replaced by those of chemical in due course of time as in the case of most crafts. The help of leather workers were needed for curing and cutting of the leather in requisite shapes. However, leather puppet shows went into oblivion and became a nostalgic memory to the older generation.

Leather in Military Service

The leather working Madiga supplied many things for the use of army in forts and military camps during the medieval period. They provided leather vests, waist belts, wrist bands, scabbards, shoes, saddles, bridles, catapults, stockings, hide ropes, leather water bags and big hide bags.[106] They supplied gun powder cases and even tents. The leather workers also provided their services to the military officers and sepoys or native soldiers of the English in the initial years. The military requirements of leather can best be understood by looking into the books on military establishments. A military communication of 1703 AD informed that ammunition was carried in leather pouch suspended by a broad buff belt over the left shoulders hanging over the right hip, a bayonet and a scabbard was attached on the left side to a broad buff waist belt.[107] A 1707 order of Fort St. George states that the leather workers were employed in the military should manufacture scabbards, pouches, cartridge boxes, gunpowder casks, binding books and painting during the times of peace.[108] Another order of Fort St. George, 28 March 1798, stated that the 'swords of the Native Cavalry shall in future be suspended by a shoulder-belt and that the cartridge belt shall be worn on the belly, the strap of the belly box to be connected with the sword-belt', which seems to be an early attempt to create a Sam Browne belt.[109] A look into the military uniform of East India Company clearly reveals the importance of leather. They include accoutrements, boots, jackboots, leather breeches, waist, pouch and sword belts, harness, leather gloves, spurs, pouch belt and brown leather belts, gun powder cases and pouches and later for cartridges and holster for pistols.[110] Apart from them, leather saddles, bridles, musket leather sling, belt with frog for bayonets, tents etc. also forthcoming from the records. It should not be forgotten that the Vellore Mutiny of 1806 was erupted due to the introduction of a new kind of turban with leather cockade and plumes.[111] It created a furore as leather was a taboo for upper caste sepoys of the Madras army. Many sepoys believed that the Company was conspiring to convert them to Christianity.[112]

In a typical colonial fashion, Chatterton commented, seems to be an European understanding also, that the output of the native leather worker was varied. "Under skilled supervision and supplied with good materials, he turns out excellent work. Boots and shoes, harness and saddlery, can be obtained in Madras, of local manufacture but of imported material as well made, in respect to finished appearance and durability, as one could wish for. But beyond the influence of European ideas in regard to the appearance of things, the work done by the native chuckler is rough and clumsy, and there are no leather workers in this Presidency whoso productions have at any time reached a standard of excellence in the least degree approaching that which is comparatively common among metal and wood workers. The reason, no doubt, is the extreme inferiority of the raw material and the uselessness of expending labour in the decoration of articles which must necessarily be of an ephemeral character. Excluding agricultural implements, the most commonly manufactured articles are sandals and shoes."[113]

Later on all harness, saddlery and accoutrements needed for Madras military were manufactured in the Madras Arsenal by using native labour mostly belonging to the leather working castes. Soon, the Government Harness and Saddlery Workshops was started in the old buildings of the Government Gun Powder Factory at Vesarpaudy to meet the increasing demand. In 1898 Government Harness and Saddlery Workshops was started in the Perambur Barracks which was the only large leather factory in the Madras Presidency by the beginning of twentieth century. The factory employed nearly 400 leather workers per day on average in 1904 AD. It manufactured the harness and saddlery for horse, field and heavy artillery, mountain artillery, British and Native Cavalry regiments, all pack transport equipment for the Supply and Transport Corps, accoutrements for British and Native Infantry Regiments and Volunteer Corps, all leather work for Field Gun Carriages, all Gymnasia Stores and Miscellaneous Equipment.[114]

Summary and Conclusion

Leather and leather workers were referred in the ancient Indian Hindu sacred lore. The Madigas were the leather working community of the Telugu speaking region. The reference to Andhra leather workers appeared nearly two thousand years ago in one of the inscriptions of Amravathi *stupa*, though not mentioned with their present nomenclature. They appeared with their caste name Madiga in the twelfth century Telugu literature. However, the Midaga caste histories (*kulapuranas*) hail them as the earliest inhabitants. They were treated as untouchables due to their occupation of removing animal carcasses, flying their skins, leather working and eating the carrion. As they were attached to the agriculturists, they too migrated with their patrons to the neighbouring Tamil and Kannada linguistic regions. Unlike other leather working castes of India, the Madigas were experts in skinning, tanning, dyeing of leather and manufacturing various leather products. They tanned and dyed the hides in traditional methods using natural products in a scientific manner known only to them. The medieval and early modern Telugu literature and the foreign travelogues mentioned different verities of artistic footwear, which were manufactured by the Madigas with their simple instruments and technology. They also made leather apparels, leather cases, water bottles, bags to carry loads and liquids and leather pots for storing ghee and oil. They also provided hides to the once famed coracles to cross the rivers and other water bodies. The Madigas played a pivotal role in the rural agrarian economy by providing various leather products useful to the agriculturists and acted as one of the members of the traditional South Indian village body, the *Ayagars*. Their technology and services were indispensible for traditional water lifting methods. With his traditional musical instrument known as *Dappu* or *Tappeta,* he kept the villagers informed about various events and played an important role in festivals associated with the little tradition. Their services were needed to the iron smelting industry for supplying bellows. The Madigas also supplied leather products to the servicing and other productive castes. Apart from preparing the musical instruments conspicuous to their community, they provided skins and thongs to percussion instruments used in public concerts and temple rituals. In the arena of public entertainment, he was the manufacturer of the puppets for once famed leather puppet shows. The leather workers also served the military during the medieval and early modern period by providing the needed material for the armed forces. It should not be forgotten that the Vellore Mutiny erupted due to the introduction of a new head dress containing a leather cockade. Due to all these activities, he received substantial income to lead a decent life apart from supporting not less than five of his dependent castes namely Nulka Chandayyas, Baindlas, Chindus, Mastis and Dakkalis. Though he was treated as untouchable, his products were sanctified for all practical purposes.

All that is stated above was the glory of the past in South India. Now the Madigas are struggling for their survival. Though there is no dearth in their technology, they lost their traditional economy. Their profession was no more lucrative. If industrialization and corporatization hit hard on their major occupations of leather tanning, dyeing and shoe making; the modernization and mechanization of agriculture took away their livelihood. The non-profitable nature of agriculture, increasing urbanization and resultant migration of agriculturists to the nearby urban localities on various pretexts made the life of Madigas miserable as they were attached to traditional agricultural communities. The substitution of metals, plastics, nylons and rubbers to leather products gave a death blow to their profession. Many Madigas left their traditional occupation for alternative professions and a few are languishing in footwear repairing and polishing works, mostly in urban localities. The deplorable condition of the Madigas is best depicted by their own traditional musical instrument *Dappu* or *Tappeta*. The process of replacing the leather head of their traditional drum by a plastic one is nearing completion.

Acknowledgement- *My profound thanks are due to Prof. Yagati Chinna Rao, Chairperson, Centre for Study of Discrimination and Exclusion, School of Social Sciences, Jawaharlal Nehru University, New Delhi for his constant encouragement in my academic activities and for forcibly dragging a reluctant person like me due to obvious reasons into Dalit Studies. I thank Dr. K. Srinivasulu, Former Head, Department of History, C.S.R. Sarma College, Ongole; Dr. Avadhanam Umamaheswara Sastry, Kamareddi and Dr. D. Venkateswara Reddy, Assistant Professor, Acharya Nagarjuna University Ongole Campus, Ongole for their inspiration and encouragement. Thanks are also due to Prof. Thallapally Manohar, Professor and Theegala Sreenivas, Research Scholar, Department of History and Tourism Management, Kakatiya University, Warangal for providing the necessary information in times of need and patiently answering my layman's queries.*

Endnotes

1 *Rigveda*, 1, 85, 5; I, 191, 10; IV, 23, 8; , IV, 45, 1; V, 34, 7; VI, 49, 18; VIII, 5, 19; VIII, 48, 5; IX, 2, 7 and IX, 70, 7. Stephanie W. Jamison and Joel P. Brereton, Tr., *The Rigveda: The Earliest Religious Poetry of India*, Oxford University Press, New York, 2014, pp. 215; 398; 594; 629; 699; 841; 1036; 1129; 1236 and1303.

2 *Rigveda*,VIII, 6, 37, Stephanie W. Jamison and Joel P. Brereton, Tr., *op.cit*., p.1037.

3 Geo w. Briggs, *The Religious Life of India: The Chamars*, Association Press, Calcutta and Humphrey Milford, Oxford University Press, London, 1920, pp. 11-12.

4 *Ibid*., p. 12.

5 *Ibid.*, pp. 12-13.

6 G. Buhler, Tr., *Manusmriti: The Laws of Manu, Sacred Books of the East, Vol. 25*, Clarendon Press, Oxford, 1886, Chapter II, Verse No. 246. The other preferable items to be gifted were a field, gold, a cow, a horse, a parasol, a seat, grain and vegetables.

7 *Ibid.*, Chapter VIII, Verse No. 289.

8 *Ibid.*, Chapter XI, Verse No. 139.

9 *Ibid.*, Chapter XI, Verse No. 167.

10 *Ibid.*, Chapter VIII, Verse No. 292.

11 *Ibid.*, Chapter X, Verse No. 36.

12 Edgar Thurston and K. Rangachari, *Castes and Tribes of Southern India*, Asian Educational Services, New Delhi and Madras, 2001 (originally published in 1909), Vol. IV, p. 292. However, Siraj Ul Hasan gives different names of the community with explanation. He says that they were also called Madigowd, Madigaru, Madru, Dher, Chandal, Antyaja, Ettlwandlu, Peddintiwandlu, Panchamollu, Matangi Makallu, Gosangi, Kamathi, Bendar and Chambhar. The name 'Ettiwandlu ', for example, signifies those who do the *etti* or *begari* (forced) work. 'Chambhar' is a corruption of the Sanskrit word 'Charmakar', which means 'a worker in leather' and the word 'Kamathi' indicates that they are menials. Some, such as 'Chandal', 'Antyaja' (lowest born), 'Gosangi, (*gao*, cow, and *hansaka*, killer) and 'Dher' are opprobrious titles applied to them by others to indicate their lowest status in Hindu society. To dignify themselves, the members of the caste have assumed such epithets as Matangi Makkalu, the children of Matangi, the daughter of their mythical ancestor Jambavan; Panchamollu or members of the fifth caste, as distinguished from the four *shastric* divisions of mankind (Brahman, Kshatriya, Vaishya and Shudra) and 'Peddintiwandlu', or dwellers in big houses. For more details see Syed Siraj ul Hassan, *The Castes and Tribes of H. E. H. the Nizam's Dominions*, Vol. I, Times Press, Bombay, p. 409.

13 The Prakrit inscription runs as follows

i. *Siddam carmakarasa Nagaupajhayaputasa Vidhikasa samatukasa sabhayakasa sabhatukasa putasa ca Nagasa sama dhutukasa sanatimitabamdhavasa deyadhamma*

ii. *Punaghatakapato*

(Translation- Success. Meritorious gift of a slab with an overflowing vase (*punaghatakapato*) by the leather worker (*carmakara*) Vidhika, the son of the teacher Naga, with his mother, his wife, his brothers, his son Naga, his daughter and with his *jnatis* (paternal cousins in the male line entitled to property) friends and relations.) C. Sivaramamurti, Ed., *Amaravati Sculptures in the Madras Government Museum*, Director of Stationary and Printing, Madras, 1977, No. 41, p. 281.

14 Pulikonda Subbachari, Ed., *Kolunupaka Nulaka Chandayyala Adi Jambava Maha Puranam* (Telugu), Dravida Viswavidyalayamu, Kuppam, 2008, p. 67.

15 Gustav Oppert, *On the Original Inhabitants of Bharatavarsha or India*, Asylum Press, Madras, 1893, p. 66. Syed Siraj ul Hassan provides three more versions as to how they were known as Madigas. See, Syed Siraj ul Hassan, *op. cit.*, pp. 409-412.

16 The caste history of the Madigas state that they became untouchable due to the removal of carcass, eating of cow meat (of Kamadhenuvu) and manufacturing of leather goods including the shoes. For more details see Pulikonda Subbachari, *op.cit.*, p. 69; Jayadheer Tirumala Rao, et.al., Ed., *Dakkali Jamba Puranam* (Telugu), Janapada Prachurana, Hyderabad, 2011, pp. 188-191.

17 H. Nanjundayya and L. Anantakrishna Iyer, *The Mysore Castes and Tribes*, The Mysore University, Mysore, 1931, Vol. IV, p. 132.

18 F. R. Hemingway, *Madras District Gazetteers- Trichinopoly*, Government Press, Madras, 1907, p. 118.

19 W. Francis, *Madras District Gazetteers- South Arcot*, Government Press, Madras, 1906, p. 75. The other Telugu speaking castes as mentioned by Francis were Komati traders, Devangas, Sales and other weaving castes, the Reddi and Kamma cultivators, Odde earth workers, the Balija shop keepers and bangle makers.

20 P.V. Parabrahma Sastry ed., *Inscriptions of Andhra Pradesh: Cuddapah District*, Part I, Government of Andhra Pradesh, Hyderabad, 1977, No. 2 and K. Srinivasulu and Avadhanam Umamaheswara Sastry. *Renati Cholulu* (Telugu), Authors, Kadapa, 2007.

21 Velcheru Narayana Rao and David Shulman, Tr., and Ed., *Classical Telugu Poetry: An Anthology,* University of California Press, Berkeley, 2002, pp. 2-3.

22 Veturi Prabhakara Sastry, Ed., *Basavapuranamu Palkuriki Somanthudu,* (Telugu) Veturi Prabhakara Sastry Vagmaya Pitamu and Tirumala Tirupathi Devastanamulu, Tirupathi, 2013; Velcheru Narayana Rao, Tr., *Siva's Warriors: The Basava Purana of Palkuriki Somanatha,* Princeton University Press, New Jersy, 1990; and Chilukuri Narayana Rao, Ed., *Sri Panditaradhya Charitra, Palkuriki Somanatha Pranithamu* (Telugu), Andhra Granthamala- 30, Andhra Patrika Press, Madras, 1939.

23 Veturi Prabhakara Sastry, Ed., *op.cit.*, pp. 218-219; Velcheru Narayana Rao, *Siva's Warriors, op.cit.*, pp. 240-241.

24 Veturi Prabhakara Sastry, Ed., *op.cit.*, p. 209; Gudavalli Venkata Subramanyam, Ed., *Dvipada Basava Puranam, Palkuriki Somanathakavi Pranitham (sankshiptamu),* (Telugu), Andhra Pradesh Sahitya Academy, Hyderabad, 1969, p.229; Velcheru Narayana Rao, *Siva's Warriors, op.cit.*, p. 232.

25 Veturi Prabhakara Sastry, Ed., *op.cit.*, pp. 217-218; Velcheru Narayana Rao, *Siva's Warriors, op.cit.*, p. 305. P.B. Desai, *Basavesvara and his Times,* Karnataka University, Dhrawar, 1968, p. 202.

26 Veturi Prabhakara Sastry, Ed., *op.cit.*, pp. 220-221; Velcheru Narayana Rao, *Siva's Warriors, op.cit.*, pp. 242-243.

27 Veturi Prabhakara Sastry, Ed., *op.cit.*, pp. 221-223; Velcheru Narayana Rao, *Siva's Warriors, op.cit.*, pp. 243-245.

28 Chilukuri Narayana Rao, *op.cit.*, pp. 116-132; Velcheru Narayana Rao and David Shulman, Tr., Ed., *Classical Telugu Poetry, op.cit.*, p. 78

29 William Methold, 'Relations of the Kingdome of Golchonda and other Neighbouring Nations within the Gulfe of Bengala, Arreccan, Pegu, Tannassery, etc. and the English Trade in those Parts' in W.H. Moreland, *Relations of Golconda in the Early Seventeenth Century,* The Hakluyt Society, London, 1931, p. 19

30 G.U. Pope, Tr., *A Description of the Character, Manners, and Customs of the People of India; and of their Institutions, Religious and Civil,* by the Abbe, J.A. Dubois, J. Higgin Bothams, London, Madras, 1862, pp. 84 and 154.

31 Kancha Ilaiah, *Post-Hindu India: a Discourse on Dalit–Bahujan, Socio-Spiritual and Scientific Revolution*, Sage, New Delhi, 2009, p.25.

32 *Ibid.*

33 N. Kanakaratnam, *Madiga: Ancient Scientist & Great Humanist*, Sujay Publications, Nalgonda, 2011.

34 Benjamin Heyne, *Tracts, Historical and Statistical on India; with Journal of Several Tours through Several Parts of Peninsula*, Black, Parry and Co., London, 1814, p. 182.

35 *Ibid.* Our enquiry revealed that during the process of tanning the flesh that was attached to the skin was removed with a knife and it was known as *jallakottuta*.

36 *Ibid.*

37 Buchanan says a fourth part of a kind of soft paste, made of 6 *Dudus* (2 456/1000 ounces or about 70 grams) weight of milky juice of the Yecada and about 6 *Dudus* weight of salt and twelve *Dudus* weight of Ragy Sanguty be applied to each skin. Francis Buchanan, *A Journey From Madras Through the Countries of Mysore, Canara, and Malabar*, Vol. I, Asian Educational Services, New Delhi, 1999 (First Published in 1807), p.227.

38 *Ibid.*

39 *Ibid.*, p. 228.

40 H. Nanjundayya and L. Anantakrishna Iyer, *op.cit.*, p. 165.

41 Benjamin Heyne, *op.cit.*, pp. 182-184. Alfred Chatterton, *Monograph on Tanning and Working in Leather in the Madras Presidency*, Government Press, Madras, 1904, pp. 24-28.

42 Benjamin Heyne, *op.cit.*, pp. 227-228.

43 *Ibid.*, p. 228.

44 Veturi Prabhakara Sastry, Ed., *op.cit.*, pp. 218-219; Velcheru Narayana Rao, *Siva's Warriors, op.cit.*, pp. 240-241.

45 Vallbharaya, *Kridabhiramamu*, (Telugu), Vavilla Ramaswamy Sastrulu and sons, Chennapuri, 1960, Verse No. 162, p. 29. Velcheru Narayana Rao and David Shulman, Tr., *A Lover's Guide to Warangal: The Kridabhiramamu by Vinukonda Vallabharaya*, Permanent Black, Delhi, 2002, p. 60.

46 *Sri Krishnadevaraya's Vishnuchittiyamanu Namantaramugala Amuktamalyada Savyakyanamu* (Telugu), Vavilla Ramaswamy Sastrulu and sons, Chennapuri, 1914, (Henceforth *Amuktamalyada*), Canto. VI, No. 71, p. 536 and Srinivas Sistla,

Tr. *Sri Krishna Deva Raya Amuktamalyada,* Author, 2010, p. 424.

47 For more details see P. Hymavathi, "Leather Technology and Industry in the Vijayanagara Empire", *South Indian History Congress Proceedings Volume of the Fourteenth Annual Session*, Tirupati, 1994, pp.229- 236.

48 Ayyalaraju Narayanamatya, *Hamsavimsathi,* (Telugu), Srungarakaya Gandha Mandali, Machilipatnam, 1938, Chapter 4, No. 76, p. 42.

49 "The Travels of Nicolo Conti in the East in the Early Part of the Fifteenth Century" in R.H. Major, Tr., *India in the 15th Century Being a Collection of Narratives of Voyages to India in the Century Preceding the Portuguese Discovery of the Cape of Good Hope from Latin, Persian, Russian and Italian sources,* The Hakluyt Society, London,1857, pp. 22-23.

50 "Narrative of Domingo Paes" in Robert Sewell, *A Forgotten Empire (Vijayanagara): A Contribution to the History of India,* Asian Educational Services, New Delhi, 2000 (First Published in 1900), p. 252.

51 H. Nanjundayya and L. Anantakrishna Iyer, *op.cit.*, p. 166.

52 Kancha Ilaiah, *op.cit.*, p.37.

53 P. Percival, *Telugu-English Dictionary, with the Telugu Words Printed in The Roman, as Well as in the Telugu Character: Intended for the Use of European Officers, Soldiers and others employed in the Several Executive Departments under the Government of Madras,* Public Instruction Press, Madras, 1862, p. 130 and P. Sankaranarayana, *A Telugu- English Dictionary,* Kameswara Rao Brothers, Madras, 1900, p. 210.

54 N. Kanakaratnam, *op.cit.*, p. 11.

55 Quoted in Alfred Chatterton, *op.cit.*, p. 18.

56 *Amuktamalyada,* Canto. VI, No. 5, p. 488 and Srinivas Sistla, *op.cit.*, p. 394.

57 Ayyalaraju Narayanamatya, *op.cit.*, Chapter 4, No. 76, p. 42.

58 "Narrative of Domingo Paes" in Robert Sewell, *op. cit.*, p. 276.

59 *Amuktamalyada, op.cit.*, Canto. IV, No. 35, p. 229 and Srinivas Sistla, *op.cit.*, p. 262.

60 *Amuktamalyada,* Canto. VI, No. 5, p. 488 and Srinivas Sistla, *op.cit.*, p. 394.

61 J. S. Cummins, Ed., *The Travels and Controversies of Friar Domingo Navarrete, 1618-1680*, Vol. II, Published For the Hakluyt Society at The University Press, Cambridge.1962, p. 306.

62 "Chronicle of Fernao Nuniz" in Robert Sewell, *op.cit.*, p. 328.

63 Charles Fawcett Ed., Lady Fawcett, Tr., *Travels of Abbe Carre in India and the Far- East 1672-1674*, Vol. II, Asian Educational services, New Delhi, Madras, 1990(First published in 1947), pp. 353-354 and William Crooke, Ed., V. Ball, Tr., *Travels in India by Jean Baptise Tavernier Baron of Aubonne*, Book I, Low Price Publication, Delhi, 2000, p. 128.

64 Kancha Ilaiah, *op.cit.,*, p.39.

65 Alfred Chatterton, *op.cit.*, p.41.

66 "Narrative of Domingo Paes" in Robert Sewell, *op. cit.*, p. 259.

67 William Crooke, Ed., V. Ball, Tr., *op. cit.*, p. 235-236. For an account of Henry Whitehead in 1906 while crossing Tungabhadra river near Hampi in a wicker boat stated as follows. "It consists of a very large, round wicker basket, about eight or nine feet in diameter, covered over with leather, and propelled by paddles. As a rule, it spins round and round, but the boatmen can keep it fairly straight, when exhorted to do so, as they were on this occasion. Some straw had been placed in the bottom of the coracle, and we were also allowed the luxury of chairs to sit upon, but it is safer to sit on the straw, as a chair in a coracle is generally in a state of unstable equilibrium." Edgar Thurston and K. Rangachari, *op.cit.*, Vol. III, p. 2.

68 James Welsh, *Military Reminiscences Extracted from a Journal of nearly Forty years of Active Service in the East Indies*, Smith, Elder & Co, London, 1833, Vol. II, pp. 194 and 263.

69 *Ayagars* were a group of village officers governing the village. It derived from a root word *Ayam*. Wilson informs that *Ayam* means "toll, tax, tribute, custom and measurement. In the Dakhin, the portion of the crop formerly paid to the hereditary village officers and servants". He also says that *Ayakar* or *Ayagar* was "a village servant or officer, one entitled to the *Aya*, or proportion of the crop, for his services to the community" and they were "the officers and servants of a village, the whole establishment, the Balute of the Maratha countries." H. H. Wilson, *A Glossary of Judicial and*

Revenue Teems, and of Useful Words Occurring in Official Documents Relating to the Administration of the Government of British India, from the Arabic, Persian, Hindustani, Sanskrit, Hindi, Bengali, Uriya, Marathi, Guzarathi, Telugu, Karnata, Tamil, Malayalam, and other Languages Compiled and Published under the Authority of the Honorable the Court of Directors of the East India Company, Wm. H. Allen And Co, London, 1855, p.41. But Soma Reddy says that *Ayagars* were the people who hold *Ayams* or fields of a certain extent granted to them free of tax by the villagers or by the state as payment for undertaking public service. The list supplied by Athavanavyavaharatantram includes 1. *Senabogu* (accountant) 2. *Gaudu* (headman) 3. *Kammari* (Black smith) 4. *Badige* (Washerman) 5. *Agasa* (Goldsmith) 6. *Panchanga* (priest) 7. *Vayidya* (Barber) 8. *Madiga* (cobbler) 9. *Agasarlu* (Carpenter) 10. *Talari* (Watchman) 11. *Neruganti* (Waterman) 12. *Kumbara* (Potter). Ibharapuram Kaifiyat of Cuddapah district lists them as 1.*Purohitudu* (Priest), 2. *Karanam* (Accountant), 3. *Nambi* (Vaishnava temple priest) 4. *Tamballa* (Saivite temple priest), 5. *Kumara* (Blacksmith) 6. *Vadlavadu* (carpenter), 7. *Mangalavadu* (Barber), 8. *Chakalivadu* (Washerman), 9. *Polimera Kapu* (Headman), 10. *Talari* (Watchman) 11. *Malavadu* 12. *Dopalavadu* (person for tom-tom /cobbler). The list of Kamalapuram of Cuddapah district consists of 1. *Purohita* (priest), 2. *Lekhaka* (Accountant) 3&4. *Devalakadvayam* (the priests of Siva and Vishnu temples) 5. *Ayakarah* (blacksmith) 6.Vadrangi (carpenter) 7. *Ksuri* (barber) 8. *Rajaka* (washerman) 9. *Padaja* (the protector of village boundary or Reddy) 10. *Padavijneya* (person who knows footprints or watchman) and 11&12. *Antejatidvayam* (the two low castes or Mala and Madiga) For more details see M.P.R. Reddy Ed., *Athavanavyavaharatantram: A Mackenzie Manuscript (April 1802)*, Mackenzie Records Vol. 154 (Fdl. 22-28) preserved in the Government Oriental Manuscript Library, Madras (Henceforth Athavanavyavaharatantram), Centre for Historical Studies, Kavali, Undated, p. 5; Athavanavyavaharatantram was collected by Kavali Venkata Borraiah, one of the assistants of Col. Mackenzie. It was a document drawn up in the 18th century by an anonymous author at the request of one of the earliest officers of East India Company, who desired to know the manner and working of the government during the Vijayanagara Empire. Hence the document explained the village administration and various taxes collected during the Vijayanagara rule. *Meckenzie Kaifiyattulu, Kadapa Jilla,* (Telugu) C.P. Brown Basha Parisodhana Kendram and Yogi Vemana Viswavidyalam, Kadapa, 2007, pp. 53-54 and R. Soma Reddy, See Chapter. 17 "The Ayagar System in Medieval Andhra Desa" in R. Soma Reddy, *Studies in the Socio- Economic History of Medieval Andhra Desa*, Research India Press, New Delhi, 2007, pp. 137- 145.

70 Edgar Thurston and K. Rangachari, *op. cit.*, Vol. IV, p. 309.

71 Gilbert Slater, Ed., *Some South Indian Villages*, Oxford University Press, London, 1918, p.21 and Benjamin Heyne, *Op.cit.*, pp. 260- 261.

72 "Machines for Irrigation" in *Gleanings in Sciences*, Vol. I, No. 10, October, 1829, pp. 298-301; Francis Buchanan, Vol. I, *Op.cit.*, pp. 263 and 294.

73 Thallapally Manohar, Ed., *Cultural History of Madigas- A Brief Study*, Pragma Publications, Hyderabad, 2016, p. 24.

74 *Athavanavyavaharatantram*, pp.5-12. See also H. H. Wilson, *op.cit.*, pp. 211 and 345.

75 H. Nanjundayya and L. Anantakrishna Iyer, *op.cit.*, p. 166.

76 *Ibid.*, p. 166.

77 *Ibid.*, p. 167.

78 *Ibid.*, p. 165.

79 Edgar Thurston and K. Rangachari, *op.cit.*, Vol. IV, pp. 294-295. For more details about the reason of opposition of Mala community see N. Sudhakar Rao, *Organised Power and unorganized Resistance*, Aravali Books International, New Delhi, 1998, pp. 205-206.

80 Henry Whitehead, *Village Gods of South India*, Asian Educational Services, New Delhi, 1999 (First Published in 1921), pp. 44 and 73.

81 *Ibid.*, pp. 54-62.

82 Francis Buchanan, Vol. I, *Op.cit.*, pp. 170- 175.

83 Benjamin Heyne, *op.cit.*, pp. 218-226.

84 Voysey, "Description of the Native Manufacture of Steel in South India", in *The Journal of Royal Asiatic Society of Bengal*, Vol. I, No. 6 June 1832, pp. 245-247.

85 Francis Buchanan, Vol. I, *op.cit.*, p. 171.

86 Benjamin Heyne, *op.cit.*, pp. 221.

87 Voysey, *op.cit.*, p. 246.

88 Kancha Ilaiah, *op.cit.*, pp.37-38.

89 Thallapally Manohar, Ed., *op.cit.*, pp.26-28 and N. Kanakaratnam, *op.cit.*, pp.7-8.

90 M. Nagabhushana Sarma, *Folk Performing Arts of Andhra Pradesh*, Telugu University, Hyderabad, 1995, p. 50.

91 Kancha Ilaiah, *op.cit.*, pp.44-45 and Thallapally Manohar, Ed., *op.cit.*, pp.21-22.

92 H. Nanjundayya and L. Anantakrishna Iyer, *op.cit.*, p. 167.

93 "Nandana Hosur Copper Plate of Saka 1232" *Annual Report of the Mysore Archaeological Department for the Year 1931*, Government Press, Banglore, 1935, p. 91

94 Modali Nagabhushana Sarma and Mudigonda Veerabhadra Sastry, Ed., *History and Culture of the Andhras*, Telugu University, Hyderabad, 1995, p. 420.

95 For the stories of Katamaraju see Tangirala Venkata Subba Rao Ed., *Katamaraju Kadhalu* (Telugu) Andhra Pradesh Sahitya Academy, Hyderabad, 1978, Vol. I and II.

96 M. Lalitha and M. Nandini, "the Divine Drone", *The Hindu*, June 16, 2017.

97 M. Nagabhushana Sarma, *op.cit.*, pp. 37-38.

98 Vallbharaya, *op.cit.*, Verse Nos. 129 and 130, pp. 23-24; Velcheru Narayana Rao and David Shulman, Tr., *op.cit.*, p. 55.

99 P. Sambamoorthy, *Catalogue of Musical Instruments Exhibited in the Government Museum, Chennai*, Government Museum, Chennai, 1998, p. 19.

100 *Ibid.*, p. 20.

101 *Ibid.*

102 *Ibid.*

103 *Ibid.*, pp. 20-22.

104 N. Devasahayam, *Puppets in the Collection of the Madras Government Museum*, Government Press, Chennai, 1999, p.2. The Madras Government Museum had started acquiring leather puppets from 1941 onwards. The collection includes 270 leather puppets representing a good variety from Andhra, Kerala, Mysore, Tamil Nadu, Malaya, Indo-China and Java. Of which Andhra leather puppets alone are 96.

105 M. Nagabhushana Sarma, *Tolu Bommalata: The Shadow Puppet Theatre of Andhra Pradesh*, Sangeet Natak Academy, New Delhi, 1985, p.24. Sarma informs that they consist of one each for head and body, two for legs, three each for hands.

106 P. Hymavathi, *op.cit.*, p.233.

107 A Staff Officer, *Historical Record of the Honourable East India Company's First Madras European Regiment containing an account of the Establishment of Independent Companies in 1645, Their Formation into a Regiment in 1748 and its Subsequent Services to 1842*, Smith, Elder and Company, London, 1843, 1843, p. X.

108 Henry Davison Love, *Vestiges of Old Madras 1640-1800 Traced from the East India Company's Records Preserved at Fort St. George and the India Office and from Other Sources*, Government of India, London, 1913, Vol. II, p. 198-199.

109 W. Y. Carman, *Indian Army Uniforms under the British from the 18th century to 1947*, Leonard Hill [Books] Limited, London, 1961, p.130. The Sam Browne belt is a wide belt, usually leather, supported by a narrower strap passing diagonally over the right shoulder.

110 Ibid,

111 W.J. Wilson, *History of the Madras Army*, Government Press, 1883, Vol. III, p. 169. For a full version of the East India Company version of the revolt see pp. 169- 234.

112 Alan Douglas Cameron says tha "If the Mysore princes were not the prime moving force behind the mutiny, it might reasonably be supposed that the introduction of the new pattern of turban and of the dress regulations was responsible for the bloodshed. This View was held by many contemporaries and has subsequently been accepted by many historians." Alan Douglas Cameron, *The Vellore Mutiny*, Unpublished Ph.D. Thesis, University of Edinburgh, 1984, p.135.

113 Alfred Chatterton, *op.cit.*, p. 39.

114 *Ibid.*, pp. 37-38.

13

Caste, Social Exclusion and Deras in Punjab

Ronki Ram*

Introduction

Punjab is widely known for its rivers, fertile land and its sacred geography speckled with Hindu, Sufi, Sikh, Christian, Buddhist and indigenous/pagan shrines. It has also earned a distinct trade-mark of being a proud food-bowl-state of north India. Its engaging role in the freedom struggle of the country and the vast amount of sacrifices made by its freedom fighters are well known the world over. The formation of the *Ghadar party* (also known as Hindi Association of the Pacific Coast) by the Punjabi immigrant in North America in 1913 for liberating India from the British rule; the rise of the *Babbar Akalis* in 1920s for self rule; the emergence of the radical movement (Naxalites) in the beginning of 1970s for furthering the cause of peasants and workers; and the rise of the Khalistan movement in the 1980s for the establishment of a separate Sikh state, all putting together represent Punjab as a land of resistance against all sorts of dominations and discriminations. Punjabi resistance draws heavily on the heroic deeds of the *Khalsa*[1], primarily aimed

* Shaheed Bhagat Singh Professor of Political Science, Panjab University, Chandigarh, Punjab, E-mail: ronkiram@yahoo.co.in

at establishing a *Halimi Raj*[2] in the name of formless God where no one would be discriminated against on primordial or ascriptive values. Another peculiarity which sharply distinguishes Punjab from rest of the country is the bloody partition forced on it on the eve of independence. Punjab partition, in fact, is one of the very few forced and violent mass exoduses the 20th century world has ever witnessed.

The above mentioned specificities about Punjab can be designated as generalities which any one even with some little interest in the region might claim to know something about it. However, there is much more beyond these generalities that characterize Punjab rather more critically but often taken note of scarcely. Farmer suicides, female foeticide, forced marriages and honour killings, craze for foreign lands, wide-spread use of all sorts of drugs among the youth, old, and women in the country-side, green revolution driven ecological imbalances and the consequent spread of cancer in the Malwa sub-region of the state, water depletion and pollution of rivers and rivulets, caste-based social exclusion and Dalit atrocities, and the mushrooming growth of different sects, *Deras*[3] and *Babas* in the state are a few of the most obvious current social concerns that remain eclipsed under the wider canvas of much talked about generalities in Punjab. They get attention only as and when something unusual happens catapulting some of them into the whirlpool of local power politics with far-reaching national as well as diasporic implications. There is hardly any scholarly literature available about them. What to talk about mainstream academic, even in the vernacular literary circles one rarely finds a reference highlighting any of such contemporary social concerns.

The present paper is a modest attempt to fill some gaps by focusing on caste and caste-based social exclusion in Punjab and the subsequent rise of Dalit identity and assertion in the form of Dalit Deras, particularly Ravidass

Deras. The mushrooming growth of Ravidass deras in contemporary Punjab, amidst mainstream Sikh dominated Gurdwara culture, assumed critical importance. It gave rise to a distinct Dalit religious sphere in the region where religion (read Sikh religion) has deeply pervaded the structures of social and political power. Given the thick concentration of Dalits in Punjab, Ravidass deras have assumed a strategic position. Dalits find themselves in sharp contradiction with Jats; a dominant peasant caste heavily concentrated in the villages of Punjab. Quite interestingly, Dalits too are heavily concentrated in rural Punjab. But despite the fact of their being in largest[4] numbers in Punjab (about 29 per cent, census of India 2001) in comparison to their counterparts in rest of the country, less than 5 percent of them were cultivators (Ram 2007; Ram 2009a). Nowhere in India, are Dalits so extensively deprived of agricultural land as in Punjab. They shared only 4.82 percent of the number of operational holdings and 2.34 percent of the total area under cultivation (1991 census). Since ownership of land assumes utmost importance in Punjab (being an agrarian economy) in determining social status, landlessness among Dalits affects their social status tremendously. Acute landlessness among Dalits along with the absence of alternate job avenues pushed a large number of them (60 percent, 1991 census) into farm labour to work on the land of landowners, who invariably happened to be Jat Sikhs. Their share in the trade, industry, financial sector, health, religious establishments and media in the state is also negligible. The relationship of landless Dalit agricultural workers with the landed peasantry, thus, is that of landless agricultural workers versus landlords, which in turn led to contradictions between them. The two communities are engaged in a protracted power struggle (Ram, 2004b; Ram 2004c; and Ram 2010).

Despite their poor record in the occupancy of land, the Dalits of Punjab, however, over the years have strengthened their economic position to some extent through constitutional affirmative action, diversification into non-hereditary skilled occupations, and ventures abroad. In addition, they have also been politicized to a large extent by the socio-political activities of the famous Ad Dharm movement during the colonial period (Ram 2004a). In the aftermath of India's independence, the Ambedkar movement further influenced Dalit activism in Punjab. Thus armed with the weapon of improved economic conditions and social-political consciousness, the Dalits mustered enough strength to ask for a concomitant rise in their social status and their due share in the local power structures. How ere, in the absence of conducive public sphere and amidst the all pervasive ambience of religious shrines of the dominant religions in the state, Dalits of Punjab too preferred to choose religious way to social mobility. This is what led them to look for alternate ways of social emancipation and empowerment giving rise to all sorts of Deras and steady upsurge of a separate Dalit identity in Punjab (Ram 2008). In search of an egalitarian religion where they can move freely without being put to any social discrimination, Dalits of Punjab expanded the mass followings of various Dalit Deras in the state emerged over the last century. The fast growing popularity of Deras and the enormous amount of wealth they receive in the form of donations from the local as well as diasporic followings eventually brought them into a sort of direct confrontation with the long established and deeply institutionalized Gurdwaras and other dominant Sikh Panthic organizations resulting in intermittent caste conflicts in Punjab over the last few years. Vienna attack and its backlash is just another violent manifestation[5].

Thus the rise of Dalit Deras in Punjab may be seen as an index of emerging Dalit consciousness and separate Dalit identity in the state. In the face of the growing caste structures within Sikhism (Ram 2009a; Ram2009b;

and Ram 2009c), a religion that theologically denies caste and known for attracting a vast constituency among the downtrodden, Dalits were but helpless to seek refuge in Deras where they were given the promise of social equality and dignity in the real sense of the term. In this paper, to be more precise, we will focus on Ravidass Deras only. Ravidass Deras are mainly Dalit Deras. They are being raised in the sacred memory of Guru Ravidass, one of several Dalit *nirguni* Sants (devotee of God without attributes) of the medieval north-Indian Bhakti movement who unleashed a frontal attack on the long tradition of social oppression and untouchability in the Hindu society and deployed bhakti as a prototype of non-violent revolt by the untouchables against the centuries-old system of Brahminic hegemony. Guru Ravidass being one of the low castes and what Omvedt called "the bhakti radical" holds a special place in the heart of Dalits, who consider him their Guru (Omvedt 2008: 7) They have built temples, gurdwaras, bhawans (memorial halls), educational institutions/chairs, cultural organizations and hospitals in his name all over Punjab. They have also founded several missions[6] to accurately establish facts about his life, times, works, and to disseminate his message of love, compassion, equality, and brotherhood in India and abroad[7] (Hawley 1988:270). In fact, the lustrous image of Ravidass has played an instrumental role in mobilising the outcastes[8], especially Chamars (leather workers), who joined the Ad Dharm movement in large numbers[9]. Chamars of Punjab in general and Punjabi Chamar/Ad Dharmi/Ravidassia diasporas in particular have organised themselves into various Guru Ravidass Sabhas (committees) and established a large number of Ravidass shrines popularly known as Ravidass Deras/temples/gurdwara/gurughars both in Punjab and abroad. The number of such Deras has been on a steady rise.

There are over sixty Deras in Punjab that have exclusive Ravidassia identity. If the small Ravidass Deras are included, the number could well cross hundred. More than half of the Ravidass Deras are located in the four districts of Doaba sub-region of the state, considered as a heartland of Adharmis – one of the thirty nine ex-untouchables castes listed in the Scheduled Castes (SCs) list of Punjab. At least forty percent of Doaba's population consists of Ad Dharmis. Ad Dharmis are not only numerically preponderant in the Doaba sub-region; they are also happened to be the most resourceful caste in comparison to the all other castes among the SCs of Punjab. They are on the top of virtually every parameter be it education, urbanization, government jobs, occupational diversification, cultural advancement or political mobilization. The management of all the Ravidass Deras is invariably monopolized by the Ad Dharmis. Ravidass deras are not merely a religious space. They, in fact, symbolise the ongoing meticulous process of concretisation of a separate Dalit identity in Punjab. Their central concern has been to present themselves as different from the Hindu and Sikh shrines and to provide an alternative religious domain where Dalit followers need not hide their identity and suffer meekly onslaughts of social exclusion. In order to look different from the shrines of Hindu and Sikh religions, and to distinctly project their separate religious identity, Ravidass deras have formulated their own sacred scriptures, religious symbols, ceremonies, prayers, rituals and messages of social protest against the oppressive structures of caste domination in the agrarian society of Punjab (Rawat 2003:589-90). Their distinctiveness also lies in the fact that they neither take refuge in any of the established theology nor do they emulate the dominant socio-cultural ethos of upper caste society. On the contrary, they proudly distinguish themselves from the mainstream religious systems and also contest the long imposed supremacy of the dominant castes over the Dalits of Punjab. These deras, in fact, have been functioning as missions to sensitize Dalits and to facilitate their empowerment (Ambedkari 2005:5).

The emergence of Dalit consciousness in Punjab and its manifestation in the form of separate Dera-based religious identity seem to have immense importance from the perspective of the interests of the marginalized sections of the society, on the one hand, and the politicization of the sacred sphere in the state, on the other. It is in this specific context that this paper aims at looking beyond the generalities in Punjab. The dominant peasant caste often interpreted the emerging Dalit assertion in Punjab as a challenge to their long established supremacy in the state. This in turn has sharpened the contradictions between the landed dominant castes in the state and the landless Dalits who seek social mobility through the mushrooming growth of Ravidass Deras. The Dalits, who for centuries have been subjected to humiliation and untold miseries, now learnt to say a firm no not only to the instances of violation of their human rights, but are also ready to take up cudgels with their tormentors face to face. The most obvious contesting site for power struggle between the landed peasantry and the landless Dalits seems to be the ever expanding religious sphere in Punjab.

Caste and Social Exclusion

Though the phenomenon of caste and social exclusion was never considered so strong in Punjab as in many other parts of the country, it has also never been alien to this part of the country. Dalits in Punjab, like their counterparts in other parts of India, have been the victims of social exclusion, physical oppression, political neglect and economic deprivations. The repeated references to and loud condemnations of caste based discriminations in the teachings of the Sufis and the Sikh Gurus is a case in point. Moreover, the roots of caste based hierarchies have been so well entrenched in Punjab that the reformatory measures undertaken by various social reform movements such as Arya Samaj, Singh Sabha and Chief Khalsa Dewan failed to weed them out. The Mazhbis of Punjab is a case in point.

> The Mazbis take the pauhl, wear their hair long, and abstain from tobacco, and they apparently refuse to touch night- soil, though performing all the other offices hereditary to the Chuhra caste.... But though good Sikhs so far as religious observance is concerned, the taint of hereditary pollution is upon them and Sikhs of other castes refuse to associate with them even in religious ceremonies (Ibbetson [1883] 1970: 294).

Even the conversion of a shudra into Muslim religion hardly relieves him of his humiliations (Ibbetson [1883] 1970: 300; see also Bagha 2001:19; and Hutton 1963:39 & 204). Moreover, in the initial years of proliferation of Christianity in Punjab, the curse of caste on the shudras remained unabated. It was they (shudras) who had to approach the missionaries for converting them into Christianity than the other way round as in the case of upper caste (Juergensmeyer 1988: 184). Christian missionaries thought of the lower castes "...as beyond the reach of the method they preferred - intellectual arguments and moral persuasion" Juergensmeyer 1988: 184). What came in the way of the missionaries not to make use of moral persuasion and intellectual argument as methods of approaching and winning the confidence of lower castes seem to be probably the prejudice on their part that the lower castes were really incapable of rational orientation? To quote Juergensmeyer

> ...lower caste requests for conversion not only baffled the missionaries but embarrassed them: they saw no sensible or moral reason for keeping the lower caste out, yet feared that allowing them in would sully the Church's reputation. In a brisk exchange of letters between the mission field and various denominational head offices, a number of missionaries warned about the consequences of 'raking in rubbish into the Church' (Juergensmeyer 1988: 184).

The indignation of being a shudra continued to follow the entry of lower caste into the Church. The upper caste converts were distinguished by the title of 'Convert'..."whereas recruits from the lower caste were known as mass movement Christians or simply Christian" (Juergensmeyer 1988: 187). To quote him further

> it was only these lower caste Christians who adopted foreign names such as Samuel, Paul Masih... and the like; upper caste converts retained their ties to the caste system by continuing to use their Hindu or Sikh names (Juergensmeyer 1988: 187-88).

In other words, the adoption of foreign names by the lower castes has doubly affected the identity of these converts in the sense that they could be easily singled out by the natives as belonged to the shudra caste by virtue of their new names which only low caste had taken on. As far as the Christian missionaries were concerned, they could also, by the same logic of foreign names, easily identify who was shudra convert. Another way of distinguishing the upper caste converts from that of the lower caste was the mechanism of sitting arrangement in the Church, whereby the upper caste converts were allowed ... "to sit at the front of the Church so that they would use the communion implements first, before they became polluted by the Christians of lower castes" (Juergensmeyer 1988: 188).

Thus, caste, as discussed above, continues to pull strings in Punjab, even though it has long boasted of a caste-free society. Rarely a day passes when Dalits are spared of a social boycott by the dominant castes in the villages of Punjab over the last few years. Caste-based social boycott, in fact, has become, rather notoriously, a routine affair in the social set up of state. Social boycotts were first imposed on Dalits in Punjab during their Ad Dharm struggle in the early decades of the 20th century (for details see Ram 2004a: 332-35) Social exclusion continued to afflict them even after India became independent. The frequency and intensity of atrocities against them increased manifolds during the green revolution as a reaction to the growing Dalit assertion for better working conditions and higher wages (Singh 1980; Sidhu 1991; Gill 2000). It is generally seen that whenever the dispossessed raise voice for their human rights, they have been greeted with severe hardships.

After the much-publicized violent conflict in the village Talhan (2003), Punjab is witnessed to a series of similar cases. The pattern of conflicts in all such cases often remained the same as it was during the green revolution phase. In almost all the conflicts, social boycott was imposed on the Dalits who were asserting for a share in the local structures of power such as partnership in the village common lands, membership in the management committees of the religious bodies, entery into the Panchayati Raj Institutions etc. Pandori Khajoor village in Hoshiarpur district, village Bhattian Bet in Ludhiana district, Talhan, Meham and Athaula villages in Jalandhar district, Patteraiwal village in Abhor district, Jethumajra and Chahal village in Nawan Shahr district, Aligarh village near Jagraon in Ludhiana district, Domaeli and Chak Saboo villages in Kapurthala district, Dhamiana in Ropar district, Abuul Khurana village near Malout in Mukitsar district, and Dallel Singh wala, Kamalpur and Hasanpur villages in Sangrur, and Jhabbar village in district of Mansa are among the prominent cases of Jat-Dalit conflicts in the state. The most recent one is about the clashes between the various groups of Sikhs and the Premis of the Dera Sacha Sauda in different parts of Punjab.

The dastardly act of murderous attack on Ravidassia spiritual leaders of Dera Sachkhand Ballan in Vienna, the capital city of Austria, during a religious congregation on Sunday (May 24, 2009), followed by a sudden and most violent protests unleashed spontaneously by their vast Dalit followers across Punjab, once again brought into light the deep undercurrents of the institution of caste in this northern agricultural belt of India. The backlash has not only brought forth the dormant contradictions between the Dalits and the dominant castes in Punjab, but also ignited the 'burning fury' of the ex-untouchables who seem to have been struggling hard in translating their newly earned wealth into a viable avenue of upward social mobility. Surinder Kaur, one of the millions of followers of Dera Sachkhand Ballan is quoted saying, "[t]his is happening to us because our community is making attempts to uplift itself"[10]. Another devotee of the Dera interprets the recent Dalit upsurge as "a fight for equality"[11]. He is quoted as saying that "[t]he dominated community is attempting to rise and the dominant community is fearful of its rise"[12].

Social Exclusion and Dalit Upsurge

Social exclusion in Punjab is unique in comparison to its observance in other parts of the country. The Brahminical tradition of social stratification has never been so effective there. The word Brahmin did not carry a sacerdotal connotation in Punjab. It was used, rather, in a derogatory sense (Saberwal 1976: 10; Tandon 1961: 77). The Jat-Sikhs, who otherwise have been *Shudra* as per the Varna system, considered themselves socially superior to the Brahmins. Brahmins, whereas in rest of the country, enjoyed the highest status in the Hindu caste hierarchy, are looked down in Punjab. The down play of the Brahmins in Punjab by the Jat-Sikhs might have diminished the purity-pollution practice to the benefits of Dalits (Saberwal 1973:256). However, it did not, in any way; help Dalits improve their socio-economic status.

Punjab is a Sikh majority state. The Sikhs constitute 63 per cent of its total population. Among them the percentage of Jat–Sikhs is the highest. About 72 per cent of the Sikhs live in rural Punjab. Although Sikhism does not assign any place to the institution of caste in its 'doctrinal principle' but the same is not true in its 'social practice' (Puri 2003: 2693). "Caste as occupational division of labour was, and is, very much a part of village life" (Kaur 1986: 229). Sikh religion is not an exception. In the Punjab censuses between 1881 and 1921 there were more than twenty-five castes within Sikh community (Verma 2002:33). Among the Sikhs, Jat-Sikhs, *Khatri* Sikhs, *Arora* Sikhs, *Ramgarhia* Sikhs, *Ahluwalia* Sikhs, *Bhapa* Sikhs, *Bhattra* Sikhs, *Ramdasia* Sikhs, *Ravidasia* Sikhs, Rahtia Sikhs, *Mazhbi* Sikhs, and *Rangreta* Sikhs are some of the most distinct caste communities.

The Jat-Sikhs in Punjab substituted the Brahmins in terms of social domination as against the purity-pollution principles developed by Dumont.

The Jat is in every respect the most important of the Pánjab peoples.... The Jat of the Sikh tracts is of course the typical Jat of Pánjab ... Politically he ruled the Pánjab till the Khalsa yielded to our arms. Ethnologically he is the peculiar and most prominent product of the plains of the five rivers. And from an œconomical and administrative point of view he is the husbandman, the peasant, the revenue-payer *par excellence* of the Province. ... But as a rule a Jat is a man who does what seems right in his own eyes and sometimes what seems wrong also, and will not be said nay by any man. ... The Banya with his sacred thread, his strict Hinduism, and his twice-born standing, looks down on the Jat as a Sudrá. But the Jat looks down upon the Banya as a cowardly spiritless money-grubber, and society in general agree with the Jat. (Ibbetson 1883, rpt. 1970: 102-103).

Jat-Sikhs are primarily agriculturists and land-owners. They are mostly concentrated in villages. They have also diversified into transport business and considered employment in the armed forces as prestigious. "The Jat might be employed as a school teacher, or service in the military but he sees his primary role as that of an agriculturist; his connection with land is what he holds most dear and what identifies him" (Kaur 1986:233). Jat-Sikhs are the backbone of the Punjab peasantry (Kaur 1986:233). Although all the ten Gurus belonged to the Khatri caste, they found majority of their followers in the Jat caste (Kaur 1986: 225). According to 1881 census, 66% of Sikhs were Jats followed by Ramgarhias (6.5%) and Chamar Sikhs (5.6%). Khatris' share was only 2.2% (Mcleod 1976: 84). Although Sikhs are prominently identified by a set of diacritical features which they are supposed to follow according to *Rahatnama* (the Sikh code of conduct), the Jat Sikhs do not always observe them strictly. Majority of them trim their beard, cut their hair, and many often smoke or chew tobacco; very few wear the *kirpan* (steel sword), *kachh* (knee length drawers), *karra* (steel bangle or bracelet) and *kangha* (comb). They rarely visit Gurdwaras (Kaur 1986: 222-23). Majority of the Jats are non-baptised Sikhs. However, the baptised ones faithfully observe all the injunctions mentioned in the *Rahatnama*. Jat-Sikhs are generally liberal in observance of *Rahatnama*. In spite of their lackadaisical approach towards the *Khalsa* discipline, Jat Sikhs in their own eyes and in those of others remained Sikhs (Mcleod 1976: 98). The Sikhs who strictly followed *Rahatnama* belong to the lower class of north Punjab (Singh 1953: 179).

Within Sikhism, Dalit Sikhs are divided into two segments. The Dalits whose profession is scavenging and cleaning are called *Mazhbis* and *Rangretas*. *Mazhbis* and *Rangretas* were *chuhras* who converted to Sikhism (Ibbetson 1883, rpt. 1970:294). "Of course a Mazbi will often have been returned as chuhra by caste and Sikh by religion; ... Mazbi means nothing more than a member of the scavenger class converted to Sikhism" (Ibbetson 1883, rpt. 1970:294). *Mazhbi* Sikhs are almost confined to the Majha sub-region of Punjab. They make good soldiers and some of the regiments in British army were wholly composed of *Mazhbis*.

The Rangreta are a class of Mazbi apparently found only in Ambala, Ludhiana and the neighbourhood, who consider themselves superior to the rest.The origin of their superiority... lies in the fact that they were once notorious as highway robbers! But it appears that Rangretas have very generally abandoned scavengering for leather work, and this would at once account for their rise in the social scale (Ibbetson 1883, rpt. 1970:294).

Their popularity in the Sikh religion has been established by a rhyme *Rangreta, Guru ka Beta* (the Rangreta is the son of the Guru), attributed to them on account of their valorous act of bringing the severed head of Guru Teg Bahadur from Delhi to Anandpur Sahib, the seat of the 9th and 10th Masters of the Sikh faith. However, in spite of *Mazhbis* and *Rangreta* Sikhs' meticulous observance of the Sikh religious principles, they were not considered equal by the other Sikh castes who refused to associate with them even in the religious ceremonies (Ibbetson 1883, rpt. 1970:294). In other words, even after converting to Sikhism they were not relieved of the taint of hereditary pollution.

The other segment of Dalit Sikhs consists of *Ramdasias* and *Ravidasias. They* are *chamars* converted to Sikh religion. Religious conversion also changes the caste name. In some cases a change of religion is also accompanied by a change of occupation (Ibbetson 1883, rpt. 1970:294). A scavenger is known as *chuhra* in Hinduism; *Musalli* and *Kutana* in Islam; and *Mazhbi* and *Rangreta* in Sikhism. A leather-worker is known as *chamar* in Hinduism; *Mochi* in Islam and *Ravidasia* in Sikhism. Weaver *chamar* is known as *Julaha* in Hinduism; *Paoli* in Islam; and *Ramdasia* in Sikhism. *Ramdasias* are also known as Khalsa *Biradar.*

The Ramdasias are confused with Raidasi or Rabdasi chamars. The former are true Sikhs, and take the *Pahul.* The latter are Hindus, or if Sikhs, only Nanakpanthi Sikhs and do not take the *Pahul;* and are followers of Bhagat Rav Das or Rab Das, himself a Chamar. They are apparently as true Hindus as any Chamar can be, and are wrongly called Sikhs by confusion with Ramdasias. (Ibbetson 1883, rpt. 1970: 300).

Most of the *Ramdasias* are *Julahas* (weavers). Whereas *Ravidasia* Sikhs are mostly engaged in the profession of leather work. Though there is a wide distinction between the *Ravidasias*, typical leather workers (*Chamars*) and the *Ramdasias*, typical weavers (*Julahas*), "yet they are connected by certain sections of leather-working classes who have taken to weaving and thus risen in the social scale…" (Ibbetson 1883, rpt. 1970: 296). *Ramdasia* (weavers) and *Ravidasia* (leather worker) are probably of the same origin. However, the distinction between them has arisen from divergence of occupation.

The *Mazhbis, Rangretas, Ramdasias* and *Ravidasias* are not equal to the Jat-Sikhs, *Khatri* Sikhs and *Arora* Sikhs within Sikhism in terms of their status. Even their status is also lower to *Ramgarhia* Sikhs, *Ahluwalia* Sikhs and *Bhapa* Sikhs (trader caste). Thus the poison of caste has also penetrated into the religion of the followers of Guru Nanak as well (Singh, Balwant 2002: 332). Moreover caste hierarchy is also being practiced among the Dalit Sikhs. *Ramdasia* and *Ravidasia* Sikhs are considered superior to the *Mazhbi* and *Rangreta* Sikhs. Although *Ramdasias* and *Ravidasias* originated from Chamars, the former considered them superior to the latter (Ibbetson 1883, rpt. 1970: 297, 302).

The evolution of Sikh community proceeded through a complex dynamics of interaction between religious principle, tribal cultural patterns of the dominant caste of Jats and their power interests. This resulted in the evolution of a Sikh caste hierarchy, distinct from and parallel to that of Hindu caste system (Puri 2003: 2693).

However, what makes caste discrimination in the Sikh community different from that of the Brahamanical social order is the absence of purity-pollution frame of relations. The centre of power in Punjab revolves around the axle of land. Much of the land is owned by the Jat-Sikhs. Although SCs in Punjab constitute high proportion of the population in comparison to the all India average of 16.32 percent (2001 census) their share in ownership of land is negligible. They cultivate only 0.4 per cent of all the landholdings occupying 0.72 per cent of the total cultivated area of the state (1991 census and All India Report of Agricultural Census 1990-91). Their being landlessness forced them to depend on the land-owning castes in the absence of alternative jobs in the agrarian economy of rural Punjab. Since cultivation involves Dalits in its various operations, it was not feasible to strictly follow the system of untouchability based on the principle of purity-pollution as was observed in rest of the country. It does not mean that the Dalits were not discriminated in Punjab. They were discriminated by the Jat-Sikhs. They were forced to remain confined to their lowest status lest they dare to ask for a share in the power structures (Puri 2003: 2698). Untouchability did exist in Punjab and its practice was tied with the scheme of keeping the Dalits away from land ownership and political power in the state. Thus Dalits in Punjab, though relatively spared from the overt impact of purity-pollution syndrome, the asymmetrical structure of the agrarian rural economy has made them subordinated to the land-owning upper castes. In fact "the Scheduled Caste population of the region has been comparatively more vulnerable in the economic structure of the village" (Jodhka 2002: 1815).

The villages are divided into upper caste and Dalit settlements. Dalit settlements are located, invariably, on the side towards which the dirt of the village flowed. Dalits were not allowed to build *pucca* (concrete) houses because the land on which they lived did not belong to them. The residential land on which they lived was claimed to be owned by the Jat-Sikhs (Virdi 2003: 2 &11). Till 1952, the Dalits along with other non-agricultural castes were deprived of landownership by the Punjab

Land Alienation Act (1901), even if a few of them have the means to purchase the land (Puri 2003: 2695, Ram 2010). In the villages, Dalits were often involved in the unclean occupations. Such occupations were like carrying and skinning dead animals, scavenging and working as attached labourer – *Siris*. Although such type of works, now-a-days, are performed on non-jajmani basis. In Malwa region, there are many Dalits who still have been working as *Siris*. According to a latest study of 26 villages in Malwa region, 21 had Dalits working as *Siris* (Jodhka 2002: 1816). However, the situation is entirely different in the Doaba region of Punjab where the majority of the Dalits have dissociated themselves from such types of menial works. Although Dalit had interaction with Jat-Sikhs, being agricultural labourers, and *siris*, they used to keep their own tumblers and plates to take meals or tea or water from the upper caste Sikhs. Many of the lower castes like *Chamars* and *Chuhras* converted to Sikhism in the hope of social equality. Even in Sikhism, the specter of untouchability kept on haunting them.

The upper castes Sikhs are a separate identity and like the upper caste Hindus they also follow the ideology of a graded human society. ... The Sikhs may take food with the Dalit-Sikhs in Gurdwaras, but they have no bond of fraternity with them (Singh Balwant 2002: 333).

To quote him further, "the impact of Hinduism and caste is visible on the adherence of Guru Nanak and they monopolised Sikhism and could not accord an equal social status to the lower caste Sikhs in Punjab" (Singh Balwant 2002: 333). Dalit Sikhs in Punjab are cremated on separate cremation grounds along with their counterparts in the Hindu religion. Even in some villages the land meant for the cremation grounds in the *Shamlat* (common land under the control of Panchayats) have been grabbed by the upper castes. "Therefore the Dalit Sikhs in Punjab are in no better position than the other Dalits within Hinduism" (Singh Balwant 2002: 334).

Dalits Sikhs, as they often allege, did not get equal treatment in the Gurdwaras of the upper caste Sikhs. "Mazhabis were forbidden to enter the Golden Temple for worship; their offering of karah prasad was not accepted and the Sikhs denied them access to public well and other utilities" (Pratap Singh 1933: 146-47, 156-57 cited in Puri 2003: 2697). Dalit Sikhs were not allowed to go beyond the fourth step in the Golden Temple and the members of the four-fold varnas were instructed not to mix with them (Oberoi cited in Puri 2003: 2697). Evidence of untouchability against the Dalit Sikhs is vividly reflected in a number of *Gurmatas* (resolutions) adopted by the Shiromani Gurdwara Prabhandak Committee from 1926-1933 (Puri 2003: 2697). Although removal of untouchability figured in the Singh Sabha movement, no strenuous effort was made in that direction. "It was not surprising. For the Jats, who composed 70 % of the Akalis, and other high castes, caste equality or removal of untouchability was contrary to their disposition for social domination and hierarchy" (Puri 2003: 2697). This has forced the Dalit Sikhs to establish separate Gurdwaras which in turn has further led to the strengthening of the already existing caste divisions among the Sikhs (Puri 2003: 2700; Muktsar 1999 and 2003). Moreover the observance of caste prejudices against the Dalit Sikhs has compelled them to 'search for alternative cultural spaces' in a large number of Deras, sects, dargahs of Muslim Pirs and other Sants (Puri 2003: 2700; for a detailed account of Sants see: Sachomer, Karine, and W.H. McLeod (eds) 1987).

Punjab has been a stronghold of Pirs and Sants, who vehemently campaigned against the system of segregation on the basis of birth. They preached unity of mankind. Farid and Bulle Shah of *Sufi* tradition, and Ravidass, Kabir, Nanak and Dhanna of the Bhakti tradition played a prominent role in diluting the substance and practice of untouchability in the state. Social reform movements led by the Arya Samaj, Singh Sabha and Chief Khalsa Dewan further bridled the impact of untouchability in Punjab.

However, even these movements and saints could not succeed in stamping out the roots of the evil of untouchability in Punjab. "The saints have never ... carried on a campaign against caste and untouchability. They were not concerned with the struggle between men. They were concerned with the relation between man and God. They did not preach that all men were equal. They preached that all men were equal in the eyes of God – a very different and a very innocuous proposition which nobody can find difficult to preach or dangerous to believe in" (Ambedkar 1995 3rd edn.: 109). The religious and social reform movements were primarily concerned with the humane and civic sense of society by transforming and elevating the individual rather than striking hard on the asymmetrical structures of the society (Grewal 1994: 116). The issue of disproportionate landholdings which has been the crucial cause of social inequalities and economic deprivations had never been taken up by the social and religious movements. In other words, the agency was prioritised over the structure. The persistence of inegalitarian structure, with the passage of time, had led to the evaporation of social and moral reforms brought by these movements. The principles and social code of conduct formulated by such movements got routinised into hard-shell traditions and rules to be strictly obeyed by the followers. These movements themselves in turn got routinised into new religious orders or political organisations. Religion has become exclusive and been paraded as an index to the deep rooted social divisions based on economic differentiation. The followers of Nanak, Ravidass and Kabir are not only Nanakpanthis, Ravidasias and Kabirpanthis in the strict sense of the term; they also represent a distinct social and economic class different from each other.

Caste with a Difference

However, what distinguishes caste in Punjab the most from the rest of the country is the primacy of the material and political factors over the principle of purity-pollution dichotomy[13]. Social exclusion has invariably remained attached with the notion of power in its varied dimensions. The concept of power in India needs to be seen in a peculiar sense as far as its socio-political and economic aspects are concerned. Power was seen as a sacred category. Its sacredness depends ultimately on something which has to be excluded from the purview of its sacred boundaries. Power sails between the boundaries but its affects are felt within the boundaries. Untouchability has provided - in a metaphorical sense - the building blocks for such boundaries. For a Dalit to cross such boundaries amounts to committing blasphemy. They were simply asked to be continuously shut within their ghettos. In fact it was the sacred facade of power which led to the evolution of untouchability rather the other way round. Untouchability is the offshoot of power. The sacred structure of power led to its institutionalization. It was not that untouchability provided stanchion to power. Untouchability has been projected as antithetical to power. Since untouchability is profane, it can not be the custodian of power; power being a sacred. In other words, the structure of power which emerged in India keeps no space at all for the Dalits to share that power. Their position somewhere resembled that of the slaves in Aristotle's Athens. Hence they have to be condemned to bear the shocks of power. In such a unique sacerdotal notion of power one need not be an entrepreneur of power. One needs to be a custodian of purity and sanctity. In ancient India the Brahmin held the key to power by way of projecting himself as the epitome of purity. Interestingly his purity has something to do with his projection of himself as a person who voluntarily abnegates (Schweitzer 1989; Thapar 2000: 876-945; Gupta 2000). The more the renouncer you are the more purer you would be. More the purer you are the more powerful you would be. The institution of "Raj Purohit" in ancient India is a case in point. Even in contemporary India one can find such a phenomenon in existence where Gurus, Saints, and Babas shower blessings for the acquisition of power. What these Babas have been doing in India the Pope used to do the same in the West until the Treaty of Westphalia. But Pope need not be the renouncer in the similar sense as the sacred men in India used to be. The sacred connotation of power and its being surrounded by purity and abnegation was so powerful that even the efforts on the part of the Dalits to break the fetters of untouchability required them to put on the mask of purity emanating from abnegation. Tukaram, Chokhamela, Ravidass, Balmiki, to name only the most prominent, were the Dalit renouncers who made significant contribution for the amelioration of the down trodden. In other words, even the sufferers of untouchability had to follow the route similar to that of upper castes to fight against their odds. These Dalits turned renouncers and gurus were the progenitor of the voice of protest and reforms against hierarchy based on purity-impurity. They were the initiators of the Dalit consciousness. Their voice was heard not because of their being the leaders of the Dalit community but for their being renouncer and so holy-men.

Castes within Caste

Caste does not only operate along fault lines between the higher and lower caste, it equally afflicts the SCs from within. The SCs are as much divided among themselves as the other various twice born castes. The similar situation applies to the Other Backward Castes (OBC) too. Baba Sahib Dr. B.R. Ambedkar highlighted this aspect of the caste system in many of his speeches and writings. He was of the opinion that SCs were as much divided house within as the division between them and rest of the twice born. Irrespective of the fact that they were socially excluded and pushed to the margins of the boundaries of the suffocating caste hierarchy, the Scheduled Caste themselves follow the same logic of social exclusion and discrimination on the pattern of Brahminical graded inequality. Baba Sahib Dr. Ambedkar reiterated that if the SCs wanted to get rid of the social exclusion and untouchability, they have to say first good bye to the social evil of untouchability within. Unless and until the internal social division is not taken care of, the requisite unity among the various Dalit castes is difficult to evolve. Unity among the various communities among the SCs is the most necessary requirement for any democratic Dalit movement to come forward to take cudgels with the Brahminical Social Order (BSO).

In Punjab at present there are as many as 39 castes among the SCs. In the 2001 Census their number was 38. Later on in 2007, another caste of Rai Sikhs was added to the list of SCs in Punjab, thus making the figure thirty nine[14]. SCs in Punjab like their counterparts in rest of India are not only divided along caste lines, they are equally splintered into various religions. SCs in Punjab are Hindus, Sikhs, Christians and Buddhists. Some of them claim to be belonging to their indigenous religion Ad Dharm; though after 1931 census Ad Dharm did not figure in the decennial census of India. The 39 SCs Castes castes of Punjab have their peculiar social hierarchical system whereby they have causally arranged themselves on low-high profile parallel to the prevalent Brhminical caste system in the rest of the country. It was against this social division within that Babu Mangu Ram, the founder of the famous Ad Dharm movement, addressed almost all the then caste members of the ex-untouchables by their specific caste names to come forward on a single platform forgetting their insidious caste factor and fight collectively the monster of untouchability.

Where SCs stand today? Are they not a divided house? Take for example marriages. There is hardly any inter-caste marriage among the different castes within the SCs. Ad Dharmi will prefer to marry within the Ad Dharmi caste. In the matrimonial advertisements it is common to find that marriage alliances are sought strictly within castes. One hardly finds marriages between the Chamar and Balmiki castes. Buddhists Dalits like all other Dalits belonging to different religions equally follow the criterion of caste endogamy in the marriages. All this has prevented unity among the SCs. Probably this may be one of the most important reasons behind the failure of the SCs in Punjab to come into political power despite their large numbers. In the absence of a unified political front and a Punjab Dalit leader, the SCs of Punjab turn to Ravidass Deras, which are indeed mushrooming over the last few decades in an unprecedented way.

Ravidass Deras: A New Mode of Lower Caste Social Mobility

The rise of Deras in Punjab is not a new phenomenon. It is rather as old as the Sikh faith, even goes beyond. During the period of the historic Gurus, different Deras of Udasis, Minas, Dhirmalias, Ramraiyas, Handali, and that of Massandis cropped up. All these earlier Deras were primarily the outcome of the disgruntled and unsuccessful attempts of the 'fake' claimants to the title of Guru (for details see: Chaturvedi 1951:360-69; Marenco1976: 28-30; Bingley 1970: 85-93; Archer 1946: 221-226; Grewal 1996:39-46). Apart from these, there were many more Deras that came up at different intervals on the long and tortuous consolidation of the Sikh religion. Some of the most prominent among them were Bandei Khalsa (Bandapanthis), Nanakpanthis, Sewapanthis, Bhaktpanthi, Suthrashahi, Gulabdasi, Nirmalas and the Nihangs (Chaturvedi 1951:361-69; Mcleod 1984:121-133). But what distinguished these earlier Deras from the contemporary ones is that they could not become the centres of Dalit mobilisation.

According to a field study undertaken by the *Desh Sewak*, a Punjabi daily published from Chandigarh, there are more than nine thousand Sikh as well as non- Sikh

Deras in the 12 thousand villages of Punjab (Tehna et al 2007). In Sikh Deras, Sikh *rahit* (code of conduct) is observed strictly. Whereas in the non-Sikh Deras, different ritual practices are followed. The Radha Soamis, Sacha Sauda, Nirankaris, Namdharis, Divya Jyoti Sansthan, Bhaniarawala and Ravidasis are among the most popular non-Sikh Deras. Almost all of them have branches in all the districts of the state as well as in other parts of the country. Some of them are very popular among the Punjabi Diasporas and have overseas branches in almost all the continents of the world. The composition of these Deras is along caste lines. Though majority of the followings in every case comes from Dalits, backward castes and poor Jat Sikh peasantry; their command is still in the hands of the upper castes (Muktsar 2007). Among them the chief of the Nirankari Deras belonged to the Khatri caste, and that of the Sacha Sauda and Radha Soamis come from the Jat Sikhs of the Sidhu and Dhillon sub-castes respectively. In the case of Sikh Deras, a large majority of their following comes from Jat Sikh community and they are invariably run by Jat Sikhs. It is rare that the head of a Sikh Dera would be a non-Jat Sikh. Even if there would be one he could never be a Dalit. At the most Dalit Sikhs' participation in Sikh Deras is confined only to various kinds of menial services as well as the narration of the sacred text (Guru Granth Sahib) and performing of Kirtan (musical rendering of sacred hymns) (for detail see: Ram 2004c: 5-7). Those who perform *Kirtan* are known as *raagis*, the professional narrators are designated as *granthis* and others who render menial service are called *sewadars*. Majority of the *raagis*, *granthis* and *sewadars* are Dalit Sikhs. Very few Jat Sikhs take up such professions [based on field conversations]. In the Sikh Deras, only Gurubani of Guru Granth Sahib is recited. But in the non-Sikh Deras along with the recitation of Gurubani from Guru Granth Sahib, other sacred texts are also referred to. Idol worship and devotion towards a human Guru is also not an anathema in non-Sikh Deras.

It is due to the presence of such non-Sikh practices that the phenomenon of non-Sikh Deras has been described by Meeta and Rajivlochan as the 'alternate guru movement in Punjab' (Meeta and Rajivlochan 2007:1910).

Ravidass Deras began emerging in Punjab in the early twentieth century. According to a field-based study conducted by Som Nath Bharti Qadian, the number of Ravidass Deras in Punjab has exceeded one hundred over the last few years (Qadian 2003). Since the publication of this study many more such Deras have been established in Punjab: twelve in 2005, eight in 2006 and seven in 2007 (calculated from the various volumes of *Begumpura Shaher*, trilingual weekly publication of the Dera Sachkhand Ballan). Paramjit Judge and Gurpreet Bal in their empirical study reported that the number of Ravidass deras has reached the figure176 (Judge and Bal 2009:106). The strength of Ravidass Deras abroad has also been growing rapidly (Singh 2003:35-40). The followers of Dera Sachkhand Ballan abroad have established their own separate Ravidass Deras different from the mainstream Sikh Gurdwaras across the world, wherever they have settled. The foundation stones of almost all the Ravidass Deras both in India and abroad are laid by the Sants of Dera Sachkhand Ballan. It is pertinent to note that these Deras have come up not merely as centers of spiritual gatherings for Dalits but have also metamorphosed slowly into epicenters of social protest (Ram 2007; Ram 2008).

Guru Ravidass has become very popular among the Ravidassia Dalit diaspora, especially of the Doaba Punjab, home to the highest concentration of Dalits in the state. A very significant part of the Ravidassia Dalit diaspora from Doaba happens to be the follower of Dera Sachkhand Ballan, also located in the same region. Some of the Ravidassia Dalits abroad are well settled and take active interest in community activities in their host as well as home country. They have constructed a large number of Ravidass shrines (interchangeably known as deras, gurughars, temples and gurdwaras) in order to assert their separate Dalit identity. Some of the most prominent Ravidass shrines abroad are in the following cities: Vancouver, Calgary, Brampton, Toronto, Montreal (all in Canada), New York, Sacramento, Pittsburg, Seattle, Fresno, Houston, Selma, Fremont, and Austin (all in USA), Wolverhampton, Birmingham, Bradford, Coventry, Derby, Lancaster, Southall, Southampton, Kent and Bedford (all in UK). In the last few years many Ravidass Temples and Gurdwaras have also come up in Austria, Italy, France, German, Spain, Holland, New Zealand, Greece and Lebanon. Sant Niranjan Dass of Dera Ballan has laid down the foundation stones of all these Ravidass Deras[15]. The Sants of Ballan pay regular visits to these various overseas Ravidass gurughars and bless the vast Ravidass naam leevan sangat (devotees of Guru Ravidass) over there.

In additions, Punjabi Dalit diaspora actively participates in various other community activities in the host countries. They organized an International Dalit Conference (May 16-18, 2003) in Vancouver (Canada), which launched a campaign in North America with a view to lobbying the MNCs in India to honour the principle of diversity for the Dalits in the private ventures. Dalit diaspora settled in the United States of America took out the float of Baba Sahib Dr B.R. Ambedkar on the occasion of the 60th India's Independence Day Parade in New York (on 19 August 2007). The float of Dr. Ambedkar organized by Shri Guru Ravidass Sabha of New York was perhaps the first of its kind in the history of Dalit diaspora.[16] The Ravidassia community of British Columbia (Canada) also created a history on February 25, 2008 by celebrating Guru Ravidass Jayanti in the Parliament of British Columbia in Victoria (based on personal communication from Jai Birdi, Vancouver, Canada, February 26, 2008). It is important to note that the planning for all the community activities and their implementation is chalked out at Ravidass Dears.

The number of Ravidass Deras has been multiplying very fast. They have been playing an important role in the on-going Dalit struggle for dignity, social justice and equality. It is pertinent to note that these deras have come up not merely as centers of spiritual gatherings for Dalits but have also metamorphosed slowly into epicenters of non-violent social protest (Ram 2007; Ram 2008; Ram 2009c). They are, in fact, a clear manifestation of the emerging distinct Dalit identity in Punjab. What distinguishes Ravidass Deras from their counterparts of other nomenclatures is that along with religious activities they also follow an agenda of Dalit empowerment. After the Vienna incidence, Ravidass Deras, primarily led by Dera Sachkhand Ballan, announced a separate Dalit religious identity based on distinct holy scriptures (Amrit Bani Guru Ravidass) and new religion (Ravidassia religion). Dalits in Punjab pegged their identity on this newly declared religion. This has led to confrontation between the mainstream Sikh religion and Dera Ballan dominated Ravidass Deras. As argued by Tracy Piersma, "[t]he announcement of Ravidassia could have been the beginning of a religious revolution; instead it emphasizes the chasm between the religious tenets of Sikhism and lack of adherence by followers" (http://rfiaonline.org/extras/article/654-Dalit-s0cietal-advancement accessed 7/13/2010).

Ravidass deras have taken the form of a new socio-cultural movement for the emancipation of the Dalits. What distinguishes Ravidass deras from their counterparts of other nomenclatures is that along with religious activities they also follow an agenda of Dalit empowerment. The Ravidass dera movement "...is silently sweeping the Punjab countryside offering a new hope to the untouchable, particularly the Chamars..." (Rajshekar 2004:3). It has generated a sense of confidence in them and provided them an opportunity to exhibit their hitherto eclipsed Dalit identity. The movement of Ravidass deras

"...reflects the fast changing socio-cultural scene of Punjab where the once powerful and revolutionary Sikh religion is failing to meet the needs of the oppressed who discovered the right remedy to cure their wounded psyche in the Ballan experiment" (Rajshekar 2004:3). The secret of the success of this movement lies in the strategy to "...sell Dr Ambedkar's socio-cultural revolution packed in an ingenious religious capsule" (Rajshekar 2004:3). Ravidass deras are, perhaps, the only religious centers where religious and political figures (Guru Ravidass and Dr. B.R. Ambedkar) are blended and projected publicly. They represent a critical Dalit space where bhakti based cultures of social protest, propounded and practiced by Guru Ravidass, get finely blended with that of the *political* spearheaded by Dr. Ambedkar. In Ravidass deras the ecstasy and reason of the song of the utopia of Begumpura (an ideal Dalit democratic state), as envisaged by Guru Ravidass, perfectly fits with the analytical resonances of the Prabuddha Bharat of Dr. Ambedkar, one of the most popular and reason based utopias envisioned by dalit-bahujan intellectuals and leaders of the anti-caste movement during the colonial period. The Ravidass deras movement in Punjab represents what Johannes Beltz, an eminent authority on neo-Buddhism, describes "a new terrain of exciting future research" (Beltz 2004: 11) whose potential strength is yet to be fully exploited.

The Case Study

For case study we take Dera Sachkhand Ballan, one of the most reputed Ravidass Deras in Punjab. Dera Sachkhand Ballan, also known as Dera Shri 108 Sant Sarwan Dass Ji Maharaj Sachkhand Ballan or simply Dera Ballan, is situated at village Ballan, seven miles North of Jalandhar city on the Pathankot road. Other equally famous Ravidass Deras are 'Temple Ravidass Chak Hakim' (Phagwara)[17], and 'Dera of Sant Jagatjit Giri' (Pathankot). The Ravidass Deras of Ballan and Chak Hakim shot into prominence during the Ad Dharm movement. They were instrumental in bringing social consciousness among the Dalits of Punjab (Juergensmeyer 1988:84-85). Mangu Ram, the founder of the Ad Dharm movement, visited the Dera Ballan and sought its support in popularizing the image of Ravidass among the Dalits of Punjab (Juergensmeyer 1988:85). The association of the Dera with the Ad Dharm movement becomes further clear from the fact that Sant Sarwan Dass, the then head of the Dera Ballan (October 11,1928-June 11,1972), offered juice to Mangu Ram to open his fast-unto-death undertaken by him as a counter measure to that of Mahatama Gandhi's against the communal award in 1932 (Bawa 2004:6). Although this movement petered out after the first general election in independent India, "...*Deras* such as that of Sarwan Das remain popular destinations for pilgrimage in the Punjab" (Juergensmeyer 1988: 85). Dera Ballan also hosted the mammoth Dalit conference (13th December, 1970) organised by Mangu Jaspal, namesake of the famous Mangu Ram, to revive the Ad Dharm movement[18]. It was during this conference that the legendry Mangu Ram many other prominent leaders of the Ad Dharm movement commended the contribution of Sants of Dera Ballan towards the emancipation and empowerment of Dalits. Sant Sarwan Dass also met Dr. B.R. Ambedkar in 1948 in Delhi at his residence and encouraged him to fight continuously for the emancipation of the downtrodden. During Dr. Ambedkar's visit to Punjab in 1951, Sant Sarwan Dass sent a message to him wishing success in his struggle for the emancipation of the Dalits (Bawa 2004:6).

Dera Sachkhand Ballan was founded in the beginning of the twentieth century by Sant Pipal Dass[19] father of Sant Sarwan Dass (February 15, 1895-June 11, 1972). Sant Sarwan Dass lost his mother (Shobhawanti) when he was only five years old. Thereafter, Sant Pipal Dass left home in search of 'truth'. He took his child son Sarwan Dass with him on the mission (Bawa 2003:4). It was during the course of wandering that the father and son reached the place where Dera Ballan is now situated. Pipal Dass found that place most suitable for spiritual pursuits. He found a dry *Pipal* tree at the site. But the tree, as per local narrative, sprang back into life after he watered it. This convinced Papal Dass that the desired truth could be obtained on this spot. Sant Pipal Dass whose real name was Harnam Dass came to be known as Pipal (from Pipal tree) Dass after this incident (conversation with the devotces of Ravidasss and the priests of Dera Ballan, 13-14 April 2004). The place, in the outskirts of village Ballan, was a thick forest. The father-son duo spent days in the forest and took shelter in a mud house in the village Ballan during nights. Subsequently the mud house was first converted into a temple, popularly known as *Ad Mandir*, and later a new concrete building was raised in its place (Bawa 2004:6). Later on, a landlord (Hazara Singh) of village Ballan donated some land to them in the forest where they built a thatched hut to begin with. "It soon became the goal of pilgrimage for lower caste and other villagers from all over central Punjab, and from its inception it was a center for the veneration of Ravi Das" (Juergensmeyer 1988:84-85).

Sant Sarwan Dass received early education from his father and learnt Sanskrit from Sant Kartanand of nearby village Kishangarh. He was in his early thirties when Sant Pipal Das died (1928). By that time he had already become a known figure not only among the people of Ballan but also in the neighbouring villages (Bawa 2004:6-7). However, what distinguished him from other holy men of his time was his devotion and veneration for Sant Ravidass. The dissemination of Ravidass bani and teachings became his sole mission. Ravidass appealed most to the lower castes probably because of his being a Chamar himself and a pioneer in the field of Dalit literature[20]. The fact that Sant Sarwan Dass was himself a chamar and a devotee of Ravidass contributed to the popularity of his Dera Sachkhand Ballan among the Chamars.

Under the stewardship of Sant Sarwan Dass, a true emissary of Guru Ravidass, dissemination of the bani of Guru Ravidass and the proliferation of the Ravidassia faith became one of the most important missions of the Dera Sachkhand Ballan. He laid the foundation stones of various Ravidass Deras and bhawans. He sponsored construction of rooms in the Shri Guru Ravidass High School, Jalandhar; Arts and Crafts Training College, Jalandhar; Shri Guru Ravidass Technical College, Phagwara; Primary school, Raipur-Rasoolpur; Bhagwan Ravidass Ashram Nirmala Chowani, Haridwar; and High School, Village Ballan (Bawa 2004:7). The Sants of Dera Ballan has meticulously kept Sant Sarwan Dass's legacy of spreading the mission of Guru Ravidas intact. They have been spreading the message of the mission to every nook and corner of Punjab and elsewhere. The construction of Guru Ravidass Temples in Seer Govardhanpur (Varanasi), Hadiabad (Punjab), Sirsgarh (Haryana), Pune (Maharashtra), Haridwar (Uttranchal), and Una (Himachal Pradesh) is a clear indication of the concerted efforts of the Sants of Ballan towards the dissemination and popularisation of the egalitarian philosophy of Ravidass (Heer 2005:4). Moreover, they have also generated a sense of cohesive belongingness among the Punjabi Dalit diaspora as well.

The active participation by the Sants of Dera Ballan in Sant sammelans (spiritual congregations) organised by the devotees of Guru Ravidass in different parts of Punjab and outside showed their deep concern for the mission of Guru Ravidass. In the last few years they participated in 52 Sant sammelans in the year 2005, 70 in 2006 and 69 in 2007 (calculated from the various volumes of Begumpura Shaher [2005, 2006 & 2007], Trilingual weekly publication of the Dera Ballan). In the sammelans, shabads of the bani of Guru Ravidass are recited and sung, and in the end *Langer* (free food distributed among the congregation) is served to all. Such sammelans have proved very useful in providing a platform for the propagation of the teachings of Ravidass and the missions of Dera Ballan. Such Sant sammelans are in fact a sort of motivating camps for the inculcation of values of separate Dalit community among Dalits based on the philosophy of Guru Ravidass. The Sants of Ballan also visited their devotees abroad regularly in order to enlighten them of the bani of Ravidass[21].

The Sants of Dera Ballan (especially the slain Sant Ramanand) have prepared a number of cassettes, compact discs (CDs), and video compact discs (VCDs) of the bani of Guru Ravidass for wider circulation among their followers (Thind 2009). Some of the most popular cassettes are: 'Mission Guru Ravidass Ji' (Mission of Guru Ravidass), 'Kanshi wich chan chariya' (Moon in Kanshi), 'Begampura Shaher Ka Nau' (City Named Begumpura), 'Rabb Dharti Te' (God on the Earth), 'Satguru Da Updesh' (Sermon of the Guru), 'Kanshi Ballan Wich Farak Na Koe' (No Difference between Kanshi and Ballan), 'Har ke Naam Bin' (Without the Name of God), 'Amrit Bani Shri Guru Ravidass Ji' (Immortal Bani of Guru Ravidass), 'Duniya de Loko Nek Bano' (Become nice, Peoples of the World), 'Jai Satiguru Ravidas' (Victory to Guru Ravidass), 'Darshan Satguru de Kar Lau' (Be face to face with the Guru), 'Begumpur de Wasia' (Residence of the Begumpur), 'Guru Da Jehrey Nam Japde' (Those who Remember the Name of the Guru), and 'Ban ke Messiah Aya' (Came as a Messiah). 'Eh Janam Tumhare Lekhe' (This Life is for You), 'Begampure Diyan Raunkan' (Festivities of Begumpura), 'Shri Guru Ravidass Amrit Bani Dohae' (Couplets of the Immortal bani of Guru Ravidass), and 'Satsang Mahina Cheet' (company of the Santsin first month of the Hindu calendar) are some of the most popular VCDs. The six-volumes set of 'Amrit Bani of Guru Ravidass Ji' is the most popular among the CDs. They are available at Dera Ballan on nominal rates and are also given as souvenir to the devotees. During one of my visits to the Dera Ballan, Sant Surinder Dass Bawa was kind enough to gift me a set of these cassettes[22]. The Dera has also composed a Gurbani programme based on the bani of Guru Ravidass. The program is called '*Amrit Bani*: Shri Guru Ravidass ji', being telecast every Friday, 6.00 – 6.15 a.m. and every Saturday, 7.15 – 7.30 a.m. on Jalandhar Doordarshan since October 13, 2003. The programme is produced in the newly built hi-tech studio in the premises of the Dera through which live telecast of the satsang is also beamed to several countries. It has a unique importance for the Dalits who in the past were forbidden to read and hear the sacred text. It has contributed significantly in building their self-esteem and confidence that in turn has sharpened their social and political consciousness.

Primary education and healthcare were the two main social service concerns of Sant Sarwan Dass, which further strengthen the surging popularity of the Dera Ballan among the Dalits. The Sant had encouraged Dalit children to study and helped them financially. He opened an informal primary school within the premises of the Dera. He taught the poor children Panjabi and trained them in reciting Gurbani (sacred text of Guru Granth Sahib) correctly. He used to feed them with rice pudding and fried loafs on every Sunday – a diet that was really a luxury for the poor Dalit. There is a common belief among the followers of Dera Ballan that whosoever was taught by Sant Sarwan Dass became an officer in Government service (conversations with the devotees of Ravidass; and Sant Surinder Dass Bawa, priest of Dera Ballan, Ballan, 14 April 2004). He urged the poor parents to educate their children so that they could earn their livelihood in a respectful way and could lead a dignified life (Jassal 2005:7).

All the subsequent chiefs of Dera Ballan who followed Sant Sarwan Dass[23] carried on the great task of philanthropy began by him for the uplift of the downtrodden. In fact, they turned these vital concerns of capacity building into long-term missions of the Dera Sachkhand Ballan. To fulfill one of these missions, Sants of Dera Ballan founded 'Sant Sarwan Dass Model School' at Hadiabad (Phagwara) in April 2004 to provide quality education to the Dalit children on nominal fee. The school is housed in a magnificent building equipped with modern instruments and materials, and has its own fleet of buses for the conveyance of the students. The medium of instruction in the school is English. What distinguished this school is that along with formal education in different streams of knowledge, students are also informed about the missions of Guru Ravidass and Dera Sachkhand Ballan (Sandhu 2005:11, and Varghese 2006:3).

Sant Sarwan Dass also established a small *Dawakhana* (Ayurvedic clinic) at the Dera for the benefits of the downtrodden who could not afford exorbitant costly treatment and medicine in the market· The Dawakhana is still in operation and Sant Surinder Dass Bawa runs the clinic[24]. This small beginning at the Dera, however, eventually flourished into a full-fledged hospital (Sant Sarwan Dass Charitable Hospital) at Dehpur-Kapoor village Adda Kathar on the Hoshiarpur-Jalandhar road (district Jalandhar). Sant Garib Dass, the then chief of Dera Ballan, founded the hospital in 1982. A humble beginning was made with a small dispensary in 1984. Soon after, it expanded into a two hundred-bed hospital equipped with latest medical technology. The hospital is famous for its expertise in surgery in the region. It provided round the clock emergency services, and has its own medical store shop, which provided medicines at reasonable rates. For the convenience of the patients and their attendants, indoor catering facilities and spacious retiring halls are also provided. A very nominal fee is being charged from the patients to partially meet the hospital expenditure, which is about 2.5 million Indian rupees per month (Kauldhar 2003: 5 & 8, and Heer 2006:4). At a time when public health services have almost turned dysfunctional, Sant Sarwan Dass Charitable Hospital has come as a great relief to the downtrodden who are incapable of fending for themselves.

In addition, Sants of Dera Sachkhand Ballan have also been regularly organising free eyes operation camps every year, in the month of February, with the support of Swarn Dass Banger, a non-resident Indian (NRI) settled in England. A team of doctors from U.K. held a 10-days (March 16-25, 2005) medical camp in Sant Sarwan Dass Charitable Hospital. The camp had the sanction of Medical Council of India, Department of Health, UK, and British Medical Association. The camp got wide coverage in the western print media that brought the hospital on the international map. The detailed account of the camp was carried in two publications: 'Trust News' of Calderdale and Huddersfield National Health Service (NHS) and the 'Evening Courier' (Heer 2005a: 4). Swarn Dass Banger has also donated 10 million Indian rupees for the construction of Sant Sarwan Dass Memorial Eyes Hospital near the Dera and 2.5-acre prime land adjacent to the Dera where a mammoth *Satsangh Bhawan* (religious congregation hall), centrally air-conditioned with a capacity of accommodating 50000 people at a time, is constructed. Sant Niranjan Dass, the present chief of Dera Ballan, laid the foundation stone of the Eyes Hospital on November 10, 2004 (Bawa 2004:7).

Dera Ballan received a large amount of offerings in the form of money as well as kind from its Dalit NRI followers in Europe and North America. Seth Brij Lal Kaler of England has donated 10 million Indian rupees to Dera Ballan[25]. The NRI followers of the Dera Ballan in Wolverhampton donated 1.5 million Indian rupees for the construction of bathrooms and an eight feet high wall around the newly added plot to the Ravidass Temple at Seer Govardhanpur in Varanasi. The sangat (followers) from Wolverhampton and Birmingham donated 2.2 million Indian rupees to the Dera Ballan for the construction of the second story of the community dinning hall at Ravidass

Temple at Seer Govardhanpur (Bawa 2005b: preface). Dalit philanthropy apart, Dera Ballan also receives rich offerings from its large number of local followings. Recently, the NRI followers the Dera from Europe and North America donated 15 Kg. Pure Gold for the purpose of making a palanquin of Guru Ravidass, which the Sants of Dera Ballan carried in the form of a mammoth procession from the premises of the Dera to Sri Guru Ravidass Janam Asthan Temple at Seer Govardhanpur (Varanasi). The procession started from Dera Ballan on February 16 and reached Varanasi in the evening of February 20, 2008[26]. The provision of excellent satsang halls and modern hospital medical facilities in the rural sectors of Punjab is what made Dera Sachkhand Ballan an exceptional religious site for the downtrodden where spiritual and social services are combined together.

Another important feature of the Dera Sachkhand Ballan that brought it in the forefront of the cause of the Dalits' upliftment was its deep interest in literary activities. The Dera has a rich library on its premises. The library contains books on the life and philosophy of Ravidass, Babu Mangu RamMugowalia and Dr. Ambedkar, bhakti movement, Ad Dharm movement, and the several projects and missions of the Dera Ballan (based on participant observation by the author; see also: Hans 2006:3-4). The books are made available to the readers on nominal charges and even free of cost. Some of the books are also given to the devotees as a souvenir along with the framed calendar prints of the Dera Ballan and Ravidass temple (Seer Goverdhanpur) with the images of Guru Ravidass and B.R. Ambedkar embossed on them. *Religious Rebels in the Punjab: The social Vision of Untouchables* (1988), a pioneer study of the Ad Dharm movement in Punjab made by Mark Juergensmeyer, is one of the most popular books that are distributed among the devotees (based on participant observation by the author).

The Dera Ballan also publishes, and sponsors books on Dalit literature. In addition, it also confers honors on

Dalit scholars as an acknowledgement of their literary contributions towards the uplift of the downtrodden. Till now, it has honoured twenty Dalit scholars with gold medals (Bawa 2005b: XXX). In addition, the Dera has also been publishing a 12 page trilingual (Panjabi, Hindi, and English) weekly 'Begumpura Shaher' since August 15, 1991. This weekly was founded by Sant Garib Dass, fourth head of the Dera Ballan, to highlight the problems of the downtrodden and to educate them about the missions of Guru Ravidass. *'Begumpura Shaher'*, the sole mouthpiece of the Dalits who were highly under-represented in the mainstream print and electronic media, has become a source of social consciousness and a symbol of self-respect among them[27]. The *Bharatiya Dalit Sahitya* Academy (Indian Dalit Literary Academy) honoured its chief editor, Sant Ramanand, recently killed in the Vienna shooting, with the 20th National Dalit Literary Award (2004) for the contribution it made in the field of journalism and Dalit consciousness. The Academy also organized a two days National Dalit Introspection Camp (9-10 June 2006) at the Dera Ballan to discuss the commonalities among the thoughts, missions, and objectives of Buddha, Ravidass and Ambedkar. Among the prominent participants who attended the Camp were Dr. Mata Parsad, former Governor of Arunachal Pradesh, Babu Parmanand, former Governor of Haryana, Dr. Satya Narayan Jatiya, former central minister of social justice and member of parliament of India, Chanderpal Sallani, former member of parliament of India, Bavanrao Gholap, former social welfare minister of Maharashtra and member of the State Legislative Assembly, and Dr. J. S. Sabar, chair Guru Ravidass, Guru Nanak Dev University, Amritsar (Sumanakshar 2006:1). The participation by such a large number of renowned personalities in the Dalit Introspection Camp – a rare occasion of its kind at a religious site – lend credence to the missions of the Dera Ballan for the upliftment of the Dalits. In a hierarchically structured society of Punjab, the literary chapter of the

Dera Ballan has proven to be of immense importance in building confidence among the downtrodden masses, who have been on the margin in the mainstream literary circles.

Of all the major contributions made by the Dera Ballan, the construction of a mammoth 'Shri Guru Ravidass Janam Asthan Mandir' (Temple of Shri Guru Ravidass's Birthplace) at Seer Goverdhanpur, a locality in the city of Varanasi is the most significant. The Sants of Ballan traced the birthplace of Ravidass to a location in the village Seer Goverdhanpur, on the outskirts of Varanasi, near the Banaras Hindu University (BHU). Sant Hari Dass of Dera Ballan had laid down the foundation stone of the temple on June 14, 1965. Dalits from India and abroad contributed enormously towards the construction of the temple. Giani Zail Singh, the President of India (July 25 1982-July 25, 1987), visited Shri Guru Ravidass Janam Asthan Temple Seer Govardhanpur on May 25, 1984 (Sachhi Kahani 2007: 11-12). The construction of the temple was completed in 1994. Babu Kanshi Ram, the BSP supremo, performed the ceremonial installation of the golden dome atop the temple. KR Narayanan, the then President of India, performed the opening ceremony of the huge monumental gate on the way to the temple, on July16, 1998.

Shri Guru Ravidass Janam Asthan Mandir at Seer Goverdhanpur has acquired perhaps the same importance for Dalits as the 'Mecca' for Muslims and the 'Golden Temple' for Sikhs (based on conversations at Deras). Every year during birth anniversary of Guru Ravidass, the Mandir attracts millions of devotees from India and abroad. The Dera Sachkhand Ballan made special arrangements for the pilgrimage of Ravidass devotees to their *Mecca* at Seer Goverdhanpur (Varanasi). Special trains were arranged from Jalandhar city in Punjab to Varanasi especially to participate in the celebrations of the birth anniversary of Ravidass. This temple serves an important purpose in reminding Dalits of silent social *revolution* led by Ravidass in Varanasi, the headquarters of Hindu religiosity. Its unique contribution lies in symbolising a vision for future and the forgotten history of the Dalit struggle for equality and dignity in the medieval India. Amidst the erstwhile headquartes of the oppressive Hindu social order, 'Temple of Shri Guru Ravidass's Birthplace' has become an important cultural and religious site for the assertion of distinct identity where the ex-untouchables can move around with their heads high and without the fear of being measured on the scale of caste hierarchy any more – in a way *Begumpura* in the making. In fact, this temple has turned out to be a repository of separate Dalit identity.

In the following part of this section, I shall explore the process of the development of the separate Dalit identity in Punjab in the context of the rituals and ceremonial traditions as formulated by the Sants of Dera Ballan, and how they are linked with the teachings and the bani of Guru Ravidass.

Dera Sachkhand Ballan became a paragon of Ravidass movement in Northwest India. It made concerted efforts for the construction of a separate Dalit identity, independent of both Sikhism and Hinduism – the two main religious traditions of the region. The architecture of Dera Ballan is unique in its outlook. It resembles both a temple and a Gurdwara at the same time. Though Guru Granth Sahib is placed in the Dera but unlike a Gurdwara, the idols of Guru Ravidass and the late heads of the Dera Ballan are also installed in its premises and are worshipped along with Guru Granth Sahib[28]. The membership of the management committees of the Ravidass Deras is strictly confined to Ravidassia Dalits only. No upper caste Sikh is allowed to become a member of the managing committees of the Ravidass Deras and Sabhas.

In Ravidass Deras, Ravidass is worshipped as Guru. Moreover, Gaddi Nashins (heads) of the Ravidass Deras are also considered as Gurus. Sant Niranjan Dass is the fifth Gaddi Nashin in the line of individual Gurus in the Dera Ballan. However, in Sikh religion, Ravidass is known as Bhakta. In Sikh religion only the ten Gurus and Guru Granth Sahib are considered the legitimateGurus. The issue of Bhakta versus Guru has not only pitted the Ravidassia community and Jat Sikhs against each other in Punjab and elsewhere, but has also led to communal polarization between the Sikh and Dalit diasroras.[29]. The recent Vienna incident is a violent escalation of this chronic communal polarisation. Another factor that distinguishes Sants of Ballan from the priests of Sikh religion (especially since the formation of Khalsa in 1699) has been their nomenclature. The titles of their last names are 'Dass' (humble). Perhaps, they inherited the tradition of suffixing 'Dass' from the very name of their Guru Ravi (Dass). The titles of the last names of the Sikhs are invariably 'Singh'[30]. Though Sants of Dera Sachkhand Ballan don turban, keep unshorn hair and flowing beard like that of the Sikh priests, still they do not consider themselves Sikhs. One of the heads of the Dera Ballan, Sant Garib Dass, was a clean-shaven. It is in this context that the Dera Ballan has emerged as an alternative religious site, separate from Hindus and Sikhs, for the Dalits with its own code of conduct that paved the way for the separate Dalit identity.

The religious insignia of Dera Ballan and of all other Ravidassia Deras is 'Har' (Supreme Being)[31]. This insignia, also known as 'Koumi Nishan' of the Ravidassia samaj. The religious symbol of the Sikh Gurdwaras is 'Khanda' (Two-edged sword over a quoit with two crossed sabers below the quoit). The insignia 'Har' is composed of a Sun-like circle with an image of forty rays on its circular edge. The forty rays round the circle of the insignia signify forty hymns of Guru Ravidass. Within the circle, there is another smaller circle within which 'Har' is inscribed in Gurmukhi script with a sign of flame on the top of it. The flame represents the 'Naam' (word) that would illuminate the entire world. The sign of flame crosses over into the bigger circle. In between the bigger and smaller circles is written a couplet *Naam tere kee jot lagayi, Bhaio Ujiaaro Bhawan saglaare* (Your Name is the flame I light; it has illuminated the entire world). This inner circle couplet is taken from one of the forty hymns of Guru Ravidass. The insignia 'Har' represents the very being of Ravidass and his teachings. The insignia *Har* is chosen after the name of their Guru [Ravi<Sun>dass<servant>] (servant of the sun) in the image. The Dalits, especially the Chamars of Punjab, proudly hoist flags with the print of insignia 'Har' atop their religious places, and vehicles during processions on the occasions of Guru Ravidass birth anniversaries and other festivities. The insignia 'Har' has become a password of the separate Dalit identity.

The format of the Ardas (a formal prayer recited at most Sikh rituals) performed in the Ravidass Deras also differentiates them from that of Sikh religion. It is comprised of a Shloka (couplet) and one of the forty hymns of Guru Ravidass. It closes with the utterance: *Bole So Nirbhay, Sri Guru Ravidass Maharaj Ki Jai* (Fearless is the one who utters: Victory to Shri Guru Ravidass). Whereas, in the Sikh religion the Ardas concluded with: *Bole So Nihal, Sat Sri Akal* (Blessed is the one who utters: True is the Immortal One). The reference to Nirbhay (fearless) in the conclusion of the Ardas of the Ravidass Deras has become a central motif of the Dalit consciousness. The inclusion of the word 'Nirbhay' in the Ardas of Ravidass Deras is thus not only symptomatic of the historical oppression of the Dalits at the hands of the upper castes, but is also reflective of their determined willingness to confront it head-on.

Like the Ardas, the Aarti (a Hindu ceremony of adoration which consists of waving round the head of an idol on a platter containing five burning wicks) that Ballan Sants perform in front of the sanctum sanctorum of their Dera differentiate them from that of Hindu temples.[32] The Ballan Sants do not wave platter of burning wicks. They blow conch-shell and rattle gong, which is followed by recitation of a hymn from the bani of Ravidass (based on participant observation). The salutations in the Ravidass Dera are also formulated selectively in order to project their unique and independent religious identity. Every religious community has its own way of greeting. *Sat Shri Akaal* (True is the Immortal One) is the greeting of the Sikhs. *Jai Ram Ji Ki* or *Jai Sita-Ram* (Victory to Ram or Victory to Sita-Ram) is of the Hindus. Ravidass *Deras* adopted the greegting: *Jai Gurudev* or *Jai Guru Ravidass* (Victory to the divine Guru or Guru Ravidass) to which the reply was *Dhan Guru Dev* (blessed the divine Guru). The short version of the greetings is Jai Santan Di [Victory to the Saints]. The forms of Ardas, Arati, and salutations adopted by the Sants of Dera Ballan have thus become distinct markers of the separate identity of the Dalits of the region. In other words, the Dera Ballan has evolved into a nursery for the cultivation of symbols, icons, signifiers, and narratives to shape the separate Dalit identity.

Despite the fact that Ravidassias and Ravidass Deras have emerged as a separate community and distinct Dalit religious space respectively, the former continued to be confused with Dalit Sikhs and the latter with gurdwaras probably because of the appearances of some of the Ravidassias, on the one hand, and the presence of Guru Granth Sahib within the premises of Ravidass Deras, on the other. Not only that, it has further led to a sort of contradiction between the long established Sikh rahit maryada (code of conduct) and observance of non-Sikh rituals and traditions within Ravidass Deras such as touching the feet of the Heads of the Deras and worshiping the idols and calendar images of bhakt Ravidass revered as Guru. This contradiction is considered to be one of the several main reasons behind the ghastly shooting incidence that took place at the Raviadss temple in Vienna on May 24, 2009. The Sants of Dera Ballan took strong objection to the gross misrepresentation of their mission and the dilution of their separate Ravidassia Dalit identity as clubbed with the mainstream Sikh religion in national as well as international print and electronic media.

It was against this crucial backdrop that the Ballan Sants decided to completely detach themselves from a long preserved tradition of reciting the holy bani from Guru Granth Sahib on the important occasions of birth and death anniversaries of the Sants of Dera Ballan and of Guru Ravidass. This was perhaps for the first time in the 109-year-old existence of the Dera Sachkhand Ballan that on June 11, 2009 (death anniversary of Sant Sarwan Dass) and again on June 13, 2009 (*antim ardas*, the last condolence concluding ceremony of Sant Ramanand, the deputy chief of Dera Ballan, who died in the Vienna shooting) the religious ceremonies were organised without the 'parkash' of Guru Granth Sahib. "The palanquin or canopy, under which Sikhs' holy book is usually placed for reading scriptures, instead held the portrait of Sant Sarwan Dass in whose name the Ballan Dera was established nearly a century ago" reported Times of India (June 14, 2009). Dera spokesperson SR Heer called this deviation a "reaction to Vienna incident' and "decision of Sants of the Dera" (Times of India, June 14, 2009). The deviation and the strategic silence about it, however, is intended to sharply focus on the separate Ravidassi Dalit identity than on distancing from close ties with mainstream Sikhism. Moreover, the deviation has also been widely perceived by the large followings of the Dera as a permanent solution to the blown up communal issue of the violation of the Sikh code of conduct at Ravidass Deras. On the 634th birthday of Guru Ravidass in 2011, the Sants of Dera Ballan celebrated the first anniversary of the newly established "Ravidassia religion" (Hindustan Times, February 16, 2011). They also appealed to the followers of the Ravidassia religion to record themselves as follower of this new Dalit religion in the forthcoming 2011 census of India (Begumpura Shaher, February 14, 20011: 10).

Endnotes

1 A religious–military order with strict code of conduct mandatory for all the followers who are to believe in one absolute but formless God. This order was instituted by Guru Gobind Singh, the tenth Master of Sikh faith, on Baisakhi Day (the first day of the Indian year) probably in 1969. For details see: McLeod 1995:121-122).

2 Humble Kingdom where no one is put to any harm. This term is associated with the Fifth Master, Guru Arjun Dev, of the Sikh faith.

3 Dera, literally mean a holy abode free from the structural bindings of institionalised religious orders, is a headquarters of a group of devotees owing allegiance to a particular spiritual person, who is reverently addressed as Baba, Sant or Maharaj. A Dera thrives on a distinct philosophy, rituals and symbol, which are inspired by the teachings and philosophy of a particular holy person after whom it has been established.

4 The proportion of the SC population is further going to increase rather significantly, as *Mahatam, Rai Sikh* – another downtrodden community – has recently been included in the SCs list of the Indian constitution [(f) in part XIV] wide Constitution (Scheduled Castes) order (Amendment) Act, 2007, No 31 dated 29th August, 2007 (Punjab Government Gazette, Regd. No. CHD/0092/2006-2008, No. 45, November 9, 2007).

5 The attack was lauched on the two topmost Sants of the Dera Sachkhand Ballan during the sermon ceremony on May 24, 2009 at Guru Ravidass Temple situated in Vienna-Rudolfsheim, the capital's 15th district near Westbahnholf, one of Vienna's main train stations. The number of the persons involved in the attack was reportedly six, who were overpowered by around 200 devotes gathered at the occasion. In the melee around two 16 people were reportedly injured. Sant Ramanand, the second-in-command of Dera Ballan later on succumbed to his injuries in the hospital (http://www.nytimes.com/aponline/2009/05/24/world/AP-EU-Austria-Temple-Shooting.ht accessed 5/25/2009.

6 The two most important missions are All India Adi-Dharm Mission (New Delhi), and Dera Sachkhand Ballan (Punjab).

For details see: Schaller 1996:111-6; Hawley 1988:271; Hawley and Juergensmeyer 1988:19-20; Juergensmeyer 1988.

7 Dera Sachkhand Ballan has established the following international charitable trusts abroad for dissemination of the bani of Ravidass amongst the Dalit diaspora: Shri 108 Sant Sarwan Dass Charitable Trust [U.K.]; Shri 108 Sant Sarwan Dass Charitable Trust [Vancouver] Canada; and Shri 108 Sant Sarwan Dass Charitable Trust [U.S.A.].

8 The outcastes were beyond the *Varna* (literally color) and were known as *Achhuts, Ati shudras, Chandalas, Antyajas, Pariahs, Dheds, Panchamas, Avarnas, Anariyas, Namashudras, Harijans* etc. They were placed at the bottom of the social hierarchy and were meant to serve the *Varna* categories - *Brahmin, Kshatriya, Vaishya* and even the Shudras. The British regime in the country clubbed them first under the legal category of Depressed Classes and then the term SCs. And in independent India the term SCs became a constitutional category. They performed hereditary menial occupation, such as scavenging, shoe-making and animal carcass removing. Some of them embraced Christianity, Islam, Sikhism and Buddhism in order to evade the oppression of untouchability. However, even their conversion to other religions could not protect them from the ruthless onslaughts of untouchability. (For details see: Ambedkar n.d.; Chopra 1982:121-2; Gokhale 1986:270; Juergensmeyer 1988:84; Puri 2004:190-224; Beltz 2005: 39; Ram 2001:146-170).

9 Though the founders of the Ad Dharm movement appealed to all the untouchables in the state, the response of the Chamars was tremendous. Majority of the total of 418,789 Ad Dharmis, who joined the movement within the four years of its origin, belonged to the Chamar caste (Juergensmeyer 1988: 77; see also Mendelsohn and Vicziany 2000: 102). Chamar is an umbrella caste category that clubs together "Chamar, Jatia Chamar, Rehgar, Raigar, Ramdasi and Ravidasi" (Census of India 1981, Series 17 <Punjab> Part IX. They comprise about twenty six percent (1991 census) of the total Scheduled caste population of the state. If clubbed with Ad Dharmis, they together comprised forty two percent of the total Scheduled caste population in Punjab (Gosal 2004:23). Since majority of the Ad Dharmis are Chamars, they are popularly called as Ad Dharmi Chamars. Chamars and Ad Dharmi Chamars are mostly concentrated

in the Doaba sub-region of the state. Mazhbis (Sweepers who embraced Sikhism) is another top ranking caste among the SCs in Punjab. They constitute about 30 percent of the total SCs population in the state (1991 census). Their Hindu counterpart Chuhras (Balmikis and Bhangis) constitutes 11.1 percent of the total Scheduled Caste population. Thus out of the total 38 SCs the two major groupings of Chuhras and Chamars together constitute 80 percent of the total Scheduled Caste population. (See also: Deep 2001:7; Puri 2004:4).

10 Mishra, Vandita, "Inside Dera Sachkhand", *The Sunday Express*, May 31, 2009, p.5.

11 Ibid.

12 Ibid.

13 For a detailed theoretical understanding of this point in a broader context refer to: Srinivas 1956: 481-496.

14 *Mahatam, Rai Sikh* – another downtrodden community – has recently been included in the SCs list of the Indian constitution (Constitution (Scheduled Castes) order (Amendment) Act, 2007, No 31 dated 29th August, 2007 (Punjab Government Gazette, Regd. No. CHD/0092/2006-2008, No. 45, November 9, 2007).

15 Based on conversations with the priests of Dera Ballan, 14 April 2004; Virinder Kumar Banger, a devotee of Guru Ravidass and follower of the Dera Ballan, Vancouver, 17 May 2003.

16 As reported in one of the most polpular Dalit web site: httop://www.ambedkartimes.com/about_Ambedkar.htm [November 11, 2007].

17 Sant Hiran Dass of this Dera established Ravidass Sabha in 1907 and published a collection of Ravidass's poems under the title *Rae Das Ki Bani,* Allahabad: Belvedere Press, 1908.

18 Mangu Ram Jaspal was an NRI Ad Dharmi of village Haryana near Hoshiarpur, Punjab. He returned from England and got settled in Jalandhar in 1970. He took active interest in reviving the Ad Dharm movement in Doaba region of Punjab and convened a Conference on December 13, 1970 at Dera Sachkhand Ballan and revived Ad Dharm Mandal

as Ad Dharm Scheduled Castes Federation. He died on February 15, 2011.

19 For biographical details see: (Bawa 2005:2 and Bawa 2005a: 5 &2).

20 Based on conversations with Ajit Chand Nimta, a poet and devotee of Ravidass, Jalandhar, 14 April 2003; Chaman Lal, a follower of Dera Ballan, Chandigarh, 17 August 2002.

21 In year 2005, the present head of Dera Ballan, Sant Niranjan Dass accompanied by late Sant Ramanand, visited Greece, Italy, Spain, Holland, and Germany from March 20 to May 31; and U.S., Canada and U.K. from July 1 to August 31. During April-May 2006 he paid visits to Europe (Italy, Greece Germany, Holland and England). This was his 4th international religious visit to Italy and probably 14th to U.K. (Madahar 2006:1, 9 & 5). In 2007 Sant Niranjan Dass along with Sant Ramanand paid visits to their followers in Europe and North America during the months of September and October (Madahar 2007). Sant Garib Dass, predecessor of Sant Niranjan Dass, also visited England six times, America four times, and Canada two times (conversation with Sant Surinder Dass Bawa, priest of Dera Ballan, Ballan, 14 April 2004).

22 Based on field notes.

23 Sant Hari Dass (June 11, 1972-February 7, 1982), Sant Garib Dass (February 7, 1982-July 23, 1994), and Sant Niranjan Dass (July 23, 1994 – Continuing).

24 Based on participant observation by the author.

25 Based on conversation with Som Nath Bharti Qadian, Dera Ballan, 14 April 2004.

26 Based on personal communication with one of the participants in the procession; see also Rozana Spokesman, February 17, 2008.

27 In the first-ever statistical analysis of the social profile of more than 300 senior journalists in 37 Hindi and English newspapers and television channels in New Delhi, the capital of India, it was found that Dalits and Adivasis (tribals, designated as Scheduled Tribes [ST] in the constitution of India) "...[were] conspicuous by their absence among the decision-makers. Not even one of the 315 key decision-makers belonged to the SCs or Scheduled Tribes" (The Hindu [Delhi Edition], June 5, 2006).

28 Based on participant observation by the author.

29 "In 1980, a Punjabi Dalit went to a Sikh Gurudawara in Vancouver to pay his respectful tribute. While speaking on the podium, he mentioned the name of Sant Ravidas as "Guru" Ravidas. The moment he mentioned this name, he faced sharp objections and reactions from the preachers and the members of the management committee. This grave sense of great humiliation of a Dalit in Sikh Gurudwara triggered a mass mobilization of Dalits in Canada. These Dalits collected donations from Dalits living in all over Canada and bought a piece of land to build their own Gurudwara. Later Shri Guru Ravidas Sabha of Vancouver built a huge beautiful Shri Guru Ravidas Gurudwara in Vancouver. ... Later these Ravidasis decided to commemorate the birth anniversary of their Guru Shri Guru Ravidas. They requested a local Punjabi Newspaper to carry a paid advertisement about the birth anniversary of Shri Guru Ravidas. That newspaper not only refused to publish their advertisement, even ridiculed them for adding prefix "Guru" with the name of Sant Ravidas. The newspaper made an issue out of it and managed to create disharmony and antagonism between Ravidassia community and Jat-Sikhs. Nevertheless another Punjabi newspaper the Indo-Canadian Times not only agreed to publish the add with prefix "Guru" with Sant Ravidas, it also wrote an editorial why should Sant Ravidas be called as "Guru" and why should Dalits have rights and freedom to call Sant Ravidass as Shri Guru Ravidas" (Singh 2003:39). I came across a similar case study during my visit to Shri Guru Ravidass Temple Sacramento (Rio Linda), California on 30 May 2008.

30 The title 'Singh' became popular among the Sikhs after the formation of the Khalsa in 1699. Before that the names of all the Sikh Gurus were not followed by the title 'Singh'.

31 However, the earlier insignia of the Ad Dharm Mandal of 1926 as well as of the All India Adi Dharam Mission (Regd.) of 1960 was *Sohang*. The Sants of Dera Ballan changed it into *Har* with the approval of the Ravidass Sadhu Sampradaya of Punjab, Ravidass Deras, and the various Guru Ravidass *Sabhas* (Committees) both within India and abroad. It was registered under the Copyright Act 1957, Government of India vide registration no. A48-807/87/CO dated March 6, 1987. Later on, the change of the insignia

became a bone of contention between the All India Adi Dharm Mission (Regd.) and the Dera Ballan. The Sants of Dera Ballan justified the change on the ground that Guru Ravidass did not use the word *Sohang* in his sacred poetry at all. On the contrary, he used the word *Har* as many as 24 times. Moreover, it is alleged that the word *Sohang*, being an article of spiritual faith, cannot be used casually and publicly in the form of an insignia. The All India Adi Dharm Mission (Regd.) refused to buy this logic of the Dera Ballan and continued to adhere to the original insignia *of Sohang* (Sachhi Kahani [The True Story] 2007: 50-66*)*. Though the insignia *Har* has become an acceptable symbol of the entire Ravidasia community in Punjab and abroad, but some of the temples abroad (Shri Guru Ravidass Temple Pittsburg [California]) still adhered to the old insignia of *Sohang* or display both of the insignia on their (Shri Guru Ravidass Sabha, New York) letter pads (based on field observation on May 25 –June 3, 2008). For a detailed account of the frequency of the word *Har* and other similar sacred names of the *Nirakar* (formless God) used by Guru Ravidass in his poetry recorded in the Adi Granth (Guru Granth Sahib) of the Sikh faith see: Singh 2001: 45-46).

32 In Sikh Gurdwaras, however, *Aarti* is not performed. Guru Nanak referred to *Aarti* in the hymn *Dhanasari* 3 (Adi Granth: 13). The entire cosmos, said he, is performing the *Aarti* of a single God. The whole sky is the platter and all the stars are its burning wicks (for details see: Deep 2001:44-46).

References

Ambedkar, B.R. n.d. *The Untouchables: Who were They and Why They Became Untouchable?* Jalandhar: Bhim Patrika Publications.

Ambedkar, B.R. (1995). *Annihilation of Caste*. Jalandhar: Bheem Patrika. 3rd Edn.

Ambedkari, Nirmal. 2005. "Dera Sachkhand Ballan Dae Manjil Whal Vadde Kadam" (The Surging Steps of Dera Sachkhand Ballan towards its Destination). *Begumpura Shaher* (weekly, Jalandhar) 2 (May): 12.

Bawa, Sant Surinder Das. 2003. "Brahamleen Satguru Swami Sarwan Dass Ji Maharaj" (Spiritually Realized Great Master Sarwan Dass Ji). *Begupura Shaher* 6 (June): 4&9.

.... 2004. "Mahan Samaj Sudharak Brahamleen Satguru Sarwan Dass Ji Maharaj" (Late SantSarwan Dass Ji Maharaj: A Great Social reformer). *Begumpura Shaher* 14 (June): 6-7.

..............2005. "Brahamgiani Shri 108 SantBaba Pipal Dass Ji Maharaj" (Spiritually Realized Shri 108 SantBaba Pipal Dass Ji). *Begumpura Shaher* 3 (October): 2.

................2005a. [Trnsl. Amarjit Jassal]. "A Great Spiritual Sant–Sant Pipal Dass". *Begumpura Shaher* 28 (November): 5 and, 5 (December): 2.

..................2005b. *Shri Guru Ravidass Amrit Bani Atey Sankeph Jiwan* (Immortal Poetry of Guru Ravidass and Brief Life). Varanasi: Sri Guru Ravidass Janam Asthan Charitable Trust (Regd).

Beltz, Johannes. 2005. *Mahar, Buddhist and Dalit: Religious Conversion and Socio-Political Emancipation*. New Delhi: Manohar.

—————————. 2004. "Introduction", in Surendra Jondhale and Johannes Beltz, (eds.), *Reconstructing the World: B.R. Ambedkar and Buddhism in India*. New Delhi: Oxford University Press.

Bingley, A. H. (1899 [1978]). *History, Caste & Culture of Jats and Gujars*. New Delhi: Ess Ess Publications. 2nd edn.

Chaturvedi, Parshuram. 1952. *Uttari Bharat ki Sant-parampara* (*SantTradition of North India*). Prayag: Bharati Bhandhar.

Chopra, P.N, ed. 1982. *Religions and Communities of India*. New Delhi: Vision Books

Deep, Dalip Singh. 2001. *Sadhan Main Ravidasa Sant: Jiwan Ate Vichar* (Sant*Ravidass among the Saints: Life and Thought*). Patiala: Punjabi University.

Gill, Sucha Singh. (2000). "Agrarian Change and Struggle of Rural Labour in Indian Punjzab", *International Journal of Punjab Studies,* Vol. 7, No. 1, January-June, pp. 73-91

Gokhale, Jayashree B. 1986. "The Sociopolitical Effects of Ideological Change: The Buddhist Conversion of Maharashtrian Untouchables". *The Journal of Asian Studies* XLV.2 (February): 269-92.

Gosal, R.P.S. 2004. "Distribution and Relative Concentration of Scheduled Caste population in Punjab". In *Dalits in Regional Context*, ed. Harish K. Puri. Jaipur: Rawat.

Grewal, J. S. 1944. *The Sikhs of Punjab*. New Cambridge University of India.New Delhi: Foundation Books.

——————.1996. *Sikh Ideology: Polity and Social Order*. New Delhi: Manohar.

Hawley, John Stratton. 1988. "Author and Authority in the *Bhakti* Poetry of North India". *The Journal of Asian* Studies 47.2 (May): 269-90.

.... and Mark Juergensmeyer. 1988. *Songs of the Sants of India*. New York: Oxford University Press.

Heer, S.R. 2005. "Proliferation of Guru Ji' Messages". *Begum Pura Shaher* 26 (December): 4.

.............2005a. "SantSarwan Dass Charitable Hospital Gets Publicity in Foreign Print Media". *Begumpura Shaher* 13 (June): 4.

.... 2006. "A Dream Fulfilled". *Begumpura Shaher*, 2 (January): 4.

Hutton, J.H. 1963. *Caste in India: Its Nature, Function and Origins*. London: Oxford University Press.

Ibbetson, Sir Denzil. [1883] 1970. *Punjab Castes*. Punjab: Language Department Punjab.

Jassal, Amarjit. 2005. "Begampura and Dera Sachkhand Ballan". *Begum Pura Shaher* 10 (October): 7.

Jodhka, Surinder S. 2002. "Caste and Untouchability In Rural Punjab". *Economic and Political Weekly*. Vol. 37, No. 19, May 11-17, pp. 1813-1823.

Judge, Paramjit and Grupreet Bal. 2009. *Mapping Dalits: Contemporay Reality and Future Prospects in Punjab*, New Delhi: Rawat.

Juergensmeyer, Mark 1988. *Religious Rebels in the Punjab: The Social Vision of Untouchables*. Delhi: Ajanta.

Kauldhar, Shinda. 2003. "Shri 108 SantNiranjan Dass Maharaj Ji Atey SantRamanand Ji Di Italy Yatra – Ik Report". (Italy Journey of Sh.108 SantNiranjan Dass Ji and SantRamanand – A Report) *Begum Pura Shaher* 11 (August): 5 & 8.

Kaur, Ravinder. 1986. "Jat Sikhs: A Question of Identity", *Contributions to Indian Sociology (n.s.)*, Vol. 20, No. 2, pp. 221-39.

Madahar, kirpal Chand. 2006. "Historic Journey of April to May 2006 Europe England By the Present (Gaddi Nashin) Chairperson of Sachkhand Ballan His Holiness, Hazoor Ji Satguru 108 Sant Niranjan Dass Maharaj Ji and His Minister

Shri 108 Sant Rama Nand Maharaj Ji". *Begumpura Shaher* 22 (May): 1 and 9; 29 (May): 5.

.... 2007. "Shri Guru Ravidass Mission Parchar and Hari Satsang in U. K., U. S. A. & Canada 2 September 07 to Ist week of October 2007". *Begumpura Shaher* 17 (September): 5.

Marenco, Ethne K. 1976. *The Transformation of a Sikh Society*. New Delhi: Heritage.

Mcleod, W.H. (1976). *The Evolution of Sikh Community*. Oxford: Clarendon Press.

——————. [trnsl & ed]. (1984). *Textual Sources for the Study of Sikhism*. Manchester: Manchester University Press.

——————. *Guru Nanak and the Sikh Religion*. Oxford: Oxford University Press.

——————. 1995. Historical Dictionary of Sikhism. New Delhi: Oxford University Press.

Meeta and Rajivlochan. (2007). "Caste and Religion in Punjab: Case of the Bhaniarawala Phenomenon", *EPW*, Vol. XLII, No. 21, May 26-June 1, pp.1909-13.

Mendelsohn, O. and M. Vicziany. 2000. *The Untouchables: Subordination, Poverty and the State in Modern India*. Cambridge: Cambridge University Press.

Muktsar, Gurnam Singh. 1999. "Every Jati has separate Gurdwara Even as Sikhs are Busy with Khalsa Fete", *Dalit Voice*, June 16-30.

——————. 2003. "Sikhs Divided into 3 Warring Camps: Upper Castes, Jats, and Dalits". Dalit Voice (Banglore) 1-15 (August): 21-22.

——————. (2007). "Sikh Dharm Banam Dera Sacha Sauda aur Dalit Peshra Logg" [Sikh Religion versus Dera Sacha Sauda and Dalit Backward People], *Himayati* (Delhi), June, p. 1.

Omvedt, Gail. 2008. *Seeking Begumpura: The Social Vision of Anticaste Intellectuals*. Pondicherry: Navayana.

Puri, Harish K. 2004. "Introduction", In *Dalits Context in Regional*, ed. Harish K. Puri. Jaipur: Rawat.

————————. 2003. "Scheduled Castes in Sikh Community: A Historical Perspective". *Economic and Political weekly*. Vol. 38, No. 26, June 28-July 4, pp. 2693-2701.

Qadian, Som Nath Bharti. 2003. *Jagat Guru Ravidass Sampradaya SantTe Sadhna Sthal* (Santsand Deras of World Guru Ravidass Panth). Jalandhar: Dera Sant Sarwan Dass Ji Sachkhand Ballan.

Rajshekar, V. T. 2004. "A Silent Socio-cultural Revolution Sweeps Punjab: Ravidass Santsgain Millions of Followers". *Dalit Voice* (Bangalore) 23.13(July): 3-5.

Ram, Ronki. 2001. "From Servitude to Assertion: Ambedkar's Subaltern Approach to Nationalism and Dalit Liberation", *Social Sciences Research Journal* (Chandigarh) 9.2: 146-170.

————. 2004a. "Untouchability, Dalit Consciousness, and the Ad Dharm Movement in Punjab". *Contributions to Indian Sociology* (N.S) 38.3 (September-December): 323-349.

————. 2004b. "Untouchability in India with a Difference: Ad Dharm, Dalit Assertion and Caste Conflicts in Punjab". *Asian Survey* XLIV.6 (November/December): 895-912.

————. 2004c. "The Dalit Sikhs". *Dalit International Newsletter* (Waterford, CT.). 9.3(October): 5-7.

.... 2007. "Social Exclusion, Resistance and Deras: Exploring the Myth of Casteless Sikh Society in Punjab", *Economic and Political Weekly*, October 6, Vol. XLII, No. 40, pp. 4066-4074

————. 2008. "Ravidass Deras and Social Protest: Making Sense of Dalit Consciousness in Punjab (India)". *The Journal of Asian Studies*. Vol. 67, No. 4, December, pp.1341-64.

————. 2009a. "Regional Specificities and Caste Hierarchies in Punjab", *Indian Journal of Politics*, Vol. 43(2), pp.15-29.

————. 2009b. "Ravidass, Dera Sachkhand Ballan and the Question of Dalit Identity in Punjab", *Journal of Punjab Studies*, (UCSB), Spring, Vol. 16, No. 1, pp. 1-34.

————. 2009c. "Dera Sachkhand Ballan: Repository of Dalit Consciousness", Deccan Herald, Monday 1 June (http://www.deccanherald.com/content/5450/dera-sachkhand-ballan-repository-dalit.html).

——————. 2010. "Burden of Tradition and Vision of Equality: Political Sociology of Jutt-Dalit Conflicts in Punjab", in Birinder Pal Singh, ed., *Punjab Peasantry in Turmoil*, Delhi: Manohar, pp. 265-95.

Rawat, Ramnarayan S. 2003. "Making Claims for Power: A New Agenda in Dalit Politics of Uttar Pradesh, 1946-48". *Modern Asian Studies* (Cambridge) 37. 3: 585-612.

Saberwal, Satish. 1976. *Mobile Men: Limits to Social Change in Urban Punjab*. New Delhi: Vikas.

——————————. 1973. "Receding Pollution: Intercaste Relations in Urban Punjab", *Sociological Bulletin*. Vol. 22, No.3, September, pp. 234-59.

Sachhi Kahani [The True Story]. 2007. Adi-dharm Mandal atye Mission da Itihas (True Story: History of the Ad-dharm Mandal and Mission). New Delhi: All India Adi-dharm Mission (Regd).

Sachomer, Karine, and W.H. McLeod, eds. 1987. *The Saints: Studies in a Devotional Tradition of India*. Delhi: Berkeley Religious Studies Series and Motilal Banarsidass.

Schweitzer, Albert. 1989, rpt. 1935. Trans. Mrs. Charley E.B. Russell. *Indian Thought and Its Development*. New Delhi: Kalyani.

Sandhu, Mohinder. 2005. "Mission Parchar Da Dhurra Dera Sachkhand Ballan" (Hub of the Propagation of the Mission: Dera Sachkhand Ballan). *Begam Pura Shaher* 27 (June):11.

Schaller, Joseph. 1996. "Sanskritization, Caste Uplift, and Social Dissidence in the SantRavidâs Panth". In *Bhakti Religion in North India: Community Identity and Political Action*, ed. David N. Lorenzen. New Delhi: Manohar.

Sidhu, H. S. 1991. *Agricultural Development and Rural Labour: A Case Study of Punjab and Haryana*. New Delhi: Concept.

Singh, Balwant. 2002. *The Suffering People*. Saharanpur: Ambedkar Mission Publication.

Singh, Master Hari. 1980. *Agricultural Workers' Struggle in Punjab*. New Delhi: People's Publishing House.

Singh, Khushwant. 1953. *The Sikhs*. London: George Allen Unwin.

Singh, Darshan. 1996. *The Study of Bhakta Ravidasa*, 2nd edn. Patiala: Punjabi University.

Singh, Bhai Jodh. 2000. *Bhagat Ravidas: Jiwan Te Rachna* (Bhagat Ravidass: Life and Works). Patiala: Punjabi University.

Singh, K.P. 2003. "Global Movement of Dalits: Dalits in North America", *The Vancouver Vision on Diversity*. Canada: The Association For International Dalit Conference Inc., pp.35-40.

Singh, Sahib. 2001. Bhagat-Bani Steek: Hisa Duja (Bani Bhagat Ravidass Ji) [Exegesis of the Sacred Verses of the Medieval Saints: Part II (Hymns of SantRavidass Ji)]. Amritsar: Singh Brothers.

Srinivas, M.N. 1956. "A Note on Sanskritization and Westernization", *The Far Eastern Quarterly*, Vol. 15, No. 4, 1956, pp.481-96.

Sumanakshar, Sohanpal. 2006. "Dalit Chintan Shiver, Ballan ka Nishkarsh" (Dalit Introspection Camp, Conclusion of Ballan). *Himayati* (Delhi) 44.18 (June):1& 44.19 (July):1.

Tandon, P. 1961. *Punjabi Centuary (1857-1947)*. New York: Harcourt, Brace and World.

Tehna, Avtar Singh *et al*. 2007. "Kyon Bandey hann Derae?" [Why Deras Come into Existence?], *Desh Sewak*, Sunday Magazine, June 3.

Thapar, Romila. 2000. "Interpreting Early India" (1992) in Romila Thapar, *History and Beyond*. New Delhi: Oxford University Press.

Thind, Amarjit. 2009. "Sant Ramanand was target: Eyewitness", The Tribune, June 15.

Varghese, Joy M. 2006. "SantSarwan Dass Model school Hadiabad, Annual Report of 2005-06". *Begum Pura* Shaher 30 (January): 3.

Verma, Archana B. 2002. *The Making of Little Punjab in Canada: Patterns of Immigration*. New Delhi: Sage.

14

Roots of Leather Working People from the 1000 BC and Tanning

Dr. Jayaram Gollapudi*

The article shows me realistic of Leather working communities in Telangana and also India; especially how they are experts in Tanning, Shoes making, repairing and also great business people also, from the beginning of the Ancient period or days dressing with different animals skins like Buffalo, Dear, Tiger and Elephants etc; with the Leather ornaments also very popular on those days.

Medieval time the Leather used as a writing Paper and covering the book binding.

Jambavan Samrjyam (Madiga /Mang/Chamar/ Matang Dynasty

Before the Varna System the Leather work is a top best Technology worldwide. First Kings and business community also leather workers; Adi Jambava is the Mula Purusha for the Madiga, Mathang , Chamar ,Mang and Dakkali etc. In the Jain religion Seventh Jain Tirthankara Supersavantha is Matanga is one of the set of Madiga.

Supersavantha

The civilization also staring with the Leather only; why it was ?

Ancient days Leather is the Platinum, Diamond, Gold and Silver etc for using of Ornaments and Coins also. several stories also in the Leather coins were issued by sakka in medieval India sakka was an age old name given to people who serve water in water bags made of leather which was called "MASHKEEZAS" he saved Humayun in a famous battle of Chausa when he jumped in river Ganga, later when Humayun reclaimed the throne of Delhi, he asked sakka for a wish, sakka wished to be a king for a day, the first thing he thought was to benefit his community who made leather bags, and announced that for a day of his rule, the coins be made of mashkeezas leather be made the currency, since his community had lots of bags ,made it coins and bought whatever wanted no became rich overnight. BUCHHA SAKKA (WATER SERVER). One day a King went for hunting and he lost his way in jungle, and got tired and about to die, he saw a small hut in jungle, he went there and asked for help. That hut belonged to Buchha Sakka, who gave water to King, and food and recovered and before returning his palace, he promised to give whatever this guy wants. Buchha Sakka asked him to make him King for One day only. And King agreed for that. When Sakka became king, he introduced leather coins in the kingdom. Mohammed Tughlak was involved heavily in monetary reform in India that included minting new gold and silver coins along with copper ones; introduced the leather currency in India.

BC 3000 year back India knows as a "Jambua Dwiwpam". In Jambua Dwipam peoples are enjoying liberal. When Aryans came to India on the basis of Migrate. They war with Jambua king. In war, Aryans are won. After arayan came to India they oppose lord shiva and jambua culture. They treated like Jambua kingsare rakshasa. Aryans all are well educated and they himself say we are brahmans.

Jambava Grufa (Cave)

Regarding of the photo/ piture the This is cave where Jambuvan know worrier of Ramayana age was residing. He was born in satyuga and seen Treta yug and Dwaper waiting for Krishna Avatar. He found diamond of precious value which was given for playing to her daughter Jambuvati. Lord Krishna was in search for same diamond which was taken away from one king by lion and reached to Jambuvan after lion was killed by Jambuvan. Lord Krishna fought with Jambuvan and ultimately him cam e to know that Krishna is nothing but same Lord Ram. He bowed to Lord and given away diamond and her doughter to Krishna with marriage with him. This jambuvan cave is situated near Ranavav town in Porbander district in Gujarat state India. There is deep cave and small light source of sun. Inside there is Shiv ling made by sand when water falls from roof of cave. We can see nature carving too. Outside cave there is Lord Shiva temple and Samadhi of Guru Ramdasji who did Tapsya there.

Jambavan /Jambava / Jambavanth (The Bear God)
Mulavasi of Jambudwipam

Peer Kho Cave Temple is one of the sacred cave temples in the Jammu region, which is dedicated to Lord Shiva. The cave temple, also known as Jamwant Cave, is enshrined with the svayambhu shivalinga. Based on the epic Ramayana, it is believed that Jamvant (the bear god) adopted the cave as a place where he went into deep meditation. The Peer Kho Temple presently comprises of two caves. Both these caves are at a depth of about 20 to 30 feet from the ground level of the temple complex. A flight of marble steps leads on to the first cave. It is not possible to cross the cave without bending. One has to stoop to cover the 15 feet long and 3 feet wide cave. At the end of this cave tunnel there is a larger cave. The naturally formed black colour Shiva Lingam is the focal point of this pentagonal cave which is 12 feet in height. This makes it possible for devotees to stand comfortably within the interiors of this particular cave to offer their prayers.

In the braman "Bram" is word come from HibUru language in Sanskrit 'bramam'. Aryans are well educated and his Kwon medicine and astrology. Because most of the peoples are fear bout Aryans (brahmans). In varna system first only three varnas after they include the last one. In varna system brahmans says that 'knowledge is power, color is supreme' but kshatriyas say that'might is right, color is secondary' it seems to first varna system opposed by kshatriya. Inside varna system, racial discrimination is there.

BC 2500 years back only three varnas like brahmana, kshatriya,and vaysha are include in the arayan social system. Native peoples like yadhava, jambua, mathya, nagulu and other are kings and war with whoever migrant people Aryans but native peoples are lost the war and they supply like slavery. Into the slavery, the shudra varna came. The brahman authority is supreme the peoples on the basis of labor and divided the work. Those who arenot doing the work god give punishment. So that's why we are opposing caste system.

In BC 2000 varnasram dhram to they implemented caste system. In the caste system,Aryan theories promote the social hierarchy system. And they promote the "God's Doctrine" as per this doctrine they implemented Karma theory means based on working process. When Aryans came to India Aryans divided peoples for his flexibility and economic needs. After BC 2000-1500 years time those who are lost the war they peoples are in slavery these peoples are in this period the Aryan authorities of brahminical system excluded the Shudras to the-shudhura called as pancham caste. In Telangana, the Madiga also was knownas mulavasi, Jambavulu, and others. They live mainly in rural areas. They speak, read, and write in Telugu. They are not vegan and consumed by alcohol but it was taken as per the dedicating of Goddess. Mochi's traditional work is footwear and leatherwork. Many are working as labourers in agriculture. Beginning of the Sindu civilization Mulavasi prayed of Puja done by the Pasupati and Ammatalli it shows the Lord Shiva is Pasupati and also Community head also group head ; hence in the Madiga community surnames are like Dunna (Buffalo), Manda (United Group) it means from the beginning of civilization we have joint action group of the people ; that's what Madigas are the Pasupalaka hence they worshiped lord Shiva in the days; Mother Goddess like Ammatalli, Poleramma, Mysamma, Maramma, Mutyalamma and Yellamma etc ; natural devotees to all for the worship one of the set or sub community of Madigas i.e Matangas doing the puja and Bali sacrificing the Buffalo. In this Puja Dakkali will be perfumed, Chindu-Madiga performed traditional song with dancing.

Madiga sitting in front of the Head, Dakkali sitting and holding Musical instuments along with Head of Madiga (Madiga Pedda/ Pedda Madiga), Madiga womenns standing with Prsadam of Pulagam / Paisannam (Mixed with Milk & Rice cooked food) on those head; and behind of the standing people are Chindu Madigas for Dancing and Bindla Pujari compliting of the Bali (Sacripising to the Godess)

That is chindhumadiga community and other sub-caste like dakkali, madiga mastine, mathangulu, jaggali communities are not there. However, most of the madiga sub-caste communities life based on the madiga community. They have their own culture like chindhu are playing street plays. Dhakkali is analysing and explaining the entire madiga History, madiga mastine's are working woodwork, and mathangas are like pujari... etc.

15

Vaishnavism and Leather Working Communities

Dr. S. Babu*

Introduction

From time immemorial, Indian social system was based on simple occupational division of labour. One among the professional classes was the leather workers who were involved in flying of skins, tanning of hides and making leather products for different purposes. They included leather chappals, garments, belts, bags, goods, bags to carry oils and clarified butter, thongs, buckets, saddles and reigns, shields and sheaths. Leather working is one of the oldest occupations recorded in the ancient Hindu literature. Various leather goods and tanneries are mentioned in the earliest known literary work Rig Veda.[1] The later Vedas, Epics and Manusmriti mentioned different leather goods used in daily life and warfare.[2] It seemed that they were organised into *srenis* (Guilds) which appeared during the Gupta period. During the early and medieval periods leather goods were used in agrarian economy to lift water and fasten the animals to the yokes for ploughing. Leather bellows were used for the smelting of iron and manufacturing of iron implements.

* Head & Associate Professor, Department of History, Avvaiyar Government College for Women, Karaikal, E-mail: drbabu1961@yahoo.com

South India is the home of different leather working communities. The Semmans were a significant caste of Tamil leather-workers found only in the districts of Madurai, Tirunelveli and Pudukottai. In the Tamil dictionaries Semman is explained as a leather-worker, living in out-of the way villages with shoemaking as their occupation. The Semmans were a sub-division of the Paraiyans, who must have been the original leather-workers of the Tamil tribes. There are many endogamous leather working communities in Tamil Nadu namely Chakkiliyar, Madigas, Pagadai, Puthurai Vannan, Vettan, and Madari. However, in the recent past all of them came under one umbrella with the nomenclature of Arunthathiyar in the Tamil region partly influenced by the self- respect movement.[3] Of late they are also known as Scheduled Castes or Dalits. They were the manufacturers of native chappals, leather bags, thongs, garments, musical instruments and *Kavalai* or *Pari*, leather buckets.[4] The leather workers, on account of their low social and ritual status, were subjected to a variety of disabilities. They were treated as untouchable, forced to live in separate hamlets or quarters away from the main villages or towns and barred to enter the temples.

The leather working community had their own gods and goddesses. They consider themselves as the descendents of Adi Jambava, who was supposedly born at the time of origin of the universe. The female deity Adi Sakthi (the Supreme Being) was born after Adi Jambava and her protegee Ellamma, Arundhati, the wife of Sage Vasista belonging to their community, was considered as one of the great *pativratas* and Matangi, the special caste and tutelary goddess, are worshipped. Apart from their own gods they also worship the village goddesses of their respective localities. Though they were considered as a part of the mainstream Hinduism, they were neither given a respectable position nor allowed to visit the sacred places nor even given the opportunity for ritual participation and were denied to attain *moksha* (salvation) as per the Hindu canon.

Buddhism was founded by Gautama Siddhartha Buddha in sixth century B.C. Buddhism was a socio-religious challenge to Hinduism. It challenged and rejected caste and strove to remove caste distinctions and as such it is a non-caste movement. It envisages that one will become a Brahmin or outcaste not by birth but by deed. Buddha preached that one can achieve salvation without any distinction of caste or creed. So it won the support of the lower order and people were taken into the Buddhist order without any consideration of caste. Hence the leather workers enthusiastically joined in Buddhist laity. The earliest record on leather workers appeared in a Prakrit Buddhist inscription belonging to the early centuries of Christian era from Amaravathi *stupa* of Andhra Pradesh mentioning them as Caramkaras.[5]

Nandanar, a devotee of Siva, was relegated to the position of one of the Nayanars and reached the godhead, even though belonging to the untouchable community. Hence, many untouchable communities willingly joined Saivism during the Bhakthi movement that took place in the Tamil region during the early medieval period. Vira Saivism, a militant form of Siva worship, was started by Basavesvara (1106-1167), the prime minister of Bijjala, the Kalachuri king of Kalyan. Basava undermined the hierarchised, ritualized and institutionalized Hinduism. The three important aspects of Vira Saivism are respect to the teacher (*guru*), who initiates a devotee into the sect, carrying a Phallus (*linga*, the stone symbol of Siva), which the devotee has to suspend around his neck and worship it five times a day by placing it in his palm with faith in the infallibility of the Vira Saiva devotee (*jangama*).[6] In this sect any person irrespective of caste or gender can receive and wear the phallus, also called *Ista Linga*. Palkuriki Somanatha, a Vira Saiva poet of Andhradesa in the thirteenth century, wrote two important

Telugu works namely Basava Puranam and Panditardhya Charitra.[7] They contain some stories of the prominent Vira Saivite devotees belonging to the leather working communities. They were emphatically called as *Pedda Bhaktulu* (great devotees). On occasions Somanatha used synonymous names of leather working community as pseudonyms for some characters and in this regard Svapachayya (from Sanskrit *Svapach* for outcaste), Godagara (same as Madiga), could be cited as examples.

Vaishnavism

Though some leather workers converted into other religions, many of them were staunch followers of Vaishnavism, one of the major religious traditions of Hinduism, even today. Vaishnavism is one of the major traditions within Hinduism and its followers are called Vaishnavas and they consider Vishnu as the Supreme Lord. The tradition is notable for its *avatara* (incarnation) doctrine, wherein Vishnu is revered in many distinct incarnations. Of these ten incarnations the most worshipped are Krishna and Rama. The devotional Vaishnava literature that emerged in Sanskrit and in Vernacular writings from the tenth to the sixteenth century continues to be part of Vaishnava worship, supplemented by later philosophical and narrative texts. For Vaishnavas, absolute reality (Brahman) manifested in Vishnu through his incarnations defending traditional righteousness in keeping with the moral law (Dharma). The worshippers of Vishnu pray to him with religious devotion for the liberation of soul to attain *moksha* from the cycle of birth and death.

The leather workers had strongly adhered to the beliefs, practices, customs and rituals of Vaishnavism in their day-to-day life with religious fervour despite their miserable socio-economic conditions. There are some mythological reasons for their belief. The leather workers consider Jambavan as their mythical ancestor and were named after him as the Jambavakula. He was closely associated with one of the *avatars* (incarnations) of Lord Vishnu. Jambavan or Jambavantha, the mythical ancestor of the leather workers, was a character in Ramyana. He was with Sugriva, the king of Vanaras who helped Rama in search of Sita and made Hanuman realize his enormous abilities and motivated him to fly over the ocean in search for Sita.[8] He also helped Rama in his fight against Ravana. For his services, he received a boon from Lord Rama that he would have a long life and have the strength of ten million lions.

In the Mahabharata, Jambavantha had killed a lion, who had acquired a gem called Syamantaka from Prasena after killing him. Krishna was suspected of killing Prasena for the gem. Hence, he tracked Prasena's steps until he learned that he had been killed by a lion who, had been killed by a bear. Krishna tracked Jambavantha to his cave and a fight ensued. After eighteen days, realizing who Krishna was, Jambavantha submitted. He gave Krishna the gem and also presented him his daughter Jambavati, who became one of Krishna's wives.[9] Jambavan, together with Parasuram and Hanuman, were supposed to be one of the few to have been present for both Rama and Krishna *avatars*. It is believed that Jambavan is the longest living of the *chiranjivis* to witness nine *avatars* of Lord Vishnu.

Tiruppan one of the twelve Alwar saints of Tamil region belonged to an untouchable community. So, many untouchables including the leather workers enthusiastically took to Vaishnava tradition. Though they were considered as the followers of Vaishnava tradition, they were not allowed into sacred shrines associated with Vaishnavism. For the first time they were allowed into the Vaishnava temples by Ramanuja.

Srivaishnavism

The founder of Srivaishnavite sect was Ramanuja (1017-1137), who was born in 1017 A.D. at Sriperumbudur in a Tamil Brahmin family in the Tamil Country and studied in Kanchipuram. On the banks of the river Kaveri at Sri Rangam he propounded his philosophy Vishistadvaita (qualified monism). He affirmed that there is unity of all souls and the individual soul has the potential to realize identity with Brahman. He then travelled around the country meeting other learned men, indulging in spiritual discourse where he defeated many pundits. The most famous occasion was in Venkatagiri where he initiated a Vaishnava *puja* in a Siva temple after he had won a particularly long scholastic discussion with the pundits there. He set up many *maths* or temples where the Ramanuja sect is flourishing even today. The followers of Ramanuja worship Vishnu and Lakshmi in their singular and twin forms. They also worship the incarnations of Vishnu.

Ramanuja had a wrangle with the Chola king Kulothunga II (1133 C.E – 1150 C.E), a staunch Saivite. Hence, he came to Mysore region in order to escape the persecution and lived there for twenty years. During his stay in the Kanarese country, he converted thousands of people to Srivaishnavism. The notable convert to the Srivaishnava tradition was of the Hoyasala ruler Bitti Deva, an adherent of Jainism. He came under the influence of Ramanuja and converted to Vaishnavism and took the name Vishnuvardhana.[10] The Mysore Census of 1871 states that "when Ramanujacharya first appeared in this part of the country we know that the religion of the Bellala court was Jain, while from the number of temples still extant, it is clear that the religion of the great mass of people was Saiva. Ramanujacharya introduced a new religion – the Vaishnava".[11]

As per tradition, Ramanuja went to Malkote to pray at the celebrated Krishna shrine. He was informed that the place had been attacked by the Turkish king of Delhi, who had carried away the idol. One day Ramanuja got a vision, in which Narayana appeared to him and told that he was in 'Delhi with the Turk Emmadu Raya. Ramanuja journeyed to Delhi and met the Raja, prevailed upon him to grant his request. The Turkish king gave orders that Ramanuja be taken to the apartments where his plundered treasures were hoarded. There were many idols, but Ramanuja failed to find among them the idol. He fell into a reverie as he pondered how to trace it. He had a dream in which Ramapriya (Krishna) appeared and said "I am with the daughter of the king. She has made a plaything of me. To her dallying and caresses, I am a living person. Come there and find me." Ramanuja awoke and reported to the king that the idol he sought was with the Sultani. The king's curiosity was roused at the revelations, a foreign Sanyasin of a different persuasion was making to him. He developed respect and adoration for the holy saint. The king took the Sanyasin Ramanuja into the seraglio where the idol of Ramapriya was found, fondled by the Sultani, his daughter, to whom he played the husband. When Ramanuja called Him by His name, the Image jumped down from the couch on which the Sultani had placed Him and walked to where Ramanuja stood, in all the glory and grace of an incarnated deity. He called him by the endearing name of Selva-p-pillai by which name the image is still called. The king, who witnessed all this procedure, was simply astonished beyond measure, and loaded Ramanuja with gifts and honours, sent him back from the scene of his holy mission. The princess, quite disconsolate for the loss of her image, mounted a horse, and followed. She disappeared the moment she neared the godhead. Soon, a monument for her was erected at the foot of the hill.[12]

In the stupendous work involved in the institution of this Holy Shrine, hard journeys to distant countries which were consequently undertaken, the low untouchable communities of the Tirukula and the Jambavakula rendered a great help to Sri Ramnuja. Also helping in recovering the image of Ramapriya when it was carried off to Delhi.[13] Hence they have the privilege of entering the temple once a year to pay their devotions. He gave them the title of "Tirukkulattar" or the "Blessed Descendants", and further allowed them the privilege of entering the Holy Temples to certain limits, viz., the out gate near the altar (Dhvaja-Stambha or Bali-pitha). This practice is remaining in force even today, in the temples of Srirangam, Melkote and Belur. They were allowed to bathe in the Holy Ponds attached to the Temples, except on the prohibited days. Ramanuja opened the doors of religious instructions for these classes, with certain modes of ritual and other privileges peculiar to Srivaishnavas, such as the Pancha-Samskara or the Five Holy Vaishnava Sacraments. It is evident how serious Ramanuja was about elevating the low-classes regarding their eligibility for salvation.

Undoubtedly one of the greatest champions of Vaishnavism in Andhradesa was Brahma Nayudu, the celebrated minister of the Haihayas of Macherla in the Planadu region of Guntur district, belonging to the later part of twelfth century. In the oral tradition of the Epic of Palnadu Brahma Nayudu was depicted as a great devotee, teacher (*guru*) and often as an incarnation of Vishnu and the builder of Chenna Kesava temple at Macherla. Hanumantha Rao put forward the view that Brahma Nayudu was a radical socio-religious reformer and he made the Macherla Chenna Kesava temple the centre of his activities and he opened the gates of the temple to the untouchables having converted them into Vaishnavism.[14] After a thorough examination of the oral tradition of the Epic of Palnadu, Roghair says that "the form of Vaisnavism championed by Brahma Nayudu of Palnadu appears, according to the epic tradition, is indebted to Ramanujacarya in several respects".[15]

The untouchables were also closely associated with the Lakshmi Narasimha temple of Kadiri in Ananthapur district of Andhra Pradesh, as attested by inscriptional evidence. A damaged inscription from a slab set up below a peepal tree in the courtyard of the Lakshmi Narasimha Swami temple provides some curious and crucial information. The inscription of 1418 AD records the decision of Samasta Pekundru, a merchant guild, in a dispute between Malas and Madigas and the ryots. The Malas were given a remission of tax payable by them in lieu of some service (details lost) and the Madigas had to do the service of providing four pillars or posts (*kambalu*) for the marriage *pandal* (of the god?) and some (details lost) bundles (*mopulu*) as per their respective caste customs.[16] It may be surmised that the services of these two communities were used for the services of one of the famous Vaishnavite temples of Andhradesa and made them parties in the temple rituals. Possibly they were professing Vaishnavism and as such their services became customary. Further, the notable feature of the annual Brohmotsava festival is that two days after the car procession the members of the untouchable communities are allowed to enter the temple after bathing in the Maddaleru river. This item of festival is known as "Mala Sparsa" (Untouchable touch) and is practised even today.[17]

Emma Clough informed a curious story regarding the origin of Charmanista sect of Madigas. Ramanuja had disciples of all castes and of both sexes and he did not initiate his followers into the mysteries of his doctrines, but wrote them in a book, which he concealed from them. At the time of his death no one was with him, and the book of secret doctrines fell into hands of the Brahmins, who characteristically kept it to themselves. But his other followers, too, wanted to know of the teaching of their Guru. Two of his disciples, who were women of the caste of dancing-women, and were, therefore, versed in the art of reading and writing, sought to meet the emergency by each writing a book. They claimed that these books contained the teaching of Ramanuja, imparted to them on his death-bed. From one of these books sprang the Ramanuja sect from the Chermanishta sect.[18] One Thatiah, a Madiga, informed Clough in the last decade of eighteenth century that in the time of his grandfather, a Guru of the Ramanuja sect had been invited by the family to come with the idols of Vishnu and perform sacred rites before them. This was repeated on special occasions, and the fees demanded by the priest were paid out of the scant earnings. When his father died, Thatiah took pride in having the funeral ceremonies performed according to the dictates of a Guru of the Ramanuja sect.[19]

Edgar Thurston informs in 1909 that one Hospet Madigas suspended round his neck, was a hereditary talisman, a big silver Venkataramana *bottu* with the *namam* in the centre on an altar, and the *chank* and *chakram* stamped on it.[20] Thurston also informs another belief of the leather workers of South India. "The god of the temple at Tirupati appears annually to four persons in different directions, east, west, north and south, and informs them that he requires a shoe from each of them. They whitewash their houses, worship the god, and spread rice-flour thickly on the floor of a room, which is locked for the night. Next morning the mark of a huge foot is found on the floor, and for this a shoe has to be made to fit. When ready, it is taken in procession through the streets of the village, and convoyed to Tirupati, where it is presented at the temple. Though the makers of the shoes have worked in ignorance of each other's work, the shoes brought from the north and south, and those from the east and west, are believed to match, and make a pair. Though the worship of these shoes is chiefly meant for the Pariahs, who are prohibited from ascending the Tirupati hill, everyone, without distinction of caste, worship them. The shoes are placed in front of the image of the god near the foot of the hill, and are said to gradually wear out by the end of the year".[21]

Nanjundiah and Ananthakrishna Iyer stated that a section of the Madigas known as Desabhagadavaru, were Vaishnavas, with satanis, or Srivaishnava Brahmans as their gurus. Some of these become Dasaris, who earn their food by begging, and whose presence is necessary on all important ceremonies. They also inform that the spiritual preceptors of the Madigas in the Mysore region were the Jambavas. The Srivaishnava Brahmins and Dasaris also recognise the spiritual status of Jambavas.

Another sub sect of the Madigas known as Dasayyas were dedicated to Vishnu and were branded with *sanku* and *chakra* and even abstain from working in leather. The presence of a Dasayya was necessary at all feasts observed by the Desabhaga section. He must repeat the word "Govinda" before he eats. His paraphernalia consisted of *sanku* (conch shell), *jagate* (gong), and *bavanasi* (begging bowl, or pouch). They generally put on beads stung to the waist-thread, and a thread with the figure of Hanumantha on the neck.[22]

Vaishnavite Tilaks

The art of marking *tilaks* (caste marks) on the forehead is a very ancient one and dates back to the time of the Vedic Aryans. Over a period of time this custom became a ritual amongst Hindus and grew in dimension and diversity as each Shiva and Vaishnava sects developed their own special marks. This practice continued down the ages and the *tilak* remained the customary symbol of all Hindus, irrespective of caste, creed and colour.

It can be observed that Vaishnavites are more particular in the wearing of tilaks than the Shaivites. They mark their foreheads either as a daily ritual or on special occasions. A devout Vaishnavite marks all the twelve parts of the body with tilaks. The different Vaishnava Sampradayas (traditional practices) each have their own distinctive style of tilaka, which depicts the Siddhanta of their particular lineage. The general tilaka pattern is of a parabolic shape resembling the letter U or two or more connected vertical lines on and another optional line on the nose resembling the letter Y, which usually represents the foot of Vishnu and the central vertical line symbolising his manhood. Another interpretation suggests that the symbol is representation of male and female parts in union. In addition to the vertical marks, figures of the conch shell, *sankha*, wheel, *chakra,* club, *gada*, and lotus, *padma,* all attributes that Vishnu holds in his four hands are drawn on the various parts of the body. The names of Radha and Krishna are also stamped on the body. The four emblems and names of gods and goddesses are carved on wooden stamps, which are used to mark on the body.

Different mantras, each specially prescribed for different parts of the body, are chanted as the Vaishnavite applies tilaks on the twelve parts of the body. For the forehead the mantra is *namaha Kashabaya namaha*, for the stomach, *namaha Narayana namaha*, the chest *namaha Madhabaya namah*, the neck, *namaha Govindaya namaha*. When tilaks are applied on the right side of the chest they chant *namaha Vishnave namaha* for the right arm, *namaha Madhusudanaya namaha*, the right shoulder, *namaha Tribikraya namaha*, for the left side of the chest, *namaha Bamanaya namaha*, the left arm, *namaha Shree-Dharaya namaha*, the left shoulder, *namaha Rishekeshayay namaha*, the back or *Prishta-desha, namaha Padmanabhyay namaha* and finally, the waist or *Kotidesha, namaha Damodarayay namaha*.[23]

It is commonly believed that every part of the body represents a particular form of god and thus every tilak is applied with the devotion a particular god commands. The most visually prominent tilak is on the forehead. This again differs from sect to sect even among the vast Vaishnavite following. This Vaishnavite forehead tilak is called the *harimandira*. According to the *Haribhaktibilasa*, the Vaishnva authority composed in 1562 A.D., "*harimandira* is really the abode of god, for the open space represents Vishnu and the two side lines represent Brahma and Siva." The trinity is thus worshipped. The Purana accepts Brahma as the creator, Vishnu or Narayana is the god who maintains the created ones while Siva destroys and paves the way for creation. This is the importance of creation.

The Vaishnava sect of South India was divided into the northern (Vadakalai) and the southern school (Thenkalai). The difference between the two schools was fierce, and was really the controversy with regard to adorning of tilak. The Vadakalai sect mark their *namam* or *thiruman* in a "U" shaped pattern with *manjal* or yellow as below.[24]

The Thenkalai sect mark it in a "Y" shaped pattern with *kunkumam* or red as below.

Thus tilaks form a prominent part of the religious rituals of the Sri Vaishnavites. The tilak symbolises not only a sect, it is also a way of life. It is an integral element of Hinduism and applied with reverence and it becomes an act of worship.

In the Tamil month of *Purattasi* everyone adorn with *Tiru Nammam*. It is also called as *moodu namalu* or *Tirumala Namalu*. It is a tilak which includes one base line drawn with *namakommu* (white in colour) and three horizontal lines on this base line of which first and second are drawn with *namakommu* one at beginning of base line and other at end of base line. The third horizontal line is made of *srichurnam* (red in colour) and is drawn from the middle of the base line.

Colonial Paintings and Photographs

The arrival of the Portuguese in India in the latter part of the fifteenth century had an impact on the development of the Company Painting style. Company Painting style was developed in line with the demand of souvenirs and visual documentation from India as requested by the employer and other actors connected with the various European East India Companies. When Manucci was living in Madras between 1701 and 1705 he collected 78 paintings made on his requirements to directly illustrate the Indian life which he referred to in his writings. The subjects of the paintings were gods, goddesses, religious ceremonies, processions, temples, and rituals, which were meant to satisfy the Europeans' curiosity about Indian society and religion. As a result of the increasing demand of paintings, Indian artists in and around Tanjore prepared standard sets of paintings that illustrated distinctive local styles and sold them at the British military stations or to travellers at halting places along the rivers.[25] In the late nineteenth century photography entered South India. A few portraits and a photo of the leather workers luckily survived as visual representation of them and their occupation along with their religious traits during the colonial period.

A Cobbler from Tamil Nadu, 1830

Shoemaker, Trichonopoly, 1850

Malabar Shoemaker, Trichonopoly, 1875

Shoemaker, Madras, Late 19th Century

Popular Tradition

Leathers workers as the followers of Srivaishnavism consider the Tamil month of *Purattasi*,(which generally falls in the months of September and October of the Gregorian calendar), to be of great importance. It is believed that Lord Venkateswara (an incarnation of Vishnu) appears on the earth in this month. *Purattasi Sani* or Saturday in the month of *Purattasi* is a Hindu festival celebrated by the Vaishnavites in South India. Lord Venkateswara is worshipped on the occasion. All the Saturdays of the month are treated as holy days. The devotees of Lord Vishnu consider this as the ideal month for thanking Lord Vishnu for preserving the Universe. The Odd Saturdays 1st, 3rd, 5th are regarded very important. Tirumala Annual Navarathri Brahmotsavam is also observed during this month where Tirumala is flooded by lakhs of devotees. Some people will take only vegetarian food during the entire month.

The leather workers as the staunch worshippers of Vishnu despite their poor economic conditions worship the Lord with their offerings like pudding of *Ragi* (*Cynosurus Coracanus*) or *Ragi sangaty* and a curry of Gongura (Hibiscus cannabinus) (pulicha keerai in Tamil), a special for the Lord from the poor devotee. They claim that the Lord is fascinated towards this than the luxurious and delicious food offered by the rich as stated by one of the leather workers from my own village.[26] On this occasion everyone in the house will keep *tirunamam* on the forehead. During pooja first Deepam will be lit followed by offering naivedhyam, agarbathi, sambrani, coconut, harathi respectively. Naivedhyam will be offered to lord Venkateswara and his wives, Sri Devi and Bhu Devi, on three banana leaves. During Harathi, everyone in the house utter the following loudly in praise of the god:

Edu Kondala Vada! Venkata Ramana! Govindha!
Govindha! Govindha!!

Apadha Mokkula Vada! Anadha Rakshaka! Govindha!
Govindha! Govindha!!

Conclusion

Leather workers were one of the occupational castes from ancient times and produced different types of goods from leather for the use. There are many endogamous groups among them. Now they are grouped under single category as Arunthathiyar in Tamil Nadu. They were considered as an untouchable caste for a long time by the ritually pure communities in the South Indian society and were barred to enter into the temples though they were considered as the mainstream followers of Hinduism. However, Ramanuja the founder of Srivaishnavism accorded them social recognition and allowed them to enter temples through his social revolutionary concept. Since then they became ardent followers of Vaishnavism and practiced the customs, traditions and rituals of Srivaishnavaism in their day to day life despite of their poor socio-economic status. Thus the leather workers are staunch followers of Vaishnavism in many parts of South India.

Acknowledgement

I express my sincere thanks to my friend and colleague Dr. B. Rama Chandra Reddy, Head, Department of History, Bharathidasan Government College for Women, Puducherry, for his constant encouragement, inspiration and support for the preparation of this paper.

Notes and References

1. Stephanie W. Jamison and Joel P. Brereton, Tr., *The Rigveda: The Earliest Religious Poetry of India*, Oxford University Press, New York, 2014, pp. 215; 398; 594; 629; 699; 841; 1036; 1129; 1236 and1303.
2. G. Buhler, Tr., *Manusmriti: The Laws of Manu, Sacred Books of the East, Vol. 25*, Clarendon Press, Oxford, 1886
3. The term Arunthathiyars was emerged during 1920's as a new identity to come out of their age old degrading nomenclature.
4. Krishnaswamy, *The Government of Madras*, Government Press, Madras, 1947, p. 72.
5. C. Sivaramamurti, Ed., *Amaravati Sculptures in the Madras Government Museum*, Director of Stationary and Printing, Madras, 1977, No. 41, p. 281.
6. Velcheru Narayana Rao, Tr., *Siva's Warriors: The Basava Purana of Palkuriki Somanatha*, Princeton University Press, New Jersy, 1990, pp. 8-11.
7. Somanatha heralded a revolutionary style in Telugu literature and in fact it may be considered as a protest against the then current dominant style. While writing these works Somanatha adopted the popular *desi* (indigenous) literary style as against the elitist *marga* (Sanskrit) style. Till then the Telugu poets used *campu* style, which combines verse and prose in one common narration but Somanatha used *dvipada* meter, which was popular in oral tradition and was closely related to the meters of folk songs. Velcheru Narayana Rao, *Siva's Warriors, op.cit.*, p. 5.

8. R.K. Narayan, *The Ramayana: A Shortened Modern Prose Version of the Indian Epic (suggested by the Tamil version of Kamban)*, Penguin Books, New York, 2006, See chapters 7 and 10.
9. For the story in detail see *Bhagavata Purana*, Motilal Banarsidas, Delhi, 1950, Chapter. 56
10. K.A. Nilakanta Sastri, *A History of South India: From the Earliest Times to the Fall of Vijayanagara*, OUP, Delhi, 1958, pp. 419-420.
11. Lalita Chandrasekharan, "Social Mobility of Scheduled Castes in Karnataka: A Study of Madigas", Unpublished Ph.D. Thesis, *Jawaharlal Nehru University*, New Delhi, 1989, p. 120.
12. Francis Buchanan, *A Journey from Madras through the Countries of Mysore, Canara and Malabar*, Asian Educational Services, New Delhi, 1999 (First published in 1807), Vol. II, pp. 70-71.
13. B. Lewis Rice, *Mysore: A Gazette compiled for the Government*, Archbald Constable and Company, Westminister, 1897, Vol. II, pp. 272-273; Alkondaville Govindacharya, *Ramanujacharya: The Exponent of the Visishtadavaita Philosophy*, Murthy & Co., Madras, 1906, pp. 189-190.
14. B.S.L. Hanumantha Rao, *Religion in Andhra*, Department of Archaeology and Museums, Hyderabad, 1993, pp. 267-268.
15. Gene. H. Roghair, *The Epic of Palnadu: A study and Translation of Palnati Virula Katha, a Telugu Oral Tradition from Andhra Pradesh, India*, Clarendon Press, Oxford, 1982, pp. 78-79. For a complete a text of the battle of Palnadu see Pingali Lakshmikantam, Ed., *Palanat Vira Charitra* (Telugu), by Srinadhudu, Mallayya and Kondayya, Visalandra Publishing House, Hyderabad, 1991.
16. *South Indian Inscriptions*, Vol. XVI, No. 24, pp. 26-27.
17. *Statistical Appendix for Anantapur District*, Government Press, Madras, 1915, p. 51.
18. Emma Raushenbusch Clough, *While Sewing Sandals or Tales of a Telugu Pariah Tribe*, Hodder and Stoughton, London, 1899, pp. 106- 107.
19. *Ibid.*, p. 116.
20. Edgar Thurston and K. Rangachari, *Castes and Tribes of Southern India*, Asian Educational Services, New Delhi and Madras, 2001 (originally published in 1909), Vol. IV, p. 294

21. *Ibid.*, pp. 310-311.
22. H.V. Nanjundayya and L.K. Ananthakrishna Iyyer, *The Mysore Tribes and Castes, Mysore* University, Mysore, 1931, Vol. IV, pp 154-163.
23. K. Rangachari, *The Sri Vaishnava Brahmans*, Commissioner of Museums, Chennai, 2000 (Originally Published in 1931), pp. 37-48.
24. Gautam Chattopadhyay and Sanjoy Chatterjee, "Vaishnavite Tilaks", in the *India Magazine of Her People and Culture*, October, 1987, pp. 20-27.
25. Laura Berivan Nilsson, Picturing the Unknown: Cultural Encounters and Visual Representations in Company Paintings from the eighteenth and nineteenth Centuries in south Indian Collections of the National Museum of Denmark, Tranquebar Initiative of the National Museum of Denmark, Denmark, 2015.
26. Interview with Gopal, A Madiga, Kodambakkam Village, Vellore District, Tamil Nadu aged around 90 years on 1-10-2017.

16

Leather Caste and Leather Trade: A Socio-Historical Analysis

Sashi Kant Rai*

Introduction

Leather workers known in different name in different part of the India. Stephen Fuchs pointed out in this regard that leather workers such as the Balahis in central India and theMahars and Mangs in Maharashtra, Chamar in north India.[1] Thallapally Manohar also says in this regard that The Chamars of North India, The Dhers of Central india, Chamagars of Karnataka, Chakkiliyans of Tamil Nadu, the Tolkollans of Kerala, and the the Madigas of both the Telgu speaking states of Andhara Pradesh and Telangana are living primarily working on animal hide (Leather)[2].

Caste Stigma

Stephen Fuchs pointed out in this regard that Indian society imposed on all leather workers the duty to deal 'with dead cattle. Some sections-and these are the lowest-skin and remove the carcasses from the village. Even among these sections there are grades: some touch no bodies but those of the cloven-footed ani-mals; others

* Associate professor, Department of Ancient History and Archeology, University of Allahabad, UP.

drew the line. at cattle and leave sheep and goats to their inferiors. Usually the hide becomes the property of the skinner and he may also cut off a portion of the animal's flesh if in his section he is not forbidden to eat carrion. Indeed, when the market for skins' is brisk, or in revenge for a slight or injustice, mortality among the cattle is apt to rise materially, and the suspicion is frequently voiced that this is due to Poisoning.[3] Bernard S. Cohen also pointed out that leather worker are considered as untouchables and face many atrocities in india. He surveyed Madhopur village which is located in Jaunpur district, U.P. He found that caste based discrimination is still prevalent. [4] My question is that why profession so bad in the eye of common Indian people. It is very difficult to kill perception.

Leather Industry

I have two working paper or report which talk about the Leather industry. One prepared by Ahmad Mukhtar on behalf of British Govt[5]. Of india and another is the planning report of Governement of india (2012-2017).Both report talk about the leather industry. However, Report informs us that the leather industry occupies a place of prominence in the Indian economy in view of its massive potential for employment, growth and exports. There has been an increasing emphasis on its planned development, aimed at optimum utilization of available raw materials for maximizing the returns, particularly from exports.The post liberalization era has generated significant opportunities for the Indian leather industry. With global players looking for new sourcing options, India stands to gain a bigger share of the global market. The leather industry has undergone a dramatic transformation from being a mere exporter of raw materials in the sixties to being a producer of value added finished products in the nineties. Policy initiatives taken by the Government since 1973 have been, to a large extent, instrumental for such a transformation. India has a 2.6 per cent share in the global leather trade and this sector ranks eighth in terms of the country's foreign exchange earnings from the industry. The composition of exports has also been changing, with more and more value added products being exported. India's share in global value added from this sector at constant 2000 prices was 2.1 per cent in2000 and declined to 1.8 per cent in 20091. Though India has distinct advantages in the leather industry in terms of availability of raw materials with the largest livestock population in the world, the tapped potential in the leather sector, particularly in the high end value chain is still limited. This untapped potential provides the sector significant opportunities for expansion and diversification.[6]

The leather industry in India is geographically well diversified, though Tamil Nadu, Uttar Pradesh and West Bengal account for bulk of the output. The major production centres for leather and leather products are located at Chennai, Ambur, Ranipet, Vaniyambadi, Trichi, Dindigul in Tamil Nadu, Calcutta in West Bengal, Kanpur, Agra and Noida in Uttar Pradesh,Jalandhar in Punjab, Bahadurgarh and Manesar in Haryana,Bangalore in Karnataka, Delhi and Hyderabad in Andhra Pradesh. The sector is dominated by micro and small units with bigger units accounting for just around 5 per cent of the total manufacturing units.

The leather industry is spread in different segments, namely, tanning and finishing, footwear and footwear components, leather garments, leather goods including saddlery and harness, etc. The estimated production capacity in different segments is as under:

Product	**Capacity**
Leather Hides	65 million pieces
Skins	170 million pieces
Footwear & Footwear Components	909 million pairs

Leather shoe uppers	100 million pairs
Non leather footwear	1056 million pairs
Leather Garments	16 million pieces
Leather Goods	63 million pieces
Industrial Gloves	52 million pairs
Saddlery & Harness	12.50 million pieces

Conclusion

We have seen that leather industry is flourishing day by day. The report says like that. Simultaneously, Caste stigma attached with profession ias also with the leather industry is also problematic.

Endnotes

1 Stephen Fuchs, At the bottom of Indian Society : The Harriman and other Low Castes, Munshiram Manoharlal, 1981, Delhi, p,196.

2 Thallapally Manohar, Cultutal history of Madigas: A Brief Study, Pragma Publications, Hyderabad,2016,p7.

3 Stephen Fuchs, At the bottom of Indian Society : The Harriman and other Low Castes, Munshiram Manoharlal, 1981, Delhi, p,196.

4 Bernard Cohn Omnibus, with foreward by Dipesh Chakra Chakrabarthy, an anthropologist among the historians and other essays with an Introduction by Ranjit guha, oup, Delhi, pp. 255-411.

5 Report on Labour Condtions in tannersries and Leather goods factories, Government of India, Shimla Press,1946.

6 Report of working group on Leather and Leather products, 12th Five year Plan (2012-2017), Department of Industrial policy and promotion, Ministry of commerce and Industry, govt. of India, p. 12.

17

Impact of Christianity and Social Transformation Among Madigas (Leather Workers) of Andhra Pradesh -1872-1947

S. Victor Babu*

The tanning of animal skin to produce leather transforms a messy, smelly, and rapidly decaying substance into one that can be experienced as sweet and clean and of great utility. It is one of humanity's major historic technological transformations, along with the smelting of metal. Today's association of leather-working with chappals, the characteristic Indian form of leather footwear, often obscures the former importance of leather items in irrigation, farming, cattle husbandry, transport, and many manufacturing processes. In a world where technological substitutes had yet to be developed, leather goods were of immensely greater significance. In India, complex values related to cattle, the main source of the skin, generated a problem but did not prevent the development of a major industry carried on in almost every village and town across the land. Profitability of leather has at times balanced ideas of religious pollution associated most strongly with its basic production process and made leather-related castes one of the major sections of the

* B.B. Ambedkar University, Lucknow, U.P.

population (Simon Charsley:2004: 269). Madigas are a large central caste of leather workers spread across three regions of Andhra Pradesh with some satellite castes sometimes regarded as sub-castes attached to them (Thurston Edgar, Vol. IV, 1909, P.92).

The primary occupation of the Madigas is the curing and tanning of hides and the manufacture of leather articles. In addition to their traditional and customary occupations, the Madigas are expected to perform certain duties for caste Hindus such as supplying sandals for the ryots, making leather belts for bulls and all other necessary items for agriculture. They were also expected to clean the streets and undertake decoration work during the village festivals and on all the occasions of officials' visits, the Madigas have to notify their entry into the village through Dandora/Chatimpu with Dappu (a percussion leather instrument. For doing all these services, they often were paid meagre and negligible remuneration, often in kind which usually consisted of cheap grains and vegetables (Y.Chinna Rao, 2009, p.70).

Next to what happened in Tirunelveli and Travancore, in no region of India were there larger mass movements than among the Madigas and Malas of Telugu country. The story of mass conversion to Christianity among Madigas began with Yerraguntala Periah, a Madiga from a small village ghetto at Talakondapadu, about forty miles south-west of Ongole, refused to engage in polluting, occupations such as leather working and menial labour.(Robert E.Frykenberg, 2010: 235). Bhakti and yogic cults prepared the ground for religious and social reform such as Yogi Vemana and Potuluri Vera brahmam cults and later Nasriah sect. (Emma Rauschenbusch-Clough, 1899:157) After being initiated in to rajayoga by an upper caste guru, he himself also became a guru. After learning about the bible (New Veda) which placed no restrictions on avarna jatis, he became a Christian and was baptized by Lyman Jowett. Afterwards, John. E. Clough visited their village in January, 1867 and baptized around twenty eight Madigas. Slowly but steadily this became a mass movement where village after village Madigas flocked to the Mission Centre at Ongole.

Apart from working in leather, Madigas also worked as agricultural labourers in the village economy. They also had a very important role in the worship of village goddesses along with Malas. Madigas were both part of the system and dependent for their survival on staying within it. However, once they converted to Christianity, they increasingly looked towards Mission centre at Ongole for various social and economic problems.

During early decades of the twentieth century there were institutions at work that regulated social relationships between groups of people with regard to caste and control over land and labour. These institutions were rooted in customary law and placed leather workers at the bottom. (Gunnel Cederlof, 1997:162). Did the presence of mission representatives in the villages make a difference to the relationship between Sudra landlords and Madigas? This relationship earlier was one of power and subordination, of control and dependence. The change of religion is thereby not merely understood as a change of gods. Whether the presence of mission and mobolisation within the Madiga community altered the relationship between Sudra landlords and Madigas (ibid.p.164).

Control and Conflict

Did the mission involvement in the villages and the Madiga's decision to convert serve to reinforce the Landlords and Madiga relationship or did it imply a threat to the prevailing division of labour and power (ibid.p. 165). In many cases large-scale conversions by members of avarna jatis were followed by conflicts with the employing landowners. The causes of these conflicts may have turned out to be different in different cases. The relationship of Madigas to the landowners is not only a question of prevailing labour relations but should include a discussion of the dominant position of the Landlords in local society with regard to the Madiga community. Search for answers to the question of mission involvement in local social relationships will lead into the context of local social and economic power structures.(ibid.p. 166)

Ideology and Identity

Thirdly, whether expressed in themes or practices, did the ideology of the mission present a viable alternative to an ideology that ascribed the lowest position in the social hierarchy to the Madigas as well as their identity as leather workers and agricultural labourers(Ibid.p.166). Without integration into the local society, the mission or its representatives would only represent a religious order in which Madigas found spiritual consolation that had no impact on local social relations. Any level of integration would mean that a new party had entered into the social life of the village. In order to further develop the question of integration, the following discussion will focus on areas of interaction with regard to social status, physical representation, material resources and mediation. (Gunnel Cederlof, 1997:178)

Social Status

Being an educated man, even though of Madiga caste, could bring a more respectful treatment from members of higher castes. However, there is nothing to show that affiliation to the mission or education anywhere replaced caste barriers. (ibid., p.178)

References

1. Simon Charsley, Interpreting untouchability: The Performance of Caste in Andhra Pradesh, South India, *Asian Folklore Studies*, Volume 63, 2004.
2. Emma Rauschenbusch-Clough, While Sewing Sandals, Tales of a Telugu Pariah Tribe, Asian Educational Services, Delhi, 1899.

3. Robert E. Frykenberg, Christianity in India: From the beginning to the Present, O.U.P, 2010.

4. Gunnel Cederlof, Bonds Lost-c.1900-1970, Manohar, 1997.

5. Thurston Edgar, Castes and Tribes of Southern India, Vol. IV, 1909, P.92)

6. Y.Chinna Rao, Dividing Dalits: Writings on Sub-categorization of Scheduled Castes, Rawat publications, 2009.

7. K.C. Suri, *Dialectic of social justice: The struggle of the Madigas,*in Y.Chinna Rao (ed.), Dividing Dalits: Writings on Sub-categorization of Scheduled Castes, Rawat publications, 2009.

18

First Leather Worker: A Fresh Appraisal

Vivek Shukla*

Introduction

Leather is made from raw skin of animals the meaning of the term leather as given in the Webster's Encyclopedic Unabridged Dictionary of the English language is "The Skin of Animals Prepared for us by tanning or similar process designed to preserve it against decay and to make it pliable of supply when dry"[1].

The Origin of the Art of leather making from the skin cannot in anyway be calculated and the art may rightly be said to have strung into existence from the misty depths of antiquity. Leather is a durable and flexible material created by the tanning of animal rawhide and skin. Primarily cattle hide. It was extensively used from the primitive times and is widely used today. Leather is not a textile used today, Leather is not a textile material but it acquires vivid use in textiles. Leather is enduringly beautiful and no piece of the leather is same. Natural grain, variation in the grains, good breath lity and other natural features are also signs that the material is genuine.

* Ph.D. Scholar in Department of Ancient History, Culture & Archaeology, University of Allahabad, Allahabad (U.P.), Email-vivekmailbox4u@gmail.com

In prehistoric times man was concerned mainly with eating or collection the food, clothing did not existed. The impulse towards the clothing is dedicated towards hunting[2]. The primitive man realized that they are not only for food but can also be used for the clothing purpose. Animals were more fortunate than human being, so they started using animal's skins to satisfy their clothing needs. Animal skin was first worn by the people in the Paleolithic period. Later on man realized that the skins rapidly putrefied and they became useless. They needed a way to preserve the hides. People found that the quality of the leather could be improved so they started preserving the hides/skins by rubbing them with fats and animal's brains; these primitive people preserved the skin by the smoke of wood fires.

For many thousands of years, modern humans (Homo Sapiens) and Neanderthals (Homo neanderthalensis) lived in western Europe. It is not known how much interactions there was between these two species of hominids. Neanderthals, far from being the slow-vitted, ape-men of victorian literature were very well adopted to living in cold climates, skilled tool makers and very capable hunters[3]. In Neanderthal fossil sites dated to near the time when this species became extinct, a ten thousand years after the arrival of modern humans in western Europe, tools and other objects have been found in contemporaneous fossil sites of modern humans. Neanderthals show behaviours similar to those associated with modern humans and have similar fine tools, such as small stone blades and bone implements.

The artifacts, approximately 50,000 years old, come from two locations in france. Modern humans are thought to have arrrived in Europe some 40,000 years ago. One of the sites is a classic Nanderthal Cave site called pech-de-l-Aze. There researchers found part of the tip of bone tool, just a few centimeters long. Archaeologists believe it part of a bone tool, because of how rounded and polished the tip is. The other site is Abri Peyromy, located about 35 kilometers away in a shallow valley up against a low cliff base[4]. At Abri Peyromy, excavators found two more fragments like the one at pech-de-l'Aze, and a complete tool specimen. Excavator McPherron said both of these sites are known to be the stomping grounds of Neanderthals because other fossils and tools characteristic of their species have been found there, and artifacts and bones from modern humans have not been uncovered there.

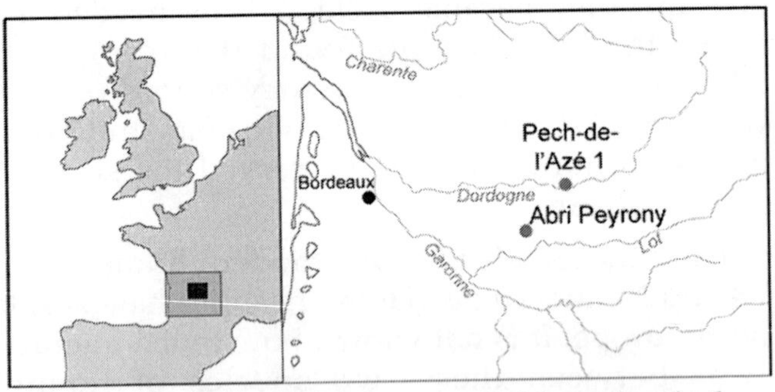

Fig. 1: Courtesy - Soressi, M.et.al. Neanderthals made the first specilaised bone tools in Europe, PNAS, 110 (35), 2013

At Pech-de-l'Aze, the skull of a Neanderthal child was found. Archaeologists already knew that Neanderthal could make bone tools, but previous specimens looked just like their stone or similar type of leather tools. Archaeologists had established that Neanderthals would take bone and remove flakes' and leather to make scrapers notch tools and hand axes. These tools didn't make use of the inherently distinct properties of bone.

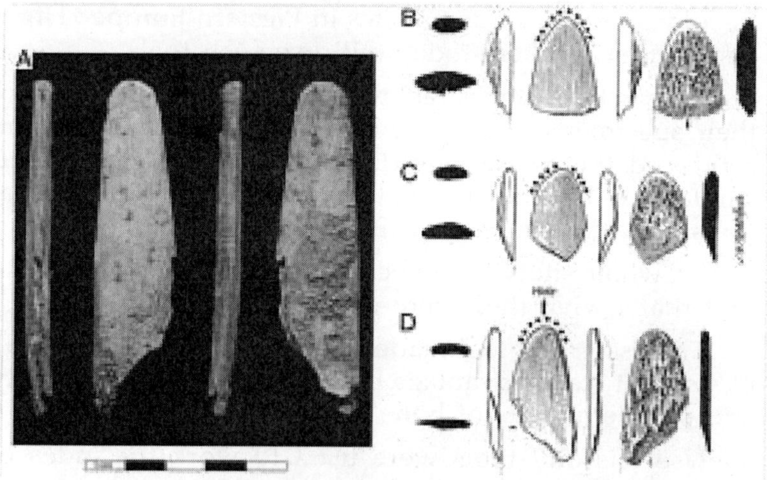

Fig. 2: Courtesy - Soressi, M.et.al. Neanderthals made the first specilaised bone tools in Europe, PNAS, 110 (35), 2013

These are four views of the most complete lissoir tool found during excavations at the Neanderthal site of Abri Peyromy, France.

Image a shows a bone tool, the dotted lines shows the original shape of the bone before it was sculpted and shaped into a tool for use in leather work. The close up images of the bones show evidence of wear as seen in modern lissoir tools used today in the fashion industry. The tools were used to smooth and burnish deer hides and make them water resistant. They were identically shaped to plastic lissoir tools used today by top fashion houses[5]. The specialised bone tools have microscopic wear patterns preserved on them, the wear is consistent with the use of lissoir in modern times to obtain supply, lustrous, and more impermeable hides.

A lissoir compacts a hide, makes the leather more water resitant and easier to work with, and gives it a shine. This type of tool is commonly found at some of the oldest modern human sites in Western Europe[6]. High-end leather workers today still use such tools.

Researchers compared the wear and tear on one of their specimens to damage to a tool that the researchers produced themselves, used against a hide. They found similarities- but they haven't proven that the Neanderthal tools were for leather crafting.

"A whole study has to be done to actually demonstrate that that's what they were used for"[7].

The lissoir is a tool made of bone that cannot be made of stone. It "take advantage of the flexibility and pliability and supple aspects of bone"[8].

Use "lissoir" tools were used to work the hides of animals and the Neanderthal bone tools predate similar discoveries made in western Europe by about 10,000 years.

On the behalf of these evidences, this phenomena may be prove Neanderthals being a skilled leather workers and leatehr antiquity goes back to earlier as a special typical technical work like other important discoveries in early period. Leather work is more specific work and its demand technical knowledge and special abilities, Neanderthals fulfill all abilities so that it may be say's Neanderthals is a first leather worker in early period and tradition continue to modern period.

Acknowledgement

It is my first and foremost duty to express my heartfelt gratitude to my esteemed "GURU", Prof. Anamika Roy. I have greatly benefited from his constructive and precious advices in the context of study, so, I am extremely fortunate to have noble, motivating. Knowledgeable and sincere guide. I express my thanks to respected Prof. Marie Soressi for her scholarly research paper published in proceedings of National Academy of sciences, Vol-110, Issue as 35, 2013. This Research Article is more useful for me.

I am also grateful to Dr. Vikram Harijan, Convener of this Seminar, for giving me an opportunity to present a paper.

References

1. Murthy K.V., "Some Important Facts of Leather Industries, Khadigramodyog, Vol. 30, No.-1, October, 1984, p.4
2. Chandra, Rowland, N.L., "Arts in Industry Through the Ages : Monograph series on Bengal, Navrang, New Delhi, 1975, p.-108.
3. CLE, Reports on Innovations in Leathers and Fashion Materials, Leather News India, Vol.2, No.4, April, 2011. p. 40
4. Yellow JE, Brooks AS, Cornelissen E, Mehlman MJ, Stewart K A middle stone age worked bone industry from Katanda, Upper semliki Valley, Zaire. Science 268 (5210), 1995, p. 553-556.
5. Lerai- Gaurhan A Doctrinaire de la prehistoric [Dictionary of Prehistory] (presses Universitiesj de france, Paris), 1968, p.63
6. Benazzi S, atal. Early Dispersal of modern humans in Europe and implications for Neanderthal behaviour Nature 479 (7374), 2011, p. 525-528.
7. Bordes F, Les gisements due pech-de- l.Aze (Dordogone). l. Le Mousteriende tradition Acheulian L. Anthropologies 58:401-432, 1994, 59:1-38
8. Soressi, M.et.al. Neanderthals made the first specilaised bone tools in Europe, PNAS, 110 (35), 2013, p. 186-190.